One Life at a Time

ONE LIFE AT A TIME

Helping Skills and Interventions

Jeffrey A. Kottler & Leah Brew

California State University, Fullerton

Brunner-Routledge

New York and Hove

Published in 2003 by
Brunner-Routledge
29 West 35th Street
New York, NY 10001
www.brunner-routledge.com

Published in Great Britain by
Brunner-Routledge
27 Church Road
Hove, East Sussex
BN3 2FA
www.brunner-routledge.co.uk

Brunner-Routledge is an imprint of the Taylor & Francis Group.
Printed in the United States of America on acid-free paper.

10 9 8 7 6 5 4 3 2 1

Library of Congress Cataloging-in-Publication Data
Kottler, Jeffrey A.
One Life at a time : helping skills and interventions / Jeffrey A. Kottler & Leah Brew.
p. cm.
Includes bibliographical references and index.
ISBN 0–415–93360–9 (pbk.)
1. Counseling. 2. Psychotherapy. I. Brew, Leah M., 1967– II. Title.
BF637.C6 K6793 2003
158'.3—dc21
2002152048

Contents

Preface

OVERVIEW

Every undergraduate and graduate program in social work, counseling, family therapy, applied psychology, human services, and related fields (nursing, education, pastoral care, medicine) offers a course (or two) on basic counseling skills and therapeutic interventions. Some would say that this is the most important unit in the program because it forms the foundation for everything else that practitioners do. This is the class where beginners learn the core skills of helping, as well as the essence of what it means to make a difference in the world, one life at a time.

Skills courses tend to be very practice-oriented, a hands-on experience in which students not only learn the basics of helping others but also practice these behaviors and interventions in simulated situations. The goal is no less than to equip students with everything they need to begin conducting interviews, planning treatments, engaging in systematic assessment and diagnoses, and structuring effective interventions. Most of this helping activity is centered on core helping skills, but in order to be truly effective these strategies must be integrated as part of an overall plan for influencing people in positive ways. This text not only teaches students basic interventions, but also inspires them to use these skills in the most powerful and ethical ways possible.

ABOUT THE TITLE

The title of this text was quite deliberately chosen to reflect the "bigger picture" that is involved in helping others. Therapeutic skills are employed within a particular context that includes the practitioner's operating theory, personality, and style, as well as the client's unique characteristics, needs, and assumptions. There are so many other dimensions that enter into the picture as well—the particular setting in which the help takes place, the sort of relationship that has been developed between the clinician and client, the respective cultural identities of the participants, the stage of counseling, and similar variables, each of which influences how skills are used and received. Yet even with broadening the place of therapeutic skills to include these other clinical factors, it is still not nearly enough to convey to beginners the incredible power of our work.

The title, *One Life at a Time*, emerged from discussions between us about our own experiences in skills courses. This training, and assigned texts, were so completely focused on learning the mechanics of how to reflect feelings or set goals that we lost all perspective about what we were actually trying to do, which is to help people make significant changes in their lives. Frequently, this is done as a result of applied skills, but just as often, transformation takes place because of many other influences and variables. (Some of them aren't necessarily even related to the counselor but to the client!)

Just think about the times in your life that someone helped you in a meaningful way. That person may have used a host of skills that were instrumental in getting through to you, but it is likely what you remember most were other things—the quality of your relationship, the caring and respect you felt, the boundaries that helped you to feel safe, the opportunities to explore new ideas, and so on. Of course, helping skills were an implicit part of all this, but they were hardly enough; the helper's personal qualities were also critical.

Although our job in this text is to teach much of what you need to know in order to *do* counseling and therapy, we also intend to remind you (constantly) that helping people is about *being* as well as *doing*. In other words, making a difference in someone's life does not often occur according to a linear, predictable path. There are times that you can do everything absolutely perfectly and not put a dent in someone's resistance; there are other situations when it will appear that you have done very little and yet the client was affected profoundly.

In order to keep your attention focused consistently on the larger context of what you are doing, and why you are doing it, we chose a title that is not only poetic and evocative but also one that we hope is inspirational. In the *Talmud*, one of the ancient Jewish commentaries written in the third through sixth centuries, there is a saying that "whoever saves one life, it is as if he has saved the whole world." This belief in the sacred value of service has been used by altruists, political figures, and religious and community leaders, in order to encourage people to give more of themselves in the spirit of helping. The essential idea is that by devoting our lives to helping others—even if we only impact a single individual—we still save a part of the world. The job for which you are preparing is one in which you will be saving the world . . . one life at a time.

UNIQUE FEATURES OF THE TEXT

This is designed to be an experiential text, one that is highly practical and student centered. It includes all the basic skills and core interventions that you need in order to begin seeing clients, but it also presents them in such a way that you can internalize them—to make them part of who you are, not just what you do when the "meter is running." The emphasis throughout this book is on ways to apply these skills to your work as well as to your life.

Although much of the book's content includes the "little" stuff, the myriad of things that helpers actually *do* to make a difference in the lives of their clients, *One Life at a Time* keeps the focus on the bigger picture we discussed earlier. All too often in texts such as this, students become so bombarded and overwhelmed with the variety of skills, techniques, interventions, strategies, methodologies, and treatment options, they might forget that the primary purpose of all this is to make contact with their clients, to help them feel understood and clarify the major issues that trouble them. Some of the most popular skills texts are so overstructured and rigidly sequenced into a series of stages that students must learn a whole "foreign language" just to be able to communicate to one another about what they are doing. In contrast, *One Life at a Time* uses a conversational tone and everyday language to help students facilitate change in clients.

Other important features of this text include:

- Combined treatment of core skills and issues related to treatment planning.
- Use of a generic model of helping that combines features of humanistic, constructivist, and cognitive theories, and will fit a variety of different settings and clinical styles.
- Diversity issues are infused into every facet of the process so that you understand the importance of adapting your skills to fit the unique needs of individual clients and cultural groups.
- Traditional helping skills are augmented with newer, more cutting-edge brief interventions.
- After core skills are mastered, they are applied to specific settings with special chapters on groups, family work, or consultation activities.
- Attention is given not only to what effective practitioners *do*, but also how they *think* and *feel*. You will be helped to increase your tolerance for ambiguity, complexity, and uncertainty.
- The text is loaded with in-class activities, structures, and assignments that help you to practice skills and help your instructors to organize lessons.
- Case examples and first-person accounts make the material come alive.
- Reflective activities, homework assignments, and application exercises help you to personalize the ideas and apply them immediately in work and life settings.
- A narrative voice uses humor, authenticity, engaging prose, practical examples, and very straight talk to communicate the passion, the excitement, and the fun of doing this type of work.
- You are guided through a self-assessment process that helps them examine their personal values and moral choices as they affect clinical behavior.

THE CONTENTS

In the first chapter, we introduce you to the overall process that is involved in helping people. We talk about what it takes for a client to be willing to change and the conditions under which such transformations can be more easily facilitated. Chapter 2 expands the context under which therapeutic skills are employed to include the individual, social, cultural, and ethical contexts for helping behaviors. This provides a framework for better understanding the kinds of issues and concerns that people bring to sessions.

Chapter 3 summarizes the major conceptual frameworks from which therapeutic skills evolved. Students receive intensive study of theory in other courses, whereas we think it is important to link counseling applications to these models so that it becomes easier to understand not only what you are doing but why you are doing it.

After this contextual overview, the next series of chapters introduce the major helping skills as applied to building and maintaining relationships (Chapter 4); assessing and diagnosing client issues (Chapter 5); exploring presenting complaints and collecting meaningful information (Chapter 6); promoting deeper understanding (Chapter 7); and moving from insight to action (Chapter 8). The final chapter of this section (Chapter 9) discusses skills for maintaining progress and evaluating the results.

Although there is considerable overlap between the skills that clinicians use during individual sessions, versus those with more than one participant present, there are some specialized strategies, interventions, and helping behaviors that supplement what you have already learned. Chapter 10 covers family therapy skills, and Chapter 11 examines those that are most useful in group leadership. The final chapter brings things to a close and provides structure for further training and development.

ACKNOWLEDGMENTS

We are sincerely grateful to the students who "field-tested" this text by providing helpful suggestions that were incorporated into the final draft: Jocelyn Frandsen, Lynnette Herrera, Judith Passy, Corrin Reynolds, Rick Thomas, Nichole Walker, and Sarah Walker.

A number of reviewers, experts at teaching the skills courses, also provided a wealth of experience and wisdom that were crucial in developing the final product. We are indebted to: John W. Seymour, Fred O. Bradley, Stephen E. Craig, Dana L. Comstock, and Marilyn Montgomery.

Finally, we thank our editor, Emily Epstein, for her support and guidance throughout the various stages of this process.

About the Authors

Jeffrey A. Kottler has written over 50 books in the field for therapists, counselors, and teachers, including *Compassionate Therapy: Working with Difficult Clients* (1992), *On Being a Therapist* (1993), *Beyond Blame* (1994), *The Language of Tears* (1996), *What You Never Learned in Graduate School* (1997), *Travel That Can Change Your Life* (1997), *Doing Good: Passion and Commitment for Helping Others* (2000), *Learning Group Leadership: An Experiential Approach* (2001), *Making Changes Last* (2001), and *Bad Therapy: Master Therapists Share Their Worst Failures* (2003).

Jeffrey is Professor and Chair of the Counseling Department at California State University, Fullerton. During the last few years, he has also spent considerable time teaching counseling throughout the world, most recently in Iceland, the Faroe Islands, Australia, New Zealand, the Philippines, Hong Kong, Singapore, Namibia, and Nepal.

Leah Brew is an Assistant Professor in the Counseling Department at California State University, Fullerton. She has presented at many conferences at the state, regional, national, and international levels in the areas of supervision, stress reduction, and attention deficit hyperactivity disorder. Leah has an interest in the areas of counseling theory, supervision, spirituality in counseling, and cultural diversity, specifically with biracial populations. She has served as the student representative of the Association of Counselor Education and Supervision (ACES) and continues to advocate for student issues.

PART I

CHAPTER 1

The Process Revealed

Before we talk about skills and interventions that are part of what therapists and counselors do, it is helpful to begin our journey by looking at the overall process involved. In this opening chapter we introduce you to the subject by covering the main ingredients that are part of most systems currently in use. We begin with a personal look at the magic of this profession through the experiences of the authors. As we will mention consistently, it is important to see the larger landscape that is involved in helping people, even when you are focused on the individual skills and interventions that are part of this complex process.

READING MINDS AND OTHER SUPERPOWERS

When I [Jeffrey] was twelve years old I spent a significant part of my life reading comic books—*Richie Rich, Archie*, but mostly superheroes like *Flash, Green Lantern, Batman*, and most of all, *Superboy*.

I used to pretend to *be* Superboy when I was a bit younger, launching myself off tables and couches with a towel tied around my neck as a cape. I really believed that if only I tried harder (like Peter Pan), somehow I could fly. Bruised and battered, my parents always scolding me for scuffing the dining room table during my progressively longer take-offs, I abandoned my attempts to leap tall buildings in a single bound but not my search for superpowers.

I next set my sights on x-ray vision, a skill I determined would be far more useful to an adolescent boy who'd never seen a naked female body, except in pictures. My prayers were finally answered one day, and of all places, in the very comic books to which I was so devoted. There, on the back page, was an advertisement for special x-ray glasses that would permit the owner to duplicate Superboy's feat of seeing through dense objects. I may have clouded memory about this, but I swear there was even an image of a girl whose outline could be seen through transparent clothing.

Five bucks, or whatever the glasses cost at that time, was still out of reach for a kid whose only outside income was shoveling snow for neighbors (this was July). Nevertheless, I begged and borrowed the money from various relatives until I finally had enough for this magical instrument that would reveal all the secrets previously shrouded from me.

Needless to say, the glasses hardly delivered what was promised and they were far too goofy looking to even wear as sunshades. Still, I refused to give up my search for superpowers.

It wasn't until years later, during my training as a therapist, that I finally realized I was developing powers that would allow me to read minds and persuade others to do my bidding. Indeed with lots of instruction, supervision, practice, and experience, I mastered the art and science of picking up cues invisible to others. I learned powerful ways to get other people to do things they really didn't want to do. I learned some tricks of the trade as well, relatively foolproof methods for diffusing anger, confronting others nondefensively, and helping people to feel heard and understood.

When I started teaching others how to do therapy—school counselors, family therapists, psychiatrists, social workers, mental health specialists—I found a whole new realm of secret powers open to me as well. I had to develop ways to keep a group spellbound, to encourage people to take risks and reveal very private things in public settings. I learned to motivate people, as well as to help them overcome fears of failure. As I began writing textbooks for beginners in the field, I figured out ways to introduce very complex ideas in ways that could be adapted to a number of practical situations and settings. Then I began doing research interviewing other therapists and counselors to find out about their own secret powers and favorite strategies.

MY PSYCHIC POWERS

When I [Leah] was an adolescent, I struggled to search for meaning in life while coping with personal problems. I felt terribly unhappy and read texts from different religions, New Age books, self-help books, and anything that would help me understand why pain and suffering were part of life. On the journey of this exploration, I stumbled on several books on psychic ability. I was drawn to this possibility, and many of the books said that *I had psychic powers.* Some books simply stated that everyone had the ability but that it was underdeveloped. Other books stated that only certain people had the ability, but since my astrological sign was/is Pisces, I should have it. I was convinced I was psychic. I bought books and started practicing. I visited psychics to understand my ability better, and they frequently told me I had "the gift." I devoted several years to developing this ability.

I imagined that with my newfound psychic ability, I could see the future. I could avoid disasters in my life and in the lives of my friends and family to avoid pain. I could make decisions more easily since I would be able to see the outcomes to avoid making mistakes. I could know people's thoughts and use them to my advantage. I could understand what's beneath what people present on the surface to respond to them better. I could amaze and astound my friends and family. I would be noticed. I would be special. In retrospect, I now realize that I just wanted to be special, to feel important. Although I am still attracted to understanding the internal experience of others, I certainly don't want to read minds . . . I don't want to know if someone thinks I dress funny or sound stupid or know anything negative without asking first, and I don't want the responsibility of seeing the future . . . too much responsibility!

I never developed my psychic abilities in the way that I had hoped, although at times I convinced myself I had a gift. However, what is most remarkable to me now is that after years of working on the skills required to become a good counselor, and working on my own issues,

I have developed some abilities that amaze my friends and family; I appear to be psychic to them. I have learned to get my thoughts and my issues out of the way (well, almost out of the way) to see the other person's point of view as much as possible. I have learned how to listen, how to really listen beneath what is being said. I've learned to pay attention to the smallest details in how a person communicates: the body language, the nuances in verbal language, and the voice inflections. Most importantly, I have learned to reflect what I see and hear from the other person in a way that seems psychic. All of these skills have helped me to be a better friend, a better teacher, and a better person in all my relationships. I have learned a way to connect with others that is natural to me now. These skills have changed me and saturated every aspect of my life. Now I finally feel special.

None of the skills taught in the first clinical course were natural to me, although some skills may be natural to some of you. I knew that I wanted to help people, and I thought that therapy was about hearing the problem and then giving advice to fix the problem. I was good at that. Was I wrong! Therapy is about building relationships, which is best done by really listening and being there for the client.

I had to learn all the skills slowly, with lots and lots of practice. In addition to my university training, I participated in an external training group. I also chose the hardest supervisors during my field experiences and internships to develop as much as possible. I would practice my skills with friends, family, teachers, coworkers, grocery-store clerks, the person next to me in the airplane, with any and all human contact. And now, here I am still developing skills, but they are strong enough to wow my friends, my family members, my students, and even total strangers (if I feel inclined to impress them).

So now I'm writing what I've read before. You, too, can become psychic. No, you won't be able to read the future. However, with a strong conviction, commitment, and tons of practice, you will appear to read minds. Amaze your friends and family. Tell them what's on their mind. You'll be surprised of how much you can know.

SECRETS REVEALED

"How'd you do that?"

"Do what?"

"You know. That thing where you . . ."

Her voice trailed off at the end, as if she couldn't quite capture what she was really trying to ask. This was a woman who was used to being in control. It bothered her already that she had been forced to ask for help about a personal matter, but it was even more frustrating to her that she couldn't figure out what therapy was all about and how it worked. It was as if she was trying to penetrate the smoke and mirrors of an elaborate hoax, or at least a magic show.

"Nothing up my sleeves," the therapist teased her, showing her forearms. She felt very much like the Wizard of Oz who was about to step from behind the curtain of the control room. The therapist didn't like to play games or hide what she was doing with clients. She wanted them to understand *exactly* what they were doing together so that if a time came in the future when clients need help again, rather than running back to someone like her, they could apply what they learned previously.

We don't mean to imply that magic and deception don't play important parts in counseling and therapy, because they assuredly do. It is a curious phenomenon that almost nobody pays much attention to us when we are not working under a cloak of expertise. In order to have some degree of influence, it is often necessary to function in a particular setting and context. You may have noticed, for example, that the offices of professional therapists and counselors are specifically designed in such a way as to display symbols of power—diplomas on the wall and impressive books on the shelves.

Therapists and counselors happen to arrange things in such a way that they increase their sense of power and status in the eyes of their clients. We appear to be magicians and wizards because we seem to *know things* that are beyond mortal beings. We can not only read people's minds, but we can predict the future and get people to reveal things that they would prefer to keep to themselves. We know just the right pressure to apply when someone proves reluctant, and when to back off when such efforts are fruitless. We have creative solutions to problems, many of which would never occur to others. We listen extremely well and hear nuances that are beyond awareness. We are able to persuade people to do difficult, risky things they prefer to avoid. We can confront them with a kind of sensitivity and diplomacy such that they don't take offense. And when we mess up or make mistakes, we are highly skilled at recovery.

We do all these things not for personal gain but because we know that the more stature we have in others' eyes, the more likely it is that they will listen to what we have to say and do what we encourage them to do. We might use a few props or special effects to appear far wiser than we really are, but it is all for a good cause.

So, when the therapist in the beginning of this section faced her client's persistent inquiries about how she managed to get through to her in a way that nobody else had before, the therapist wanted her to understand the process, but not to the point where it lost the magic. Once clients see behind the smoke and mirrors, the trick can be ruined. Magic only works when the illusions are maintained.

Of course, counseling is a discipline that is firmly lodged in science. Almost all of our theories, and the skills you are learning, have been developed as a result of empirically based studies that were designed to test their effectiveness and usefulness under various conditions and circumstances. Counselors do not fly by the seat of their pants, or operate by intuition

---

Think About It

Either in your journal, or talking to classmates, discuss the extent to which you believe the impact of counseling is mediated by what is currently known through scientific inquiry versus what appears to be magical because the factors are not thoroughly known and understood. As an example that might guide your exploration, consider a time recently in which you experienced some sort of personal change. Try to account for all the reasons and influences that may have contributed to that transformation. Now, consider your level of confidence in those explanations: How certain are you that the changes you experienced did, in fact, result from those causes and not from other things that may be beyond your awareness and understanding?

alone. Every intervention you choose, and every skill you employ, should be supported by a clear rationale. You will constantly consult the literature to determine whether your current practices are consistent with the latest research. And you will conduct your own studies to measure the impact of what you do. So, although there is an element to what we do that might *appear* magical, there is a much larger component that is supported by scientific principles.

Like most professionals, therapists and counselors consider themselves part of an elite guild. We have our secret handshakes, our special codes, and our unique rituals. Like wizards and magicians, in order for us to create illusions that lead to change we must keep our methods private. The trust and confidence we inspire is based primarily on others' beliefs that we really do *know things*, that we have *The Answer*, and that we have access to *A Cure*. We convey these impressions partly through the highly trained skills we use to foster confidence and inspire trust, but also through a number of strategies that are far less obvious.

HOW THERAPISTS ENHANCE THEIR MAGIC

I [Jeffrey] have spent some time doing research with witch doctors in the Amazon region of northern Peru, with indigenous healers in the Kalahari Desert of Namibia, and in several regions of Asia. I have been interested in making sense of how it was possible that healers and therapists in so many different parts of the world seemed to operate in such different ways. We're sure you have already heard many of the endless debates among members of our profession about the best way to help people. Some practitioners insist that you must make sense of the past while others look to the future. There are therapists who work only with thinking patterns, or repressed feelings, or observable behaviors. There are those who think therapy should take a long time and others who see it as a very brief encounter. There are therapists who prefer to work with individuals, or in groups, or with whole families. There are experts who have a style that is confrontive, and others that are nurturing. Some see their role as a teacher, or a coach, or a consultant, a surrogate parent, or a provocateur. The really amazing thing is that there isn't a lot of evidence to support the effectiveness of one of the hundreds of therapeutic approaches over others; they all seem to work pretty well, depending on the situation. Needless to say, we've always found this a bit peculiar. It also makes learning how to do this complex craft extremely challenging when we can't agree on the best way to do it.

So Jeffrey was off in the jungles or deserts observing and interviewing healers to identify some of the strategies that he might recognize in his own work. It occurred to him that in spite of their claims otherwise, maybe all good therapists do essentially the same things. Regardless of what they call themselves, and where they work, there are some universal ingredients that operate in all therapeutic approaches (see Kottler, 1991; Prochaska & Norcross, 2003).

Jeffrey noticed immediately that witch doctors in the Amazon did not have framed diplomas on their walls (they didn't actually have any walls because they worked on mountaintops) but they did display a stuffed condor, the greatest symbol of power in their culture. On the surface, it appeared as if they were practicing a very different sort of helping than he was familiar with. They led chants and dancing and prescribed the most awful-tasting hallucinogenic cactus pulp that was blown up one's nose through a long tube. They waved wands and old skulls over a person's body, repeating incantations. They kept their clients up all night until they finally agreed they were cured of their maladies.

We might subscribe to a different theory of what causes emotional problems, and might have different methods for working our therapeutic magic, but there are indeed some similarities between what healers do all over the world. First of all, we all capitalize on a person's expectations by instilling a sense of hope and increasing our power in their eyes. If you act like you know what you're doing, if you believe in your powers to help others, and if you can convince them to believe in you as well, then almost whatever you say may be perceived as useful.

POWER AND INFLUENCE

We don't wish to reveal all our secrets and magic tricks—at least right away—but here are just a few of the ways that therapists and counselors enhance their power in the eyes of their clients so as to maximize their influence.

It is one of the most annoying qualities of therapists that we so rarely give direct answers to questions. There is a very good reason for this (besides the fact that we rarely know what truth is for any given individual). Once we are caught as being mistaken, or fallible, then people may very well lose confidence in our abilities. How would you like your physician to admit that she doesn't have the slightest clue what is wrong with you? At the very least, she has got to venture some reasonable hypotheses. It is the same with therapy; the most ambiguous responses are most likely to give us the most room to maneuver.

"What should I do next?" the client asks with desperation in his voice.

The counselor's first thought is: "How the heck should I know what you should do? I barely know what's best for me most of the time. I agonize for ten minutes before I can finally decide between the chef's salad and chicken stir-fry. And I'm supposed to know what you should do with *your* life?"

Exercise in Advice Giving

With a partner, take turns telling one another about a personal problem or concern that you are currently struggling with in your life. After the person has shared, respond by telling him or her everything that you think he or she should do to fix it. Then reverse roles.

Hopefully, what you learned from this exercise is that although well intended, giving advice doesn't work very well. Even if people do hear what you are saying, they will rarely act on what you told them to do. And if they do follow your advice, they may end up blaming you if things go wrong, or, worse yet, coming back to you every time in the future when they feel stuck.

Second, even if the counselor did know what the client's best course of action should be, it is unlikely that the client would listen, much less act on what was suggested. Our most recurrent fantasy in sessions is imagining ourselves telling clients exactly how they should straighten out their lives—change their wardrobe, lose the glasses, quit their jobs, get rid of that loser of a boyfriend, show better posture, stop raising their voice at the ends of their sentences. People want advice (because they don't want to be personally responsible) but they rarely take it. It has gotten to the point that the only time therapists give people advice these days is when they want them to do the exact opposite (this clever strategy is called a *paradoxical intervention*).

Think About It

Think of a time where you were struggling with a decision, perhaps with a job or to start or end a relationship. As you spoke with your friends and family, did they offer you plenty of advice? Was the advice contradictory? Was it helpful? And think of the many times you followed the advice of others. I [Leah] can think of the many times that my parents so strongly advised me to do certain things . . . end this relationship, take that job, stop going to school and get a real job (especially during my doctoral work). Most of the time their advice led to arguments. At other times, I would simply listen patiently and still not follow it. What has been your experience? I once had a professor who said something quite profound: "Take my advice, I won't be using it."

So, ask a therapist or counselor a direct question about what you should do, and you'll most likely get a response like the following:

- *"That's a very good question. What do you think?"* Doing therapy is often like ping-pong. Keep the ball in the other person's court.
- *"You aren't sure what to do so you're hoping I will decide for you."* This is called a reflection, but is often used as *def*lection.
- *"Going back to what you were saying earlier . . . "* Changing the subject often works.
- *"What you are searching for has always been within your grasp."* Going mystical is a great way to put the focus back on the other person.
- *"When you leave here today you will find yourself, almost against your will, coming back to some things that were said here that will begin to make more sense, or less sense, than they do now."* We love this one a lot as it makes predictions about the future that, one way or the other, have to be confirmed.

We know this sounds cynical, and we don't wish to reduce the important work that therapists do to a bunch of tricks and gimmicks. Most of all, therapy is about a relationship with a person that forms the core for the other skills that you use. Within the context of that trusting alliance, the skilled expert is able to help people to experiment with new behaviors, take constructive risks, learn about new ideas, make sense of the past, and plan effectively for the future. This process does not take place when the therapist plays games with people, quite the opposite actually. The therapist goes to great lengths to make him- or herself as transparent, authentic, honorable, and dependable as possible. Ultimately, what Jeffrey learned from his own research with witch doctors and other healers around the world is this: *It is not so much what therapists do that matters as much as who they are.* In other words, personal characteristics are just as critical as their clinical skills. We help people not only through our skills and interventions but also through the sheer power of our personalities.

Exercise on Personal Qualities

Get together with a partner or in small groups and discuss what you consider the most powerful aspects of your personality. This is no time for modesty; you must increase your awareness and understanding of how you impact and influence others.

Each person takes turns identifying the prominent features of his or her personality that have been reported to be inspirational to others. Leah, for instance, has been told that she seems to be open, nonjudgmental, and intelligent. Jeffrey uses his sense of humor and playful spirit.

After everyone has shared what they observe about themselves, then give each person feedback on other qualities that you have observed or sense.

Under ideal circumstances, therapists and counselors are able to model for their clients the same degree of personal effectiveness that is being taught and nurtured in the sessions. This is the real magic of therapy: that two (or more) people can spend time together talking about life difficulties, and within a relatively short period of time, perhaps just a few conversations, the pain and discomfort go away. Sometimes forever.

It isn't magic that heals people, but it is important that clients have strong beliefs in the power of those who help them. This is the first and most important principle to keep in mind in any helping relationship: Unless you can convince others that you know what you are doing, and that you are very good at what you do, your efforts are not likely going to be of much use. Of course, before that can happen, you must first believe in yourself.

YOU GOTTA BE DESPERATE

If you wonder how it is possible that people manage to make such stunning changes in counseling and therapy, it all starts with candidates who are *very* motivated. By the time anyone actually seeks the services of a professional it is likely that a whole lot of other options have been tried first. Nobody sees a therapist as a first choice but usually as a last resort after everything else has failed. The person has likely tried sweeping the problems under the rug and pretending they don't exist. He has tried blaming others for the difficulties. He has consulted with friends and family, hoping for attention and sympathy. He has already exhausted every alternative within grasp. With nowhere else to turn, or perhaps being pressured to seek help by others, the client limps into the office feeling desperate.

Generally speaking, people don't change because they want to, but because they have to. Nobody walks out of a relationship, quits a job, or relocates to another city when they are feeling quite satisfied with the way things are going. People initiate changes when they are at the end of the line. It all starts with discomfort. Desperation is even better. Unless you are unsettled by the status quo there is little motivation to change anything. When present strategies aren't working, when things start to fall apart, when there seems no other alternative, that's when people seek change. And it ain't pretty.

Change means being awkward and uncertain. It means facing the unknown. It feels like taking a giant leap into thin air, without a net. That is an important secret about the way that change in general, and therapy in particular, tends to work. Most people will get better anyway, over time; a professional guide just makes it happen more quickly. It is the same thing with a therapist. It is not as if most of our clients actually need us in order to get to where they want to go; it's just that we help them to get there a *lot* quicker, with a lot less aggravation.

Exercise in Change

Get into groups of three or four and talk about a time when you made a major change in your life (change of relationship, change in career, moving far away). Discuss what led up to the change and the amount of courage it took to risk the change over remaining the same.

IT'S ALL ABOUT LEVERAGE

When someone is experiencing some personal distress—let's say a moderate case of depression, anxiety, confusion, or loneliness—there is a strong drive to reduce this discomfort. Drugs or alcohol might work for a little while, but they have side effects. People "medicate" themselves with other things as well—excessive sleep, exercise, food, or work—any place to hide from the pain. All of these strategies work pretty well, although they all have significant disadvantages in that they tend to create other problems that are also annoying.

The favored preference, by far, is for the person to deal with the situation so that no big changes are needed. It may be uncomfortable to remain stuck in an empty or unsatisfying relationship but things could also be far worse.

Once a client feels that perceived options are limited, and favorite coping strategies don't work, then the person may be ready to *consider* significant change. Keep in mind, however, that the client may not be nearly to the point where he or she will actually *do* anything differently, but at least that possibility will be taken under advisement.

This is what we might call "leverage." It is what gives us some starting momentum to get things moving in a constructive direction. After all, it is really the client who does most of the work in therapy, and also it is the client's motivation, commitment, and resources that best predict a positive outcome (Tallman & Bohart, 1999).

A Few Things to Remember

It is difficult to influence anyone in a therapeutic relationship unless the following conditions are in effect:

1. The person is not satisfied with the current state of affairs.
2. The person realizes that he or she can't cope with things on his or her own.
3. You are recognized as someone who can provide needed assistance.
4. You believe strongly in your own power to help.
5. You can convince the other person of your usefulness.
6. You must be able to deliver on what you promise.

So a very important thing to understand about change is that it is most likely to occur—and last—when a person doesn't see another choice. It's easy to walk out of a job or relationship if you can't stand another second of the predicament without imploding. And it is much easier to help someone when this individual feels lost and is willing to acknowledge this state of helplessness.

AMATEURS VERSUS PROFESSIONALS

You already have the broad strokes, but there are a few more details to fill in. If the therapy process were as simple as we are making it sound, almost anyone could do it with little training or practice. You would hardly need a whole course on skills, nor would you require a textbook on the subject. In fact, almost everyone *does* act as a therapist at times. Professionals hardly have a monopoly on helping relationships. Taxi drivers, bartenders, hair stylists, and friends are also known to engage in helpful conversations with people during times of difficulty. The main difference, though, between amateurs and professionals is that we professionals are far more likely to have a positive impact in the briefest period of time.

Contrary to popular belief, helping people is not at all natural. It takes a *lot* of training and hard work to put your own needs aside, to focus completely on this other person. You must be able to concentrate so intently on what the person is saying and doing that you can fluently decode the underlying meanings that are being expressed. At the same time, you are reviewing a host of options from which to select the best intervention.

For instance, someone says, "I just don't know what I want to do next. It's like . . . I don't know . . . No matter what I do, it's not going to work out."

The initial reaction to this statement is to feel flooded with options. It is not that there is a shortage of possibilities; it is that there are too many. Here are a few options:

1. You could reflect the content of what you hear to let him know that he was heard and also give yourself more time to think about other things you could do or say next. *"No matter what choice you make, you still think you're going to end up back in the same place: stuck."* This isn't elegant but, at short notice, it does encourage further elaboration.
2. You could reflect the underlying feelings you hear: *"You are feeling so discouraged and hopeless that you wonder if it's even worth trying. You have faced so many disappointments in the past."* This might seem similar to the previous response but it actually takes the person deeper, exploring some of his or her frightening feelings.
3. You could help this client to examine some of his thinking patterns that are getting in the way. *"First of all, you are telling yourself that you should know what to do and that you are somehow inadequate because you don't know. Secondly, you are predicting the future based on very limited information."* Now you would be helping the client to look at his or her illogical and self-defeating thoughts that are sabotaging efforts to move forward.
4. You could try a mild confrontation. *"You say that no matter what you do, it's not going to work out, but we've both already seen a lot of progress you've made by taking similar risks in the past. It seems like you are reluctant to risk making a mistake so you'd really rather prefer to stay stuck so you have an excuse for remaining miserable."* This encourages the person to look at the excuses he or she is giving for avoiding action.

don't like this approach

5. For something completely different, you could use self-disclosure. *"I remember a time in my life when I was feeling much the same way that you are. I wanted to give up. I wasn't happy but at least it was familiar. I wondered if that might be better than risking something new that could turn out far worse. Then I decided that I couldn't possibly be worse off, took the risk, and then never looked back."* This shows the client that he or she is not alone and also gives him or her hope that good things are waiting for those who take constructive action.

We could go on at great length and list no less than two dozen other responses that might be used in this situation, but the point is that skilled therapists are trained to sort through the various strategies and select the ones most likely to be helpful. Although this takes years of education, training, practice, and supervision, the basics can be learned and applied rather quickly—even in a single course.

A FEW MISSING INGREDIENTS

Before we get into the actual method of using therapist skills, it is important to understand that there are several other ingredients involved in the process. These same elements would be evident not only in therapy relationships, but in any helping encounter.

Altered States of Consciousness

If you are thinking about a drug or hypnotic state, you're not far off. There are particular times and situations when people are more open to being influenced than others. What therapists attempt to do is create an environment that is maximally conducive to people hearing what is said and acting on what they declare. In order to do this, therapists use the setting as a stage and their voice as an instrument of influence. They speak in such a way as to command attention and suggest things in a way that they are more likely to be acted on. In that sense, therapy itself is a trance state wherein clients are encouraged to relax, let themselves go, trust in the expert, and then do what they are directed to do (Havens, 1996).

Some therapists use their voice to calm clients down, or get them emotionally activated. The very choice of language is made based on what is most likely to match what given individuals will respond best to. The whole object of the encounter is to establish confidence, build suspense, facilitate awareness, provoke insight, motivate action, and then sustain interest. As you will see later, these same stages can be employed in any relationship that is designed to influence another person.

Placebo Effects

Long ago in medical studies (Beecher, 1955), it was established that the client's own expectations for a cure are often more important than the actual treatment. Give someone a pill, especially a tiny, green specimen, and tell the person that it is powerful medicine and, sure enough, the person will likely feel better in the morning. Even if the pill contained nothing but sugar, food coloring, and binding agents, it may still have solid effects if the person believes it is useful. Things work even better if the doctor prescribing the pill believes in his or her own heart that the medicine is just what is needed, and says with utter confidence to the patient, "Take this pill and you will definitely feel better in the morning."

If placebo effects (derived from the Latin, meaning "I shall please") work with medications, they can be equally effective in helping relationships (Fish, 1973; Snyder, Michael, & Cheavens, 1999). If the therapist communicates confidently that what he or she is about to do is going to be helpful, *and the client believes the therapist*, then the intervention will more likely work quite well. This has extremely important implications for other relationships as well. In any situation in which you want to have an impact on others, it is crucial that you believe in what you're doing. Not only that, you must be able to communicate this confidence effectively.

Compare, for instance, how differently you might respond to the following two introductions to an idea:

1. *"Well, uh, I'm not sure if this will work or not, but let's give it a try. I think it might help, but then again, maybe not."* This person is covering himself, protecting against anticipated failure, but also reducing the likelihood that the intervention will prove useful.
2. *"I am about to do something that works very well in these situations. I am certain you will see a significant difference within a short period of time."* Obviously, you wouldn't want to say something like this unless you could deliver on what you promised, but in this confident language the situation is set up in a way to play off others' positive expectations.

So often, results are in the eyes of the beholders. The same outcome can be judged a success or failure depending on others' expectations. If a helper tells you that you are probably feeling better already, and this is said with assurance and convincing evidence, then you will probably start to feel better. This is the case even if the helper didn't do anything else other than tell you that you have improved.

Healing Relationships

One of the mistakes made most often by beginning therapists is that they think that their job is to learn and apply the most elaborate, powerful interventions possible in order to provoke changes. In fact, therapeutic techniques and strategies are less important than the quality of the relationship established with the person you are trying to help or influence. If you can establish a close, trusting, accepting connection with another, a relationship in which the person feels valued, respected, and honored, almost anything you try is going to be useful (Rogers, 1951).

Even more importantly, once you have a solid relationship, you have a lot of flexibility to make mistakes, experiment with new strategies, and take the time you need to discover the best solution. We rarely get things right the first, second, or even third time. But that hardly matters if the person we are helping gives us the benefit of the doubt and allows us to work together as a team until we come up with the right combination to set things on the right path.

If you think about the most successful helping encounters you ever had, whether they were with a counselor, teacher, therapist, coach, family member, or friend, it is highly probable that what the person did or said was less critical than the quality of the relationship you felt with that person. If you felt heard and understood, if you felt safe enough to try new things, if you could risk talking about difficult subjects, if you were pushed and motivated, then you profited from the encounter. Furthermore, the helper could have tried an assortment of different strategies, any one of which may have worked.

Exercise in the Power of Relationships

With partners, or in small groups, talk about the most healing relationships that you have ever experienced. These may be people who have made lasting changes in your life, shifted the course of your life, or helped you through something difficult.

This principle is certainly confirmed by your own experiences. In a public forum, you may agonize about the best way to express yourself, rehearse the absolutely perfect lines, but what makes all the difference is the relationship you develop with your audience. The same holds true for any situation in which you hope to impact others. If you can build solid connections with others, get them to trust you and feel confidence in your abilities, what you actually do is a whole lot less important than you think.

Cathartic Processes

Good ol' Sigmund Freud noted a century ago that people feel a lot better if they are allowed to tell their story to someone who listens well and allows them to dump all their pent-up thoughts and feelings (Freud, 1936). This sounds rather simple, but it is actually quite rare that anyone allows you to talk without interrupting, giving advice, shifting the conversation onto them, or doing other things at the same time. Other therapists since that time believed that catharsis was so powerful, especially if it involved strong emotions, that this was quite enough to produce a cure. As it turns out, this is not strictly the case. It may be helpful to be able to talk about your troubles, but it is not often enough without being helped to take things to the next level of action.

The lesson at this point is that if you do nothing else, or perhaps even don't know what to do or say, it is a great first step to encourage the person to simply express him- or herself more fully. This will often produce immediate relief and works wonders in establishing that relationship that is so critical to anything else you do.

Consciousness Raising

Listening is great, but not nearly enough for situations when something more is required. All therapies, in whatever form they take, attempt to produce some sort of new understanding. They seek to help people look at the world, or their own lives, in a different way.

Often people who are experiencing difficulties feel stuck because of a perceived lack of choices. They don't see a way out of their predicament, at least a path that is within easy walking distance. Of course, this is not necessarily the case. There may be a hundred alternatives available, not just those that appear possible at the time.

Because there are over a hundred distinctly different kinds of therapies, each one approaches this consciousness raising in a slightly (or radically) different way. As you are already aware, psychoanalysts approach this task by helping people to understand their past and how it continues to exert influence in current patterns of behavior (Freud, 1936). So-called cognitive approaches help people to realize the irrational ways they think inside their heads, substituting other, more useful internal strategies (Ellis, 1973). The Gestalt approach believes that the client does not have sufficient awareness or experiencing so, in turn, the therapist helps to enhance that awareness (Perls, 1969). Some approaches look at the advantages people enjoy for remaining stuck or at the larger implications of their behavior on their whole family "system" (Bowen, 1978). In whatever form this insight takes, the goal is to increase a person's understanding of his or her situation, leading hopefully to new solutions.

Using Intuition

You have heard of intuition, and experts define what intuition is differently, depending on whom you ask. However, there is something that happens at times where you have something in the back of your head nagging you, you want to say something or ask something, and you're not sure where that's coming from. That's your intuition, and it can be extremely beneficial when you use it wisely. Whether intuition is your brain's ability to assimilate a vast amount of information and deduce new information from that data, or whether you have some ability that science has yet to explain, intuition is something that is helpful in therapy. Every once in a while, you might hear a therapist say, *"I'm not sure why I want to say this or where it's coming from, but . . . ,"* and sometimes whatever that is, it is right on the nose. Intuition helps you to see things or express things that might not be explained through any other means. So, rather than trying to determine the source of it, just appreciate it and use it. That inner voice can sometimes stimulate a powerful process and response in your client.

Reinforcement

All therapies encourage those behaviors that therapists think are good for people and extinguish those that are deemed self-defeating or counterproductive. There might be different goals with this in mind, but the object is to support progress in desired directions.

Behaviorists taught us that there are strategies that can be used to increase or decrease outcomes (Wolpe, 1958). The hard part is figuring out what is reinforcing for one person, because it may not be all that rewarding for others. This may seem pretty obvious, but you would be amazed how often people fail to do this. Someone does something that they don't like. They respond in a particular way, designed to stop further repetitions of this annoying behavior. Rather than having the desired effect, the behavior persists, or even increases. Although it might be apparent that the response so far is not working, and perhaps is even inadvertently rewarding the obnoxious behavior, the individual still fails to alter the strategy by trying something else. As you no doubt have noticed in your own life, some people actually enjoy the attention they get from acting in annoying ways. In order to alter this pattern, you must come up with some other way to extinguish the behavior.

Task Facilitation

It isn't enough to talk about things. You've also got to *do* some things. All good therapies structure ways for people to follow up on conversations by applying what they learned and realized to their lives. In fact, such therapeutic tasks are part of the procedures favored by most healers around the world from witch doctors and shamans to medicine men and sages (Keeney, 1996).

You've probably heard enough discouraging stories about people who have been in therapy their whole lives, or at least many years, without any noticeable change in their dysfunctional conduct. They may have perfect insight into their unconscious motivations, or understand all too well why they do such destructive, stupid things, but they still engage in those behaviors. They still drink too much, or obsess about the future, or pick losers in relationships, or feel depressed. They might perform like trained seals when they are in sessions, saying all the right things, but once they leave, nothing much changes.

The best helping encounters are those that focus not so much on what people do during the talk, but rather what they do after they reenter their lives. Even if you attended a session every day, five days a week, that would still only represent less than 1% of your waking time. What matters most is how you apply what you learned in the reality demands of daily life.

Talk is cheap. It's action that really matters most.

THE PERFECT COUNSELING STUDENT

Frequently, in our counseling skills classes, we have students practice their skills with each other as clients and therapists. We ask the students to discuss real issues and real frustrations so that the student/therapist has an opportunity to better develop counseling skills. In addition, the student/client gets the benefit of becoming more aware of his or her own issues that may or may not need more work with an experienced therapist. In fact, doing your own work is one of the most important skills you develop as a therapist. For some students, this can be problematic.

One of the common qualities of many graduate students is the need to look good, especially in school. In fact, many graduate students of counseling and psychology score high on the lie scale of the Minnesota Multiphasic Personality Inventory or MMPI, indicating they are faking to look better than they are. One student in my [Leah's] practicum was an excellent example of this. I was watching two students practice their reflecting skills, when the therapist stopped and said she felt stuck. Her client didn't seem to want to reveal anything. I finally decided to model what I would do after many attempts to guide the student/therapist. It turned out that the student/client proudly stated that she must be perfect. She thought this to be a positive quality about herself. She even stated that she must be the perfect student, and in order to appear perfect, she could not reveal her weaknesses. After stopping my role-play and discussing my approach to the students, I let the student/client know that she would have quite a challenge in our counseling program. I told her how we valued the ability to show some vulnerabilities and the willingness to work on weaknesses as part of her growth as a therapist. In order to become a good therapist, I told her that she must be actively willing to work on her own issues. Therefore, in order to be the perfect student, she must show her imperfections. The student assured me that she wanted to be the perfect student and would risk showing imperfections. How ironic! However, through painstaking work, she managed to accept her vulnerabilities and even allow them to be exposed at times in the interest of being the perfect student.

Inside a Therapist's Head: Processing Skills

What's going on here? The guy seems pretty strung out, as if he is going to fall apart any moment. Look. His hands are shaking. He can't maintain eye contact for more than a fleeting moment. His complexion is wan and his lips are pressed tight. It is almost as if he is hemorrhaging inside, which I suppose he is, at least emotionally.

So, should I let him go on a little longer, finish his story, or interrupt him at this point and offer reassurance? It's not clear yet whether we are dealing with a situational response to stress or a chronic, ongoing personality characteristic.

I could reflect his feelings at this point, his sense of terror and hopelessness, but I sense that this would only push him deeper into his despair. And he is already emotionally activated, too much so.

Maybe what I should do next is offer some structure. I can slow him down and we can back up and talk about goals. I bet it would help if we worked one step . . .

Wait! There are tears forming. What does that mean? His voice is so devoid of any affect yet his body is positively exploding with emotional energy that now seems to be leaking out of his eyes. Should I comment on his tears, which will only encourage him to lose control even more, or would things be better off if I continue with the plan to introduce structure and incremental steps of progress?

As you readily see and hear from this therapist's internal dialogue, there is quite a lot going on inside a practitioner's head in the course of any interview. It might have seemed to you that therapeutic skills were mostly about what you do—your behavior and action—but perhaps you didn't consider the extent that doing can also involve what is in your mind.

REFLECTIVE ACTION

So much of what we therapists and counselors do takes place inside our heads. Unlike other professionals such as physicians, attorneys, architects, and engineers, much of our work is reflective activity.

In a sense, one of our primary jobs is to understand people and then to communicate that understanding. In order for us to be able to accomplish this task, we must have a fairly clear grasp of several things, including:

1. What clients are experiencing.
2. A comprehensive inventory of their complaints and symptoms.
3. A reasonable hypothesis about the origins of their problems.
4. A diagnostic formulation that pinpoints the core issues.
5. The cultural, familial, and contextual background for the client's experience.
6. A treatment plan for what will be done and how it will be done.

In the internal dialogue mentioned earlier, you got a sense for the kind of overwhelming pressure that is often felt by therapists, especially during first interviews. We feel tremendous pressure to figure out what the heck is going on, to reassure clients that they will be okay, and to reassure ourselves that we know what we are doing when we often feel some doubt. Unless we can quickly establish trust and a working relationship, we are not going to be able to convince the person to return. And all throughout the time that we are busy doing stuff—listening carefully, asking pointed questions, offering reassurance, reflecting feelings, summarizing content, leading, directing, guiding, following a structured agenda—our minds are racing with ideas. We are sorting out possible hypotheses to account for what we observe. We are accessing our intuition and "felt sense" about what we believe might be going on. We are sorting through complex data, linking what is observed to other things we know, and otherwise just trying to get a handle on the situation. We are so busy on the inside that it is a minor miracle that we ever choose anything to do or say on the outside. But such are the demands of a skilled therapist.

APPLICATIONS TO SELF: INCORPORATING SKILLS INTO YOUR DAILY LIFE

All of this understanding of how therapy works might be interesting, even enlightening, but what good is it unless you take what you learn and do something with it?

Take inventory of your life, including the aspects that feel most satisfying and those you sincerely would like to improve or change. There are likely some relationships that are not going as well as you would prefer, perhaps some conflicts you find disturbing. There are probably some other personal challenges and difficulties that give you trouble. Some of these arise from the daily demands of your family, leisure, and work life; others stem from unresolved issues from the past.

If you are serious about mastering the skills of a therapist to apply to your life, the first place to start is with yourself. You can't very well help or influence anyone else if you can't make headway with your own personal struggles.

One of the reasons that self-help books and self-improvement efforts don't often last very long (just look at all the books gathering dust on your shelves) is that people take in the ideas they've read, resolve to use some of them, but then "forget" to apply them after the effects wear off. In other words, the new concepts never really became part of them.

In order to behave more effectively in your life, to act like a therapist in the sense of being a model of personal and professional effectiveness, it is necessary to personalize the concepts in such a way that they become part of you. This means that you must find ways to integrate the ideas into your daily thinking and, more importantly, your behavior. Daily journaling is an excellent tool to begin processing what's often in the back of your mind, hidden from your view, and sometimes a strong facilitator of your behaviors.

In this first chapter, you've read about the process of therapy, what ingredients are often present, and how it usually works. The question now becomes: So what? What does all this mean to you? How can you use this stuff in the areas of your life that matter most to you?

If you really want these skills to stick, to remain with you for the rest of your life, you are going to have to figure out a way to practice what you learn. For one thing, this means sharing what you are learning with friends and loved ones. We are sure you realize that you can't learn this stuff from reading a book if all you intend to do is rehearse things in the privacy of your own mind. More than any other class you will ever take, the learning of therapeutic skills involves daily practice in which you apply ideas to your work and your life, as well as to your personal relationships.

You must find ways to try out what you are learning, and then get honest feedback on the results. This means recruiting others into your study efforts, describing to them what you are doing, and finding out what is most effective. If our job is to introduce you to ideas that will prove valuable, it is your responsibility to customize and personalize them in such a way that they fit best.

Think About It

Take a moment to think about what areas in your life you need to work on. What holds you back? What is it that is difficult to change? What recurring issue keeps getting in the way of your relationships? Now think about how far you've come, and how far you have to go. Think about what you haven't changed and why. Now you understand the position of your clients.

SUMMARY

In this chapter, we have introduced you to some of the secrets and magic behind therapy. We have covered some of the reservations that clients have in coming to sessions, and the tools you will need in order to encourage them to proceed. We have introduced you to the world of being a therapist and, hopefully, elicited some excitement about learning the basic skills required to be a good therapist. The next chapter introduces you to cultural sensitivity as well as ethical and legal considerations related to basic counseling skills.

A CHECK ON WHAT YOU LEARNED

1. What kind of power do the authors talk about that may seem magical to clients but can actually be learned? *listening attention to class*
2. Therapists, witch doctors, and all healers have two things in common that facilitate healing. What are they? *hope & power*
3. What is counterproductive about giving advice when things go wrong?
4. What is counterproductive about giving advice when things go well?
5. People don't change because they want to, they change because *they have to*
6. If you and the client believe that an approach or technique will work, and it does, this is sometimes not due to the treatment, but due to *placebo effect*
7. Change is usually not only influenced by powerful techniques, but also by the _____.

8. *intuition* _____ may be the ability to assimilate a vast amount of information and deduce new information from that data or an ability that is not yet explained by science. Regardless, it is a powerful tool that should be used and appreciated.

9. Catharsis is helpful in therapy, but frequently it isn't enough to facilitate change. Instead, the client must *increase understanding*.

10. In order to communicate understanding to clients, we must have a clear grasp of six primary things. List them.

SUGGESTED READINGS

Frank, V. (1963). *Man's search for meaning.* New York: Beacon Press.

Hubble, M. A., Duncan, B. L., & Miller, S. D. (Eds.). (1999). *The heart and soul of change: What works in therapy.* Washington, DC: American Psychological Association.

Kottler, J. A. (1993). *On being a therapist.* San Francisco: Jossey-Bass.

Kottler, J. A. (2000). *Doing good: Passion and commitment for helping others.* New York: Brunner-Routledge.

Kottler, J. A. (Ed.). (2002). *Counselors finding their way.* Alexandria, VA: American Counseling Association.

Lindner, R. M. (1955). *The fifty-minute hour: A collection of true psychoanalytic tales.* New York: Rhinehart.

May, R. (1953). *Man's search for himself.* New York: Dell.

Prochaska, J. O., & Norcross, J. C. (2003). *Systems of psychotherapy: A transtheoretical approach.* Belmont, CA: Wadsworth.

Rogers, C. (1980). *A way of being.* Boston: Houghton Mifflin.

Yalom, I. (1993). *When Nietzsche wept: A novel of obsession.* New York: Basic Books.

CHAPTER 2

Clients in Need:
Individual, Social, and Cultural Factors

I t often sounds like it is the counselor who does all the work and determines whether the experience is helpful or not. In fact, clients have at least as much say, if not more so, about the outcome. When clients are highly motivated, taught appropriate roles and behaviors, and helped to become actively involved in the process, it is their own self-healing efforts that are as important as anything the therapist does in sessions (Tallman & Bohart, 1999).

You can be the best clinician in the world, with every possible intervention at your disposal, and still not make a dent in a client's situation if he or she is not on board with the negotiated program. Likewise, a therapist or counselor can be an absolute master at applying a particular skill or intervention, but if the effort is not customized to fit the client's unique needs, cultural background, personality, and situation, then the effort is likely to be less than optimally effective.

There are features related to the client's own readiness levels, developmental stages, needs, preferences, attitudes, skills, and personality characteristics that also impact the possibilities for change. A key part of your job involves helping people to make the most of their strengths, as well as building on their weaknesses. You might also keep in mind that what might look like significant deficiencies and obstacles might also be viewed as opportunities for learning and growth. Such a resilient attitude is best exemplified in the life of Lance Armstrong, one of the greatest bicycle racers to ever dominate the Tour de France. After contracting cancer that appeared to be fatal, with his body debilitated by chemotherapy, Armstrong successfully fought the disease and recovered to the point where he became one of the most fit people on Earth. Surprising an interviewer about the lessons of cancer, Armstrong said, "It was the best thing that ever happened to me. Now I have a template for how to overcome something, how to prepare for something. I looked at the illness as an athletic event. The cancer was the competitor. And I was mad. I wanted to win . . . When I recovered, I applied that focus and ethic to cycling. It taught me a new level of commitment" (Zimmerman, 2002, p. 73).

One can almost hear the words of a therapist in Armstrong's testimony. Just imagine how you would help a client with such a life challenge to reframe and reconstruct a narrative in which he or she is heroic rather than a victim. When dealing with any trauma, loss, or life challenge, your job is often to help people to create or construct meaning from the experience in such a way that they feel empowered rather than discouraged from the experience (Neimeyer, 2001).

CULTURAL CONTEXT OF THE CLIENT EXPERIENCE

In order to make a significant and lasting difference with a client, helping skills are certainly important but rather useless without the sensitivity and ability to appreciate the context of that person's life. There is no way you could help someone with a life-threatening illness like Lance Armstrong without understanding his cultural background. This may often include factors like ethnicity, race, and religion, but in Armstrong's case, it would most likely involve his dominant cultural beliefs imbedded in his identity as a world-class athlete. For each person you will ever see, there is a complex tapestry of cultural themes that play a significant role in shaping that person's attitudes, life experiences, and identified problems. Certainly these involve ethnic and racial backgrounds, but also one's gender, sexual identity, spiritual beliefs, socioeconomic background, family background, even such things as one's profession, hobbies, and geographical location (Ivey, D'Andrea, Ivey, & Simek-Morgan, 2002).

When I [Leah] was completing my education to become a counselor, I decided to try out counseling and see what it was like to be a client. I vividly recall being nervous going to my first session with the designated practitioner assigned to my case. After all the intake information was exchanged, I told the therapist that my purpose for seeing her was to reduce the stress in my life. I was aware that I put a huge amount of responsibility upon myself to produce far more work than my coworkers, and to do so perfectly. The consequence was daily headaches.

Eventually, the topic moved to my childhood. I told my counselor about some of my struggles growing up. Then, to my horror, she started to cling to the idea that I was emotionally abused and neglected because my parents weren't attentive enough. This, she believed, was the reason for my problems. I left the relationship after two sessions (yes, she made this assessment in less than two meetings).

I later discovered that my main issue wasn't about childhood neglect—it was about being culturally different and struggling with those differences. My mother was Japanese, and as much as she wanted me to be an American, her cultural influence bled into my upbringing. Specifically, expressing strong emotions was considered to be self-indulgent and an imposition to others. So, at home I was expected to behave one way (neutral or moderately happy), and among my peers, I was criticized for being stoic and unemotional. I might have actually remained in counseling if my counselor had considered my cultural background before applying such a harsh label as abuse.

Exercise in Cultural Identities

We all consist of multiple selves rather than a single, stable identity. For instance, Leah's cultural identity just described may be as a biracial Japanese American, yet there are also other cultural identities that influence her values and behavior. If you were going to see Leah as a client, you would need to know her strong identity as a Texan from a small, rural town. You would also need to understand her strong cultural identities as a professor, a feminist, and a Gestalt therapist. In each case, whatever presenting problem she might present

> *in counseling, her multiple cultural identities would become the landscape for the journey you walked together.*
>
> *Consider your own strong cultural identities related to your race, ethnicity, religion, socioeconomic class, geographical location, hobbies, and so on. In a small group, share those features that would be most important for a counselor to know and understand in order to help you.*

CULTURAL SKILLS AND COMPETENCIES

There are certain competencies that are considered essential for the culturally sensitive practice (Axelson, 1999; Horgan-Garcia, 2003; Lum, 2003). Among them are understanding the client's unique worldview, including core beliefs, being aware of one's own biases and values, and an understanding of how methods must be adapted to fit the needs of each person.

Clients present themselves in one way, and their helpers receive them according to their own perceptions. These are influenced by our values, our own experiences with people who are similar, our biases and prejudices, and our sensitivity (Tseng & Streltzer, 1997).

According to the authors, there is:

- *The problem as experienced by the client.* This is what the person is feeling, his or her core experience in its most raw form.
- *The problem as identified by the client.* This is what is noticed and labeled. The person takes the raw experience and converts it into verbal and visual images, then gives the problem a name. This identification may or may not be a full and complete representation of all the issues.
- *The problem as presented by the client.* This is what is revealed and told as a story using words. The limitations of language will influence what and how the experience is reported.
- *The problem as understood by the therapist.* This is what is heard by the clinician. Considerable distortions may take place as a result of this "translation." In other words, what the therapist hears may not be closely related to what was said, much less what was experienced.
- *The problem as diagnosed by the therapist.* This is what is labeled by the clinician and what is focused on as clinically significant. The client tells a long, complex, and multitextured and layered story that includes infinite facets. The therapist then must decide what part of this presentation is most important.

Each of these steps is both influenced and distorted by each participant's individual and cultural worldview. Both participants in the relationship come from different life experiences that each shapes what they understand about one another and how they respond to one another. That is one reason why it is so crucial for you to have a clear handle on the influences within your own cultural identities and how they impact your beliefs and behavior. Although true objectivity is impossible, this journey of self-discovery will better help you to become aware of your biases, confront your prejudices, and manage your beliefs in the best interests of those you are trying to help (Baruth & Manning, 2003).

Exercise in Self-Awareness

Let's start with the assumption that everyone is prejudiced, meaning that everyone makes prejudgments about others based on limited data related to appearance, first impressions, and prior experience. Such behavior is not only normal but sometimes quite helpful: Humans had to evolve some way to quickly and efficiently make evaluations about whether someone represented a threat or danger.

If you follow this reasoning (you don't have to agree with it), then we all not only have prejudices but certain biases toward and against others, based on our prior experiences. I [Jeffrey] drive a small car and I have frequently felt intimidated (persecuted?) by rather large vehicles, especially pickup trucks that seem to delight in running me off the road. Now, whenever I see a pickup truck on oversize tires, I immediately form negative judgments toward the driver inside. Do I know this person? Of course not. But it doesn't stop me from forming prejudgments based on my previous encounters with some representatives of this group. In a similar vein, most of us have preferences to associate with others "like us," and to avoid those "not like us." This could be related to your religion, sexual orientation, political affiliation, or whatever.

Either in a journal, or in small groups, talk about some of the prejudgments you have toward people of particular religious, racial, or socioeconomic backgrounds, or other factors such as their labels. For instance, what immediately comes to mind when you consider working with a new client who is a pedophile? Or a member of the Libertarian or "Green" political parties? Or a transvestite? Or a tax accountant? In each case, you have an initial impression, perhaps one that won't last long after you actually meet the person, but nevertheless you have certain expectations, beliefs, and attitudes, some of which are strongly biased. You would be very naive indeed not to understand the ways your own cultural background and attitudes impact your relationships with others.

BECOME FAMILIAR WITH CULTURAL DIFFERENCES

Who will your clients be? Most of them will be different from you, whether due to gender, socioeconomic status, sexual orientation, ethnicity, religion, or other cultural differences. That your clients will be similar in all of those areas is highly unlikely. Therefore, learning tolerance for differences and educating yourself about cultural issues will help you to provide better therapy. More importantly, enhancing your awareness of and articulating your own values may prevent you from creating barriers between you and your client.

For example, when I [Leah] was in high school, I had a friend who was ethnically 100% Italian. He was physically just like you see in the movies (olive skin, dark hair, dark eyes, Roman nose), and you would be certain of his heritage except for missing the accent. I remember going to his house after school one day; it was my first time to visit his home. The place smelled wonderful: garlic and spices—well, you know—like Italian food. His mother was in the kitchen cooking. While I waited in the living room, my friend entered the kitchen to talk with his mother briefly. Then, much to my surprise, I heard lots of yelling and screaming. I didn't know if I should leave. I thought he was certainly in big trouble about something. I was frightened for him. Maybe five minutes later, he returned, although it seemed like hours later. We walked silently out of the house and to the car to head to our destination. Once in the car, I nervously asked him if he was in trouble. He looked at me very confused and said, "No, why?" I told him I heard all the yelling and screaming in the kitchen and didn't know what to do. He said, "We weren't yelling, we were just talking. We weren't even disagreeing about anything. What are you talking about?"

Exercise in Confronting Cultural Biases

Make a list of all the cultural groups that you might expect to encounter in your work. Include such dimensions as race, ethnicity, national origin, and religion, but also other cultural identities related to sexual orientation, profession, avocation, geographical location, and so on. Make the list as exhaustive as possible and include almost anyone you might expect to see in counseling.

Circle those groups with whom you have little experience or understanding. For instance, you might have a fair degree of contact with people from the southern region of Vietnam but no experience with the Hmong peoples of the highland mountains. Or, you might know a little bit about gay men but nothing about transsexuals or lesbian women. Or, you might be reasonably familiar with middle-class professional African Americans but have had little contact with those who live and work in the inner city.

Now, here's the hard part, because it requires a degree of honesty that is not often politically correct to admit. Put an asterisk (*) next to those groups with whom you feel uncomfortable working. If a transgendered individual came to see you, how would you handle that? What if a new client walked in who was an Orthodox Jew, a devout Muslim, or a Jehovah's Witness? Some of your discomfort may be related to ignorance and lack of experience, but another part may result from prior encounters with particular individuals of a particular culture.

Now the really hard part: Make a commitment to educate yourself about the groups that you circled, and to challenge your biases and prejudices towards people of a particular culture. This is not the kind of assignment you will complete in a week, in a semester, or even in the years of your training; it will take you a lifetime.

In my family, we were emotionally less expressive than any of my friends' families; I was taught that raising my voice was *always* inappropriate. What a shock it was for me to discover that other families talked in loud voices, just talked that loud. I couldn't imagine what it might be like to hear them yell at each other in anger! I totally misconstrued the situation because of a simple (or not) cultural difference.

Thank goodness for that experience! I remember during my training as a counselor leading a group where the members were students in a group counseling class. Several weeks into the group, family-of-origin issues formed where group members were projecting experiences of their siblings onto each other. Specifically, two members were yelling at each other as if they were siblings. I definitely recall hearing one say, "You're just like my brother." As the volume of their voices increased, I was acutely aware of my cultural beliefs about yelling and tried not to interfere until I felt what they were saying was no longer productive, although every cell in my body wanted to stop the conversation and keep the voices at a more civilized volume (notice I used a culturally biased word about the volume: civilized). I was incredibly uncomfortable, but as a therapist, I realized the process wasn't about keeping my comfort level. Instead, I realized that they needed to express, I suspected, repressed anger. Today, I'm not sure that allowing that process to go so far was most productive, but at least I was aware to some degree of my own cultural values.

One caveat exists about learning cultural differences: Learning about cultural stereotypes and abstaining from making absolute assumptions about certain groups is a delicate balance that counselors need to learn. Certain beliefs or assumptions may hold true for many within a particular group, but your client may be the one exception. I [Leah] remember supervising a session with one student who thought her client was gay. She made this assumption because he was slightly effeminate and used the term "partner" because he was not married. At one point, she referred to his partner as "he," and the client reacted negatively to her assumption that he was gay. A few sessions had to be devoted to repairing the relationship between the client and counselor as a result of this mishap.

Exercise in Prejudices (Prejudgments)

Post several sheets of paper up around the classroom. At the top of each page, write down a particular cultural identity, whether it is an ethnic group (African Americans, Asians, etc.), religious group (Christians, Muslims, etc.), sexual orientation (homosexual men, lesbians, straight men), or any other issue that you think is relevant. Make sure to include middle-class Caucasian Americans. Each student is to walk around the room and then write down particular stereotypes about each group (not personal beliefs). Go around the room as many times as is needed. When everyone has written something, process the experience.

Several areas can be important with regard to cultural differences. Here is a list of the most common areas about which new counselors tend to make assumptions. This list is not exhaustive by any means.

Gender

Have you ever found you and your friends saying, "Men are this way," or "Women are that way"? So often, we state or believe gender stereotypes. This is one area where we may already hold assumptions, especially regarding the opposite sex. Whatever assumption you hold, many individuals do not fit your stereotype. For instance, think of people you know who are exceptions to these stereotypes:

- Women are too emotional.
- Men aren't communicative enough.
- Women love shopping.
- Men love sports.
- Women are the victims of abuse.
- Men are the abusers.

Differences obviously do exist between men and women; even our brains develop differently (Carlson, 1998). Nonetheless, we are all thinking, feeling, behaving beings with many of the same wants and needs. Too often, our biases about the opposite sex, or even the same sex, can get in the way of modifying our approach to fit the client.

Socioeconomic Status

Many stereotypes exist based on socioeconomic status (SES). The truth is that all dysfunctions and problems exist regardless of the client's income level. Some common stereotypes might be:

- High-SES clients will be prompt.
- Low-SES clients are more likely to abuse their children.
- High-SES clients will pay their bills.
- Low-SES clients are less motivated.

Regardless of your client's SES background, the problems will be similar. It's essential to be aware of these incorrect stereotypes so that they do not interfere with your ability to work with your clients.

Sexual Orientation

The issue of sexual preference is one that can stimulate a lot of debate among students in counseling. Many students have strong beliefs about homosexuality. Strong beliefs against homosexuals, lesbians, bisexuals, or transgendered clients can interfere with a therapist's ability to provide professional care. As a therapist, your job is not to decide whether or not your client is acting in a moral way, but rather to help your client deal with whatever issues are relevant for him or her. If you are unable to feel unconditional positive regard for your client, you may want to refer him or her elsewhere.

Three common problems occur with regard to student therapists working with homosexual, lesbian, or bisexual clients. First, some students, upon discovering the client is homosexual, will try to convert the client to become straight. Obviously, this can create a significant amount of problems for the client and for the therapist's relationship with the client. A second challenge is when the new therapist believes that all of the client's problems are related to his or her sexual orientation. Just because your client is gay does not mean that all of his or her problems will necessarily be related to sexual preference. Finally, student therapists hold incorrect stereotypes about gays, lesbians, bisexuals, and transgendered clients that can interfere with therapeutic effectiveness. Just because your client is gay does not mean that he is promiscuous, or that she does not like to wear makeup. As with any population, individual differences must be taken into consideration. Accepting your client for who he or she is and responding to him or her in a respectful way is an essential component to good therapy.

Religion

Religious differences are another touchy issue for students. Many students have strong beliefs about their religion, and their values are intricately interwoven with their particular belief system. Furthermore, many religious behaviors are frequently misunderstood and misinterpreted. These differences in values can trigger a therapist who may feel challenged by a client who maintains different values. For example, which of these beliefs stir something up in you?

- Polygamy.
- Abortion.
- Homosexuality.
- Eating pork.
- Dressing provocatively.
- Premarital sex.
- Capital punishment.

Many religions hold strong opinions about these listed areas. You may find some to be absurd issues whereas others may seem more important to you. Whatever your opinion, your client has the choice of his or her opinion as well, and a most challenging skill is to support your client's worldview even if it contradicts your own.

Ethnicity

Cultural differences can often be most obvious because of the client's ethnicity. Students can err in two ways when working with ethnically different clients. One common error is for students to hold certain stereotypes about an ethnic group that may not necessarily fit the client. To assume intelligence, motivation, or anything else about a particular ethnic group is simply dangerous, and frequently inaccurate.

On the other hand, students may not be appropriately educated about cultural differences of different groups and may misinterpret a client's behavior. This is the more common error. For example, you may have a young female client from India come to your office frustrated with her traditional family because they want her to enter into an arranged marriage when she is in love with another man:

> *Therapist:* So, your parents don't approve of this man because they did not select him for you?
> *Client:* It's not so much that the marriage must be arranged. And that's not exactly why they don't approve of him. It's because he's from a lower caste.
> *Therapist:* What would be the consequences if you did marry him without your parents' approval?
> *Client:* Why would I do such a horrible thing! I must always do as my parents ask.

The therapist in this case made an assumption that the client is trying to decide whether to marry in spite of her parents, when instead she may be coming to therapy to learn how to get over the man she loves. If the therapist isn't careful, the therapist may find biases of valuing independence creeping in when the client firmly believes in her cultural traditions. Therefore, you must not only learn about cultural differences, but respect them as well.

ASSESS STAGE OF CULTURAL IDENTITY

Now that we've told you that some stereotypes exist for each group, and to be cautious of the stereotypes you hold, how do you assess the level of acculturation? There are several authors who have created stage theories for levels of acculturation (Downey & Roush, 1985; Helms, 1984; Ruiz, 1990; Sue & Sue, 1973). These models have been based upon the African American or Caucasian cultures. However, a look at these stages would be relevant for any ethnic group. Loosely described, the stages of the Minority Identity Model, which can also be used for White Identity Development, are as follows (Atkinson, Morten, & Sue, 1989):

- Conformity—discriminatory.
- Dissonance—conflict between dominant views and views held by minority group.
- Resistance and immersion—conflict between empathy for minority group and feelings of culturocentrism.
- Introspection—concern with ethnocentric basis for judging others.
- Integrative awareness—group appreciating.

Therefore, in working with some clients, you may want to be familiar with these models to determine where your client might lie when cultural issues arise. However, these two particular models may not be appropriate for some groups who have emigrated from another country.

Check Out Level of Acculturation

We have presented a popular stage theory. Now let's look at acculturation from an immigration perspective. A first-generation immigrant in the United States, for example, who has English as a second language and still is steeped in the cultural values and norms of home, would be in a different place than a fourth-generation minority who cannot speak the language of her ethnic background and is steeped in American culture. The former client may be struggling primarily with the adjustment to cultural differences in the United States. The latter client may struggle with her parents forcing traditional cultural norms when she does not identify with the culture at all.

Even more complicated is when a client is biracial. He may not fit in either culture. Both ethnic groups to which he belongs may see him as belonging to the others, leaving him to feel culturally homeless (Vivero & Jenkins, 1999). To further complicate the issue, his parents only know their culture and may be totally ignorant of the specific concerns of being biracial.

For example, as I [Leah] have mentioned, I am half Japanese and half American. My mother was born and raised in Japan. My father was born and raised in the United States. Neither of them experienced any racism growing up, and my mother was only mildly exposed to some racism on one occasion once we moved to the United States. So, when I started complaining about problems with kids at school who were making fun of the way I looked, they dismissed it. I was devastated not to be able to receive any empathy for my situation. It was only when I reached the graduate-level counseling program that I finally understood the causes of misery from my childhood. But, in a way, I don't blame my parents (although I'm not pleased either), because they had no idea what it was like to experience racism. They were in that first stage of cultural identity development. However, I think it is relevant here to say that I still have issues associated with this experience beyond the occasional discrimination I now experience as an adult. You can imagine that if your clients have painful memories associated with being culturally different, at some point in therapy this issue will likely arise.

Okay, now we've given you three different perspectives on acculturation: identity models, immigration, and biracial issues. There are many variations and combinations of conceptualizing acculturation. Fortunately, you will likely have a full course in it. As you take that course, think about how you can assess where your client falls into these areas in order for you to respond to her needs appropriately. And just as important, think about where you are in your cultural development and awareness.

Exercise in Raising Your Personal Cultural Awareness

As we have discussed, culture involves far more than your ethnicity. Depending on your background and experiences, your religious affiliation could be most dominant, or perhaps your sexual orientation, professional identification, geographical location, or even your strong association with a particular thing (i.e., owning a Harley-Davidson motorcycle or being a stamp collector).

Reflect on your most dominant cultural affiliations. Try to think of at least three of them that have been most influential in your thinking and your development.

Next, list some of the assumptions that you hold that originated from your racial, religious, family, or other cultural heritage. For example, how do you view being on time? How do you express feelings? What feelings are most appropriate or inappropriate for you to express? Is doing what's best for the group or the individual more important? What gender-role stereotypes does your culture hold? What biases, prejudices, and beliefs do others hold about members of your culture? What assumptions do you have that are based upon your religious upbringing? How does your culture view counseling? With what aspect of your culture do you most identify (your cultural home)? How do you treat strangers? Should you always be polite or should you always be honest and direct?

Then get into small groups and share what you wrote down. Talk about your similarities and differences. Be aware of how you respond when others have different assumptions. Are you offended? Are they wrong? Are they simply different?

By clarifying your own culture and comparing it with the cultural differences from others in a nonthreatening environment, you may be less likely to offend others. You may become more educated about yourself and see others as having differences, rather than seeing them as wrong.

Review Cultural Norms

In order to determine the level of acculturation, you will need to be familiar with cultural norms. The course you take regarding culture will likely cover the following groups: gay/lesbian population, African American, Asian American, Native American, and Hispanic/Latino. Because this is not a culture class, we won't go into the norms for each of these groups. However, this is worth mentioning so that you can be mindful of the need to assess these norms when working with culturally different clients. And while you learn about the different cultural norms within these categories, keep in mind that there are some limitations. First, within each of these groups is a great deal of variation. A Mexican American has differences from a Cuban American. A Japanese American may be very different from a Vietnamese American. Second, the groups you cover will certainly not be a comprehensive list of all cultures. Many culture classes don't include Western cultures because we assume, as Americans, that we are very similar. Although some truth to that exists, there are many differences. If you have ever traveled or made friends with someone from Europe, for example, you may be acutely aware of their cultural differences.

With all of this in mind, as you come across clients who are culturally different, start by briefly reviewing what you learned in your culture class, but don't stop there. Also obtain some information about the specific cultural norms of the specific group from which your client comes. You might consider looking at the following areas:

- *The value of family.* Some cultures put the family's needs above the individual's, whereas in the United States we believe that self-care has value as well. An awareness of the importance of family can keep you from imposing your own beliefs about how a person should behave with his or her family.
- *Individual focus versus group focus.* Related to valuing the family, some cultures believe that an individual must consider the group first and self second; in other cultures, an emphasis on the group is not as essential.
- *Gender-role stereotypes.* In the United States, we strive for more equality between men and women, but in some cultures different roles are clearly defined. These differences might be especially important if working with couples who are first-generation immigrants.
- *Influence of religion.* The values of Christianity vary from those of cultures that are based in Buddhism, Hinduism, Judaism, or Islam. In a way, the view of life and its purpose can be quite different with each of these groups, and if you have a client with existential issues, you'll need to be sensitive to these differences.
- *Social structures.* Unlike in the United States, in some cultures the language or words used are determined by status (authority or age), and in others language differs for gender. This may appear on the first session with how the client wants to address you or how you should address your clients.
- *Emotional expression.* Some cultures value the open expression of emotions whereas others believe expression should be reserved. Be careful not to misinterpret someone who is emotionally reserved as resistant or someone who is emotionally expressive as unstable, because these may vary depending on the cultural background of your client.

These are just a few areas that come to mind when thinking about cultural norms. There are others; the list could be virtually infinite. What we most want to convey here is that you must understand the norms of your client's culture before making diagnoses or setting goals. It's vitally important to be sensitive to these values.

Assess Language Skills

Clearly, if your client has an accent, you will probably assume that English is not his or her first language. And so you might think, *"Am I able to understand this person?"* If you can understand the words, you may think you're off the hook. But you are sadly mistaken. Unfortunately, a lot must be considered if English is the second language of your client. For example, we frequently have idioms or colloquial phrases that are difficult to understand if translated literally. For instance:

- I'm fix'n to make some notes.
- She's breaking your heart.
- He got your meaning.
- They are flat broke.
- She was fuming!
- He lives over yonder.

You see how some of these phrases might be confusing. In fact, some of them are regional, so if you are not from the region that uses it, *you* may not understand it. Imagine how hard it will be for someone who speaks very little English.

Another challenge is that language is influenced by or influences culture greatly. I [Leah] roughly speak two languages, and many of the people in my life speak at least two languages. What I have recognized is that some expressions are weakly translated, at best. Because each culture has a different paradigm, a different way to view life, its language reflects those differences. We will not always be able to translate or describe things from language to language. In fact, some of our students have struggled doing therapy in a different language because there are not words that can translate from English to Spanish or Japanese or Chinese or whatever. And when we have supervised these students, they have had difficulty translating what the client is trying to express. They may translate the words, but then they have to elaborate for five minutes about the cultural context from which that phrase comes and how it should be understood in English. Therefore, whether you are doing therapy in another language or with someone in English where English is not the first language, you will be better served if you understand the nuances of language.

Finally, if your client's English is very weak, he or she may understand very little of what you are trying to convey. You may want to do lots of reflective listening (discussed in the Exploration chapter) and go very slowly in these cases. Ideally, you want to find a counselor who can speak your client's native language. However, we know that isn't always possible. This problem can be further complicated if the culture from which your client comes values externally agreeing with persons in positions of authority, whether they internally agree or not. You may never know that your client doesn't understand. He or she won't be able to tell you. So go slowly. Reflect a lot.

Consider Views of Culture Toward Treatment

We hope that because you are studying to become a therapist, you value the process of therapy—but you can't assume everyone does. In fact, some of you reading right now believe therapy is good, is valuable, and yet you won't go yourself. You don't think it's good for you, but it's okay for others. Many of your clients from the majority culture will also struggle with what it means to be in therapy. They might be afraid that people think they are sick, that they are incompetent to handle their own problems. Worse, some people may think they have problems! (You get the point?)

Well, in many other cultures, going to a stranger for help is looked on with great dismay and even shame. Some cultures think that you should be able to cope on your own, that focusing on your own problems is self-centered. Other cultures may believe that you should go to family members or other experts within their own culture if help is needed. Finally, other cultures believe more in a medical type model of healing, taking herbs or going through ceremonies to heal the "sick."

I [Jeffrey] teach counseling in other parts of the world, traveling several times each year to Hong Kong, Singapore, Australia, and Nepal. It never ceases to amaze me the kinds of transformations I must make with different sets of students. In Australia, the favored therapy is: "Crikey, get over it!" In Hong Kong, the favored method is often family therapy, but ancient Chinese methods including the use of herbs, palm reading, and such are also common. In Nepal, there are no mental health services whatsoever, yet any interventions must be consistent with both Buddhist and Hindu practices prevalent in that area.

The point we wish to make is that very few of the skills or interventions you will use are culturally neutral; each one reflects particular ideas about what is good for people. It will be your job to make necessary adjustments to what you do, depending on the client's background.

Respecting Client Beliefs

These are only a few areas in which therapists and counselors will encounter cultural differences; many others exist. And the most difficult challenge is to be educated about cultural differences while not maintaining a rigidity about those beliefs so that your stereotypes or beliefs do not prevent you from acknowledging or looking for individual differences. If you learn nothing else about working with culturally different clients, learn this: You must respect your client's beliefs, values, and ways of being in order to provide good therapy. If the client does not feel some level of unconditional positive regard, he or she may not trust you enough to share her innermost secrets or to share the parts of him- or herself that the client sees as most repulsive. Without that trust, your contribution toward the client's growth is stunted.

Exercise in Values

Get into small groups of five to eight people and rank the following values from most important (1) to least important (9). Your group must come to a consensus, which means that you do not vote. You have fifteen minutes to finish this task.

- *Patriotism*
- *Friendship*
- *Freedom*
- *Family*
- *Money*
- *Spirituality*
- *Intimate love*
- *Education*
- *Competition*

After completing the exercise, think about and discuss what this experience was like for you. What was it like to come to a consensus?

OVERVIEW OF A CLIENT CONCERN

Now that you are beginning to understand that you need to learn about what to expect from various culturally different groups while remaining sensitive to individual difference, how do you make the most of this information? Imagine a couple comes to therapy who has just moved here from Mexico.

Therapist: What brings you to counseling?
Husband: My wife is having difficulty living here without her family.
Therapist: [looking at the wife] Tell me about your difficulties.
Husband: She cries often and is always sad. [The wife is looking down and very sad.]
Therapist: [looking at the wife] Can you say something about your sadness?
Husband: She just doesn't know what to do with herself while I am at work. In Mexico, we lived close to her family and she spent most of her time with them. Now she's alone. We have only lived here a few months, and we do not have any friends yet. We know no one here.
Therapist: [looking at the husband] I notice you keep answering questions that I direct toward your wife.

In this case, the therapist did not make any assumptions about why the husband continued to answer questions directed toward his wife. What's your first assumption? Your response may tell you something about your biases. There are many possible reasons for this type of behavior:

- The wife does not speak English.
- The husband is controlling.
- The wife is shy.
- The wife reflects on her responses more slowly than her husband.
- This is culturally appropriate behavior.

By simply expressing what the therapist noticed, the client was free to respond as to why he was answering for his wife. How he responds may provide some information about their response patterns (and perhaps even her depression if he is controlling). If the therapist was culturally aware of this population, he or she may have known that the responding husband is typical in many Latino cultures (Sue & Sue, 1990). However, the therapist cannot assume this because this couple may not fit the stereotypical, traditional family system. He or she must check it out before moving forward.

Another way in which cultural sensitivity may help you work with clients is to be clear about any value differences you have with your clients. Imagine that a male client comes to your office to work on his marriage. Following is an example where the therapist's agenda can get in the way:

Therapist: You state that you are here to work on your marriage. I think it might be helpful if I see you and your wife together.

Client: We can't do that because I'm having an affair and she doesn't know about it. She accuses me of having an affair, but I won't admit it. So, I guess she kind of knows, but not for certain.

Therapist: Tell me why you haven't admitted to your affair.

Client: It will cause so many problems. I love my wife and don't want to lose her. I don't think this other relationship interferes with my family. If she wasn't so suspicious, then we wouldn't have these problems. I'm tired of listening to her accusations.

Therapist: Of course having the affair interferes with your marriage. There is no way to repair the marriage until you are willing to give up the other relationship and be honest with your wife.

Clearly, the therapist has strong values about extramarital affairs and honesty in a relationship. Although this example is not about an obvious cultural difference, value differences are apparent and can still interfere with your productivity as a therapist. In this example, the client is not likely to return for a second session. A better response would have been, *"You believe that your wife's suspicion is the cause of your marital problems, not your affair. Say more about how you experience your wife's suspiciousness."* At least this improved response validates the client's experience, and perhaps through further investigation the client may discover his own level of responsibility for his marital problems.

Therefore, you may use the skill of cultural sensitivity in many ways. Becoming sensitive to specific cultures will help to prevent you from saying something offensive, which can decrease your power and influence in therapy. Cultural sensitivity may also help you to understand the experience of your client more deeply and clearly. Awareness of cultural differences, especially the values that are held by various cultures, may help you to be clear about your own biases so that they are less likely to interfere with your therapeutic goals. Finally, understanding cultural differences expands the way in which you look at people in general, enhancing your ability to be empathic. This is not something that you do that is optional; sound, ethical practice is grounded in understanding the cultural differences of your clients and responding to them in appropriate, respectful ways.

ETHICAL CONSIDERATIONS IN THE PRACTICE OF HELPING SKILLS

The ethical codes for therapists provide specific information about cultural sensitivity. According to the American Counseling Association (ACA, 2002), the American Psychological Association (APA, 1992), and the National Association of Social Workers (NASW, 1999), therapists must be knowledgeable about cultural differences and respect the diversity of all individuals. Very specific statements are made in all of these ethical guidelines with regard to respecting and understanding diversity. In addition, all of these organizations, plus the American Association for Marriage and Family Therapy (AAMFT, 2001), state that therapists are to avoid discrimination based on age, gender, ethnicity, religion, sexual orientation, religion, or any other factor. Therefore, understanding and respecting differences is not just an opinion of the authors but an ethical guideline regardless of the organization with which you are affiliated. That is one reason why you will hear this theme echoed in every one of your classes and mentioned in every text.

Ethical Considerations Applied to Practice

Although you will probably have an entire course on ethical and legal considerations, we want to briefly discuss some hot topics here that are directly related to practicing therapeutic skills. We wish to introduce them as early in your skills training as possible because they guide everything else you do. Although you may have already had a class in ethics, or will have one later in your training, there are many excellent resources that you may wish to consult to prepare you to conduct yourself in highly moral, ethical, and professionally appropriate ways (see Baruth & Manning, 2003; Corey, Corey, & Callanan, 2003; Cottone, & Tarvydas, 2003; Remley & Herlihy, 2001; Welfel, 2002).

First of all, you may belong to a variety of organizations, each with their own ethical guidelines. In addition, you will have legal guidelines that are prescribed by your state for your particular license. You might assume that these guidelines agree, but in fact, they sometimes contradict one another. When you find yourself stuck in a situation, probably the best thing to do is follow the most conservative guideline. However, if you feel that your client might benefit from something more, we highly recommend that you consult with several of your colleagues (and supervisor) to assure that what you are doing is in your client's best interest. For example, imagine having a client who is HIV positive and is having unprotected sex with his spouse. Some ethical guidelines state that you have a duty to warn the victim if she can be identified, because HIV can be life-threatening. Other ethical or legal codes may specifically state that you cannot break your client's confidentiality to warn the potential victim. What would you do? All ethical and legal guidelines agree on one singular fact: Promote the welfare of the client (ACA, 2002; APA, 1992; NASW, 1999; AAMFT, 2001). Just how that is defined may differ with your ethical and legal codes.

Before You Schedule the First Session

A client calls and leaves his name and phone number. Can you schedule him right away? Maybe not. You have some ethical and legal considerations that must be followed first. For instance, are you within your scope of practice? In other words, does your license allow you to practice with this particular issue? In addition to scope of practice, you must consider scope of competence. For example, you are expected to avoid harming the client by only providing services for which you have been trained and supervised (ACA, 2002; APA, 1992; NASW, 1999; AAMFT, 2001). In other words, you must feel confident that you have the knowledge, skills, and abilities to help your client. If you are not sufficiently trained or supervised, then you need to refer your client to another more appropriate therapist.

Although the ethical guidelines make this sound clear and simple, it's a difficult guideline to follow. If you work in a clinic that takes a variety of issues, each client will come in with different backgrounds and circumstances, and you cannot be an expert at everything. The abuses alone are overwhelming: child abuse (physical, emotional, and/or sexual), domestic abuse (violence), alcohol or drug abuse. Some therapists have a specific area of interest and become experts working only with a single population. However, many therapists have to be able to work with a variety of clients and situations (individuals, couples, groups, families). In addition, if you are going to use assessment instruments, you must have competency to administer, score, and interpret them (ACA, 2002; APA, 1992; NASW, 1999; AAMFT, 2001). Therefore, once you have taken all of your required coursework, and hopefully mastered the basic counseling skills, you will need additional training for more advanced skills and training for a variety of populations. Your education will continue for the rest of your career. When is the situation fully beyond your scope of competence, requiring a referral? That's a difficult question to answer.

There are some obvious answers on when to refer. First, if you have education/training and have been supervised working with a particular issue, you do not need to refer the person elsewhere. For example, if a client comes in because she just ended a long-term relationship, most new practitioners will be qualified to handle a simple case like this. This situation would be considered within your scope of practice.

A little more tenuous is when you have the training/education, but have not seen this particular issue under supervision. As long as you get that supervision, then you can see the client. One example might be working with a client who not only just ended a long-term relationship, but also is medicated for depression. In this case, if you have not yet worked with a depressed client, you could probably continue to see this client under supervision, assuming you had training in depression.

If you have no training/education, you may or may not be prepared, depending on the issue. Again, supervision and/or consultation might be a good way to determine whether or not you need to refer the person elsewhere. One situation where you would not be qualified regardless would be to administer Eye Movement Desensitization and Reprocessing (EMDR), a technique for working through emotionally laden issues. EMDR requires specific training and supervision. On the other hand, doing traditional therapy with an extremely emotional client wouldn't require special training or supervision.

If you have no training and no supervision, and the topic requires expertise, then refer the client elsewhere. EMDR would be a good example of this. If the issue triggers countertransference issues for you, and you can't seem to separate your own issues from the client's, then refer the person to someone else. For instance, you are seeing a couple where the primary issue is active infidelity, and you just discovered your spouse or partner has been cheating on you for the past year with the same person. You probably will have some difficulty, just after discovering your partner's infidelity, in being unbiased with the "cheating" client partner.

Are you ready to schedule your client yet? Nope. You have at least one more primary consideration. Is this client an actual or potential multiple relationship? The ethical and legal guidelines all specify that you are discouraged from providing therapy to clients you know, whether as closely as a family member or spouse, or as distant as your hairdresser (ACA, 2002; APA, 1992; NASW, 1999; AAMFT, 2001). When you have a potential or existing relationship with a client other than as a therapist, you have a multiple relationship, and having such a relationship can cause many problems.

Exercise in Multiple Relationships

In groups of four or five, discuss the potential problems that might exist in multiple relationships with clients. See if you can come up with at least four reasons why being a therapist to a friend, partner/spouse, family member, or hairdresser (or any other service provider) is a bad idea. Share your ideas with the class.

Your First Session

Okay, you have called your client, who is a total stranger and with whom you believe you have the competence to help. You have scheduled your first session, and you are ready to go. Can you just jump right into why the client came to therapy and begin working on the issues as soon as the client walks through the door? You guessed it; the answer is "no." There are a variety of issues that need to be covered, preferably in the first session, and a number of other concepts that you will want to be clear about even before you see your first client (Rosenthal, 1998). These issues are covered in general in a later chapter, but for now, let's talk about the legal and ethical requirements. First, the ethical guidelines require that you cover confidentiality and its limits with your client. The client is to be informed that everything discussed in therapy is confidential, with some limitations. It's the ugly truth; you don't have complete confidentiality. The client must be informed of those limitations:

- Intended harm to self.
- Intended harm to others.
- Reports of abuse to a child, an elderly person, or a person with a disability.
- If records are subpoenaed by a court of law.
- If the client requests information be released.
- If you are being supervised and will discuss your client's case with others.
- If you are recording the session, the client must be informed of the recording itself and how it will be used.

In addition to confidentiality limits, an informed consent is required. This is a document stating that the client (or client's guardian) understands the conditions of therapy and is giving consent to participate. Many agencies combine the limits of confidentiality with the informed consent on one form. Typically, the client and the therapist sign these documents, and both the client and the agency keep copies. This document is usually presented in the first session.

Okay, assuming you were able to cover this information at the beginning of the session, you can start to talk about the reason(s) the client came to therapy. Easy, right? Wrong again. When do you speak and what do you say? Everything you say during a session directs the client, even if only minimally, including silence. Therefore, how you respond to your client is absolutely essential. As a therapist, your greatest tool is the art of interacting with a client. Although this book covers some basic skills that are considered essential to all theories of counseling, the basic skills may not be sufficient to help your client. Where are we going with all of this?

Well, one common theme to all ethical and legal guidelines is that your job as a therapist is to provide therapy with the best interests of the client at the forefront of everything you do. This seems simple enough, because you came to this field with an interest in helping people, but it's not that simple. Who determines what is the best course of action to help your client? You and your client do. Well, who made *you* an expert? Think of how the different schools of thought contradict each other. For example, one theory states that insight is necessary and sufficient for change, whereas another states that insight is neither necessary nor sufficient. Specifically, in

Gestalt therapy, fully experiencing and emotional catharsis are said to help the client most (Perls, 1969). In cognitive-behavioral therapy, changing thoughts that result in new behaviors helps clients most (Beck, 1976). Finally, in person-centered therapy, creating the right conditions for the client is sufficient for growth (Rogers, 1951). Therefore, as you learn some of the basic skills of counseling, think about where you will go beyond those basics. What are your beliefs about how people change? How will you utilize your theoretical orientation to conceptualize your client and justify what you do?

Now that we've added a portion of the ambiguous and complicated ethical guidelines to scare you a bit, we have some suggestions to ease your fears. First, make sure that you are intimately familiar with the ethical and legal guidelines. Second, we suggest you keep in touch with the colleagues you meet in school and go to conferences and workshops to meet more people so that you can consult with several other professionals when you are unsure about the appropriate course of action. If for any reason you have to go to court, evidence of consultation (without breaking confidentiality) may go a long way to support your case. Third, many organizations whose guidelines you will be following provide liability insurance in case of a lawsuit. As a result, these organizations sometimes provide free legal consultation in case you have questions. Fourth, continually obtain education about new research and trends in therapy to stay abreast of what may be more or less effective to be congruent with standards of practice. Finally and most importantly, maintain a strong relationship with your client throughout the therapeutic process by showing empathy. If the client likes and trusts you, he or she will be less interested in litigation and more interested in working through any concerns. Then the only challenge left is to know when to ask for help, and that's left up to your good judgment.

HOW TO BE A GOOD CLIENT

Strangely enough, one of the most important skills of being a good therapist or counselor is being a good client. Unless you know how to get the most from therapy in a consumer role, how on earth are you going to teach others to do the same? That is one reason why we believe the single most important thing you can do to prepare for your profession is to gain some experience as a client. You must understand what it's like to sit in the client's chair, to feel the same apprehensions, the same exhilaration. You must understand, from the inside, the games that clients play, the ways they try to keep therapists from getting too close. You must know intimately what it feels like to have someone probing and pushing you beyond the point where you feel comfortable.

Part of a therapist's job is to teach clients how to behave. Most of what people know about being good clients they have learned from watching television and movies. They think that they are supposed to come and tell you their problems and that you will listen to them and tell them what to do. They assume you will agree with them, or be their friends. They may assume that you will have a magic solution in the form of advice to "fix" their problem. They don't understand how therapy really works, and it is your job to teach them (at least to the point that you understand it yourself).

> **Exercise in Therapy Stereotyping**
>
> *In small groups, talk about several movies in which therapists were involved. Just to get you started, consider films like* Ordinary People, What About Bob?, Analyze This, The Prince of Tides, Don't Say a Word, K-Pax, *and* Good Will Hunting. *Talk about the ways that therapists and therapy are portrayed in the media and what assumptions people have about what it is that we do. This may give you an idea about what your clients will expect.*

One of your first missions will be to teach new clients how to get the most from their experience. You will want to assess their expectations, many of which will be wildly unrealistic. If they were truly honest they would tell you that they want you to wave a magic wand and fix them, and that they want you to do it fast. They want you to agree that they are right and others are wrong. Most of all, they want you to be gentle and give them your undivided attention—not just during the session, but they'd like you to be on call 24 hours a day!

Once you have discovered what they expect (just ask them), you will next correct their misperceptions by telling them what therapy is and how it works. This sounds something like the following:

Client: So, I was hoping you'd tell me what to do with my kid. He's just out of control. I've tried about everything I can think of. That's why the teacher at his school suggested I see you. She said that you could fix things, that you've done this before.

Therapist: I appreciate your confidence in me but perhaps I should tell you something about what I do and how I work.

Client: Okay.

Therapist: Although I am very good at helping parents deal with problems related to their children, it is not my job to fix things but rather to teach you how to do that.

Client: What do you mean?

Therapist: Just that I don't have a magical solution that I can just tell you to make things better. I need to spend some time with you, and your son. I suspect that he has quite a different story to tell about what is going on.

Client: You're not going to take his word over mine, are you?

Therapist: What I'm going to do is help both of you to understand one another better. Then I'm going to help you negotiate better with one another. Obviously, your son is acting up in school for some reason. We have to find out what that is about.

Client: I told you, I already know what the problem is. He just doesn't have any discipline. He needs . . .

Therapist: Yes, I heard what you said. And I heard what you want me to do. But what I'm telling you is that I work differently than that . . .

As you can tell from this dialogue, there is a lot of negotiation that goes on during this early stage. Therapists sometimes forget that all the time we are trying to influence clients and convince them that their dysfunctional beliefs are misguided and counterproductive, they are doing their best to convince us to join their side. There is, thus, an intrinsic conflict in therapy wherein we are trying to get clients to be one way that we think is good for them and they are trying to get us to be another way that they believe works best for them. As you can imagine, things can become quite conflicted as the two partners in this process both struggle for control.

Think About It

There are many different skills that are involved in being a "good" client. Here are some important ones to consider:

- How to ask for what you want.
- How to talk about thoughts and feelings.
- How to be painfully honest.
- How to understand and speak therapy language fluently.
- How to get the most from sessions.
- How to be patient.
- How to take risks.
- How to convert talk into action.
- How to let the therapist know you aren't satisfied.
- How to protect yourself from becoming dependent on your therapist.
- How to recognize when you are having a setback.
- How to know when it's time to stop.

DECISIONS, DECISIONS

During or after an initial interview, the therapist is presented with a variety of decisions that need to be made. Often there is paperwork to fill out—progress notes, treatment plans, intake summaries—that provides a structure for some of these decisions. Basically, you will be asked to make the following decisions:

- *Is the client in the right place?* Are you the best person to work with this person? Can you deliver what is needed? Is there a reasonable match between what the client needs and what you can offer?
- *Does the client require a medical consultation?* Is the client presenting symptoms that could conceivably be the result of a biologically based disorder? Some kinds of depression, anxiety, and other complaints do not respond to counseling alone but may require medication to manage the symptoms.
- *What is the risk of suicide?* If you suspect that clients may be at risk to harm themselves or someone else, then this will kick in a series of actions that must be followed to safeguard human life.

- *Is this a short-term or long-term case?* You may very well change your mind in the middle of treatment, but you will often be expected to estimate time required to meet the desired goals. Is this a case that will take a few weeks, a few months, or even longer? Is this a candidate for brief therapy?
- *What therapeutic modality is most appropriate?* Is it better to use individual therapy, group therapy, or family therapy? If the latter, which member(s) should be included?
- *What kind of therapy is likely to be most helpful?* Most therapists can work in different ways, depending on the situation and the client. Even practitioners who favor one theoretical orientation are still able to adapt what they do according to their clients' needs and styles. Basically, you will be trying to sort out whether a case is a candidate for relationship-oriented work or perhaps a more action-oriented model. For clinicians who employ a variety of approaches, decisions might be made for one client to use a feminist approach dealing with power issues, another client who is struggling to find meaning in her life might respond best to an existential approach, and still another client with reactive depression might be more amenable to a cognitive-behavioral approach.
- *What style of intervention should you employ?* Does this client primarily need support or confrontation? This is not an either/or proposition because both modes are often helpful at different times.
- *What sort of supervision and resources will be needed with this case?* Who would be the best person to work with you on this case? What books and resources might you consult? Who are experts you could consult with as needed? What are some areas of weakness in your ability to work with this case? Needless to say, it is crucial that you be honest with yourself about what you can and cannot do on your own. In some cases, you might decide it is best to refer the case to someone who has additional training or expertise in areas where you fall short.

APPLICATIONS TO SELF: WHO YOU ARE VERSUS WHAT YOU DO

One of the challenges of becoming a therapist or counselor is that the line between who you are and what you do is not so clear. As you learn to develop counseling skills, your communication style will change (and hopefully improve) in your ordinary life. Furthermore, as you become more aware and sensitive of clients, you will become more aware in your life as well.

Another way in which "who you are" and "what you do" becomes blurry is in your contact with clients. You have a strong set of values, beliefs, and ways of moving through life. Concurrently, your client has strong values, beliefs, and attitudes that will likely be different than yours. One challenge is to become vividly aware of your *self*. You must be clear about what you value and how you believe one should behave. Once that is articulated, a greater challenge is to accept that the client's way of being, of doing things, is not necessarily wrong . . . just different from yours. Sometimes one of the most difficult aspects of being a counselor is fully accepting your client's differences, or fully accepting where your client is at in her process of growth. By pushing who we are onto the client, you inhibit the client's growth experience.

Interview Exercise

Learning to be a counselor or therapist transforms you in a number of ways. You not only master certain professional skills that are useful in building trust when you are at work, but your interpersonal style and personality may also be altered in your personal relationships. Under the best circumstances, you become a far more compassionate and patient listener. You become more sensitive and responsive. You develop a far greater capacity for reading others' internal reactions and communicating at a deeper level of intimacy. Among many other things, you learn how to confront people effectively and how to summarize what you've heard.

Talk to friends and family members who you trust to be most honest with you. Ask them about changes that they have already witnessed in you as a result of your professional training. What are some aspects about this development that they especially appreciate and value? What about parts that they find uncomfortable or challenging to adjust to?

What can be most difficult is when your client believes or behaves in a way that you vehemently dislike, such as a disowned part of yourself. For example, let's say that your client is from a culture where emotions are not acceptable to express in public. As a person, you have struggled with this same issue. You have difficulty allowing your feelings to be not only experienced, but expressed. However, because you've been trained as a therapist to honor feelings, you dislike that aspect of yourself. And here you are, working with a client on something you have yet to master in yourself, and even worse, you dislike that aspect of yourself. One dangerous consequence could be that you don't like your client because he or she is so "cold." Until you become accepting of your own coldness, you may have some difficulty accepting your clients. The line between who you are and what you do is blurred.

Another example of this line blurring is when the client holds different values than you do. Remember the earlier example of the man who was having an affair? Think about how it might be for you to work with a client like that. Perhaps you are someone who values fidelity. How will you handle this client? Will you refer him out? Will you try to sway him to change his values? Will you find a way to work within his experience? We are not advocating that you give up your values. However, you may have to remember that they are *your* values, and others have a right to theirs. This can be a challenging task, but it is possible. In this case, you must clearly draw a line between who you are (a believer in fidelity) and what you do (unconditional positive regard for your client). Just make sure and get supervision or consult with someone when these issues arise . . . and they will.

SUMMARY

In this chapter, we have covered cultural factors that must be considered in order to provide effective therapy. In addition, some ethical and legal considerations were presented to add to the formula of good therapy. Both require an awareness of your own values to work effectively with clients and to help you make ethical decisions. And finally, individual considerations such as how to be a good client and what directions to take in therapy were included. All of these factors form a foundation needed before applying the basic skills of counseling. The next chapter focuses on how theory and skills combine into the phases of counseling.

A CHECK ON WHAT YOU LEARNED

1. Learning cultural stereotypes is helpful to understand your client better. However, taking _____ _____ into account supercedes the stereotypes you learn.
2. List the five areas described in the chapter where cultural sensitivity must be taken into consideration.
3. What are the two ethnic cultures that have specific identity development models listed in this chapter?
4. When working with clients who are immigrants, you must not only consider the cultural norms from which the client comes, but you must also consider the level of _____.
5. List at least three areas of norms with which you will want to become familiar when meeting a new, culturally different client.
6. One function you will have as a therapist is to teach your client how to _____ _____ _____ _____.
7. Ethical and legal guidelines state that you must be _____ about cultural differences and _____ diversity.
8. List some considerations you must make before scheduling a client for therapy.
9. Communications between you and your client are confidential except under what six conditions?
10. Because clients are likely to have different values from your own, it will be important that you do your own work by undergoing what process?

SUGGESTED READINGS

Baruth, L. G., & Manning, M. L. (2003). *Multicultural counseling and psychotherapy: A lifespan perspective* (3rd ed.). Upper Saddle River, NJ: Prentice Hall.

Cottone, R. R., & Tarvydas, V. M. (2003). *Ethical and professional issues in counseling* (2nd ed.). Upper Saddle River, NJ: Prentice Hall.

Corey, G., Corey, M.S., & Callanan, P. (2003). *Issues and ethics in the helping professions* (6th ed.). Pacific Grove, CA: Brooks/Cole.

Horgan-Garcia, M. (2003). *The four skills of cultural diversity compentence.* Pacific Grove, CA: Brooks/Cole.

Ivey, A. E., D'Andrea, M., Ivey, M. B., & Simek-Morgan, L. (2002). *Theories of counseling and psychotherapy: A multicultural perspective* (5th ed.). Boston: Allyn and Bacon.

Pedersen, P. B., & Carey, J. C. (2003). *Multicultural counseling in schools: A practical handbook* (2nd ed.). Boston: Allyn and Bacon.

Remley, T. P., & Herlihy, B. (2001). *Ethical, legal, and professional issues in counseling.* Upper Saddle River, NJ: Prentice Hall.

Robinson, T., & Howard-Hamilton, M. (2000). *The convergence of race, ethnicity, and gender: Multiple identities in counseling.* Upper Saddle River, NJ: Prentice Hall.

Welfel, E. R. (2002). *Ethics in counseling and psychotherapy: Standards, research, and emerging issues.* Pacific Grove, CA: Brooks/Cole.

CHAPTER 3

Models of Helping

Professional preparation programs are often structured according to two basic approaches. In the first option, you may be studying helping skills before you take a course in theory. It is reasoned that these professional behaviors are so universal among practitioners that it is not necessary to understand their theoretical base before you begin practicing them. Because they take considerable time to learn well and make part of your interpersonal repertoire, the idea is that you should have as much time as possible to master them. Although some of the skills may be learned proficiently in a matter of weeks, mastery of others will take you the rest of your life.

A second training approach requires you to study theories before you learn applied skills. In this approach you postpone learning how to do counseling and therapy until you are first exposed fully to the conceptual base that supports practice. Of course, other possibilities are that you are taking both classes concurrently or as part of an integrated unit in which theory and skills are linked.

In any of the scenarios, the outcome is the same: It is necessary to master both the underlying conceptual base of the profession, including the major theoretical approaches (see Corey, 2001; Ivey, D'Andrea, Ivey, & Simek-Morgan, 2002; Kottler, 2002; Seligman, 2001) *and* the applied interventions that emerged from these models (see De Jong & Berg, 2002, as one example). There are distinct advantages and disadvantages to each preparation method and no clear consensus as to which is best.

THEORIES AND THEIR OFFSPRING

Theories of counseling and psychotherapy provide several distinct uses for practitioners. First of all, they give you a foundation for understanding what you are doing. Second, they provide an organized framework for diagnosis and treatment. Third, theories help you to articulate what your values are about why clients come to therapy and how clients change.

Finally, every theory supplies an inventory of techniques, skills, and interventions that become the means by which the model is applied. For instance, you have probably heard that psychoanalytic theory stresses that it is important to help clients uncover their unconscious desires and repressed wishes (Freud, 1936). This means essentially that the

47

therapist's job is to increase client awareness, especially of things in the past that have been buried, as well as internal thoughts and feelings that are not currently accessible. It is reasoned that bringing such material into view will help people to come to terms with the unresolved issues in the past that are disrupting current functioning and producing annoying symptoms.

It is one thing for Freud and his disciples to present ideas for the best ways they believe therapy should be practiced, and it is quite another when they provide specific methods and skills by which this plan can be carried out. In the case of psychoanalysis, Freud (1936) did introduce certain techniques like dream analysis and specific skills like the use of interpretation to increase client awareness of hidden patterns. Most of the other theories you have studied, or will study, have also spawned particular skills; many of these have now become integrated into mainstream practice and are not restricted to practitioners of that one theory. Many therapists and counselors, from a variety of schools, now use the skills of interpretation in their work even if they don't apply it in the direction that Freud first preferred. Interpretation can be used for a variety of other purposes, such as to offer alternative explanations for patterns or behaviors that may seem puzzling to the client.

Although we used this one example of a skill from psychoanalysis, almost every other theory you have heard about has generated a few other skills that have migrated beyond their original territory. In Table 3.1, we list examples of some prominent theories with corresponding skills that have now entered widespread practice.

Exercise in Brainstorming Skills and Common Concepts

If you have already had the theories course or are concurrently taking it, get into groups of four or five people and list concepts and skills that are found in each of the theories. See if you can connect some common concepts or skills from one theory to the next. For example, projection *is a term found in psychoanalytic as well as Gestalt therapy.*

Table 3.1 provides only a sampling of theoretical approaches and the skills that they produced. There are also many counseling skills that did not emerge from a single theory but rather resulted from observing what therapists actually do with their clients in sessions. It is one of the paradoxes of our profession that it is often difficult to tell which theory a clinician is using just by watching what is going on; often, a theory is more an organizing set of assumptions rather than a blueprint for how to behave. Examples of these universal skills include open-ended questions in which you might elicit information or summarizations in which you tie things together.

What Using a Theory Looks Like

Throughout your studies, you will probably hear about how important it is to align yourself with a theoretical orientation. This may seem like a challenging task because so many theories present clear strengths. In addition, you may think that being eclectic can serve you just as well. However, your theory provides you with a structure, a foundation as to why people do what they do, and how people change. Each theory will offer something useful, and you can actually use any technique in any theory. What your professors are advocating when they

TABLE 3.1

Therapeutic Models and the Skills They Spawned

Theory	Skill	Example
Person-centered	Reflection of feeling	You are feeling overwhelmed by the volume of new ideas that you are being exposed to.
Strategic	Reframing	It's not so much that you are helpless as you have chosen to let others make decisions for you.
Psychoanalytic	Interpretation	The problems with your daughter seem to parallel those you had with your mother.
Behavioral	Goal setting	What is something specific that you can do between now and next week?
Cognitive	Disputing	Where is the evidence to support your belief that you are a worthless person just because of this one mistake?
Gestalt	Enhancing awareness	You are tapping your foot vigorously. If your foot could speak, what would it say?
Existential	Immediacy	I'm aware that right now as you talk about your fears of intimacy you are pulling away from me.
Problem solving	Looking for exceptions	Describe a time recently when the problem did *not* dominate your life and you were able to maintain control.
Adlerian	Socratic dialogue	Tell me more about the anger you feel toward your husband.
Reality	Choice making	What are the consequences of continuing that behavior?

want you to use a theory (and by the way, most state licensure exams expect you to align with one as well) is for you to have a direction in therapy. Every thing you say directs the session. So when a client tells you a story with many different important facets, which one do you focus upon? Your theory may help you answer this.

This is obviously not a theories class, but perhaps we can entice you to really study at least two or three of them well when you take that class. To further illustrate the use of theories, we'll conceptualize several models from the perspective of a character that everyone will be familiar with. Darth Vader, from *Star Wars*, was the villain in the original trilogy of these movies. The more recent *Star Wars* films portray him during his younger years, before he "went over to the Dark Side." We look at Darth's life through the lenses of three theoretical orientations: psychoanalytic, person-centered, and cognitive.

Darth Vader: A Brief Biography

You may know Darth Vader from *Star Wars*, but that was only after his "transformation." Before he became Darth Vader, Anakin Skywalker was raised by his single mother in an implied immaculate conception. During his formative years, he lived in slavery, but had a loving mother who fostered his interests and natural ability to become a talented pilot. At age 9, he was given the opportunity to fulfill his dream of becoming a Jedi warrior, but in order to do so, he had to leave his mother behind in order to undergo rigorous training. He left his home and mother in great sorrow, relieved at having escaped his own fate as a slave but still feeling guilty that his mother had been left behind. As you probably realize, 9 years old would have been a rather traumatic time to be separated from your only living parent.

At age 19, we see Anakin again, still mourning the loss of his mother. During the ensuing decade, he has found love in the arms of a woman senator, and also a mentor and father figure in Obi-Wan. As much as he loved and respected his mentor, Anakin became rebellious (typical of later adolescence), feeling that Obi-Wan did not appreciate his abilities as a Jedi knight. Anakin's rebellion evolved more into anger after the death of his mother, where we see, for the first time, his rage take control over him. Finally, he suffered a traumatic physical injury in the loss of his arm during a battle.

Eventually, Anakin suffers a number of other experiences that move him further toward the "Dark Side." He becomes embittered, rageful, vengeful, and sustains other injuries that require mechanical parts. At one point, he becomes more of a cyborg than a man; Anakin eventually "dies," and Darth Vader is born, complete with the trademark black mask, cape, labored breathing, and voice of James Earl Jones.

Psychoanalytic Theory (Freud) Conceptualization of Darth Vader

According to Freud's (1936) theory, Anakin experienced a strong *oedipal complex* consisting of *unconscious* incestuous desires toward his mother, especially without a father to guide him. These unresolved feelings caused him to be *fixated* in the *phallic stage* of his development. His father figure, Obi-Wan, was considered the enemy, starting with *unconscious wishes* for Obi-Wan's death that eventually became *conscious* and acted on. His mother contributed to his *narcissism* because during his childhood he was indulged as much as possible, enhancing his feelings of grandiosity. Thus, his *ego* was unable to inhibit his strong *id impulses,* enhancing his narcissistic personality.

Anakin/Darth exhibits many of the classic psychoanalytic *defense mechanisms* through the traumas in his life. First of all, he evidenced *denial* that he could have done something to prevent his mother's death. He *displaced* much of this anger onto the Jedi Council, and especially toward his mentor, Obi-Wan. Furthermore, he *projected* his own undesirable arrogance onto Obi-Wan, completely denying his own inflated arrogance. Anakin *rationalized* his conversion from being good to giving over to the Dark Side because the Dark Side provided him more perceived power, when actually he was trying to *compensate* for his weaknesses. Once transitioning to the Dark Side as Darth Vader, he *introjected* the value of power over good and *identified* with Emperor Palpatine, the creature symbolizing the Dark Side.

Person-Centered (Rogers) Conceptualization of Darth Vader

Rogers (1951) would have conceptualized Anakin differently. Anakin was held in *high regard* because of his ability to be a good pilot, creating a *condition of worth*. He believed that if he was a good pilot, he was a worthy person. In addition, when he worked under his mentor, Obi-

Wan, his conditions of worth increased having to behave according to the Jedi standards. This may have been further complicated by the fact that Obi-Wan was someone he respected early in their relationship so that he perceived Obi-Wan as a father figure. This need to please his mentor/father figure was *incongruent* with his own wants and needs, enhancing the gap between his *ideal self* and *self-concept*. Thus, his *organismic valuing process* was externally driven, causing him to have a *regard complex*. As a result, Anakin was unable to *symbolize* positive experiences accurately, causing a *breakdown* and *disorganization* in his *self-structure*, and eventually leading him to feel *confused* and *anxious*. This anxiety and confusion consequently made the Dark Side more tempting in order to enhance his perceived *self-worth*.

If Anakin had been able to express his feelings in a *trusting* relationship where he experienced *unconditional positive regard, warmth, genuineness*, and *empathy*, he might have been able to cope with the loss of his mother and his body image in a more *fully functioning* way, releasing his natural *self-actualizing tendency* to support good, rather than dark forces.

Cognitive Therapy (Beck) Conceptualization of Darth Vader

Beck (1976) might have conceptualized Anakin as having several *cognitive distortions*. First of all, he made an *arbitrary inference* that he could have prevented his mother's death. In addition, he made another *arbitrary inference* that Obi-Wan's intentions were not in his best interest. Anakin *overgeneralized* his negative experience of his mother's death and the loss of his arm that the world was a bad place where he must become powerful in order prevent feeling hurt. He *magnified* Emperor Palpatine's position and *minimized* the power of the Jedi Council, especially his mentor, Obi-Wan. Futhermore, he *personalized* Obi-Wan's criticisms as trying to decrease his personal value rather than seeing Obi-Wan's influence as educational and helpful. He evidenced *dichotomous thinking* by seeing people in one of two ways: powerless or powerful. Thus, wanting to be powerful, he aligned with the Dark Side. After the death of his mother and the loss of his arm, he probably was clinically *depressed*. His probable *automatic thoughts* with regard to his *cognitive triad* were that *he* was worthless without power; that the *world* was out to get him; and that the *future* would be bleak unless he aligned with the Dark Side. These *beliefs* in his triad and his cognitive distortions were probably related to a *dysfunctional* underlying *schema* that he must be all-powerful to be worthy of love.

You may notice a difference in the use of language. You may also observe some commonalities. In all three scenarios, Anakin's negative experiences (mom's death and body injuries) contributed to his angst. Furthermore, he was unable to or not given the right conditions to cope with these losses in a healthier way, leading him to make a poor decision to join with the Dark Side. We believe that if he had undergone counseling, Anakin might have never needed to become Darth Vader. But then, if that had happened, there would have been no *Star Wars* movies, and what fun is there in that?

So you see that although these three theories are quite different in language and what they emphasize, they also use common sense to determine what went wrong with this client, Anakin Skywalker, a.k.a. Darth Vader. Therefore, we hope to encourage you to find a theory or two that emphasizes what you think are important contributors to behavior, and we hope that you will become familiar with one or two in order to help guide you in conceptualization and treatment planning as you work with clients.

THEORETICAL FRAMEWORKS AND MODELS OF PRACTICE

Not only are there different theoretical orientations adopted by practitioners, but even within these schools of thought there are several different ways they may be applied. If we temporarily put aside the notion that there are more than a dozen major theories currently in use (it has been estimated that there are actually several hundred of them), we can concentrate instead on what clinicians do rather than on their underlying conceptual paradigms. Other courses examine the philosophies and theoretical assumptions that guide therapeutic practice, whereas our job is to focus on skills and interventions.

During the past few decades, a number of authors have developed generic models of practice that formed the basis for the instructional methods. Each of these approaches attempted to integrate what is known about "good practices" and then constructed a systematic method for applying the skills. The goal of these endeavors is essentially to provide beginners with most of what they might need to conduct a helpful interview when a client walks in the door.

In one of the first systematic attempts to teach counseling skills in a sequential, problem-solving way, Robert Carkhuff (1969) combined the skills that emerged from Carl Rogers's person-centered approach with a series of studies undertaken to identify those behaviors most associated with positive therapeutic outcomes (Carkhuff & Berenson, 1967). The model that emerged from these efforts is one in which helpers were taught a very structured problem-solving approach that moved from one stage to another, each composed of a series of steps and related skills (Carkhuff & Anthony, 1979).

Thomas Gordon took much of the same material and developed a system for teaching parents (1970) and teachers (1974) the major skills of helping. Parent effectiveness training and teacher effectiveness training thus introduced a whole generation of non-professional "counselors" to the value of active listening and reflecting skills. Students were taught the basics of several specific interventions:

- *Active listening.* This set of skills involves learning how to listen effectively, "decode" underlying affective messages, and then reflect back to the client what was heard. The goal is to promote deeper exploration of issues and lead clients to solve their own problems.
- *"I" messages.* If active listening works well when the client "owns" the problem, then using the pronoun "I" is appropriate when it is the teacher, counselor, or parent who has a problem with what others are doing. If a student is carving his initials in a desk, for example, the teacher might first try saying something like this in a rather stern, scolding voice: "Young man, do you have a problem?"

The student, of course, doesn't have a problem at all. He *likes* defacing the desk with his initials. About the only problem that he has is that the teacher is in his face. In fact, it is the teacher who has a problem. And until the teacher is willing to recognize that in reality, any intervention is not likely to be very useful. He or she can punish the child, send him to the office, make him clean up his mess, but there are considerable side effects to this way of "solving" the problem. If instead the teacher were to use an "I" message it would sound something like this: "Excuse me. I have a problem with what you are doing to that desk. I appreciate that you are expressing your artistic talents, but I am the one responsible for this property. So we have a problem that we are going to need to work out."

This may not sound like much of a difference to you from the first statement, but its approach clarifies who owns the problem. If it is the student's problem, then active listening is indicated; on the other hand, if it is the teacher's or parent's problem, then active listening is not going to be particularly helpful.

Note the use of both skills in the conversation that follows between a father and his 9-year-old daughter:

Daughter: No I won't get dressed! I hate this dress. And I hate these shoes. And besides, you said I could stay home and I didn't have to go.

Father: I can see you're really upset right now. You're mad at me for making you do something that you'd rather not do. [active listening]

Daughter: Well, you told me before that if I didn't want to go, I didn't have to. And I sure don't want to go. So that's the end of it.

Father: So, if I understand what you're saying, this argument isn't really about which dress to wear, but our disagreement about whether you have to go to dinner or not. [active listening]

Daughter: That's right! I don't want to go. And that's it.

Father: Okay. I'm in a bit of a bind and I need your help. I did tell you that you didn't have to go if you didn't want to. You're right. But if you don't go to dinner then I can't go either. And then your mother and brother will be pretty disappointed. So, I wonder if there is something we can do to help me with my problem? ["I" message]

You can see in this brief interaction how the father starts out by resisting the urge to be scolding, to use power and discipline to enforce his will on his daughter. Instead, he listens carefully and compassionately to her, trying to sort out what is really going on. He reflects back to her what he hears her saying. Once he thinks he has a handle on what might be going on (this is only a tentative hypothesis that must be checked out), he then "owns" his share of the problem. Notice he does not become defensive or accusatory. He does not argue with his daughter. He does not yell at her. He simply maintains an active listening stance until the point that he realizes that he is the one with the problem, and until he articulates this reality, he isn't going to get much cooperation from his daughter.

Exercise in Who Owns the Problem

For each of the following statements made by a student to a teacher, who "owns" the problem?

1. *"I'm just so angry at my mother. I can't believe she won't listen to me."* student
2. *"Teacher, you gave me the wrong grade on my exam. I know I did better than this."* Student/Teacher
3. *"You want me to clean up this mess? No way! I didn't do it."* Teacher
4. *"But I was standing in line. Are you blind?"* Teacher

The models introduced by Carkhuff and Gordon revolutionized the ways that counseling skills could be taught. A very complex process was reduced to a few basic skills and a half dozen progressive stages. This made it possible to teach a method previously restricted to psychiatrists and psychologists to a host of other helping professionals: nurses, crisis intervention workers, supervisors, teachers, parents, and others. It also made it possible to take a similar systematic approach to teaching skills for therapists and counselors.

Among the predominant models of training counseling skills that are currently in use, perhaps one of the most popular was developed by Egan (2002). His text on helping skills, now in its seventh edition, presents a very detailed problem-solving method that includes a series of successive steps. This "flow-chart" model follows a tradition first introduced by Gottman and Lieblum (1974) in a manual for mostly behavior therapists that described a series of clinical decisions to be made, such as decide whom to see, negotiate a therapeutic contract, or find out the source of client resistance.

Although not to everyone's taste, there is a certain comfort to a structure like Egan's that prescribes for Stage I, Step I-B—help clients to become aware of their blind spots—or for Stage II, Step II-A—help clients to explore possibilities for the future.

Some models are slanted according to one particular theoretical orientation. For instance, Cormier and Nurius (2003) introduce a system for conducting interviews heavily steeped in the principles of cognitive therapy, Watts and Carlson (1999) favor an Adlerian approach, and Ivey and Ivey (1999) use a constructivist orientation. Still other models for learning helping skills have tried to be more integrative and synthesizing (see Mikulas, 2002; Okun, 2002; Young, 2001).

This text is both similar to its predecessors and also quite different. We have followed the trails blazed by the aforementioned models but also included a number of unique features that we hope will make the learning experience more fun, interesting, and engaging.

STAGES IN THE PROCESS

Stage theory had dominated the fields of psychology and education ever since Sigmund Freud first proposed an integrated theory of psychosexual development (remember the oral, anal, genital, and phallic stages?). Others jumped on the bandwagon and introduced his or her own stage theory to account for some facet of human behavior. Jean Piaget (1967) described stages of cognitive development, followed by a disciple, Laurence Kohlberg (1976), who used a similar template to account for the development of moral thinking. Erik Erikson's (1950) influential theory of psychosocial development was organized around a series of struggles between polar opposites (i.e., trust vs. mistrust, or integrity vs. despair). Since this "golden age" of stage theory, there have been many others describing career development, gender development, sexual development, and cultural identity development. It will therefore come as no surprise to you that counseling and therapy have been organized according to stages as well.

How Many Stages Are There?

I [Jeffrey] was once giving a lecture about counseling skills to a group of nurses in Katmandu, Nepal. I had a total of one hour to teach them everything that might be useful to them in their work with sick and dying patients. Because in Nepal there are very few medications or medical procedures that are readily available to the population, a nurse's compassion, caring, and interpersonal skills form a large part of the medical care that is provided. Needless to say, it felt a bit daunting to try to teach them everything I know, or at least everything I thought they might need, in a single hour.

After reviewing some of the basic concepts mentioned in this text, I tried to save a few minutes at the very end for questions—about four minutes, to be exact. Someone in the audience raised a hand and asked politely how many stages of counseling there were. At first I started to panic because I couldn't remember how many stages there were—the numbers four, five, seven, and nine all kept popping into my head. When I calmed down, I recalled that were a number of different ways of looking at this question, depending on the preferred model.

When I glanced at my watch and noticed I had less than three minutes left, I took a deep breath and gave in to the reality (and absurdity) of the situation. "Look," I told them, talking as fast as I could and hoping their English was good enough to understand anything I had been saying in the previous hour, "there are basically three main stages: a beginning, a middle, and an end." I was about to get into details about which might be included in each stage, but the questioner seemed satisfied with the answer and sat down.

After considerable thought it occurred to us that this simple answer is not far off the mark. In a sense, all counseling *can* be reduced to these three basic stages. But because we have considerably more time than an hour to teach you what we know, and what is known about therapeutic skills, we have expanded these stages to include a few more factors that might otherwise be overlooked. We see no reason to make this organizing model needlessly complex (especially when you are first learning the basic skills), but neither do we wish to minimize all the complex ingredients that go into the mix.

AN INTEGRATED MODEL

We have synthesized many of the different models that have been used over the last few decades into a generic outline that we believe most practitioners could live with. What you need most at this point in your development is a framework that helps you accomplish several critical tasks:

1. *Assess what is going on with your clients.* This includes but is not limited to their presenting complaints, other symptomology that is operating behind the scenes, family history and background, cultural identities and personal values, and anything else that helps you to understand their worlds.
2. *Formulate a diagnosis and treatment plan.* This becomes the outline for organizing the work you will do. Diagnoses can be developed according to a number of different models, some of which might concentrate on personality attributes, behavioral descriptions, developmental functioning, systemic patterns, or other factors. The treatment plan addresses systematically whatever you identified as clinically significant in the diagnosis.
3. *Establish a solid working alliance.* This is the therapeutic relationship that allows you to develop trust and reach treatment goals. The relationship may be structured differently according to client needs and preferences, the nature of the presenting complaint, the length of the treatment, and the particular stage in which you might be operating. Therapeutic relationships evolve over time according to what is needed.

4. *Make good choices about which skills and interventions to use in which situations.* As we have said before, the major problem you will face is not a scarcity of choices but far too many to sort out in the time you have available. A client says or does something and you must respond—immediately. You need some way to simplify and organize your choice efforts.

5. *Figure out where you are in relationship to where you wish to be.* Regardless of which model you are following, you still will need some way to assess accurately the impact of your interventions. In any given moment you must have at least a rough idea of the stage you are operating in and what your goals are. It is also a very good idea to have a defensible rationale for anything you do or say, one that you can explain if called on by a client or supervisor.

Of course, what sort of model you use to organize your work depends on your own stage of development as a professional. These stages can be presented according to a series of questions related to a beginner's fear of failure (Kottler & Blau, 1989):

Stage 1: What if I don't have what it takes to be a therapist?

Hopefully, you are now past the point where you question constantly if you have the stuff it takes to make it in this profession. You may have some doubts and insecurities about how good you will be as a practitioner, especially when you make comparisons to others who seem more poised, confident, and experienced, but deep in your heart you trust that with sufficient training, practice, and hard work, eventually you will reach a point where you can do somebody some good. On a good day, you will notice a few things you do very well; on a not-so-good day you will question all over again whether you made the right career choice.

If you are still feeling stuck in this very first stage in which you are having serious reservations about whether being a therapist is a good fit for you, then the helping model you choose should be one that is very basic and simple to operate. You already have enough to worry about without adding to your stress by making things unnecessarily complicated.

Stage 2: What if I don't know what to do with a client?

If you are feeling okay about your relative abilities to function as a skilled practitioner, the next stage is one in which you are fearful of making a mistake. The usual fantasy is that you will say or do the wrong thing, resulting in the client becoming so distraught by your ineptitude that he or she immediately jumps out the window, cursing your name all the way down.

As a beginner, of course you won't know what do with a client. We have been doing this work for many decades and we still don't know what to do a lot of the time. The experience of doing therapy is one of living continuously with ambiguity, complexity, and uncertainty. When you think you might be helping someone you might find out later that the effects didn't last, or that the person was just deceiving you and himself. Other times you will be sure that you have screwed up big-time only to discover later that what you thought were misguided efforts turned out to be a brilliant strategy. Then there will be other times when the client thanks you profusely for your masterful interventions—only you will have no recall whatsoever about what you supposedly did. The question is not whether you will feel uncertain at times but rather how you will handle these doubts.

Stage 3: What if my treatment harms a client?

If in the previous stage you are wracked with doubts about not knowing what to do in a given situation, in this stage you are concerned more with the consequences—most of them negative—of making a huge mistake. At this point you recognize the awesome power of what you have learned; the concern is how to harness this power.

If you get inside the head of a therapist at this stage, you might hear something like the following:

Therapist: Where would you like to begin? [What a stupid way to say that. I should have just asked what he wants to talk about today.]

Client: Um. I don't know.

Therapist: You don't know? [What am I, a parrot? All I can think of to say is to repeat what he says?]

Client: Remember last time what I was talking about things my supervisor said?

Therapist: Sure. You were talking about how angry you were feeling because she wasn't being fair to you. [Oh no. I'm putting words in his mouth. I don't think he was saying that at all; rather, that was where I wanted to lead him.]

Client: I was?

Therapist: Um, so what would you like to talk about then? [I'm such an idiot! Now what did I do?]

This therapist is obviously being unnecessarily hard on herself but it gives you a sample of how concerned any of us can be with making mistakes. If there is an overriding fear of failure, then the clinician is going to try to proceed in a way to minimize risks and errors.

Stage 4: What if I'm not really doing anything?

This stage is for more experienced therapists who have been practicing for some time. Once you have mastered the basics and become comfortable with the major skills, you have time to wonder about the relative value of your work. Are your clients really changing or maybe just pretending to change?

Stage 5: What if my life's work doesn't really matter?

Here you are trying to change the world, one life at a time, but perhaps none of this really matters.

Given the stage of development in which most readers might be currently operating (somewhere in the first three stages) we have organized the process of helping (and this text) according to four basic stages. We believe that this outline for understanding the therapeutic process is neither needlessly complicated nor simplistic. It represents our best efforts to preserve the wonderful complexity of what we do, yet does not (yet) burden you with things you probably don't need at this stage.

1. The Beginning Stage

Think through this logically and analytically. A new client walks in the door. What are the first things you need to do and the first tasks you must accomplish in order to get any productive work done?

This is not rocket science to figure out some lengthy, hidden formula that takes brilliant minds all their best efforts to find the answer; it is all quite obvious: Unless you can get clients to respect you and like what you are doing, they won't come back a second time, and that makes it very difficult to help anyone. So your first task is to inspire some sort of trust and confidence. You must establish rapport and a working relationship that is designed to elicit the information you need and yet also help the client feel comfortable and safe enough to talk about some very threatening and personal issues (Rogers, 1951, 1961).

You have four main tasks to accomplish in this first stage:

1. Establish a working alliance.
2. Complete an assessment and formulate a diagnosis.
3. Conduct a treatment plan.
4. Negotiate a contract and mutual goals.

The major skills that you will be learning and using that are linked to this stage incude questioning and reflective listening. These are behaviors that are specifically designed to elicit information efficiently, as well as to develop a relationship with clients that builds trust, intimacy, and respect.

This is what the beginning stage looks and sounds like in the middle of the first session with a new client, about twenty minutes into the interview.

Therapist: When did you first begin to notice that you were having difficulty sleeping? [open-ended question to elicit more information on the symptoms of anxiety]
Client: I can't really recall. It seems like it's always been like this.
Therapist: So your sleep has been disrupted for some time. [restatement]
Client: I guess so. I don't really know. All of this is just so overwhelming that I can't remember things anymore. I don't even know what I'm doing here.
Therapist: You're having some doubts about your decision to come for help and you're feeling like things may be hopeless for you. [reflection of client's most terrifying feelings]
Client: [nods head] So, what do you think I should do? Can you help me or not?
Therapist: I think that your decision to seek help at this time is a sign of your resilience and strength. [reassurance and support] You have been feeling so alone and already you will notice that some of that has diminished. [instilling confidence and planting favorable expectations] Yes, I can help you. I've worked with issues like this many times before. Before we proceed further, I'd like to ask you: what would you like to have happen as a result of our work together? [question about expectations and treatment goals]

The therapist is trying to accomplish several things simultaneously. At the same time, he or she is learning as much as possible about the symptoms and when they occur, while also offering support and reassurance. There is a lot more the therapist will want to explore: what the anxiety feels like, when it first occurred, what has worked and not worked in dealing with it, whether these symptoms have occurred before, whether there is a history of this disorder in the family, what the consequences are of having these symptoms, and so on. Yet gathering all this important information to satisfy the therapist's curiosity and needs is worthless unless the client feels heard and understood. It is absolutely crucial that the initial exploration of the problem is balanced with sufficient efforts to build a good working relationship.

Building a good working relationship involves reflecting, reflecting not only the content and the feelings expressed by the client, but the meaning and emotions beneath what is being presented. We are not the only people who believe that the working alliance is a necessary condition of therapy. All of the other primary theorists believe it is the foundation of therapy. As stated before, if the client does not like you or have confidence in what you do, why would he or she be motivated to return for more sessions? It is difficult enough for most clients to make it to the first session. If the client can find a reason not to return, he or she may not. So, you have to create a strong working alliance and maintain this relationship throughout the therapeutic process.

Exercise in Building the Relationship

Get into pairs and have one person talk for five minutes about an emotionally charged issue (client role). The other person (therapist role) is to reflect a feeling and some content in one sentence that is most essential about what the "client" said. Have the client respond with agreement or a correction, and repeat until the reflection is accurate. Once complete, switch roles.

---

2. Exploration and Understanding

What you began in the first stage is continued as things develop further. The relationship is deepened. More and more data are collected about the client's presenting complaints and annoying symptoms, preexisting conditions, relevant family and cultural background, and other important areas of personal functioning. Essentially, you are exploring what is going on now and what has been going on in the past. This is not an activity that is taken solely for the therapist's comfort and curiosity; rather, the very process of getting significant background information is also related to helping promote greater awareness and understanding in the client.

Just as you might expect, there are as many ways of promoting this understanding as there are approaches to therapy. Some systems like behavior therapy or brief treatments minimize this stage, believing that insight is, at best, needlessly time-consuming and irrelevant, and at worst, downright dangerous. We would certainly agree that the realities of contemporary practice sometimes require us to abbreviate our treatment to a few sessions. However, we also find that when it is feasible to include some component of insight, such efforts often help clients to generalize what they learned to other areas of their lives.

Depending on your own therapeutic style and theoretical allegiances, insight can be promoted in a number of different ways. A cognitive therapist would concentrate on helping clients understand how problems are the result of distorted and irrational thinking patterns. The nature of the insight work is focused on helping them to identify those dysfunctional beliefs that are getting in the way and learning to substitute alternative perceptions that are more reality based (Beck, 1976).

Once a strong working alliance has been established and maintained, the therapist would help the client to explore the current problem by looking for patterns of behavior that were established in childhood. Once an awareness of where the patterns stems from is reached (usually based upon a mistaken belief or beliefs), then the client can choose to see self, others, or the world in a more realistic way and act accordingly. Insight is not reached until awareness, cognitive change, *and* behavioral change occur (Adler, 1963).

A classical psychoanalytic therapist might encourage the client to free associate to hopefully bring about a catharsis. This process allows the client to bring unconscious material into consciousness, enhancing his or her insight to what has driven the client unconsciously in the past (Freud, 1936).

Within Gestalt therapy, one of the assumptions about what brings people to therapy is that they have not fully experienced something. They feel resistant and fearful to go deeper into a certain experience, such as pain or despair. They are stuck at an impasse. A Gestalt therapist, then, would help the client move into those feelings (or thoughts) in a way that allows a deep immersion into those experiences and the freedom to express what the client has previously feared to release. Once the client has moved through the impasse and experienced and expressed what was lying underneath, usually an insight occurs helping the client understand what has kept him or her stuck (Perls, 1969).

The type of insight that is promoted depends not only on therapist preferences but also on client needs and time parameters. One of the first questions we like to find out in the early stages of treatment is: How much time do we have together to work this out? Obviously, you would structure therapy differently with a client who was only coming for one meeting versus another who was committed to attending sessions for several years. So if the first question you

TABLE 3.2

Types of Insight

Theory	Type of Insight
Psychoanalytic	Uncover unconscious desires and make sense of the past
Existential	Create meaning to human existence
Person-centered	Access, understand, and express feelings
Cognitive	Identify and confront cognitive distortions
Reality	Examine avoidance of responsibility for choices
Gestalt	Enhance awareness to complete gestalts
Adlerian	Changing mistaken beliefs and consequent behaviors that perpetuate the problem
Narrative	Tell the story in a different way

end up asking is, "How can I help you?," one of the next things you will wonder about, if not ask aloud, is, "How much time have we got?"

Compare the different ways you would manage the Insight Stage according to these client responses:

- "Look, I'm kind of in a hurry. I'd prefer that we finish this thing today, but if you really think it's necessary, maybe I could come back another time."
- "I understand that therapy takes a long time, maybe years. I'm not looking for a quick fix. I really want to get to the bottom of things and I'm prepared to do whatever it takes to make this happen."
- "My kids are both sick. I'm out of money. I've got nowhere else to turn. I just think that I might as well give up. I think everyone would just be better off if I wasn't around anymore."
- "I've been sent here by my probation officer. I'm here to serve my six sessions and then get on with things."
- "I keep getting myself into these awful relationships. I dump one loser and then end up living with another one who is worse off than the one before. It's almost like I can't help myself."
- "I'm really not satisfied with my life. I'm in my mid-thirties and I can't keep a steady job. I don't have a career, a family, or anything to show for myself. I feel like a loser."
- "Look, my parents think I need to be here just because my grades aren't perfect in school. I don't have a problem; they do. I'm just busy with hockey. That's all."

Exercise in Insight

With partners, or on your own, develop a plan for the kinds of insight that you might promote for each of the clients who are presented in the above scenarios. Role-play each scenario.

We don't wish to give the impression that we are "selling" you insight as a necessary and sufficient condition for change to take place. This particular phrasing of "necessary and sufficient" was exactly the phrasing used by Rogers (1961) in his research, in which he believed that it was quite enough to help clients access, understand, and express their feelings (i.e., insight). However, like Rogers, many of the great theorists believe that insight is an important condition of therapy. For example, Freud (1936) proposed that "good" therapy helps people to understand their pasts as a way to free them from dysfunctional behavior in the present. Although Rogers believed that most of the action took place in the realm of feelings, Freud was far more concerned with understanding unconscious and repressed desires. Cognitive therapists also subscribe to the philosophy that insight is critical for change, but, as we mentioned, they are concentrating on underlying belief structures (Beck, 1976). Existential therapists value insight tremendously as well, but they are interested in uncovering the meanings to life (May, 1953). Gestalt therapists are interested in enhancing awareness so that clients can fully experience an incomplete gestalt, creating an insight not only at a cognitive level, but at a full mind, body, and spirit level (Perls, 1969). Within individual psychology, insight is the final stage of therapy where a change occurs not only in awareness, but also in the way a person thinks and behaves externally (Adler, 1963).

It is our position, and the one we take throughout this book, that insight is important and valuable but it is often not enough to promote lasting changes. You probably know several people who have been in therapy for a long time, may understand perfectly why they are so screwed up, but still persist in their self-defeating behavior. It is therefore entirely possible to understand what is going on but still be unable to do much to change the situation. A particularly good example of this has to do with addictions. A substance abuser *knows* that doing drugs or drinking all the time is not a good thing to do. But he or she is still unable to stop. An even more common example has to do with smoking. Every smoker today understands all too well the health risks of continuing to engage in this behavior. Most people would love to break this habit. But they still can't stop.

When there is time to foster some kind of insight, this stage offers a number of advantages:

1. It satisfies the human urge to make sense of life.
2. It helps people to generalize what they learned to other areas of their life.
3. It teaches skills for working systematically to deal with problems in the future.
4. It can sometimes foster change.

Given the variety of ways that insight and understanding are employed in different therapeutic systems, you can appreciate that there would be a lot of diversity in the skills that are used most often. If the skills in the previous stage are centered around exploration, then the ones at this juncture are designed to increase awareness and help move clients to a different level of understanding about themselves and the world. This means that people must often be provoked and challenged in order to give up comfortable but ineffective coping strategies in lieu of others that are more fully functioning. The major skills employed include confrontation, challenging, reflecting discrepancies, and information giving.

In the following vignette, some of the major features of the insight stage are evident.

Client: I guess the anxiety that I've been feeling is nothing new for me. When I was much younger—I think when I was in elementary school—I had problems going to school. And my parents tell me I was always afraid of strangers.

Therapist: So what you are experiencing right now is part of an ongoing pattern in your life that began when you were quite young. The risks that you avoid at work, and in your most important relationships, represent your best efforts to protect yourself from being hurt.

Client: Yeah. I'd say that is probably true.

Therapist: You think of yourself as rather fragile, as if you can't take much stress or you'd fall apart.

Client: [nods head]

Therapist: But if that was really the case then how could you possibly have learned to live with your anxiety for so long?

Client: What do you mean?

Therapist: I think you are a lot tougher than you give yourself credit for. You are amazingly resourceful in the ways you have learned to live with your fears. Somehow you've managed to keep your job and your friendships. You strike me as pretty competent in a lot of areas—in spite of your handicap.

Client: You really think so?

Therapist: Well, what do you think? Let's look at the evidence.

This gentle confrontation is intended to help the client to examine alternative ways of looking at his or her situation. The therapist is introducing another way of viewing the situation: Instead of weakness, things have been reframed as a kind of strength. The client has not yet agreed to this interpretation, but this conversation is typical of the negotiations that take place in therapy. In part, our job is to teach clients alternative ways of looking at their lives. We do this through an assortment of different skills that are all designed to challenge thinking, clarify feelings, and provoke people to consider alternative viewpoints that are more helpful. And all of this must be accomplished while still being mindful of the relationship with the client.

3. Action Stage

This component of the process isn't so much about what clients think or feel but how they will act. The bottom line for clients is the question: "Based on what you now understand, what are you going to do?"

Like the previous stages, this part of the process is interpreted differently according to the practitioner's favored theoretical orientation. One therapist might explicitly ask each client about structured homework assignments after sessions, each of which is designed to build specific behaviors and work towards established goals. Another therapist might interpret action to include things that the client will think about between sessions.

Although there are, occasionally, clients you will see who are less interested in making specific changes in their lives than they are just spending some time understanding themselves better, the vast majority of your caseload will have rather annoying symptoms they wish to eliminate. Your job is to help them to do so by making successive progress towards their preferred goals.

An adolescent boy has been talking for several weeks about his interest in making more friends. The counselor helped him to look at the origins of this problem, how being a loner became an established pattern when his younger brother was hospitalized and his older sister went away to college. He was also helped to look at his fears of rejection and the consequences of this protective strategy. In this fourth meeting with his school counselor, he is pressed to translate what he now understands into some form of action.

Client: So, what I was telling you is . . .

Counselor: Excuse me but I see we're almost out of time today.

Client: Oh. Sorry.

Counselor: No problem. I just wanted to bring that to your attention so we could save some time to think of some ways that you could apply what we have been talking about to your life.

Client: I'm not sure what you mean.

Counselor: Just that we could talk about this stuff on and on, but unless you make some changes in the way you do things, nothing much is going to be different. You're still not going to have many friends.

Client: So, what do you want me to do?

Counselor: The question isn't what I want you to do but rather what you would be prepared to do.

Client: Go on.

Counselor: That's just it. Talk is great but my question for you is what you intend to do about the things we've been discussing.

Client: You mean I should just go up to people and ask them to be my friends.

Counselor: You could try that, of course, but it isn't likely to work very well. I had in mind that you start out with something that might be a small step in that direction. What could you do between now and next week when we next talk? Ideally, this would be something small but important, something that would make you feel like you are making definite progress in the right direction.

The major skills used in the action stage are those designed to increase client motivation and momentum, as well as provide structure for reaching goals. Although some theories, such as psychoanalytic (Freud, 1936), person-centered (Rogers, 1951), and existential (Yalom, 1954), pay less attention toward an action stage, many of the theories specifically address this process. For instance, in individual psychology, the final stage of therapy is insight (as stated before), but insight is not only an understanding of the problem, it's practicing new ways to be in the world or with others (Adler, 1963). With Gestalt therapy, the client frequently experiences the action stage in the session with the therapist to enhance awareness such as the empty chair technique, where a client might imagine speaking to her father (Perls, 1969). In cognitive therapy, action is seen in the homework that might be assigned to clients to increase their awareness of how they think and react in certain situations, and then finally to change the thoughts or cognitive distortion in the moment (Beck, 1976). Behavioral therapists might challenge the client to make changes in session and, subsequently, out in the world once a certain level of confidence is built (Wolpe, 1958). Both cognitive and behavioral changes are expected to occur within reality therapy (Glasser, 1965) and rational emotive behavior therapy (Ellis, 1973).

The reality of being a therapist is that you will be accountable not only to yourself or your client for evidencing change, but also to the agency you work for and any insurance company or health maintenance organization (HMO) that might be helping to pay for your client's sessions. Although insight can be wonderful, actual change in the client's behavior or experience *must* occur in order for therapy to be deemed successful in the opinion of most agencies and insurance companies/HMOs. Therefore, regardless of your theoretical orientation, you will need to define goals and have some sort of evidence toward reaching those goals to proceed with therapy. Of course there is an exception to this rule. If you have the luxury of working with a client in a private practice and the client is self-paying, then you can do whatever is comfortable for you and your client. However, you will find that, as you gain more experience as a therapist, you will want to see evidence of change to know that your interventions are helpful to your client. After all, that's what you came to this field to do: Change one life at a time.

Exercise in Action

Using the scenarios role-played earlier, see if you can generate specific goals for each and role-play a technique that might move the client toward that goal.

---

4. Integration

As things move toward closure, clients are helped to prepare for the end of treatment. Concerns and apprehensions are addressed. An assessment is made to determine the extent that original goals were met. Clients are taught to apply what they have learned to other areas of their lives. They are encouraged to have relapses so they can practice recovering from them. They are prepared in every way possible to be their own therapists in the future.

In the following conversation you can see the integration stage in action:

Client: That's about it for now. So where do we go next?

Therapist: It sounds like we are moving to a point where you can imagine a time when these sessions will no longer be needed. You've been making some solid progress and we're almost done with our work, or at least the goals that we originally established.

Client: Are you kicking me out? [laughs]

Therapist: No, not at all. We can keep talking as long as this is helpful to you. I'm just concerned with you being able to do more and more of the stuff we've been doing on your own. All along you've been learning how to be your own therapist.

Client: I guess that's so. But I'm just worried that once we stop I'll revert back to the way things were.

Therapist: That's not only possible but highly likely.

Client: Excuse me?

Therapist: Of course you will have slip-ups. I can see how anxious you look even thinking about that possibility, but consider that when you do have setbacks you can simply apply what you've already learned. In fact, I think that a good place for us to go next would be to arrange for you to mess up deliberately so we can see how you handle this situation.

The therapist is implementing a strategy in which he or she is prescribing a relapse in order to improve the client's confidence and ability to resist deterioration once the therapy ends. This client's fears are entirely reasonable. During this final stage, the therapist's job is to help the client to handle whatever might come up in the future. Even after the treatment ends, follow-up sessions can be scheduled on a monthly basis to make sure that the momentum has continued. Frequently, therapists see clients over the course of years. The client may come for six or eight sessions, then terminate for a year, and reappear when a new challenge occurs. Therapy does not have to be something static with a single beginning, middle, and end, but rather therapy can be something dynamic that's taken when needed, like aspirin for a headache.

So when does therapy end? That's a good question. If you are in training, it could end at the end of the semester. It could end when the HMO or insurance company stops paying, which is sometimes around six sessions. Therapy could end once a concrete goal is established.

However, the ending is usually more vague and nebulous. Termination is something that is agreed on between the client and therapist and should always be left with an invitation to return, if needed in the future.

APPLICATIONS TO SELF: CHOOSING AND USING A THEORY

Many programs require that you choose a theory to utilize when you begin working with clients. Some state licensure boards require proficiency with at least one theory, and most licensure exams require some familiarity with all of the primary theories. So, the question is: How do you choose a theory?

Before discussing how to choose, let's start with your resistance to this process. One common response from many students is that they like several theories and find many techniques useful from all theories. They feel frustrated that they must choose one and prefer, instead, to be eclectic. The problem is, in order to provide good therapy, you must have a rationale for applying certain interventions, an underlying structure that motivates the direction of mutually negotiated goals. Without that structure, you will have difficulty justifying what you do. So, even if you choose to be eclectic, you are likely to have some beliefs about how to treat each client, a foundation from which to work. Thus, you are still using a theory, a theory of eclecticism (Slife & Williams, 1995). So it's difficult to escape the fact that utilizing an underlying structure or theory is necessary.

The good news is that research indicates that the choice of theory is far less important in determining therapeutic outcomes than the ability to use the theory effectively. Therefore, choosing a theory to learn well is what's most essential because there is no right or wrong approach; rather the best theory is the one you feel most comfortable with (for now). Remember, you can always change if it doesn't fit. You aren't stuck with it for life.

In addition, we have found that good therapists all look basically the same, but differ in how they explain what they do. Most theories are essentially getting at the same task of finding underlying causes of behavior that must usually be understood and then consciously changed. That's why we presented our eclectic stage theory as a way to provide a structure for *what* you do. The other primary theorists give the motivations for *why* you do what you do.

Okay, let's assume you have, reluctantly or not, agreed to choose one. Let's talk about how you choose, before discussing the best way to use it. First, you must think about what brings people to therapy and how people change.

If you believe that clients come to therapy because of unconscious drives and can change once those drives are made conscious, then psychoanalysis might be the theory for you. On the other hand, if you believe people feel discouraged because the feelings of inferiority are ineffectively dealt with by striving for significance in a socially useless way, and that change occurs once the client has the courage to accept his or her feelings of inferiority that are overcome in a socially useful way (by belonging), then individual psychology (Adler) might be your theory. Existential therapy might be more your cup of tea if you believe that people come to therapy because they lack meaning in their life, and change can occur once they realize they have the freedom to choose meaning and take responsibility for their lives. Or you may be attracted to person-centered therapy, which focuses on how the client's ideal self and perceived self are incongruent due to conditions of worth, and once the appropriate conditions of warmth, empathy, genuineness, and unconditional positive regard are provided to the client, he or she will be able to realize his or her actualizing tendency to become a more fully functioning person.

If you see that individuals get stuck at an impasse because they feel fearful to fully experience something painful, and by fully experiencing that pain through some sort of expression, the client can increase his or her awareness to change how that pain is experienced, then Gestalt therapy might be more interesting to you. Another possible paradigm that might parallel your belief system is of cognitive-behavioral therapy, where people come for help because they have cognitive distortions, and once the schemas that hold those distortions are confronted and changed, then the client's affect and behavior change as well. Finally, if you believe that all of our problems are found within a system and must be changed by working within that system, then family systems therapy might be more appropriate for you.

You may have noticed that in each of the descriptions just given, a special language was used to say that the client comes to counseling because of some problem (i.e., unconscious drive; discouragement; meaning; conditions of worth; impasse; cognitive distortions; or systemic dysfunction), that an exploration must occur to gain insight to that problem (i.e., the techniques of each of these theories), and finally, that some kind of change will occur once a shift takes place (i.e., unconscious material made conscious; courage and belonging; responsibility; fully experiencing; changing schemas; or change in a system). And the beauty of it is that you can use any technique you want as long as you can rationalize how you are using this process within your theoretical framework. So the hard part is exploring your value system, and then studying each of the theories that you think might best align with your values. After learning the top two or three really well (we're talking about reading more than what your theory textbook describes) then you are more prepared to choose one and learn to use it. In addition, we recommend talking with practitioners or professors who align with the theories that interest you to gain a deeper understanding. And so we get to how to best use your theory of choice.

Once you master (if that's possible) the basic counseling skills, especially of building a solid relationship with the client, you will need to do other things with most clients to bring about change. Your theory helps you to understand why your client is experiencing this problem. Once you are able to conceptualize your client's problem and identify the consequent goal, then you use your theory to help explain why you say what you say to the client, why you apply certain interventions with the client, or why you suggest a certain homework assignment. Your theory provides you with a rationale and direction for therapy. Theory is one of your best tools for understanding the therapeutic process, which you must usually share with your supervisor(s), teacher(s), or HMO/insurance company in the form of case notes and other paperwork. Therefore, although identifying your own values and studying the theory that matches you best is a daunting task, you will be better prepared to serve your clients effectively.

SUMMARY

In this chapter, we have covered some information about how skills and theory work together within the therapeutic process. We talked about how many theories have specific stages in the process, and how other writers have worked to create an eclectic model for working with clients. Finally, we examined our own model for conceptualizing the therapeutic process with four primary stages: the beginning stage, conceptualization and understanding, the action stage, and the integration stage. These stages are broken down in the following chapters, with more detail to help you work with clients more effectively.

A CHECK ON WHAT YOU LEARNED

1. What are two skills that can be used with teachers and counselors to facilitate deeper exploration and assign appropriate ownership of issues?
2. The two basic interventions used regardless of theory are what?
3. According to the authors, how many stages are there to therapy?
4. What is the most important task of therapist in the beginning stage of therapy?
5. True/false: All theorists agree that insight is a necessary step in therapy.
6. The authors believe that insight is an _____ and _____ part of the therapeutic process.
7. The primary skill of the action stage is to increase client _____ and _____.
8. Relapses in the therapeutic process toward reaching a goal are _____ and _____.
9. Research indicates that the _____ of theory is less important than the _____ of theory for determining therapeutic outcomes.
10. _____ is one of the best tools for understanding the therapeutic process.

SUGGESTED READINGS

Corey, G. (2001). *Theories and practice of counseling and psychotherapy* (6th ed). Belmont, CA: Wadsworth.

Egan, G. (1998). *The skilled helper: A problem-management approach to helping* (6th ed.). Pacific Grove, CA: Brooks/Cole.

Ivey, A. E., D'Andrea, M., Ivey, M. B., & Simek-Morgan, L. (2002). *Theories of counseling and psychoanalyzing: A multicultural perspective*. Boston: Allyn and Bacon.

Kottler, J. (2002). *Theories in counseling and therapy: An experiential approach*. Boston: Allyn and Bacon.

Mikulas, W. L. (2002). *The integrative helper: Convergence of Eastern and Western traditions*. Pacific Grove, CA: Brooks/Cole.

Okun, B. (2002). *Effective helping: Interviewing and counseling techniques*. Pacific Grove, CA: Brooks/Cole.

Seligman, L. (2001). *Systems, strategies, and skills of counseling and psychotherapy*. Columbus, OH: Merrill Prentice Hall.

PART II

CHAPTER 4

Skills for Building
Collaborative Relationships

Although this is a chapter about relationship skills in a book about counseling skills, we want you to know from the outset that building relationships with people involves far more than applying a few helping behaviors. Although it is true that some of these actions are conducive to constructing closer connections with people, human intimacy and trust develop in far more complex and mysterious ways. You can do all the right things with a client, apply your relationship skills with perfect mastery, and still fail to establish any sort of meaningful connection.

YOUR BEST RELATIONSHIPS

Think about the most powerful and influential relationships you have ever experienced. Aside from your parents, who were the teachers, coaches, and mentors who made the most difference in your life?

As you reflect on these relationships, now consider: What was it that these powerful individuals did that helped you the most?

Our strong hunch is that some of the following attributes played a prominent role:

1. *You felt safe.* You were allowed to make mistakes and learn from them. You were not manipulated, abused, or taken advantage of. You felt essential trust.
2. *You felt respected.* You were treated with essential kindness and caring. Even if the mentor was a strict taskmaster, you still felt that this structure was enforced for your welfare.
3. *You felt valued.* You were treated as if you were important and as if what you thought and felt and did really mattered.
4. *You felt understood.* It was clear to you that this mentor heard you, responded to your needs, and demonstrated high levels of empathy.

USES OF THE THERAPEUTIC RELATIONSHIP

It might seem to you as if the only function of your helping relationships with clients is to build sufficient trust so that they will tell you what is really bothering them, but that is only a small part of what is possible within this alliance. It is certainly true that without a solid relationship, it would be hard for you to accomplish much. You must keep in mind, however, that there are very different sorts of relationships that can evolve and prove useful, depending on such factors as (a) what the client needs, (b) what the client would respond best to, and (c) the stage of counseling that you are operating within. Keep in mind that in the very beginning of your contact one sort of relationship is appropriate, whereas in the latter stages you would wish to construct a very different sort of alliance.

Imagine, for instance, that you are greeting a helper for the first time. What would you like from this person to help you feel most comfortable? You would probably want someone who is polite, careful, reassuring, supportive, and who makes it clear that things will move at your pace. Yet once you have established some degree of rapport and trust with this person, you might very well be open to a more directive, confrontive, and perhaps less structured interaction. The ways you use the relationship with your clients thus depend on where you are in the process and which treatment goals are currently being addressed.

If a client presented himself for treatment because he was shy, withdrawn, and friendless, you would probably create a different sort of relationship with this person than you would with another client who was embroiled in conflicts because she was overly verbal, gregarious, and controlling. In the first case, you might try to allow the client to take more responsibility for the process in order to bolster confidence and teach assertive skills, whereas in the latter instance you might wish to install more structure and boundaries to offer constructive feedback. Therefore, let us cover some of the basic uses of the client–therapist relationship.

Diagnostic Aid

How a client behaves with you in session offers clues as to how this person interacts with people in the outside world. You can observe very closely the patterns with which your relationship evolves, and how the client responds to you, and use this valuable information to generate hypotheses about what may be happening in other relationships.

A client says to you that he wishes to have more intimate relationships with people. You invite him to tell you more about how this isolation feels to him. He then becomes angry with you for being intrusive and withdraws into a pouting posture. When you attempt to draw him out he lashes out and calls you incompetent. There may, of course, be many reasons to account for this conflict, but one possibility is that this behavior is characteristic of the ways he deals with personal overtures. Perhaps, you surmise, what he has just done with you he does with others. You will have to check that out, naturally, but your close observation of the ways your clients establish relationships with you gives you pause for consideration about ongoing patterns in their lives.

Interpersonal Engagement

Your relationships with clients can act as powerful vehicles for influencing them in a variety of ways. In a sense, one of your jobs is to impact clients in as many ways as you can within the limited time you have together. This is a daunting mission, given all the other influences (many of them counterproductive) in the client's life, the short period of time you spend in sessions, the client's fears and apprehensions, and the tendency to backslide to old, familiar habits.

Through your engagement with clients, you develop the leverage to influence clients in ways that you think would be good for them. Basically, most clients don't want to take risks, don't want to do things that might be difficult, and don't want to experience any discomfort. They even prefer the pain they know over the prospect of other pains associated with the unknown that could be worse. So they often dig in their heels and may resist your efforts to get them to do things or complete therapeutic tasks. Your job is to develop as much influence as you can to motivate people to do things that they would prefer not to do.

A client complains that her job is meaningless and unfulfilling. She says over and over she wishes she had the courage to quit her present situation and find employment elsewhere where she would have more responsibility and opportunities for growth. "So," you say to her, "why don't you do just that?"

"Do what?" she answers.

"Quit your job. Why don't you find a better opportunity?"

The client supplies lots of excuses and reasons why this isn't possible at this time. You point out that she has been unhappy and dissatisfied for over two years and yet still hasn't taken any significant steps to move on.

It is clear in this situation that the client feels some ambivalence about changing her situation. She is fearful and apprehensive. Her job is not good but she has learned to live with the mediocrity. She wonders if things might be worse somewhere else.

In order to motivate her to take action, you will need a high degree of interpersonal engagement and influence with her. Your relationship with her becomes the leverage by which you are able to get her to act, one small step at a time.

Unfinished Business

Sigmund Freud and his psychoanalytic legacy were instrumental in sensitizing us to the power of the past in shaping present behavior. People respond to others in particular ways, not just because of what is happening right now, but what has happened before. We sometimes don't see another as they are but how we imagine them to be. These perceptions are often distorted. They are also "grooved" as a result of patterns that were established long ago, often during childhood.

Clients will sometimes respond to you in ways that may seem way out of proportion to reality. Called "transference," these reactions represent client fantasies about who you are. As an authority figure, as someone in a position of power in their lives, you may resemble others they have known (parent figures, other helpers) in the past. You may do or say something that evokes an extreme response. When you replay the scene you are puzzled by why the client reacted so negatively, or even why the client has attached himself so closely to you. After all, you hardly know this person. Countertransference reactions, that is, the distorted ways that you see your clients based on your own fantasies and past experiences, further complicate matters.

Once you can accurately read and identify the ways that unfinished business from the past plays itself out in sessions, you can use your relationship to act as an instrument of healing. Imagine, for example, that a client has never had a positive relationship with an authority figure before in which she has not suffered as a result of her misplaced trust. No matter what else you do to help this person, your relationship with her, if it is structured in a way to help her to feel safe, can help to restore her faith in others who may serve in an authority role in the future.

Problem-Solving Collaboration

There are some approaches to therapy, especially the brief and cognitive therapies, which construct relationships that are based on a collaborative model. Partners in this process both work together to sort out what is going wrong and then put their heads together to figure out what can be done instead. The role of the therapist is structured more as a consultant rather than as benevolent parent figure or expert teacher.

Regardless of the kind of work that you do, there will be times when you will slip into this role of consultant and structure the kind of relationship that is more egalitarian with shared responsibility for content and process. In the previous example of the woman unhappy with her job, the clinician first tried direct intervention but encountered resistance. He then decided to abandon this kind of relationship as ineffective and redesigned an alliance in which they would work together as collaborators on a problem that was "externalized" so as to feel less threatening to the client.

"Let's approach this situation as if the problem is not yours," the therapist introduces, "but rather belongs to someone else. How might we tackle this challenge?"

Note in the use of the pronoun "we," the therapist is making it clear that this is a partnership, a relationship in which they will work together to solve a problem in a systematic fashion.

Personal Support System

It would be difficult to underestimate the importance of our role as a source of support in clients' lives. Apart from anything else you do, any interventions you use or any techniques or skills you employ, standing in a person's corner provides immeasurable benefits. So often, clients feel isolated and alone in their pain. They lack confidence. They are dispirited and demoralized. They feel little hope for the future and sometimes want to give up.

One of the most consistent things we can do to help clients is support them in their efforts to change. We communicate, as strongly as possible, the following messages:

- "I am here for you."
- "No matter how bad things get, you can always count on me."
- "Even if I don't approve of some of the self-defeating things you do, I still support you as a person."
- "I am utterly reliable and dependable."
- "I will never take advantage of you or do anything deliberately to hurt you."
- "I have no vested interest in the choices you make; my only job is to help you to get what you want."

It feels wonderful, more comforting than words can ever describe, to be involved in a relationship with a professional who is so completely trustworthy and supportive. We inspire faith. We teach people that it is indeed possible to be involved in a relationship with someone who will cherish you. Although our commitment is a professional one, in a sense we hope our clients will become so used to this sort of relationship that they will expect support from others in their lives. Keep in mind that many people, and especially many folks who come to therapy, may never have experienced very many healthy, supportive relationships. If you do nothing else, your job is to provide this net.

Novel Interaction Experience

Once support and trust are established, it becomes possible to use the relationship to experiment with alternative ways of functioning, called immediacy. Let's say, for example, that a client has trouble asserting herself with others, especially older authority figures in positions of power. Characteristically, she has allowed herself to be steered in whatever directions others have wanted, silently fuming to herself, building resentment over time. In one session, you notice that she seems a bit reluctant to go along with a suggestion you have made that you think would be helpful. Knowing her history, you could back off at this point and nudge her along slowly. Instead, you decide to use your relationship as an object lesson to practice new behaviors.

"No," you tell her, "I must insist that you do this. I really think this will be good for you."

"Well," the client hesitates. "I don't know."

You can see that she is becoming angry at your prodding but she is far too polite and deferential to say no in a direct way. You decide to push her further and even exaggerate things to the point that she will have to confront you. Finally, with her back against the wall and her resentment boiling to the surface, she tells you in no uncertain terms that she has had quite enough of this. You will please respect her wishes and stop pushing her.

The therapeutic moment has arrived. You applaud her courage and reinforce her strength in standing up to you. You make the point that if she can do this with you, if she can set limits within the therapy, why can't she do so in other areas of her life with her husband, her children, and her coworkers? This novel interaction with you is the beginning of a new pattern of assertiveness that the client is learning.

Enforcement of Boundaries

Some people come to you with more severe personality disorders or extremely irritating, controlling interpersonal styles. With diagnostic labels like borderline, narcissistic, or sociopathic personality, these are individuals who are used to controlling and manipulating others to get their way. They are often very self-centered and sometimes exploitive. They have a strong sense of entitlement.

Even in less extreme forms than full-fledged personality disorders you will recognize some clients who will play lots of games and test the limits of what they can get away with. They will come consistently late to sessions and then expect you to accommodate them by running over into your next session. They will not pay their bills and then argue over charges. They will cancel appointments at the last minute. They will call you at home with constant emergencies. You may feel them get underneath your skin in a variety of ways, haunting your fantasies, invading your sleep. You will notice yourself spending a disproportionate amount of time thinking about these very few individuals.

In such cases, a very different sort of therapeutic relationship is called for. Specialists who work with such "disorders of self" believe that the primary instrument of treatment is a special sort of relationship that includes a "holding environment" and clearly enforced boundaries. This means that although you might ordinarily be flexible and adaptive with your clients, in some cases it is absolutely imperative that you establish very structured rules that are enforced without exception.

I [Jeffrey] recall one young woman who I knew fit the description of a borderline disorder. I don't like those labels and prefer not to use them because they get in the way of my seeing these people as individuals who are just doing the best they can to get along in a world that feels terrifying to them. One day, as our session came to an end, she asked me if she could send me a note during the week summarizing what she got out of the session.

At first, this struck me as a fabulous idea. It showed how motivated she had become to work on herself and reflect on our work between sessions. I was very keen to get ongoing feedback from her about what was getting through to her and what was not working at all. I was even thinking this might be a good thing to try with all my clients.

A warning buzzer went off in my head but I chose to ignore it. After all, previously this woman had tried many other ways to get me to demonstrate to her that she was my most valued and important client. She would save her best stuff for the last five minutes of the session to see if I would give her more time (I didn't). She would threaten suicide to see if I would spend extra time with her (instead I referred her for a psychiatric consultation to see if hospitalization was in order). She called my office occasionally in immediate crisis to see if I would see her outside of her scheduled sessions (I would not). Ordinarily, I am extremely responsive to any of these requests from most of my clients, but with this woman I had learned the hard way how important it was to stick to our agreed-on rules. As is so often the case, we found that she was improving not so much by my brilliant interventions as simply by the enforcement of these boundaries, which helped her to realize that relationships could indeed be dependable. I "held" her in an environment that was safe, predictable, yet I was impervious to her manipulations—that is, until this next ploy.

Sure enough, the two-page summary of our session came in the mail. She was insightful, concise, and entirely on target in identifying the main themes we had covered in our previous session, what she had learned, what she was working on, what helped most and least, and a review of the assignments she would complete before we saw one another next. Needless to say, I was quite pleased with this new development.

When after the next session the client asked if she could again send me in the mail a summary of what she learned, I again agreed. Frankly, I was really enjoying this process. Of course, she knew that, and knew exactly how to get me to make exceptions to our contract of no contact outside of regularly scheduled sessions. When her next letter arrived a few days later, it was again extremely impressive. This time it was four pages long. This concerned me a bit, and again a warning bell chimed in my head, but I was already planning how I was going to write this up for an article.

I'm sure you know where this is going. The next week, the letter was 12 pages long and no longer appropriate in length or content. When I told her in the next session that I would no longer accept or read these letters, she became hurt and indignant. "But I don't understand," she accused me innocently, "at first you said this was okay and now you are changing your mind. I thought you said that you would be consistent with me, that this was part of my treatment."

She got me.

We are including this story not to warn you to mistrust your clients but rather to alert you that there are some cases, such as personality disorders, that require a different kind of relationship than what you might ordinarily construct. In such situations you will want to use the relationship as a way to teach these clients how to live within boundaries. This is a task many of them will find very difficult and they will test you in every way possible.

Authentic Engagement

Last but hardly least, Carl Rogers was among the first to advocate the value of therapeutic relationships to provide genuine human encounters between people (Rogers, 1951). We have always lived in groups of people, been nourished and sustained by these interactions. Among all the things that we do to be helpful to people, one use of the therapeutic relationship is to provide caring and love. We are not talking about love in the romantic sense, of course, but rather as the genuine and real affection and respect that we feel for those we help. We are communicating to them in many ways that they are important to us, that they are not "just" clients but real people who are involved with us in real relationships.

It is true that there are many clients you will work with who you don't like very much, and will certainly not like some of the crazy, hurtful things that they do, but you will nevertheless come to care about them deeply. There are other clients you will see with whom you will have among the most intimate relationships that you will ever experience in your life. They will tell you their deepest, darkest secrets. They will show a degree of honesty and openness that you will rarely experience in any other relationship in your life. If you think about it, even your closest relationships with family members and friends rarely (unfortunately) involve meeting on a weekly basis (without interruptions!) to talk about feelings and innermost thoughts.

Remember, in therapy sessions, almost everything is private, secret, and confidential (unless someone exhibits dangerous behavior or potential). There are no interruptions or distractions. You listen to one another with perfect, hovering attention. You talk about the most important things, all of them very personal. You become a perfect confidante and listener for your clients, and they will feel very grateful to you for this. They will tell you a lot about how much you matter to them. And you will reciprocate.

The nature of the authentic engagement between clients and therapists makes for some very intimate, powerful encounters. In some ways, your clients will be among the most cherished people you will ever be privileged to know.

ABOUT EMPATHY

The glue that holds everything else you do together in your therapeutic relationships is empathy. This is that state where you enter into other people's experiences and sense their worlds from their points of view. It is when you can see, hear, feel, and sense what someone else is going through, yet at the same time you are able to preserve your own sense of self. You can feel what another is feeling at the same time you can feel yourself.

Economist Adam Smith was actually one of the first writers to sort out empathic reactions. Although what he called "fellow feelings" was more closely aligned to sympathy, Smith believed that this uniquely human state occurs when two conditions are met. One is the observation of someone else in the midst of emotional arousal, whether that is elation, despair, or frustration. Second, there is the imagination necessary to share this affective experience.

Empathy originates from the German use of aesthetic transcendence in which the observer projects herself into the object of beauty. American psychologists then borrowed the term, translating it into English in order to describe what happens when one person experiences another emotional reaction to those under stress.

There has actually been considerable debate among psychologists and philosophers about what constitutes empathy. Is it a cognitive process in which thinking and interpretation are involved or solely an emotional reaction? Like so many such intellectual debates, it probably doesn't matter as much as the theorists believe.

You may experience empathy in your head, your heart, or more likely in both places. You are moved at a profoundly personal level and are also making sense of this experience with your senses and mind.

What we do know is that empathy is a uniquely human experience. At its most primitive level, infants only a few days old are known to cry in response to others' distress (Acebo & Thoman, 1992). According to several theorists (Buss, 1999; Glantz & Pearce, 1989; Kottler & Montgomery, 2001), humans have developed this capacity for a number of reasons that ensure our continued survival:

1. Increased sensitivity to others' moods allows us to predict their behavior or avoid direct conflict.
2. Empathy allows us to recognize and anticipate others' needs, making for a more cooperative society.
3. It allows for mutual support and help-giving when one person is in distress and benefits from the "tribe."
4. Empathy creates interpersonal bonds that are useful in community action.

5. It is a vehicle that elicits altruistic behavior in which one sacrifices personal safety for the greater good of the community.

When it comes to empathy, we are definitely not created equal. And when we say "created," we don't just mean the capacity you are born with but also how you are trained. There are, in fact, vast individual differences, in which some people bleed emotionally at the slightest provocation of another's discomfort and others feel nothing at all in the presence of human suffering. They feel no pity, no sympathy, no concern, not even any guilt and shame if they were the cause of others' pain (these people are often called sociopathic).

First and foremost, empathy must be applied to yourself before turned toward others. How on earth can you tell what other people are feeling if you don't recognize such states inside yourself? Awareness of the world and its inhabitants thus begins with the self. Sometimes this is one of the most difficult tasks for individuals to learn. In order for you to be more in tune with your client, you have to be self-aware, which engenders feeling pain, sadness, despair, anger, fear, and a myriad of other unpleasant feelings we so frequently like to avoid.

It was Carl Rogers (1961, p. 2), the first systematic geographer of the empathy landscape, who noted that it isn't necessary to be attuned to everything within any more than "the centipede that becomes aware of all his legs," but it certainly helps to sense the general movement.

When Empathy Hurts

People sometimes feel sorry for themselves to the point where they almost enjoy staying stuck in their predicaments; they may even invite you to join them in their feelings of helplessness. "If you put all your moods in a shoebox and placed them on a scale," points out novelist Jim Harrison (2000), "you'd only get a reading on the shoebox. Moods are only self-indulgent emotional whims and fuel for sloth" (p. 236).

Harrison's protagonist is speaking about the excuses that people use for avoiding work and movement. After all, if one is crippled by pain, then others will carry you or, at the very least, let you sit around and feel sorry for yourself.

Empathy can be counterproductive under the following circumstances:

1. When it becomes intrusive and threatens a person's sense of privacy.
2. When boundaries collapse and a person is not allowed to express individuality.
3. When there is a loss of control and overidentification on the part of the helper.
4. When the helper's own needs are neglected.

During empathy, the fences constructed between you and others are dismantled or, at the very least, a gate is opened. What pours through next is the intensity of emotion felt on the other side. During the best of circumstances, a close connection is felt; the suffering person not only feels less alone, but also supported, held, and understood. At least this is the way that empathy is supposed to work.

But what happens when the gate remains stuck in the open position, unable to close when the force and power of the emotion become overwhelming? What if the person on the other side of the fence, for reasons unknown, wedges the gate open so it cannot be closed?

Protect Yourself

When I [Leah] started my training as a counselor, I had an assumption that because I was able to dissociate from my feelings so well (as was taught to me indirectly in childhood), empathy would be difficult. However, I had it all wrong. After a lot of conscientious work, I realized the feelings were always there, and I only needed to remove the cover that I pretended was there to shield myself from pain. I realized I wasn't actually shielded from pain, but rather pretending it wasn't there. As the veil was lifting (and trust me, this took years), I started to learn the skill of empathy, of not only feeling it, but also expressing it verbally. What seems most interesting to me, though, was that I felt a great deal of pain that did not belong to me. It was my sensitivity to others, sometimes, that I felt. (Think of times when you can feel that the tension in a room is so thick that you could cut it with a knife.) All along I had the ability to pick up the feelings of others, but when I was younger I didn't realize they weren't my own. Once I came to that understanding, it was much easier for me to allow myself to feel, and my new task was to develop a strong sense of what feelings were generated internally versus what I was getting from the people around me.

Therefore, when you get close to others, especially individuals who are wounded and bleeding emotionally, it is hard not to become profoundly affected by the experience. It is important that you are able to open yourself up to feel the pain and express it without identifying with it as if it was your own. In this way, you are able to allow it to leave the room with your client, although you may still feel sadness. However, the depth of the wound does not become yours. Only the compassion for your client will be left behind after the session. This is certainly a concern that many therapists-in-training have. Imagine how many times when you've told someone that you want to be a therapist, they responded with, "I could not do that, listen to people's problems all day. How do you keep from taking it home with you?" So how *do* you do it?

First, you must become clearly aware of your own feelings and reactions toward others. Learning to differentiate between your own feelings and what someone else is experiencing is essential. One way to help establish these boundaries is to take in the feelings of others so that you will be able to reflect them back, and, at the same time, be aware of your response to what that person experiences. This helps you to differentiate your feelings from your client's.

Second, enforce those boundaries. Each time you interact with individuals, and especially clients in pain, be mindful of your boundaries, of what's yours and what's the other person's stuff. Work hard not to let that guard down until it becomes second nature to you. It may seem like a lot of work, and that's because it is. However, in time, you will not need to be as mindful of it as often.

Finally, confront your own need for distractions. We frequently use distraction to avoid uncomfortable feelings. First, you have to be willing to feel your own emotions without distractions before you are receptive to the emotions of others. Then, you have to get yourself out of the way; you must put your needs aside (of hunger, of feeling tired, of wanting to talk about yourself) to fully listen to your clients. Once the distractions are put aside, you will be more fully able to feel what the client is expressing without identifying with those feelings. As long as you are not clear, you have a risk of taking ownership of what the client feels as if it is your own. Clarity is another essential component of protecting yourself.

RELATIONSHIPS SKILLS

The skills of building relationships are the same as those that would be needed to communicate effectively. The various behaviors are divided into several successive stages. First we cover the skills required to read nonverbal behavior, followed by the skills required for good attending.

You Are Watching the Client: Reading Nonverbal Behavior

Before clients even open their mouths, your observational skills kick into gear. You note their dress and appearance, the way they carry themselves, the way they walk. You observe how they present themselves and form a first impression. You listen to the sound of their voices. You feel the firmness of their handshakes. You note which chair they take in your office. You observe their posture, their gestures. And inside you, there is a whirlwind of reactions going on that might sound something like this:

> Nice haircut. But what's with that hair color? Why does she keeps touching her hair? Is that a nervous gesture or more a grooming thing?
>
> Interesting that she wore such a short dress. Is that the usual way she dresses, I wonder, or rather a seductive gesture? Or perhaps this is my own projection? She seems rather feminine in her mannerisms but she could be overcompensating. Bet she's having relationship problems.
>
> Careful now. Don't jump to conclusions. Wait to hear her story.
>
> She seems kind of passive, waiting for me to take charge. Is this a pattern in her life? Does she defer to men characteristically?
>
> Her voice is rather throaty, as if she has a cold. Maybe she's a smoker. She does look rather nervous, even for a first session.
>
> I like this woman. I wonder what that's all about? There is something about her that is instantly endearing. Could it be a vulnerability or is it something deeper? Must watch my reactions in this area.
>
> She is smoothing her dress, as if she is ready to begin. But she is still waiting for me. Her foot is moving, a nervous gesture. It seems coordinated with her hair grooming. Should I let her off the hook or wait for her to begin? My sense is that she wants me to start. Okay. Here it goes.

In this brief example, which lasted about a 20 seconds in a therapist's head, you can begin to get a sense of the observational skills that are used to begin the therapy process. It all starts with reading nonverbal behavior.

Reading Body Language Skills

The first information at your disposal includes what you notice and observe about the ways clients present themselves. In those first few minutes, you will be paying close attention to whatever cues you can read from the ways that clients stand, walk, sit, and conduct themselves. The face alone presents a staggering 5,000 different expressions, many of which can be recognized as far away as the length of a football field. Although there are cultural variations in what nonverbal cues can mean, and also the possibility of deception (fake smile), many human facial expressions such as smiles and anger are universal.

Body language can be grouped according to several categories:

> *Facial expressions.* What can you read in the client's face? Smiles, head nods, frowns, tiny movements in the mouth, eyes, cheeks, and brows, all signal internal states.
>
> *Gestures.* Look for hand movements that accompany speech. What do they communicate that supports or contradicts verbal speech?
>
> *Body movements.* Notice restless feet, wringing hands, or any other movements that may be significant.
>
> *Posture.* Is the client's body tense? Relaxed? Slumped?
>
> *Visual orientation.* This includes eye contact and movement.
>
> *Physical contact.* Handshakes, hugs, pats.
>
> *Spatial behavior.* How does the person position him- or herself? How close or far is the person standing or sitting? In family sessions, how do members position themselves in relation to others?
>
> *Appearance.* Clothing, grooming.
>
> *Nonverbal vocalizations.* Uh huhs, ums, exclamations, sighs.

Body Language Exercise

Get together in small groups. Each of you take turns expressing some internal state only through nonverbal behavior and vocalizations. The other members of your group will try to guess what you are feeling inside.

Each of you take turns telling a story that involves some emotional response. Frame your body language so it is inconsistent or incongruent with the way you are really feeling as you relate this story. For instance, if you were actually feeling quite anxious inside you would say that you handled the situation quite well and felt no nervousness whatsoever. In fact, you are still feeling quite calm about the situation. All the while you are saying this, your behavior is showing agitation (wringing hands, darting eye contact, nervous foot tapping).

So, what are you looking for and what are you thinking about when you observe clients systematically? Here are some general guidelines:

1. Assessment of general mood: How does the person appear to be feeling? Check energy level, emotional states, and variation of affect.
2. Clues as to inner states: What does nonverbal behavior tell you about what the person might be feeling inside? How does what you observe fit with what the person reports is going on?

TABLE 4.1

Reactions to Stress

Physical	Cognitive	Emotional
Fatigue	Poor concentration	Guilt
Sleep disruption	Obsessive thoughts	Helplessness
Lethargy	Flashbacks	Anger
Appetite changes	Violent fantasies	Depression
Lowered sex drive	Memory disturbance	Moodiness
Headaches	Self-blame	Numbness
Hyperactivity	Poor reasoning	Irritability
Startle responses	Irrational thinking	Fear
Muscle tremors	Impulsive decisions	Anxiety

3. Mental status: What is the person's relative functioning level in terms of memory, behavior, and control?
4. Verbal and nonverbal congruency: What are the discrepancies between what you see and hear?
5. Signals of distress: What are overt and subtle symptoms of acute distress? (See Table 4.1)
6. Elaboration of verbal expression: What is the person's communication style?
7. Unconscious reactions: What are some things the client is doing about which he or she may be unaware?
8. Communication of underlying meaning: What are some of the symbolic and metaphorical communications that are accompanying the surface messages?
9. Evidence of deception: This is a difficult area to recognize (see Table 4.2). Even professional police investigators can only tell when suspects are lying about two-thirds of the time. In our work, we aren't as concerned with finding out the "truth" anyway because this is a relative concept strongly influenced by people's imperfect memories and perceptions.

TABLE 4.2

Examples of Nonverbal Deception

Averted gaze
Rapid blinking
Rambling responses
Nervous foot and hand movements
Self-touching
Stressed voice
Long and frequent pauses

The Client Is Watching You

Think about what happens when you meet a person for the first time. Now imagine that this stranger has come to you for help. He or she takes a seat in your office and tentatively begins to tell you what is desired. As this scene unfolds, the very first thing you do is observe the individual and form some initial impressions. Remember that your clients are doing exactly the same thing. They are watching you carefully and asking themselves several questions:

- Will I like this person?
- Will this person like me?
- Can I trust this person?
- Does this person know what she is doing?
- Will this person judge me harshly?
- Will this therapist agree with me or give me a hard time?
- Will this person make me do something I don't want to do?

All of these observations are based on nonverbal cues. The client is looking at your dress and manner, the way you furnished your office, the diplomas on the wall, the books on your shelves, the way you sit, your voice and manner, your posture, all the innumerable ways that you present yourself. Do you convey a sense of confidence and essential competence? Do you seem attractive and trustworthy? In these first moments, the client is still trying to make up his or her mind about whether he or she wants to continue this enterprise.

First Impressions Exercise

In small groups, get together and share your first impressions of one another the first day you met. Talk about the personal reactions and opinions you formed during that first contact and what shaped most of those impressions. Mention the ways that dress choices, hairstyles, posture, voice tone, body language all provided cues.

Discuss the impressions you presented to others compared to the ways you see yourself. Discuss the values and limitations of first impressions. For instance, such quick, instinctual reactions are programmed into us as a way to react quickly to perceived danger.

We mention this to remind you that the assessment process in the first interview is a mutual process; while you are checking out your client, he or she is also making up his or her mind about you.

What's Beneficial About These Listening Skills?

You would be amazed how much information you can collect and how well you can develop a relationship with clients by relying solely on listening skills. What you are attempting to do is the following:

1. Help the client to tell his or her story.
2. Draw out appropriate background and contextual information.
3. Communicate understanding.
4. Facilitate deeper level exploration.
5. Make connections.
6. Demonstrate empathy.

Attending Skills

Now that you have an idea of how to read the client's nonverbal behavior, you must also use this knowledge to let your client know you are listening. This is going to be a *lot* harder than it looks. We are talking about those nonverbal behaviors in which you *communicate* your complete and total interest in what the client is saying. Sounds simple, doesn't it? What's the big deal? You just look at the person and nod your head a few times.

The truth is that most people don't have the slightest idea about how to attend fully to others. Watch others (even more educational: watch yourself) during their conversations and you will see people who are engaged in multiple tasks at the same time. They are nodding their head in acknowledgment all the time they are looking around them, fumbling with notes, glancing through pockets for lost objects, signaling to passersby.

Even when they are giving their full attention, you would never know it. It is important not only that you are attending fully to what others are saying but also that you appear to be attentive. The difference may elude you, but it won't do you much good to be concentrating on others if they don't think you are listening at all. So there must be congruence between what you are doing and what you appear to be doing.

What does someone look like who is attending effectively?

- *Body posture.* You will notice body positioning and posture that signal attention. This means facing the person fully, often leaning forward, using your whole body to communicate intense interest.
- *Eye contact.* You will observe that the person is making relaxed but focused eye contact.
- *Facial expressions.* The face is showing appropriate responses to what is communicated.
- *Acknowledgments/minimal encouragers.* Head nods and other gestures communicate nonverbal encouragements.

You may notice that these are precisely the same characteristics that you use to read your client. Obviously, the message you convey is just as essential as what you are observing from your client. Therefore, even though you haven't even opened your mouth to say a word, you are still using every part of your being to say to the client: "I am hanging on your every word. There is nothing else that exists for me in this moment except for you and what you are saying. I am using all of my concentration and all of my abilities to listen intently to everything you say. I am picking up the slightest nuances of what you are expressing. You have never had anyone listen as carefully as I am doing right now."

Exercise in Observation

Spend an evening watching reporters on television conduct interviews. Watch the ways they use their bodies and gestures to communicate to their interviewees (and the viewing audience) that they are attentive listeners. Note which things each interviewer does well in addition to weaknesses you observe.

Exercise in Attending

Get into triads: a client, a helper, and an observer. While the client talks for about five minutes, the helper should try to attend to the best of his or her ability without talking. The helper should practice attending as much as possible and at the same time, be aware of how thoughts, feelings, and other distractions seem to get into the way of the ability to fully listen (Are you hungry? Do you need to scratch an itch? Do you want to talk about yourself?).

The observer should observe the helper (not the client who is talking). Pay attention to body posture, eye contact, facial expressions, and acknowledgments/minimal encouragers.

After five minutes, the helper should talk about the experience of attending, followed by the client sharing his or her experience. Finally, the observer can talk about what was noticed during the interaction. Rotate until everyone has played each role.

Exercise in Feedback

Ask people who know you well what things they like best and like least about the ways you listen to them. It is going to be difficult to get people to be really honest about this, so in order to get useful feedback you need to impress on them the importance of giving you specific suggestions.

When I [Jeffrey] did this assignment recently, a number of students told me that I have a very blank rather than animated expression on my face when I'm listening. I suppose this is because I am concentrating so hard on what they are saying. They have told me that this look is off-putting because they are talking and talking and they can't tell how I am responding inside. In actuality, I am just listening, but it feels to them as if they are being judged. They feel more and more uncomfortable until some of the brave ones will stop abruptly and just ask me what I'm thinking. After hearing this feedback I have been working hard to show more vividly on the outside what I am thinking and feeling inside. I don't show everything, of course, but I do now signal more actively that I am hearing and understanding what is being said.

Passive Listening

So far, we've been talking about establishing a relationship with someone by demonstrating solid listening skills. We have been covering those skills that are involved in this process. You may have noticed that we haven't even gotten into the realm of speaking aloud, and we won't for a bit longer. Before we get to active forms of listening, you must first master passive listening. This includes all the nonverbal things that we cover in this chapter in order for you to encourage and to keep the client speaking.

Make sure that you are positioned in such a way as to listen and respond in the best way. Try not to have any big objects (like a desk) between you and the person you are helping. Face the person fully but in a relaxed position. Make eye contact in a natural way.

With a clear mind and gentle spirit, allow your face to be as animated as possible, to let the person know you are tracking appropriately what is being said. Your face shows sadness or delight or concern, depending on what the client is trying to convey at the time.

Head nods are particularly important. In a natural way, you nod yourself up and down (or side to side if you are in parts of Asia) to let the person know you are hearing what is said. You smile when appropriate (when the content is happy, not with nervous or avoiding laughter). And you use "verbal encouragers" like "uh huh" to keep the person talking.

Exercise in Passive Listening

Sit opposite a partner. Your partner talks about something, anything, for about five minutes. During this one-way conversation you are not permitted to speak. No questions. No prompts. You are only allowed to use passive listening skills to track the conversation. Obviously, this is not what you would do during a normal session, but it is a first step before moving on to more complex skills. A good analogy is learning the proper grips for holding a tennis racket before proceeding on to the correct way to stroke the ball.

This will feel awkward and even silly but it is important to get into the habit of practicing sound listening skills. In addition to using your eyes and facial expression and body posture to communicate your interest, you are only allowed to nod your head and say, "uh huh."

After about five minutes of this (which is about all you can take), switch roles.

Internal Assessments

The empathic attitude described earlier in the chapter would now be applied full force. With your attention focused and your listening skills brought to the forefront, your main job at this point is to stay with the client.

To start, you must listen to your own heart. Put yourself in a state of maximum receptivity in which you are fully open to what is coming from others. Open your eyes, your ears, your senses, and most of all, open your heart. So, before you sit with your client, you should feel and exhibit certain characteristics.

- *Be confident.* Your client needs to have confidence in you, and the first way that can occur is if you have confidence in yourself. You may feel like you still have so much to learn, even after receiving your degree, and you do; that learning never ends. However, regardless of where you are in your program when you see your first clients, you still know more than they do. You know how to attend and build a strong relationship.
- *Be flexible.* One of the most valuable qualities you will need as a therapist is to be flexible. You may hold certain opinions about your client that should easily change with new information. You may have a way that you prefer to work with most clients that doesn't

work with one particular client. You must be flexible enough to try something different. You may set goals that seem inaccurate or inappropriate as you develop your relationship with your client. You must be willing to adjust your goals with your client. No matter how you might get set in your ways, you will inevitably need to change at some point since individuals are so unique.

- *Be assertive.* Many people who come to the field of counseling really want to be liked and can sometimes neglect to assert themselves in exchange for popularity. However, as a therapist, you must be sometimes willing to assert yourself, even if it upsets your client. You must set boundaries for appropriate behavior in therapy, especially with couples, families, and groups. You must end your sessions on time, even if your client was late. You must sometimes assert yourself by confronting your clients. Finally, asserting yourself is an excellent way to model this important life skill to your clients.

- *Be nonjudgmental.* As we covered in Chapter 2, you will find that being nonjudgmental may be difficult at times, especially when your values are substantially different from your client's. However, if you are aware of your values and biases, you can be more prepared to handle all kinds of client issues. Furthermore, realize values are not necessarily objectively correct or incorrect; rather, values are something we decide is right for us. If you can perceive values as choices we make, then you may find it easier to accept value difference. Another recommendation we can make about trying to be nonjudgmental is that you accept that the client is ultimately responsible for his or her own life. Your job is not to make decisions for or judge the client. Instead, your job is to provide a supportive and fostering environment. You must trust that the client has the ability to find his or her own solutions in a way that is best for him or her.

- *Be focused.* In the first chapter, we discussed a little about how you attempt to put your client in an altered state of consciousness. You can only do that if you are focused. That's why it's a good idea to take a deep breath before beginning. If your mind is wandering about what you'll eat for dinner or your last client, you aren't really fully listening to your client. This is a skill that can be difficult to learn at first, and as you encounter personal problems while trying to do therapy, focusing can be quite difficult. However, you must work to develop your ability to give your attention fully to the client. Otherwise, you might miss something important!

- *Be caring.* You may like your client; you may not like your client. In either case, you must care for your client and be interested in his or her welfare. You must maintain a loving attitude as a parent would for a child, but without the responsibility. When you care deeply for your client, your loving attitude comes across, and clients feel valued. Feeling valued, a client not only feels safe to explore unpleasant aspects of him- or herself, but also experiencing that caring can enhance his or her self-esteem.

Related to this internal assessment process, your job is to carefully check out how well the relationship appears to be going so far. This allows you to make adjustments as things proceed further. Here is a list of questions you might wish to consider at this time.

- How is the relationship evolving so far?
- How am I reacting internally to this person? What personal reactions am I having?
- What have I done so far that seems to be working well? What have I tried that has not worked that well?

- What is the client avoiding?
- Before I respond, what do I know and understand so far?

You have not really been allowed to say much yet. So far, the skills you have learned are all designed to position you in a way that you can demonstrate maximum receptivity and sensitivity. Although in the "outside world" most people associate helping with giving people advice—telling people what they are doing wrong and what they could do—instead, the professional concentrates as much on listening as on talking. In fact, the skills you learn in this chapter account for more than half of the counseling skills you will use in your work to build collaborative relationships; add a few responding skills to your repertoire (which are covered in the Exploration chapter), and you will be amazed at the results you will get.

BEFORE YOU BEGIN

When you begin an interview, or any conversation, the first thing that you must do is clear your mind of all distractions. This is very much like what happens during the practice of meditation, yoga, or any martial art. The goal is to gently push aside anything going on within you or around you so that you can remain fully present with the person you are facing.

In yoga there is a ritual called a "cleansing breath" that is used to begin any activity. You close your eyes for just a moment and take a deep breath through your nose. As you exhale slowly through your mouth, you focus on the sensation of the air moving out of your body. You then allow yourself to breathe normally, increasing your awareness of the sensations of your breath moving in and out of your body (the heat as you exhale through your mouth, the coolness as you inhale through your nose, the rise and fall of your abdomen and/or chest with each breath, etc.). As you do this, you will find your mind wanders or that other sensations in your body interfere with your breath awareness. Acknowledge the interruption without judgment and gently return your attention back to the task of breathing. Let us warn you: Concentration on a singular task is difficult to accomplish, and those that do it well practice for hours each day for years and years.

> ### Exercise in Meditative Listening
>
> *Several times throughout the day, notice how your attention wanders when you are speaking to someone on the phone or in person. Each time you observe yourself "leaving" the conversation, thinking about something else, gently return yourself to the present. Close your eyes for a moment and take a "cleansing" breath in order to remain focused.*

In this preparation phase to begin helping, your goal is to lead yourself to an "altered state of consciousness," a place where you will be hypersensitive to what you hear, observe, and sense. You do this by following five steps:

1. Clear your mind.
2. Resist distractions intruding from within and outside.
3. Stay neutral and centered.

4. Focus your concentration.
5. Take a deep breath.

Exercise in Testing Your Listening Skills

Now that we have introduced you to observation and attending skills, let's see how you are doing. Sit with a partner so you are facing one another. One of you tell a story about something personal that happened to you recently. Pause at least every minute or so, selecting spots that lend themselves to transitions. The listening partner will then summarize what was heard thus far while using observation skills and demonstrating good attending skills. The storyteller will then fill in any details that were left out before continuing with the narrative.

After doing this for about five minutes, switch roles so that each of you has the chance to practice listening.

Talk to one another afterward about what this was like.

PITFALLS AND COMMON MISTAKES

We are into the section of the book where you will learn specific skills related to being a therapist. As you learn each skill, you may be prone to make certain errors that are common with beginners. In the next several chapters, we present a list of these pitfalls. Following is a list of some of those mistakes related to observation and attending skills. Perhaps by our presenting these pitfalls, you will be more conscious in trying to avoid them.

Using Minimal Verbal Encouragers or Nodding Too Much

Earlier in the chapter, we recommended the use of minimal encouragers and nodding to let the client know you are following her. However, there are a few caveats. First, be aware not to overnod or over-"uh huh," as this can sometimes convey that you feel impatient. If you record yourself listening to someone, fast forward the video as you watch your recording. You will quickly identify if you nod too much. Listen to the session for five minutes, and if you hear yourself saying "uh huh" to the client frequently, you know it's too much. Finally, some new therapists say "right" or "good" as minimal encouragers. Although these may be intended to be neutral, they imply a judgment that increases an external locus of control. In other words, by your saying judgment encouragers, the client may think you approve and begin interacting with you in a way that seeks approval. Your goal is not to judge or approve of your client; instead, your goal is to provide understanding and caring regardless of what your client says.

Maintaining a Stoic Face

Like Jeffrey, I [Leah] was given feedback during my training that my face was too serious when I worked with clients. I was concentrating. Of course I looked serious. I didn't really understand the problem until I started supervising others and saw that no matter what the client said, the therapist looked serious. The nonverbal facial expression did not convey empathy to the client when something light or fun was shared. So we recommend that you practice making faces in the mirror if you tend to be serious. Spend time with infants and toddlers because for some reason, we seem to parallel the expressions of infants naturally (probably because language is not yet developed). Make your face congruent with the client's topic so he or she feels more understood. Record yourself talking with someone to see what you do.

Making Your Face Too Animated

A similar problem to the stoic face is the one with too much animation. If you appear overly happy or overly sad, your expression may not match what your client is feeling. As a result, the client may not experience accurate empathy. The best way to develop appropriately modulated expressions is to record yourself in a conversation with someone, and then make the appropriate adjustments.

Closed Body Language

We all have habits on how we sit. Pay attention to how you sit in your office, when waiting for something, and in the passenger seat of your car. If you tend to be cold a lot or if you are feeling angry or sad, you may cross your arms in front of you and cross your legs. Have someone sit like this in front of you, and describe your reaction. Most likely, you will perceive that person as having closed body language. Everything crossed may communicate: "Get away, I want to be alone." So you must always be aware of what your body says.

Sitting Too Relaxed

If you tend to slouch in your chair or lean on something as a usual habit, this may convey to clients that you aren't interested in them. You are a professional, and as such you must convey a demeanor that presents professionalism and confidence. That's not to say that we want you to sit perfectly straight with your legs down and your hands on your knees; rather, be comfortable, but professional. You are not selling an object; you are selling yourself as a service to your clients.

Staring Too Much

You have read above that keeping relaxed eye contact with the client indicates good attending behavior. What does that mean? Well, it doesn't mean staring at the client without ever looking away. You may find that when people listen, they tend to make stronger eye contact than when they talk. When people talk, they tend to look up when they think or down when they feel. So it's okay to look away when you are talking, but only on occasion. And it's okay to briefly look away sometimes when the client talks to avoid staring too much. There are cultural differences related to this behavior as well.

Exercise in Staring

Choose a partner and face each other. For three minutes, stare into each other's eyes without talking. Afterward, talk about your experience. You may find that you had difficulty not laughing because of feeling embarrassed. You may have found that staring was quite intimate. You may have been aware of thoughts about what the other person sees when she looks at you. You may have been aware of your thoughts about the other person based upon their appearance. You may have noticed your mind drifting to avoid the discomfort of such intense contact.

Matching the Client's Face Rather Than the Tone of Content

As stated before, socially we tend to smile when people laugh, even if the content of the information is sad or serious. This is to match where the other person wants to be. It's polite. However, this is therapy and the rules for politeness are different. In order to help the client feel his or her feelings, you would best serve the client by matching the content rather than what his or her face or tone of voice projects. Now if it's the first session, you may want to smile a little and make a mental note. Eventually, though, you will want to match the content. If the client still tends to do this even though your face and tone are matching content, then let the client know he or she does this. For example, "I notice that when you talk about something difficult, you tend to laugh a lot." The client is avoiding feelings, and by helping clients in a gentle way to feel those feelings, they may be served better.

Applications to Self: The Effects on All of Your Relationships

"So, what is the client trying to say? What does that facial expression mean? Is my facial expression appropriate? Am I leaning forward and showing that I'm attentive? How am I reacting to what the client says? How can I convey empathy while facilitating the depth of the client's expression?" Learning how to focus on so many aspects of the client while still attending to your own reactions may seem like a daunting task. That would be because it is. However, you don't have to learn all of these skills in one class for a mere 3 hours per week. These skills are something you can practice each day in all of your relationships, with all of your interactions with others. Each time you interact with a person, whether with someone you know or not, pay close attention to their nonverbals and what they are attempting to convey. Practice listening to others while expressing good relationship-building skills, such as appropriate minimal encouragers, focusing your attention fully, having appropriate nonverbal expressions, and so on. The more you practice, the better you will become. Eventually, most of the time, most of these tasks will become second nature.

By now, we recommend that you start recording some sessions with a partner to practice these skills. If you are not already assigned a client, find a classmate with whom you can practice these skills. Meet with him or her each week to record a 15- to 20-minute session. Then immediately review your tapes to see if you are applying what you learn as we present new skills each week. Most of the skills you learn will be cumulative. Because you have now been introduced to nonverbal attending skills, you should evaluate your progress in this area each week until the end of the semester.

We also recommend that you save these tapes so you can compare your early sessions to later ones. As you start to feel a little overwhelmed, it helps to look at previous work in order to see your progress and, hopefully, build your confidence as well. In fact, at the end of the book is an exercise designed to compare three tapes: your first, a middle tape, and one of your last tapes.

So practice at home. Practice in class. Practice on tape. Review your progress, and you will find that some skills become second nature.

SUMMARY

In this chapter, we introduced the various uses of the therapeutic relationship. We covered the important concept of empathy, the definition of it, the facilitation and advantages of it, and the risks associated with it. We also introduced to you how to listen—listen to your clients as well as yourself. Hopefully, you will begin to practice your nonverbal listening skills so that in the Exploration chapter, you will be more prepared to learn how to respond verbally as well. Finally, we presented a perspective on how you can use these skills in your daily life.

The next chapter introduces you to the intake process. At the same time when you are building a solid, collaborative relationship with your client, you are also collecting relevant information and assessing with the client what is going on. In order for this to proceed in an efficient and helpful way, your relationship skills must be highly tuned so that you can better respond to client needs while you also attempt to meet the needs of treatment planning.

A CHECK ON WHAT YOU LEARNED

1. How a client behaves in the session is probably how they behave in the outside world. Which use of the therapeutic relationship does this statement apply to?
2. Transference is an example of which use of the therapeutic relationship?
3. Genuine affection and respect by the therapist for the client facilitates which use of the therapeutic relationship?
4. Before being able to provide empathy to clients, you must first apply empathy to _____.
5. List the ways to protect yourself from risks associated with empathy.
6. List the four ways you exhibit good attending skills.
7. The authors recommend what for clearing the mind and preparing for each client?
8. Which is more important for therapeutic effectiveness: matching the client's behavioral expressions, or matching the client's content?
9. The skills you learn in this chapter account for more than half of the counseling skills you will use in your work to _____.
10. How can you strengthen the skills presented in this chapter?

SUGGESTED READINGS

Brammer, L. M., & MacDonald, G. (1999). *The helping relationship: Process and skills* (7th ed.). Boston: Allyn and Bacon.

Chen, M. W., & Giblin, N. J. (2002). *Individual counseling: Skills and techniques.* Denver, CO: Love.

Ciaramicoli, A. P., & Ketcham, K. (2000). *The power of empathy.* New York: Dutton.

Feltham, C. (1999). *Understanding the counseling relationship.* Thousand Oaks, CA: Sage.

Gelso, C. J., & Hayes, J. A. (1998). *The psychotherapy relationship: Theory, research, and practice.* New York: Wiley.

Kahn, M. (1997). *Between therapist and client: The new relationship* (rev. ed.). New York: W. H. Freeman.

Kottler, J. A. (1994). *Beyond blame: A new way of resolving conflicts in relationships.* San Francisco: Jossey-Bass.

Kottler, J. A., Sexton, T., & Whiston, S. (1994). *The heart of healing: Relationships in therapy.* San Francisco: Jossey-Bass.

Okun, B. F. (2002). *Effective helping: Interviewing and counseling techniques* (6th ed.). Pacific Grove, CA: Brooks/Cole.

Rogers, C. R. (1980). *A way of being.* Boston: Houghton Mifflin.

Stark, M. (2000). *Modes of therapeutic action: Enhancement of knowledge, provision of experience, and engagement in relationship.* Northvale, NJ: Jason Aronson.

CHAPTER 5

Skills of Assessment and Diagnosis

Among the first things you must do in a new relationship with a client is to figure out what the most important issues are to deal with and to develop a plan to address them. This is a collaborative effort in which you enlist the client's help to determine desired goals and treatment objectives. It is also a process that makes use of a number of structures to help you to organize your efforts.

In this chapter we present a number of skills that will be useful in conducting assessments with your clients, formulating diagnostic impressions, and planning treatment strategies. There are several different structures that are currently in use, depending on the setting (i.e., hospital vs. school vs. crisis center), the professional identity (family therapy vs. psychiatry vs. psychology vs. counseling), or even the theoretical orientation of the practitioner (i.e., cognitive-behavioral vs. psychoanalytic vs. existential vs. constructivist). Rather than confusing you with all the various possibilities at your disposal, we will concentrate on those assessment skills and strategies that are somewhat universally employed. The most commonly used such structure originally evolved from medical practice, especially in inpatient psychiatric units.

MENTAL STATUS EXAM

In medical and mental health settings, a standard clinical examination is often used to assess mental functioning. This is especially important for clients who are manifesting extreme symptoms of disorientation or unusual behavior. Although you may not be required to use this assessment structure (it is more universally applied by psychiatrists, medical practitioners, and psychologists), it is still helpful to understand the various areas that are covered. Even if you are specializing in adjustment and developmental disorders, it is still helpful to examine client behavior systematically.

> *Appearance:* How does the client present him or herself? Look at hygiene, clothing, nutrition, weight, and alertness.
>
> *General behavior:* Examine characteristic mannerisms, facial expressions, eye contact, voice tone, and general attitude. Take into consideration gender, cultural, and individual differences in the ways these mannerisms are manifested.

Mood: Assess the types and intensity of moods displayed. Are these emotional reactions appropriate to the situation?

Flow of thought: Note the rate and rhythm of speech. Is there a flight of ideas, incessant rambling, disjointed thoughts?

Content of thought: Is there evidence of delusions and hallucinations that might indicate psychotic thinking? Are there obsessions present in thought? Is there suicidal ideation?

Orientation: Make sure the person is oriented to time, place, and person. This means that the person knows where he or she is, what day it is, and what he or she is doing in your company.

Language: Note comprehension and fluency of language. If there is some concern about whether the person is understanding and speaking well, check out first languages used in home.

Memory: Assess both short- and long-term memory functions. Simple exercises are available for this process.

Attention and concentration: Is the person able to track the conversation appropriately?

Abstract reasoning: Can the person grasp symbolic or metaphorical ideas?

Insight and judgment: Does the person appear to have the capacity for self-reflection and insight?

Cultural background: What are the client's dominant cultural identities and how might they influence the behavior previously considered?

Okay, so now the question remains: What do you *do* with this information you've collected so far during a mental status exam? Let's say that you are pretty skilled at asking good questions according to the format just presented. The most important part involves using this data to help you formulate a clearer notion of the client's presenting problems and underlying processes. This is crucial in order to create a sound treatment plan.

The mental status exam is only a quick, relatively crude initial evaluation of a person's mental, emotional, and cognitive functioning. It is a highly structured format that allows you to compare responses to a rather large database and determine the extent of impairment in certain areas. A more extensive intake procedure is needed, however, to get a more in-depth picture of what is going on.

THE BASICS OF CONDUCTING AN INTAKE INTERVIEW

Although a mental status exam is a fairly structured process to assess cognitive as much as psychological functioning, other procedures are used for general practice. Basically, you might ask yourself what you need to know in order to help someone.

Reflective Exercise

Imagine that you could only ask a new client three questions. Based on the answers you get to those queries, you would have to construct a plan for being most helpful. In small groups, or on your own, settle on the three most important questions that you would want to ask.

In this section, we teach you the mechanics of how to do a first interview and illustrate the steps with sample dialogue from a beginner who is meeting a client for the first time. You will wish to customize these steps to fit the needs of your clients, clinical style (as it evolves), and work setting.

Phone Contact

So, this is your first meeting with a client. You may feel a bit excited and nervous. Many clinicians feel that anticipation each time a new meeting occurs. However, your client will likely be very anxious about meeting you. So it is essential that you help the client feel more comfortable. This is a challenge, though, because you need to collect a significant amount of information while trying to convey empathy, concern, and hope.

Several approaches exist for conducting the intake interview, and you will have to develop your own style. However, there are some basic guidelines that might be helpful to get you started. First, when contacting the client by phone, you may want to let him or her know that this session will be a little different than the others and to arrive early to fill out any paperwork prior to meeting with you. If you have the liberty to do so, you may also schedule the first meeting for an hour and a half so that the client will have more time to talk about what brought him or her since so much of the first session requires a certain amount of formal procedures to cover. In addition, you may want to review the cost of services at the agency. Before you hang up, reiterate the day, date, and time of your session, and say something to the effect of, "I'm looking forward to meeting you."

Keep in mind that the therapy begins with this first phone contact (actually it began as soon as the client first considered reaching out for help). Some clinicians even use this first conversation to begin the work by planting a favorable prognosis, instilling a sense of hope, and encouraging the person to think about how to use the time in the most efficient way possible.

The Greeting

Next, in the waiting room, you may want to introduce yourself. Tell the client what you would like to be called (i.e., by your first name, by title, etc.), and ask what your client what he or she would like to be called. It's best to ask because some clients may come from different cultural backgrounds and may have certain expectations about how to address one another. Therefore, if you offer your client to call you by your first name, but she chooses to call you by a more formal name, just go with it. The one possible exception is if your client wants to call you doctor and you are not a doctor.

Once the client arrives, we recommend that you don't begin any conversation while in the waiting room but rather wait until you get into the therapy room to continue. Waiting is not only important during the intake interview but during all sessions, as sometimes clients begin the session right in front of other people. Waiting will assure your client's confidentiality. (The one exception might be that if you have a long walk to your therapy room from the waiting room, you may want to let the client know.) Remember, your client will most likely be unfamiliar with your procedures and the layout of your clinic. Many clients don't know how to be clients (except what they have seen on television or the movies), so it is your job to teach them the appropriate behaviors to get the most out of the experience.

The Opening

Once reaching your office, ask the client to sit anywhere he or she feels comfortable (that choice may provide you with interesting data) and close the door. After sitting down, begin to help your client feel at ease. You might start with telling him or her what to expect from this session that may be different from other such interactions. In addition, we recommend not starting this session (or any other session) with "How are you?" because that statement frequently elicits a social atmosphere rather than a therapeutic one. Here is an example of an opening conducted by an intern:

> Hi, Maria. I am happy to meet you. This conversation may be very different from others you have experienced before with friends you have talked to, with doctors, or other professionals. I will start by telling you about some of our agency procedures and some of your rights as a client. After we get some paperwork completed, we can talk about what brought you to visit us. During all other sessions, we will be spending our time together working on helping you achieve your goals.

Taking Care of Ground Rules

Telling your client what to expect can help him or her be more comfortable with the process of therapy. Informing the client that this session is different is also essential because he or she may think that every session will be like this one. If you don't articulate the difference of this session, clients may not want to come back. After all, you will be doing the majority of the structuring during this first session, which is not necessarily helpful toward the client's goals. The intake continues with:

> I would like to start by informing you that all of our sessions will be confidential, but there are a few limitations to that confidentiality. For example, you need to know that all of our sessions will be videotaped. I am a graduate student in a counseling program, and my experience here at this clinic is the final part of my training. Because I'm in training, my supervisor and this agency require the use of videotapes to provide you with the best possible services. So consequently, you will get the benefit of my supervisor's experience as well as my own. Once the videotape has been reviewed by my supervisor, I will erase it immediately. Therefore, my supervisor and I will be the only people to view your session, and my supervisor is bound by confidentiality just like me.

If you are videotaping your session, it may be helpful to start with that information, especially if the video camera is in full view. Stating that the video is a requirement by the agency for your and the client's benefit with confidence will limit the amount of resistance the client has with this procedure. However, if you sound unsure or lack confidence, your client may become reluctant and apprehensive. The session continues:

> Another limitation to keeping confidentiality is if you inform me that you will hurt yourself or another person. Your safety is essential to me, and I am bound by my ethical guidelines to report any harm you intend toward yourself or others. In addition, if you reveal any abuse to a child, an elderly person, or a person with a disability, I am legally bound to contact the authorities. Furthermore, if you request that your records be released or if your records are subpoenaed by a court of law, I will release your records to the appropriate person(s). Do you have any questions? [if your client does not] Well, if any come up, please do not hesitate to ask. Here is an informed consent that I need you to sign. I have one copy for you and one copy for our agency files. Once you take a moment to read over it, let's both sign them.

Now you have covered your limits of confidentiality. Starting with this will let the client know immediately that some limits exist. If you have agency policies, this might be a good place to cover those. For example:

> As I covered on the phone, each session is $50. I would like to meet with you each week at this same time for our sessions. Our sessions will be between 45 and 50 minutes. If you notice me checking my watch, it's not because I'm bored, but because I need to make sure we finish on time since this room is used immediately after our session. If you need to cancel, please provide me with 24 hours' notice. The agency phone number and my name are on this form. Our agency requires that you pay the fee if you do not show without canceling. Another agency policy is that if you do not appear for three consecutive sessions, your time will be given to another client, and you will need to call us for a new day and time. This policy is in place to assure that I obtain my training hours and to provide as many clients as possible with services. Do you have any questions about our agency policies so far?

Perhaps your agency will not have these policies, but if they do, you need to cover them explicitly. Forms with these policies that your client signs will be important to keep in your client's file, and you may want to give a copy to your client as well with the agency phone number and your name.

Checking and Correcting Client Expectations

The next section is something that may help eliminate some confusion about the counseling process, especially if your client has never been to therapy. However, if he or he has received counseling before, the previous therapist or agency may do something different. What is it we're leading up to? Checking out the client's expectations about your role as a therapist. For example:

> Before we talk about what brought you here, I would like to find out what you expect my role to be as your therapist. In your mind, what do you think is my role as therapist and your role as client?

Sometimes clients believe that your role is to provide advice or concrete answers to their problems. Sometimes clients believe that you will be "psychoanalyzing" them. Once your client responds, reflect what you heard, and then make any corrections to how you see your roles. You may want to use your theory to help define your role here, or you can be more general. For instance:

> You believe your role is to tell me your problems and that I will provide you with solutions to those problems. [if the client says yes, then . . .] Well, my style is a little different than that. I believe that clients come to therapy when they feel stuck and are unsure of how to proceed in their lives. They may feel depressed, frustrated, or any variety of emotions. I believe that my role is to help facilitate your exploration to clearly identify the source of your problems, and that source may not be as obvious as you might expect today. I believe that once I help you to clearly identify those emotions or thoughts that cause you to feel stuck, then we can work together to find the best way for you to cope with your situation. I may be reflecting some of what you say to make sure I understand your position, and I may ask you some questions to help you explore deeper. In addition, I may have you do some activities in or out of therapy to help enhance self-awareness. How does that sound? [wait for client response and reflect if necessary] Any questions?

Exploring the Presenting Complaint

Now your client is a little clearer about how you do therapy. He or she will now be ready to explore what brought him or her to therapy and what to expect from your sessions together. However, if you have a structured interview, you may need to proceed with that paperwork. If not, an open invitation to talk about what brought her to therapy would be appropriate now: "We have covered the basics, and I would like to invite you to tell me what brought you here today."

During this first session, whether structured or unstructured, practice your feeling and content reflections (covered in the next chapter). Even if you have many questions for your interview, reflecting not only assures that you are hearing what your client is saying, but also helps the client to feel your empathy and consequently establishes a strong therapeutic bond between you and your client.

Inventory Exercise

Team up with a partner or two. One of you agree to be the client and your partner will help you to take inventory of all those areas of your life that could profit from some sort of reflection, deeper exploration, and possible constructive action. Using some simple open-ended questions and reflections, help the "client" to review all the ways that he or she might utilize counseling to improve personal functioning.

If I [Jeffrey] were your partner, for example, I might talk to you about needing greater balance in my life as a result of being overstressed. I'd tell you about wanting to temper my ambition. I'd mention struggling a bit with adapting to changes in my body as part of the aging process and accepting the limits of some things I can't do anymore. I'd want to talk

> *about the generativity stage of life that is now part of my job as a mentor for others. Well, I could go on and on, but you get the point: Help each other to get in the habit of taking inventory with others (and yourself) of all the multiple areas where personal work could be done.*

If time allows, do not be afraid to get into deep material during this first session (sometimes one session may be all you have to make a difference). Frequently new practitioners feel hesitant to explore things in great depth because the relationship is new. Trust the client. He or she will not go any deeper than feels safe, especially if you respect his or her pace and moderate your own impatience. As long as you display good empathy, you can frequently help the client with something during the first session. If the client feels like something has been accomplished, then he or she is more likely to return.

Discuss the Treatment Plan

After reviewing the situation, the presenting problems and primary issues, you will want to discuss with the client the plans for future sessions. This is a negotiated process because the client may want you to do things that you are unable or unwilling to do ("I want you to tell my wife that she is wrong and agree with me that she is the problem" or "I want you to tell me what I should do"). Likewise, you may have expectations for your client that he or she is not amenable to ("We are going to take our time and get to know one another pretty well before we attempt to resolve this difficulty").

Treatment plans include both short-term goals (those to be worked on before the next session) and long-term objectives (those targets that are to be worked toward before therapy ends). You will want to discuss both with your client.

We wish to emphasize that this stage of a first session does *not* involve simply telling the client what you think is going on and what you have in mind to make things better. There is often a negotiation involved in this process. The client has one set of objectives in mind and you might have quite another. Note in this dialogue how the therapist attempts to find common ground between their discrepant goals for treatment.

Therapist: Given what we have discussed so far, what is it that you would like to accomplish before our work is done?

Client: Well, that you'll be able to straighten out my kids and get them to stop acting up and all.

Therapist: Yes, I heard quite clearly that you are frustrated and unsatisfied with the way your children are behaving. Rather than me doing the work to fix them, though, my job is to teach you the skills to handle things much better.

Client: You mean you are going to tell me what to do with them?

Therapist: I will certainly work with you to develop some more effective parenting strategies, but ultimately you are the one who lives with them every day, and you are the one that your children love and respect.

Client: Sometimes I'm not so sure about that.

You can see that the therapist and client are trying to come to agreement about what work will be done, and which roles each will play. It is quite important before you end your first session to make sure that you both (or in the case of family therapy, all of you) have reached a consensus.

Closure

Once you have arrived at your last five minutes, let your client know that your time together is almost over. First check to see if your client has any questions before you go. Finally, some therapists and counselors like to take the last five minutes to solidify the relationship and reiterate any goals. For example:

> Well, our time is about up, and before we go, I wanted to check with you to find out if you have any more questions. [if the client says no] It sounds like you want to improve your relationship with your husband. I believe we could work well together to help you with this goal. How do you feel about us working together? [if the client feels good about it] Good. Then I will see you next Monday at 2 p.m. It was very nice meeting you today, Jane.

Then take the client to the door or the waiting room, but be sure not to allow the client to continue the session outside the room. If you can, stay in the room after the client leaves to prevent any further conversation; if not, just walk to the waiting room silently. Now let's explore some information that might be covered in a structured intake as well as any diagnostic information.

STRUCTURED INTAKE INTERVIEWS

Many clinical settings will require you to follow a standardized procedure for conducting first interviews with clients (such as a mental status exam). These protocols are designed to help you collect background information in an organized and systematic fashion. If a specific form must be completed that will require you to ask lots of questions, make sure to do some reflecting along the way to establish a good working relationship with your client. Typically, such structured intakes include the following components that can also be used to write up case reports.

> *Identifying information:* This category includes the client's name, marital status, occupation, interests, and cultural background.
> *Background information:* Include educational and work history, developmental history, and how and why the person was referred for help.
> *Medical history:* List physical symptoms present, sleep and eating patterns, and any relevant medical conditions. Include all medications that are taken regularly.
> *Mental health history:* Included might be any information regarding the client's previous mental health diagnoses as well as any family history of mental health issues.

A Practice Exercise

Team up with a partner and practice interviewing one another during an abbreviated 20-minute first session. Try to accomplish a few basic goals: (1) put the person at ease, (2) help the person to tell his or her story, (3) collect some basic background information, and (4) close the brief session by asking the person what this was like. Debrief one another afterward and then switch roles.

A Reality-Based Counterpoint

The previous section describes the way initial interviews are often taught in training programs. You are supposed to cover all these details, informed consent, rules, norms, roles, confidentiality, and so on. We would be amiss to tell you any differently.

But. . .

What's coming next? you wonder.

Just this: What a surprise it was to find out when I [Jeffrey] started practice that many clients would never give me a chance to take care of all the "business" before they launched into a heartbreaking story of why they were there. I was fully prepared to deliver my definition of counseling, to review the limits of confidentiality, to talk about billing procedures, client rights, and all that good stuff just reviewed, when a torrent of emotion would come bursting forth. I could hardly interrupt the person and say, "Ah, excuse me. Could you hold that in for a few minutes? We've got some things we have to cover first?" ·

Likewise, I was taught that clients should fill out their paperwork first and then get to their problems. Just like in doctors' offices: You fill out the forms, you give them your billing information, then you get seen, or then you get to talk about what is bothering you. Well, as a patient I never liked this process. I felt it was dehumanizing. And now being in the role of a professional helper I prefer to *first* make contact with my clients, first to connect with them in some way, first to hear a little bit about what is troubling to them, and *then* I will go back and take care of the business end of things.

We don't wish to confuse you by presenting two very different ways of doing a first interview. Rather, we wish to demonstrate that there are a multitude of styles and formats that are employed in various clinical settings depending on agency rules and supervisor preferences.

Exercise in Obtaining Information

Using the categories described in this section, conduct a conversation with someone in which you attempt to get background information in each of the areas. For now, don't worry so much about the skills you use to elicit this information as just trying to get some experience in what it's like to assess areas of someone's life.

After you are done with the interview, write up the results into a case report that follows this outline.

Family history. *Who lives with the client? Who is he or she close to and in conflict with? What are the intergenerational patterns, support systems available, sibling positions,*

---

coalitions, and power balances? Who else has a vested interest in the outcome of the counseling?

Presenting problems. *What are the initial complaints? When did they begin? What happened right before the onset of the symptoms? When, where, how often, and with whom do the symptoms occur? When do the problems not occur? What are the client's accompanying thoughts, feelings, and reactions to the problems?*

Expectations for treatment and goals. *What does the client expect from treatment? What are the desired goals and outcomes?*

Treatment history. *What have been the client's previous attempts at getting help? What have been the types, kinds, and lengths of treatment? What has worked best and least? How does the person engage in self-medication? This includes illicit drugs, exercise, stress reducers, and perhaps self-defeating coping strategies.*

Behavioral description. *How did the person behave and respond during the interview? What stands out most to you? What are your overall impressions?*

Summary and recommendations. *In this final section you summarize the main points and themes of the case. You also specify the kind of treatment recommended—short or long term? Group, family, or individual sessions? Is a medical consultation needed?*

Exercise in Practicing an Initial Interview

Take turns with partners conducting a 15-minute initial interview. In this limited time, try to collect as much information as you can about the presenting complaint and relevant background. Take notes during the process. When you are done, consult with your "client" about things you did well, as well as important things you missed.

SPECIAL CONSIDERATIONS IN ASSESSING ALCOHOL AND SUBSTANCE ABUSE

There are a number of issues to look at with any high-risk client population (Summers, 2003). For instance, substance use and abuse present some special considerations for clinicians that must be reviewed. You would want to assesses client behavior in several domains:

- Behavior patterns—acting out, self-control, consequences, relapses.
- Health status—accidents, injuries, illnesses.
- Psychiatric disorders—depression, anxiety, personality disorders, psychotic symptoms.
- Social competence—social skills.
- Family system—conflicts, parental supervision, marital quality.
- School performance—adjustment, grades.
- Work adjustment—competence, motivation.
- Peer relationships—social network, gang involvement, friendships, support system.
- Leisure activities—recreation, hobbies, outlets, interests.

In addition, it is critical that a detailed substance use history be collected in which you determine which substances are being used, how much, how often, in which circumstances, and with what effects (Lewis, Dana, & Blevins, 2002).

All of this would be taken into consideration in formulating your treatment plan. For instance, if your client is actively abusing a substance it is unlikely you will wish to treat the person with weekly hourly sessions alone. You may decide that inpatient treatment is indicated or, at the very least, use of a 12-step program in Alcoholics or Narcotics Anonymous.

SPECIAL CONSIDERATIONS IN ASSESSING PHYSICAL OR SEXUAL ABUSE

You will be required by law in most jurisdictions to recognize, identify, and report evidence of abuse toward children, the elderly, or spouses. This includes sexual abuse, physical abuse, neglect, or emotional maltreatment.

Most programs will require you to go through specific training to develop the skills of identifying and reporting abuse. In most states this means that if you have reasonable suspicion of any abuse going on, you *must* report it in a timely way to Protective Services or a law enforcement agency. You are usually protected from breaching confidentiality in such circumstances and you are given immunity from legal action. It is when you *fail* to report such suspicions that you can get in a lot of trouble, as well as put others at risk of further harm.

There are several things you should look for in assessing possible abuse (Table 5.1). None of these symptoms by themselves signal that abuse is taking place, but in combination, or as part of a consistent pattern, you would wish to investigate matters more carefully.

TABLE 5.1
Indications of Abuse

Emotional Symptoms	Physical Evidence
Sadness	Poor dress and grooming
Guilt	Bruises or injuries
Fear/anxiety	Bandages
Irritability	Camouflaged clothing
Anger	Ligature or binding marks
Behavioral Indications	**Systemic Factors**
Seductive behavior	Overly clingy behavior
Inappropriately sexualized behavior	Isolation in family
Phobic reactions	Scapegoat
Regression	Exploitation of power
Aggression	

SPECIAL CONSIDERATIONS FOR HIGH SUICIDE RISK

Another important assessment that must be done is the risk for suicide. You are obligated ethically and by law to protect your client from self-harm. Like abuse, most programs will have a more thorough description of how to assess suicide in other classes. However, we briefly cover the topic here because of its obvious importance.

First, many applications and/or assessment instruments screen for this type of risk. However, if you don't have the luxury of those tools, or even if you do, start your assessment by identifying if your client seems depressed. Is his or her affect sad, energy low? Does the client seem to have a sense of hopelessness and helplessness about life? You might even ask if the client has thought about dying as an escape from his or her pain. In this way, you introduce the concept of suicide without mentioning the word if your client hasn't thought of it yet. If he or she has considered dying, then ask if he or she has considered suicide. Make sure to practice your reflecting skills a lot here (you will learn more about reflections in the next chapter). It's essential that your client feel understood at this point.

If your client has considered suicide, ask if he or she has a plan. The more detailed the plan, the greater is the likelihood of suicide. Does the client know what method he or she will use? "I will run the car in the garage until I die from the fumes." How lethal is the method, such as taking aspirin versus shooting oneself? Does the client know when he or she will do it? "I will do it after everyone has just left for school and work so that I have plenty of time alone." If the plan is detailed and the method highly lethal, then you may want to have the client sign a written contract with you that the client will call you (or a suicide hotline) if he or she feels that hopeless. You may want to come to some agreement or plan for the client if his or her feelings seem out of control. If the lethality is too great, then you are obligated to call the authorities.

Reflective or Discussion Exercise

Most people, at some time during their lives, have considered suicide, or at least entertained fantasies of self-annihilation. Of course, contemplating suicide and actually following through with a plan may be two quite different things. Nevertheless, there may have been a time in your own life when you were feeling despair and hopelessness, when the prospect of putting an end to the pain seemed very attractive. Either in a journal, or in a discussion in small groups, talk about what this experience is like. In other words, start to become more comfortable talking to people about deep, uncomfortable feelings. Of course, you will want to use sound judgment regarding how much you share with others depending on trust developed.

In any case, providing lots of empathy and understanding can be very beneficial to a depressed client. We find it helps to acknowledge how the pain seems so devastating that death may seem to be the only escape, but death is permanent and the pain does not have to be. In addition, a psychiatric evaluation might be recommended to determine if antidepressant medication might be indicated.

OBJECTIVE AND SUBJECTIVE SOURCES OF INFORMATION

In order to supplement your subjective perceptions and information gathered during clinical interviews, you will also wish to use psychometric and other objective assessment tools. Such tests and measures may be far more reliable (consistent) than just relying on your own perceptions; at the very least, they provide additional data to consider in forming your diagnostic impressions. In addition, each instrument has a distinct "way of thinking" that may emphasize more standardized, empirically based administration that helps one to maintain a certain distance and objectivity.

There are a number of assessment tools at your disposal, including objective personality tests like the MMPI or Beck Depression Inventory, subjective personality tests like the TAT or Rorschach, or other measures like the Draw a Person or Bender Gestalt. You might also use genograms to assess systematically clients' family history and configurations.

Some Useful Clinical Instruments

Even if you do not become trained in the administration of psychological instruments (or choose to use them), you must still become familiar enough with what they can offer so they might guide your practice and help you make sound clinical decisions. In one sense, such tests represent just another sample of behavior, one that is offered in a normative context that helps you look at things in light of what you might expect. Obviously, such instruments have their limitations and biases, but they are still valuable tools to help you assess client functioning. You will also have to consider that instruments like the MMPI and projective measures (TAT, Rorschach) are only to be administered and interpreted by advanced-level practitioners (usually with a PhD in psychology).

Some of the major clinical instruments are reviewed:

Minnesota Multiphasic Personality Inventory (MMPI)

- Ten clinical scales.
- Hypochondriasis, depression, hysteria, paranoia, social introversion, schizophrenia.
- Lie scales—validity, deception, test taking style, faking, malingering, eccentricity, carelessness.
- Subscales that assess anxiety, hostility, gender role, posttraumatic stress disorder (PTSD), social responsibility.

Strong Vocational Interest Inventory

This is based on John Holland's theory, which associated personality types with particular categories of jobs. It classifies people as essentially:

- Realistic (tools and machinery).
- Investigative (science).
- Artistic (self-expression).
- Social (helping).
- Enterprising (business).
- Conventional (clerical).

Wechsler Scales

This so-called intelligence battery looks at verbal and performance scales using a series of tasks, not just to measure IQ but problem solving, memory, reasoning, even underlying brain damage. There are versions designed for adults (WAIS), children (WISC), and preschoolers (WPPSI).

Myers–Briggs Type Indicator

This is the most widely used personality measure. It contains 16 specific personality types according to:

- Extraversion/introversion.
- Sensing/intuitive.
- Thinking/feeling.
- Judging/perceiving.

Genogram

A genogram plots the relationships among and between family members, both in the current family and in the family of origin. Such information as ages, marital status, names, occupations, degree of conflict, or affiliation can be included. Like in any new system, genograms or family diagrams have their own unique symbols and language. The following standard symbols are often used and were devised from the theory of Murray Bowen, one of the originators of family therapy:

- Circles—females.
- Squares—males.
- Number—age of member.
- Birth dates, occupations, education entered to side of squares or circles.
- Slash—shows divorce between partners.
- X through square or circle—deceased member.
- Jagged lines—conflicted relationships.
- Bold lines—strong affiliations.
- Two lines—enmeshed relationships.
- Thin lines—weak affiliation.

MODELS OF DIAGNOSIS

So far we have been looking at some of the practical aspects of what therapists and counselors do to launch an effective therapeutic relationship and collect necessary information. All this data must somehow be processed in a meaningful and constructive way in order to formulate a diagnostic impression of the case.

Therapists conceptualize their work in so many different ways. You might think that there is universal agreement on a diagnostic system, but there are actually several such models depending on one's professional identity and theoretical orientation.

- *Medical:* categories of psychopathology, uses a disease model and a biologically based perspective, mental disorders.
- *Psychodynamic:* a disease model as well, ego functioning, defense mechanisms and coping styles, looking at past, unconscious, diagnosing.
- *Developmental:* stages of growth, assessment of current levels of functioning in all dimensions.
- *Phenomenological:* complex descriptions of person, personal strengths and weaknesses, freedom, autonomy, responsibility.
- *Behavioral:* specific descriptors of behaviors, reinforcers, consequences, specific goals.
- *Systemic:* contextual dynamics and family structures, power, coalitions.

Each of these diagnostic models might be applied in different ways, depending on the perceptual filter of the clinician. For instance, a client complains of frequent stomachaches that are believed to be brought on by excessive stress. Working backward from the list of diagnostic options, a systemic model might conceptualize things in such a way that the identified client is a scapegoat of a dysfunctional family system. Because of weak boundaries between interfamily coalitions, a chaotic system of communication between members, and an inappropriate power hierarchy, the client's symptoms represent a call for help to realign the family system. Given this conceptualization, a treatment plan would follow that attempts to address these issues.

A behavioral model, on the other hand, would focus specifically on the presenting problems, identifying as clearly as possible what is bothersome, when, where, with whom, and in which situations the behavior occurs. You would be looking for ways this behavior is being rewarded—in other words: How are the stomachaches helpful to the person? You would attempt to define, in very specific terms, exactly which behaviors are going to be targeted, what the behavioral goals will be, how they will be reached, and what consequences will result from each prospective outcome.

A phenomenological model is far more global and encompassing. Rather than seeking to reduce a person to a diagnostic label, the intent instead is to retain the essence of a person who is far more than his stomachache. This would be only one small facet of the total picture, and the goal would be to describe (and conceptualize) what is going in the language of the person. If the behavioral and systemic models focus on the presenting complaints, then this model is equally concerned with the client's experiences and perceptions of these symptoms. Such an approach is favored by not only a phenomenological approach but also so-called "constructivist" models that look at presenting problems in a much broader cultural/social/political context.

Developmental diagnosis refers to the identification of a client's functioning in a host of areas including physical, emotional, cognitive, social, cultural, moral, spiritual, and gender dimensions. If you can diagnose accurately where a person is currently functioning you can make predictions about where the person needs to go next. Treatment follows to design experiences that will help facilitate movement to the next stage of development. For instance, if the stomachaches are seen as an example of low-functioning coping skills in dealing with social situations, then efforts may be directed to help the person move to the next stage of developmental functioning in that area.

A psychodynamic model evolved from the work of psychoanalysis. Although many of these concepts have been integrated into mainstream generic practice, this diagnostic approach focuses much more on patterns of the past: How is what the person is experiencing now related to unresolved issues? Thus diagnostic impressions include characteristic defense mechanisms and an assortment of other coping strategies.

The medical model is the one that has given rise to the diagnostic system now favored in the mental health system. When it is combined with a few of the other systems just described, you will have at your disposal an assortment of powerful tools for conceptualizing cases and making sense of what you encounter. All of these diagnostic models are useful in some ways in providing a structure for exploring, investigating, and finding meaning in what clients present.

Learning the *DSM*

Other courses will teach you how to use the *Diagnostic and Statistical Manual* (*DSM*) that has become the "bible" of our profession. Regardless of the setting in which you will eventually work, whether in a school, mental health center, hospital, community agency, or private practice, you will still be expected to master the nomenclature and structure of the *DSM* (APA, 2001; Spitzer, 2002).

Most human problems that could show up in therapy are sorted and classified into one of 17 different categories and then further divided into subclasses. Because the *DSM* was authored primarily by psychiatrists, it is consistent with a medical model, a very different kind of approach than the other diagnostic models described in the previous section.

A *DSM* diagnostic assessment looks something like this:

TABLE 5.2

Sample *DSM* Diagnostic Assessment

Axis	Description	Example
I	Clinical disorders	Disorganized schizophrenia
II	Personality disorders	Borderline disorder
III	Medical conditions	Multiple sclerosis
IV	Psychosocial problems	Health care and legal problems
V	Assessment of functioning	Impairment in reality testing

You can see from this example that the *DSM* classification system is useful in assessing the client's presenting problems in a host of areas covering all facets of human functioning. As another example, let's take the case of a young man who presents himself to you complaining of chronic stomach problems. There are a number of possible sources for these problems. Perhaps there is some genuine organic problem that is contributing to the symptoms (Axis III). The pain could also be the result of extreme anxiety as a result of an upcoming exam (Axis IV) or perhaps a cry for attention as part of an ongoing manipulative interpersonal style (Axis II). It would be important for this case, and all others that you work with, that you proceed with caution and consider many different dimensions of the difficulty.

You should also be aware that there are certain biases associated with the use of the *DSM*. As we have already mentioned, it is clearly slanted toward a medical model and favors approaches used by psychiatrists, and to a certain extent those of psychologists. Because it is empirically based, it may also take some work to make it fit those who prefer a more "constructivist" or "humanist" orientation. These are examples of theories that downplay labeling and prefer to operate within the client's frame of reference.

The cultural and gender biases of the *DSM* are not unlike those of any diagnostic system, or choice of therapy. That is why it is so critical that you take a client's cultural background, gender, ethnicity, spiritual beliefs, and other factors into consideration when assigning any diagnostic labels. What may be auditory hallucinations in one person might very well be a transcendent religious experience in another. Or what might strike you as antisocial behavior in one adolescent might very well be entirely normative within that person's peer group. That is why all of your thinking and internal processing should take place within the cultural context of the clients you are seeing.

REMEMBERING WHAT YOU SEE AND HEAR

One of the most important aspects of developing your skills related to conceptualizing cases and evaluating the impact of what you do is related to keeping accurate, comprehensive, descriptive, and meaningful records (Prieto & Scheel, 2002). Basically, after every intake interview you will want to write extensive notes that include a diagnostic impression, a detailed treatment plan, and working guidelines for future sessions.

In this first session and all succeeding sessions, you will need to maintain case notes on what occured. Keeping records of your sessions can be helpful to remember details that may be forgotten from week to week. For example, referring to last week's notes prior to meeting with the client can jog your memory as to what you might want to follow up on, such as homework assignments. In addition, sometimes the details of two similar clients in a large caseload can become confusing early in the process. Keeping notes will help you to avoid a huge blunder by mixing up information between clients.

I [Leah] remember a time when I had two clients that started at about the same time, were of similar age, and had similar issues with their children. I confused some details with one client from another's situation. I felt so foolish making that mistake. My client was really confused! Now, I always look over my notes if I'm at risk for confusing two clients. Furthermore, there may be times when your notes will be subpoenaed or requested by your client for a variety of purposes. Keeping good records of sessions is essential in protecting you if you are accused of an ethical violation. Finally, your ethical guidelines require that you maintain case notes.

Some therapists choose to keep notes during the session while the client is talking. This can be helpful in that you will retain all the details of the session, forgetting nothing. However, there's an extreme disadvantage to doing this. If you are keeping notes while your client is talking, you can't listen as well.

> **Exercise in Note Taking**
>
> *Get into triads: The talking person should tell a story with lots of details, the second person takes notes on the story as a therapist might, and the third person listens without taking notes as a therapist might. After five minutes, both listeners make notes about the speaker's content in details, the essence of the content, and any nonverbal messages. Compare notes. Then get feedback from the speaker about what he or she preferred: the person taking notes or the person just listening. Rotate until everyone has played each role, and then discuss the experience overall.*

After completing this exercise, you may find that taking notes can interrupt the client's process. The client might slow down his or her story so that all the details can be written down, thus staying in his or her head to tell the story and avoiding emotions. In addition, the therapist taking notes may miss important nonverbal information. And finally, believe it or not, when you get so involved in taking notes, you sometimes don't really attend to what's being said. Think of a time when you have been so busy taking notes in class that you have no idea what you just wrote down. If you feel it's important to get the details, you may want to record the session instead; it's less invasive. However, a good therapist is more interested in the process than in the content. How does the client convey his or her story? Does he or she do so without feelings? Is the client animated when he or she tells it? What patterns are you seeing from previous stories? Rarely will the details like names, ages, or cities be important to the overall problem.

Whether or not you decide to take notes during the session, you will need to make some notes afterwards. The amount of detail is up to you. Some therapists prefer to just take notes on processes, such as, "The client seemed to be gaining insight about why she chooses domineering men." Other therapists prefer to report only the facts, such as, "The client discussed the relationship between her mother and father, and stated that her father seemed to be 'controlling' with regard to her mother and her." One popular format is to use is called a SOAP: subjective, objective, assessment, and progress (Sommers-Flanagan & Sommers-Flanagan, 1999). In the subjective section, the therapist would indicate information about how the client was dressed, overall mood, or anything else that he or she perceives or observes. In the objective section, the therapist would note the content of what was discussed during the session. The assessment section might include an interpretation of how the client is doing. This section is most conducive to include information using your theoretical orientation. The final section, progress, includes how the client is doing relative to meeting short-term and long-term goals (see Figure 5.1).

We have a few pointers in keeping case notes. First, especially during training, you may want to only have the client's name at the top in case you need to replicate the progress notes for your supervisor or professor, or the HMO or insurance company paying for sessions. This way you can cover the name and not give away the identity of the client. Second, when stating information that is not factual, you may want to use tentative language because you are only speculating. Finally, you want to keep your information secure and safe from hazards. If you keep hard copies, the file cabinet should be locked at all times and fireproof. If you are keeping notes on the computer, the diskette should be locked up or, if on your hard drive, your com-

Counseling Services Agency, Inc.

Client Name: <u>Jane Doe</u>   Therapist: <u>Leah Brew</u>

Date: <u>January 21, 2002</u>   Session Number: <u>6</u>

Subjective: The client came in dressed much nicer than usual. She wore makeup and seemed unusually cheerful. Her energy level was high, and she smiled frequently.

Objective: The client reported that she had just met a man this past weekend. She discussed how he was different than her ex-husband and previous boyfriends in that he had a full time job and a home. She reported how they met and how they have spent every day together since meeting last weekend. She stated that she was hopeful that this relationship could be different than all of her previous relationships. She talked of hopes of marriage.

Assessment: The client seemed to have a lot of positive self talk with regard to this new relationship. However, she also seemed to have unrealistic expectations about the future by hoping for marriage after knowing him only one week. The client has evidenced this pattern of belief before. When confronted about this pattern of wishing for marriage after one week, the client denied ever having this experience before and was quite defensive.

Progress: The client may be making progress toward meeting her short-term goal of wanting to meet more people. However, the client does not seem to be meeting her long-term goal of getting into a healthy relationship at a slower pace. She seemed to be making decisions about the future in a short period of time as she has done in the past.

_____
Therapist Signature

_____
Supervisor Signature

FIGURE 5.1. SOAP

puter should have a password that is changed monthly to assure security. Keeping the records confidential is required by your ethical guidelines and each state requires that you maintain your client notes for a certain number of years.

The preceding example is just a sample format for keeping case notes. If you work for an agency, as you most certainly will during your practica and internship experiences, the agency will have a format that you must follow. In addition, your supervisor may have specific requirements about record keeping because the case notes are a vital part of the supervision process.

MAKING THINGS FIT YOUR STYLE

In this chapter, we have exposed you to an abundance of information involved in the beginning phase with your client: the mental status exam, the intake interview, the assessment instruments, and the *DSM*. How you perform your intake interview may be predetermined by the agency in which you work. They may require a very structured intake process. In other agencies, someone else might complete your intakes. However, most agencies give you the freedom to obtain relevant information in whatever way you see fit. In any case, you will need to develop a style that fits your personality and your values and works with your unique qualities. When you sit down with your client for the first time, you will have to figure out what works best for you. Hopefully, we have given you some tools from which to choose your own personal style. In the next section, we alert you to some traps and errors that you will want to watch out for as you learn to conduct assessment interviews.

PITFALLS AND COMMON MISTAKES

As with any new skill, mistakes are made by new practitioners. By exposing you to some of the more common mistakes and pitfalls, we hope you can begin to work on avoiding what we have seen does not work. Let's start by letting you know that we make mistakes, too.

A Personal Tale of Woe

I [Jeffrey] had just opened my office in private practice. I had exactly two clients with a new referral due any minute. My rent and overhead were more than I could afford and I had no other sources of significant income. Unless I could build my practice, and do it rather quickly, there was no way I could survive. I was desperate. And I badly need to keep this new client, who would represent a 50% increase in my caseload.

When I heard the door to my waiting room open and close, I took a deep breath and went out to greet my new client. She looked up and smiled shyly. I greeted her warmly and handed her a clipboard where I had attached my "intake" form containing a series of questions about billing information and many of the areas of inquiry mentioned in this chapter. I then retreated to my office and waited impatiently for the woman to fill out the forms so we could begin.

About five minutes elapsed before I heard the outside door of the waiting room open and close again. I wondered who that could be as I was not expecting any other visitors. I peeked into the waiting room and found to my surprise that it was now empty. Perched on the chair where my client had been sitting was the clipboard I had handed her. I picked up the form and saw written on the cover sheet the following message: "I am sorry but I can't go through with this."

I was crestfallen: I had lost my new client and my only present opportunity to build my struggling practice. As I sat in my empty office during the next hour, and for the rest of the afternoon, I thought about what I had done wrong. I wondered what I could have done differently and whether that would have mattered. I resolved at that moment that forever after I would make certain that my very first interactions with new clients would be geared toward building a solid relationship *before* I asked them to fill out any forms. I realize that many, many agencies and doctors' offices have procedures similar to those that I had used without losing clients. Nevertheless, the lesson I learned from this episode was that I had forgotten how important it is to create a working alliance before proceeding with anything. Sometimes therapists become so focused on collecting information that *they* need to fill out their forms that they forget what clients need most during those first critical minutes—to be treated with caring, respect, and hovering attention.

Thinking Too Much Instead of Listening

As we've said before, the experience of doing counseling (in case you haven't noticed) is one of feeling confused and overwhelmed. In any given moment there are at least a dozen things you can do or say, and whichever one you select, you will wonder what you should have done instead. The client is speaking. You are doing your best to demonstrate solid attending and listening skills. You are trying to figure out the underlying meaning of the communications: What is the client *really* saying by this? You are making connections between what is being said and other things you have heard before. You are considering how what is going on fits within your overall scheme of things. You are planning where you are going to go next. You are reviewing options in your head, rejecting some, choosing others, then making adjustments as the client changes directions. Something the client says sparks a recollection of something you must do later in the day. This reminds you of something that you forgot to do earlier in the morning. Then you think about the client you saw last hour, and the one you will see in the next hour. Then you realize that for the last several minutes you haven't been really listening to what the client has been saying.

You can ask the client to summarize what the main points were—and this is a clever way to catch up when you have been falling behind—but the main point is that you must stay centered and focused on listening above all else. At least a dozen, maybe even a hundred times, in any session you are going to find your mind racing behind, or darting backwards and sideways. You will have the most brilliant realizations and insights—about the client, about the world, about yourself, about the meaning of life. You will be juggling so many different ideas, theories, and revelations at the same time. And all this time you are nodding your head, *pretending* to listen to the client. Remember that you can't help someone very well if you are not paying close attention to what they are saying. All your amazing theories and insights are useless if they do not correspond with where the client is at any moment in time. Listen now and save your thinking for later.

Failing to Engage the Client

Beginners, in particular, are so focused on their diagnostic and assessment skills that they forget that being with the person is as important as what you actually do. Unless you manage to create strong connections with your clients, relationships in which they feel valued and understood, then nothing else you do is going to work very well. We are giving you fair warning that there will be times when you have the most accurate, comprehensive, and utterly brilliant diagnostic grasp of what is going on with a client, and such conceptualizations will be utterly useless when the person doesn't return. You will be left with your detailed case notes and your meticulous clinical judgments, all of which will get tucked away into a case file and then later thrown away. Almost all other mistakes can be forgiven, *if* you have built a good relationship with your clients.

Being Judgmental

As humans, we have a natural tendency to make assumptions or judgments about people when we meet them. Making these presumptions is our way of organizing the world. We even study cultural stereotypes to help us be more sensitive with our clients. However as a therapist, if your judgments about your client are rigid or inflexible, you will not be able to see him or her clearly. You will have difficulty demonstrating empathy and consequently building a strong therapeutic alliance. Therefore, although it may be necessary for you to develop some theories about your client, make them just that: theories. Theories are flexible and require supporting evidence. They can change, and we can assure you that some of your first assumptions about most clients will change over time.

Trying to Do Too Much

The problem that most beginners have is not in doing enough but in trying to do too much. People come to you in pain and you want to do something to take away their suffering. You have visions of being a healer, of saying a few magic incantations, and voila!—the person is cured. We are not saying that quick relief is out of the question, especially in this era of brief therapy, but rather that you must honor the pace of your clients. When you force things, when you push too hard, that is when clients can be hurt, or fail to return. And remember, if you don't get clients to come back, you can't help them!

The more work that you do in the sessions, the less there is for the client to do. That is a problem in many couples relationships in which one partner complains that the other is too passive in bed, in social situations, or in other areas. In such situations, the goal is to get one partner to back off so the other can step up and become more active and involved. This same analogy holds true for counseling relationships.

How do you know if you are pushing the client too hard or working harder than your client? You will experience a lot of resistance from the client. The resistance indicates either that you are wrong, or more often that you are way ahead of your client. Your client is not ready to see what you are presenting or to do what you are suggesting and more work needs to be done right where the client is stuck.

When you catch yourself working really hard to convince a client about the merits of your brilliant interpretation, and you notice that the client isn't buying it, then back off. In most situations where you observe that you are working furiously while the client is sitting back watching the show, it is time to make adjustments so those roles can be reversed. In spite of what you have been led to believe, in therapy it is the client who does most of the work.

Neglecting to Offer Help

Here is an opposite problem of the one just discussed. In this case, rather than trying to do too much, you don't do what is needed. Let's say that a client comes to you in the midst of a crisis. There has been a recent tragedy and this person is experiencing profound grief and loss. She is barely holding things together. You quickly find out that she is acutely depressed and unable to manage the most ordinary daily tasks. She clearly needs immediate relief and crisis intervention.

Instead of responding to the immediate situation, you persist in the usual data collection that is part of an assessment interview; after all, you have forms to fill out and procedures to follow. Through dedication and Herculean efforts, you manage to get the information you need while keeping the client focused on the task at hand. The session ends and you have what you need—but the client is still just as lost and distraught.

We'd like to repeat one more time the most important thing to remember in doing a first interview: *The object of a first session is to get the client to come back for another one.* Unless you can do this, then all the information you have collected, and diagnoses you have formed, will be worthless. This means that you must deliver some constructive help in the session, even though your own goal is to get the information you need to create an intelligent treatment plan.

Failing to Collect Relevant Information

Another common mistake is to follow a procedure such that the more information you collect, the better. You can fill volumes of notebooks with data on your client, but unless these details are clinically meaningful and relevant, you have just wasted a lot of paper and time. Throughout the interview, keep in focus where you are going and what you need to get there.

Your principal job during the initial contact is to find out what is bothering the client the most and what is desired after the treatment is over. That is the big picture. The subgoals are to find out: (a) when, where, and how the problem started, (b) what has been tried previously with which effects, and (c) how what is being presented connects with other facets of the person's life. There are indeed other things you will want to learn about the client, many of which have been previously reviewed, but keep in mind that time is very limited. You have only 45 or 50 minutes in a first session, or even 90 minutes if it is scheduled that way, so you must be disciplined in finding out the basics as efficiently as you can.

For school counselors and crisis intervention specialists, who don't operate in neat time segments, you will have to be even more focused in your assessment efforts. There are times when you might have only 15 minutes total to figure out what is going on and create some sort of intervention. In some cases, this might be an only contact with this client. Plan the assessment according to the time that is available and the realistic constraints that are in place.

Thinking That What You Missed Was Important

After you complete the interview, and reflect back on what you did (and didn't do), you may very well find that you missed a lot more than what you captured. This is not only normal, but just what you should expect. A first contact is just that—the initial attempt to figure out what is going on and start building a collaborative relationship. Unless you are doing single-session therapy, or are limited to very brief therapy (less than three sessions), you will have plenty of time to fill in gaps.

In addition, the client will first present what is most relevant at the moment. You cannot force the client to talk about anything until he or she is ready. In supervising new therapists, we have found that many clients keep going back to the same topic, the topic that is most essential to them at the moment, no matter how often the beginning therapist goes off the primary topic to explore some tangent. You might as well give in and allow the client to lead. By reflecting well, you will obtain an abundance of information.

The beauty of the pace that therapy sets is that you usually meet with clients once (or even twice) per week. After they walk out the door, you have plenty of time to reflect on the session, consult with supervisors, and do your homework to prepare for the next meeting. Anything and everything that you missed the first time, you can often pick up the second or third or eleventh time. It is very important that you have realistic expectations about what you can do, and what you cannot do, or you will set yourself up for failure.

Forgetting to Find Out How You're Doing

Never forget that clients are your customers. They pay your salary directly, or indirectly at taxpayer expense. Clients, or those who referred them in the case of involuntary participants, must be satisfied with the way things are going or you will be "fired."

In your zeal to conduct your assessment you must keep at the forefront of your agenda the reality that clients (as well as their parents, significant others, and referral sources) must have confidence in your plan; if they have their doubts, they will go somewhere else or, worse yet, abandon their efforts to seek help altogether.

You are not expected to read clients' minds, even with your advanced skills in reading body language and discerning underlying meaning to their communications. You are not only permitted, but encouraged to find out how you're doing. Such an inquiry might look something like this.

> *Therapist:* Now that our session is over, I'm wondering what this has been like for you.
> *Client:* Excuse me?
> *Therapist:* How did you find this conversation?
> *Client:* Oh. It was fine.
> *Therapist:* What I'm asking is, what about this meeting was most helpful to you? I am very interested in making sure that what we do together meets your needs. In order to do that, I need feedback from you—not just now but all along the way—about what you liked most and liked least about what we are doing. Specifically, I'd like us to spend the last few minutes reviewing what we did today and then figure out how we could best proceed in the future. That means it would be helpful to hear what your reactions were to the session.

This was a fairly realistic glimpse into how this conversation might go. Clients don't know what we are looking for and often don't know how to respond to your queries. In your efforts to conduct ongoing assessment about progress and satisfaction with services you must teach your clients how to give you feedback as honestly and clearly as possible.

In one of my [Leah] classes, the instructor proposed using an interesting statement at the end of every session, including the intake. He would ask, "Did I do or say anything today that offended you?" He said he liked using this statement to give the client ample opportunity to discuss any problems. I would imagine that using this question shows the client that you care about your relationship, and it can help bring to light any problems you might have been unaware of. Consequently, you have a better chance for the client to return the following week.

There is nothing more frustrating than having a valued client one day cancel an appointment, refuse to reschedule, and then never learn what happened and why. What did you do to drive the person away? What did you neglect to notice and respond to? Or perhaps the person didn't return because she already got what she wanted from the sessions. Unless the person returns for a future session, you will never know.

Misdiagnosing

If a diagnosis represents a clinician's perception of what is disturbing to clients, then there is always potential to misread the situation. Under the best possible circumstances, even among very experienced clinicians, there is often disagreement about what the "real" problem is. You have seen this in the medical profession, of course, but in our own field, the potential for error is even greater because what we are observing and measuring is often elusive and imprecise. At times, even the client can't say exactly what is bothering him or her.

A client says that he is depressed. But that can mean a whole assortment of things. Is this a temporary or chronic situation? Was there a precipitant to the symptoms or did they begin without a particular stimulus? Might the depression be masking other conditions? In other words, is the depression the problem, or is it the result of what is really most bothersome? Is the depression biologically based or is it sparked by something in the person's life? In addition, there are at least a half dozen kinds of depression (dysthymia, reactive depression, major depression, bipolar disorder, etc.) that might be operating, and each one might involve a different treatment regimen.

If even experienced therapists struggle with formulating accurate diagnoses, then imagine how difficult it will be for you. The good news is that a diagnosis is only a working hypothesis that is altered in light of new data. The key feature is to make sure that you don't become so vested in your reading of the situation that you fail to make adjustments as things develop further.

Trying to Fix the Problem

There are some styles of practice, especially some forms of brief therapy, where the therapist's job is defined as identifying the presenting problem and then fixing it in the shortest, most efficient period of time. At the very least, this is the way many managed care organizations describe our preferred roles—we are problem solvers.

We leave it to other courses for you to resolve this dilemma as to what your main role is to be—as a problem solver, consultant, teacher, confidante, surrogate parent, mediator, or per-haps combination of all them. Frankly, much will depend on where you work and what the mission is of that health care organization.

For our purposes in this class learning basic helping skills, we would like you to learn sound procedures for *not* getting in the habit of fixing other people's problems for them. There are several good reasons for this. Number one: If your efforts to "cure" or fix the problem are unsuccessful, you will be blamed as the culprit. In fact, positive outcomes are most likely the result of what clients do or don't do; *they* are the ones who primarily determine the outcome. Granted, we can do a lot to improve their motivation, resilience, and strategies, but ultimately, *their* efforts will influence the result.

Because many clients don't want responsibility for their lives and choices in the first place, they will be delighted to blame you when things go wrong. The implicit message is that you failed them because of your incompetence or inadequacies. We much prefer to communicate a very different message to our clients that goes something like this:

Client: What we talked about last time didn't work at all. I'm worse off now than ever!
Therapist: What is it that you did this week and how did that work out?
Client: I just told you: What you told me to do didn't work.
Therapist: I'm a little unclear about what I told you to do. What I remember is that you said that you wanted to try approaching things with your mother a bit differently. You said that you were tired of arguing with her and that you were going to try backing off a little to see how that worked instead. I told you at the time that this first strategy of yours might not be as successful as you'd like, at least the first time you tried it. I also told you that I could help you to come up with some other things that you might invent to work things out. So, let's figure out where things fell apart, and what you did that wasn't all that helpful. Also, let's look at what you did that you liked and might want to continue doing.

Think About It

Reason through why you think that the authors are saying that giving good advice could be dangerous. After all, if you tell someone what to do, and it solves the problem, isn't that what we're paid to do? What could possibly be wrong with that?

To understand the reasoning behind the authors' point, consider the consequences of giving someone good advice. The person comes to you, feeling helpless, frustrated, at a loss as to how to proceed. He tells you what is wrong and you say, "Hey, no problem. Have you thought about trying this?" The client goes home, uses your advice, and it works out beautifully. Now, what has the client learned from this experience?

Notice the way the therapist continues to emphasize the pronoun "you." It is what the client did, or did not do, that matters. The therapist does not directly argue with the client about who is at fault but instead turns the conversation to a review of progress. This continues to reinforce the idea that the client is the one who fixes his or her own problems; the therapist is the guide, the consultant, the partner along the way.

The second reason why trying to fix the client's problem is generally a bad idea (except when using paradoxical directives that are the kind of advice designed to be disobeyed) is that what you tell the person to do might work out. You heard us right: Giving good advice could be even more dangerous than giving bad advice.

When you tell someone what to do with their lives, you are essentially saying that they don't know what is best for themselves and they need someone like you to figure it out for them. They are either too stupid or inept to sort this out themselves so they need someone like you, an expert, to fix things. You have just reinforced their own inability to take care of themselves.

Because things appear to have worked out so well, they have now learned to come back to you, or another expert, the next time they have problems. They have learned to distrust their own problem-solving ability and have learned very little about the process of taking care of their own business in the future. In contrast, if the client does not take your advice, the client may feel too ashamed to return the next week. The client may feel like you will not approve of them if he or she did not take your advice.

These points are the reasons why it is very important to choose your language very carefully. Following are some examples of how you might intervene in response to some client statements:

Client: You really helped me last week with that suggestion.
Therapist: You mean that you really helped yourself by adapting what we talked about to that situation.

Client: Thank you so much for all your help!
Therapist: You're quite welcome. But I want to remind you that you are the one who did all the work. You are the one who took the risks and tried so hard to change this pattern.

Client: That idea you gave me last time worked perfectly.
Therapist: Tell me, how did you take what we talked about last time and make it fit in this situation?

Client: I'm really going to miss you when these sessions end.
Therapist: I will miss you as well. Remember, though, that what you have managed to do here you can continue to do once we stop these meetings.

Note that in each of these cases, the therapist continues to reinforce the idea that it is the client who solves his or her own problems, with the able assistance of the therapist.

Liking or Disliking the Client Too Much

A final common mistake we would like to mention again is related to the countertransference reactions that we talked about earlier. At a more basic level, you will find yourself having a number of personal reactions to your clients. Some you will find immediately attractive and others may repulse you. Some you would enjoy as friends and others you would hope to never run into again. You may have vivid sexual fantasies about some clients—when you are with them in session and when you have idle moments on your own. All of this is normal, natural, and part of what comes with the territory of being a therapist. Of course, if your fantasies are frequent and persistent, then you would have to consider a pattern that could be dangerous to the people you are paid to help.

You are probably well aware that your personal reactions, if left unchecked, can wreak havoc in your work as well as other people's lives. At this beginning juncture, just as the relationship begins, you will want to make sure that you present yourself as warm and accessible without being perceived as seductive. Depending on the client's age, cultural background, and individual style, you will wish to adapt your demeanor to match that of the person you are helping.

The warning we wish to issue is that although it is permissible, even desirable, to like your clients, you don't want to like them so much that you enable their manipulative behavior or disrupt your own life by thinking about them when you are off duty. Likewise, when you must work with individuals whose behavior you find abhorrent (think sex abusers, murderers, spouse batterers, obnoxious people) you will want to guard your strong negative reactions so they don't compromise your work. In spite of what you might believe, you will often not have the luxury of referring elsewhere people to whom you have a negative reaction. Not only does this send a strong message to your supervisor about the nature of your biases, but it suggests that you have a hard time accepting people who come from different backgrounds.

Conceptualizing Client Presenting Problems

If only therapy were as easy as simply asking what is bothering clients and then proceeding to fix things up just like an auto mechanic or a surgeon. Unfortunately, even when clients do articulate clearly what is most bothering them (and that is usually not the case), we still can't be certain that this is the core issue that must be addressed. At times, clients may wish to test you first, find out if you are trustworthy and competent before they trot out the "real" concern. In other situations, they genuinely don't know what is wrong. They might just feel uneasy or depressed or unhappy but can't point to the source of the difficulty. Sometimes they will come up with some explanation just because they know it is expected. Finally, at other times, clients will present only the symptoms of some underlying issue. Remember, what is presented is usually not the problem, but the symptom of some pattern that was developed earlier in life but isn't working today.

Before anything else is done, the therapist must come up with at least a working hypothesis and structure for figuring out what is going on. This is often called "case conceptualization and treatment planning" and involves the mental activity of gathering needed information, synthesizing the data, and generating reasonable assumptions about what is most likely going on (Cormier & Nurius, 2003). It involves generating hypotheses about what caused the problem, what precipitated it, and what continues to maintain it. Based on these hypotheses, the therapist's next job is to plan what needs to be done and how this can be best accomplished (Seligman, 2001).

Applications to Self: Diagnosing in a Variety of Settings

The skills you develop from this chapter will be helpful in a variety of ways to you, professionally and personally. The ability to build a relationship while collecting information as thoroughly as possible in a limited amount of time is essential in the helping field. You can use these skills in a variety of environments, such as private practice, agencies, schools, at work, or at home. You can use these skills with a variety of people, such as with individual clients, couples, groups, families, organizations, colleagues, or with your friends and family. You can use these skills with a variety of roles, such as therapist, mediator, consultant, friend, or family member.

Let's start with how diagnosing skills are helpful in various environments. You may assume that once you graduate, you'll open up a private practice. The reality is that you will probably work in more than one setting. Some individuals work in a private practice while still having a connection to an agency. Others consult with schools while maintaining a private practice. It does not matter what kind of office you work in, you will need to develop a proficiency at obtaining information and organizing it while maintaining a good relationship with the individuals in that environment.

You might also assume that you will only use these skills in the context of individual therapy, but you can and will use them with many populations in many roles. For instance, your client types may include individual adults, children, groups, families, or couples. In all cases, diagnosis will be a necessary beginning to the process of therapy. You may choose to work as a consultant or a mediator with organizations. In these situations, you will still need to develop a thorough understanding of the problem while being mindful of the relationship to establish trust and to inspire confidence in your clients. Furthermore, you will most likely consult with colleagues and interact with coworkers in a way that requires strong diagnostic skills. Finally, these skills may be helpful in your personal life. We are all social animals, and life is full of problems. Whether you have a conflict with someone or just happened to be a shoulder for a friend to cry on, you will probably find these skills being used once you learn them. In your life, you will have personal challenges, and developing these skills with clients helps you to work on your own issues, an essential component of becoming a good therapist.

SUMMARY

Our goal in this chapter was to introduce you to the first steps involved in your initial client meeting. We provided an overview of some concepts that you will likely learn more thoroughly in other courses such as the Mental Status Exam, assessing for special conditions of abuse or suicide risk, different modes to diagnose, and the *Diagnostic and Statistical Manual*. All of these subjects are relevant to the intake interview. We attempted to provide you with an overview of that process with specific examples. Finally, we introduced some common mistakes of beginners for you to be conscientious of during your first meeting with your client. The next chapter introduces you to the exploration phase of therapy.

A CHECK ON WHAT YOU LEARNED

1. A clinical exam used to assess mental functioning and including assessing appearance, general behavior, mood, flow of thought, orientation, and other areas is called what?
2. Don't start your conversation with the client where? Why?
3. If possible, you may want to first cover the _____ to help your client be more comfortable knowing what expect.
4. True or false: You must always cover all the limits of confidentiality with the client before going into what brought the client to therapy, just in case a need to break confidentiality is necessary.
5. Three areas that require special considerations during the first meeting are:
6. The *DMS* is based on what kind of model that differs from other models used in therapy?
7. One pitfall that will interfere with your ability to really listen to the client is _____.
8. You may come up with a brilliant diagnosis for your client during your first session, but if you fail to _____ the client, he or she may not return, making your effort a waste.
9. True or false: You should attempt to collect all the information necessary from the client in the first session to make an accurate diagnosis and good treatment plan.
10. List the two reasons why it is not good to attempt to fix your client's problem.

SUGGESTED READINGS

Hood, A. B., & Johnson, R. W. (2001). *Assessment in counseling: A guide to the use of psychological assessment procedures*. Alexandria, VA: American Counseling Association.

Paniagua, F. A. (2001). *Diagnosis in a multicultural context: A casebook for mental health professionals*. Thousand Oaks, CA: Sage.

Seligman, L. (1998). *Selecting effective treatments: A comprehensive, systematic guide to treating mental disorders* (2nd ed.). San Francisco: Jossey-Bass.

Simeonsson, R. J., & Rosenthal, S. L. (2001). *Psychological and developmental assessment*. New York: Guilford.

Spitzer, R. L. (2001). *DSM–IV–TR casebook*. Washington, DC: American Psychiatric Press.

Welfel, E. R., & Ingersoll, R. E. (Eds.). (2001). *The mental health desk reference*. New York: Wiley.

CHAPTER 6

Exploration Skills

"So," the client begins the second session, "I was wondering where we go next?"

Good question, you think, considering yourself what direction to proceed. "What were you thinking about since our last conversation?" You ask this partially to stall, but also to get a sense of what has transpired during the intervening week. It is important to get an accurate reading on the current situation rather than make assumptions that may no longer be valid.

"I felt better after our talk. I mean, it feels good to know you can help me and all. Last time you said some interesting things about what might be going on. That all sounds good to me. So, what do we do next?"

AN OVERVIEW OF THE EXPLORATION PHASE

With the working diagnosis in place, and a basic assessment process completed, the next step is to learn more about what is going on, study relevant background, and help to facilitate a deeper-level exploration of the problem and its meaning in the client's life. Several questions may immediately come to mind:

- Why is this problem occurring now?
- How is what is going on related to other issues in this person's life and other themes in the person's past?
- How is this problem connected to other things going on within the client's family and identified cultures?
- What feelings and thoughts are going on of which the client may be currently unaware?
- What unconscious motives and forces might be operating?
- What hidden agendas might be going on?
- How can I help this person to understand his or her story in a way that is more personally meaningful and clinically useful?

You may recognize the theoretical roots to some of the questions that reflect the assumptions of a particular orientation. For instance, wondering about unconscious desires is part of psychoanalytic theory (Freud, 1936), or wanting to know about underlying thinking patterns may stem from cognitive therapy (Beck, 1976), or constructing the client's story in a more helpful way may be an extension of narrative therapy (Monk, Winslade, Crocket, & Epston, 1997) or constructivist therapy (Neimeyer & Mahoney, 2000). Almost every other therapeutic approach has its own priorities of material that are considered most important to explore. Regardless of where you go, and what paths you take, there are still a few generic skills that will be most useful to you.

You should know that including some skills in this chapter on exploration and other skills in the next chapter on promoting insight was somewhat arbitrary. All of the skills used in the search process are also part of deepening a client's understanding. While delving into a client's background, connections are made, new ideas are generated, and greater self-awareness is initiated. Likewise, exploration is hardly restricted to the beginning stage of helping but is recycled again and again as new material is introduced. So, although we are talking in this chapter about a half dozen skills that are most often associated with exploration activities, you should know that you will use them during every other stage of the process.

STRUCTURING THE CONVERSATIONS

Exploration is not something you do *to* a client, but rather *with* a client. It is a mutual process of searching for valuable and useful information and collecting important background information. When at its best, this process proceeds in a systematic, progressive, and logical fashion, but also at a pace and direction that is fluid and flexible. At its worst, it comes across as an interrogation in which the therapist fires one question after another.

Compare two examples of a structured exploration.

Therapist: Can you tell me when this problem first started?
Client: I'd say about a week ago.
Therapist: Would you say that was, what, about last Monday?
Client: Yeah. About then.
Therapist: And did the symptoms begin gradually, or all of a sudden?
Client: I'm not sure. Maybe gradually?
Therapist: This is the first time you've experienced anything like this?
Client: I think so.
Therapist: And how would you say this has been affecting your life? Would you say that you are having difficulties sleeping and eating?
Client: Uh huh.

You can see that this therapist is going after some very critical information, but is doing so in a way in which he retains full control. The client is reduced to providing brief responses and is clearly not involved except as a reluctant participant. You may recognize this pattern as similar to what happens with a physician when he or she asks a series of rather specific yes–no questions: "Do you have pain here, or here? Would you say the pain is radiating or centralized? Does it hurt when I do this?" Such questions are appropriate when you are trying to find out very specific answers to questions that help with differential diagnosis but are not especially useful in counseling settings when are you trying to foster a spirit of mutual responsibility for the outcome.

In this next example, the clinician goes after the same information but in a less interrogative, more open way.

Therapist: Talk about what has been bothering you most and when it first began.
Client: Um, I guess about a week ago, more or less. I was visiting my parents and I started to feel uneasy, like I couldn't catch my breath. I felt dizzy and, I don't know, kind of funny.
Therapist: So this really took you by surprise and scared you.
Client: Yeah, you could say that for sure. And I wasn't sure what to do. I didn't know what was happening to me.
Therapist: It sounds like you felt particularly upset because this was a new experience for you.
Client: Well, once before something like this happened, but it was in a different situation.
Therapist: This wasn't completely unfamiliar to you but you still felt caught off-guard.

Notice in this second example, the therapist is not even asking questions to elicit information and encourage exploration. Instead the therapist is reflecting back both the content and feelings of what he or she hears. This is a preferred way of proceeding that encourages a mutual process of exploration while showing empathy for the client's situation.

OPENING WITH THE STORY

Typically, therapy and counseling begin with clients telling their stories. They talk about what is wrong and their theories about how these problems started. There is a history to the story. There are antagonists and supporting characters. There is a complex plot and there are many subplots. There is a beginning, a middle, but no end in sight.

During the exploration phases of therapy, your job is to help the client tell the story well. This includes a richness in detail and texture. It means including as many details and as much context as possible. Most of all, it means helping the client to feel comfortable during this process.

It could be said that if you do nothing else, helping people to tell their stories can be intrinsically therapeutic. It capitalizes on what Freud and other psychoanalysts described as catharsis—the emotional release of pent-up energy. It feels good to tell someone safe about one's life story. If you have ever been in therapy or counseling yourself (and we encourage this strongly with our own students), then you know how wonderful it is indeed to have an attentive audience for hearing how you ended up in the mess—er, life—that you now find yourself enjoying.

Inviting the storytelling is just about the easiest thing you can do. People have seen enough movies and television shows about therapy that they pretty much know what is expected. They will come in fully prepared to dump the sad tale on your lap; it takes little to get things going other than the opening prompt: "How can I help you?" or "What's on your mind?" or "What would you like to talk about?"

The truly difficult part, which includes advanced skills covered later, involves several structuring actions to keep clients on track, to prevent digressions and rambling, and to elicit depth and as much useful information as possible. You will do this with a few good questions, but mostly with reflective skills described later in the chapter.

ASKING QUESTIONS

The main thing to remember about asking questions is that beginners ask far too many. It is a direct but inelegant way to get information, to probe particular areas, or to invite exploration. It is certainly direct to say to a client: "What were you thinking when that happened?" As you will learn, there are also other options at your disposal that are more indirect and inclined to let the client lead things. After all, you don't want to get in the habit of being defined as the one who does all the digging with the client in the role of reluctant participant. In addition, the client does not feel heard when you are shooting one question after another. Reflecting helps the client feel heard and consequently, continues to strengthen the collaborative relationship.

When to Ask Questions

There are some specific times when asking questions is not only unavoidable but highly desirable. This would be in the following situations:

When the session first begins: "Where would you like to start today?" or "How can I help you?" or "What would you like to talk about?"

When you need more clarification: "I wonder if you could say some more about that?" or "What do you mean by that?"

When you need to get things back on track: "Earlier you had been talking about this reoccurring problem with avoiding new situations. What is a recent example of that?"

When you want to check out how things are going: "What are your reactions to what we've been doing today?"

When you want to bring focus to present-moment reactions: "What is this like for you right now?"

When you must find out specific information: "What help have you sought in the past for this problem?"

When you want to make connections: "How is this related to what you were talking about earlier?"

When you want to bring attention to a significant point: "What were you thinking and saying to yourself right before you backed down?"

When you want to clarify goals: "Given the various things you've mentioned, what do you want to focus on most?"

When you want to move the person to take action: "What are you prepared to do about this right now?"

These examples highlight the ways that questions are actually used in every phase of the therapeutic process. They not only gather information and foster exploration, but they can also be used as subtle forms of confrontation and goal setting.

Good and Bad Questions

There are effective and ineffective ways to ask questions, just as there are times when they are most and least appropriate. For instance, you wouldn't want to interrupt someone in the middle of an important story to ask about a particular detail.

A Homework Assignment

Listen to your favorite talk show interviewers on television or radio conduct celebrity interviews. Now that you are more familiar with what it takes to ask good questions, as well as what makes for lousy inquiries, notice how spectacularly unskilled and ineffective most talk show hosts really are. They ask a series of closed-ended questions ("So, did you find the experience making this film rewarding?"). They follow written scripts, often without even listening to the previous answers. The only reason they are able to elicit any entertaining interaction whatsoever is because their subjects are so highly motivated to promote their products. It doesn't even matter what the interviewers ask, or how they ask it, because the celebrity authors, actors, or athletes have already prepared their canned self-promoting answers.

Start paying closer attention to good and bad interviews in the media. Notice what professionals do best, as well as their common mistakes.

Just during the time I [Jeffrey] was working on this chapter I was driving in the car with a friend. She was telling me about some recent problems she was having. This was how the conversation went:

Friend: So I've been carrying more than my fair share of work lately. That's why I am always in such a hurry.
Jeffrey: What has been going on with you?
Friend: Well, my husband has been out of work so the burden fell on me to carry the load.
Jeffrey: Oh, what kind of work does your husband do?

What is wrong with this? Why did Jeffrey kick himself afterward for making such a simple error in judgment, especially when he was in the process of writing about how questions can get in the way?

You will notice that the first question, a probe, was appropriate and useful: "What has been going on with you?" It is leading, and somewhat general and ambiguous. These are often good characteristics of leading questions because they allow the person to interpret the question in different ways. Sometimes you will find that how the person interprets the question is as revealing as how it is answered. That's one reason why therapists respond in that maddening way when their clients ask them, "What do you mean?," and then respond, "What does it mean to you?" We are not playing mind games by being evasive but rather allowing the client to go wherever seems most important.

Back to the questions. The first leading question was appropriate: "What has been going on with you?" Jeffrey patted himself on the back for that one. It is concise, to the point, and very inviting. It creates space for the other person to elaborate, and yet does so in a way that there is a lot of latitude. Sometimes (like with friends) you don't want to be intrusive. So far, so good.

Then the friend shares a very emotionally laden statement about her stress and pressure supporting her family with her husband out of work. Rather than following up on this disclosure, or even acknowledging that he heard her, Jeffrey instead asks a question that is irrelevant and distracting. At the time, of course, it made perfect sense to follow this up because Jeffrey was curious (and he wasn't in the role of a therapist). But the price paid for this needless and mistimed question is that the conversation remained superficial (which is maybe where he unconsciously wanted it to stay).

The lesson implicit in this story is to make sure that the questions you ask do not distract the client from the central story, nor ignore important feelings and thoughts that should be explored further.

Don't Ask "Why" Questions

Why, you ask? Because most of the time people don't know why they do things. The most common answer you will get after asking someone why is: "I don't know."

Teacher: May I ask why you carved your initials on the desk?
Student: [Shrugs] I don't know.

What the student is really thinking is something along the lines of: "Because it was fun. Because it felt wicked and naughty. Because I could express my artistic talents. Because I wasn't really thinking one way or the other. Because I wanted to piss you off. Because I'm mad at this damn school and I can't fight back any other way. Because I don't value furniture the same way you do. Because I just felt like it." In any of the cases, there isn't much likelihood you would hear any other response except "I don't know," always the easiest way to evade the query.

The truth is that most of the time people don't really know why they do things, or don't do things. If we asked you why you wait until the last minute to do your studying for class, what would you answer? If we asked you why you remain stuck doing certain things that don't work for you, what would you say? We are sure you would come up with some sort of intelligent answer or explanation, but that doesn't mean it is meaningful.

That isn't to say that there are not times when you can and should use "why" in your questions, just that it is ordinarily not very useful compared to other options available. Some exceptions might include when you are provoking exploration but not really expecting a definitive answer: "I wonder why you keep getting yourself into these situations from which you have trouble extricating yourself?"

Open Versus Closed

A "closed" question is one that can be answered with a single word, usually yes or no. Such questions tend to cut off communication and set up a pattern wherein the client becomes a passive respondent. Listen to the following conversation between a parent and her young child who just came home from school.

Parent: So, did you have a good day in school today?
Student: Sure.
Parent: Would you say you had a good day or a bad day?
Student: Pretty good.
Parent: Did you go on that field trip?
Student: Yup.
Parent: And did you get to sit next to Lisa like you wanted to?
Student: Uh huh.
Parent: Were you able to talk to her like you wanted to about coming to your birthday?
Student: Not really.
Parent: The time didn't seem right to you?
Student: Yeah.
Parent: Um, okay then. Can I make you snack?
Student: Okay.

This parent will then complain that her child was uncommunicative and resistant. So much depends on the way you probe and ask questions designed to open up the interaction. One way to do this is by using "open-ended" questions, the kind that cannot so easily be answered with one word.

Compare the closed questions that were asked to the ways they could have been framed differently, shown in Table 6.1.

TABLE 6.1

Open Versus Closed Questions

Original Question	Open-Ended Version
"So, did you have a good day in school today?"	"What was your day like today?"
"Would you say you had a good day or a bad day?"	"What was the best thing that happened in school today?"
"Did you go on that field trip?"	"What was the most interesting thing that happened on your field trip?"
"And did you get to sit next to Lisa like you wanted to?"	"What things did you do and talk about on the bus?"
"Were you able to talk to her like you wanted to about coming to your birthday?"	"I remember you said you wanted to talk to Lisa. So, what happened?"
"The time didn't seem right to you?"	"How do you feel about that?"
"Can I make you a snack?"	"What would you like to do right now?"

With a particularly uncommunicative child, it might very well be the case that these new questions would not elicit much more information, nor would they facilitate deeper exploration, but they certainly increase the probability of a more balanced conversation. Closed-ended questions create an atmosphere in which the therapist is the expert, the authority, the problem solver, who is controlling the proceedings. They also elicit very limited information.

This may sound very basic to you, and easy to learn, but we can tell you from years of experience watching counselors, teachers, and therapists in action that most professionals have very bad habits in asking closed questions. Check this out for yourself.

It is difficult to catch yourself asking closed questions, and to remind yourself to rephrase them, unless you monitor yourself very closely. Do you understand what we mean?

See what just happened? Oops, we did it again. In both cases, we asked questions in ways you could answer them with "yes" or "no." It would have been far better to ask, "What about this confuses you the most?" or "What just happened?"

As with any rule, there are also exceptions. As we already mentioned, there are indeed times when closed questions are useful, especially when you need rather specific information. Let's say that someone says that he has trouble sleeping. You ask what he means by this because the kind of sleep disruption may signal a variety of problems that may be treated in different ways. Early-morning wakening is different from trouble falling asleep, which is different from frequent awakenings in the middle of the night. It might be entirely appropriate to ask: "Would you say you have more trouble falling asleep or staying asleep?"

Another example of the use of closed questions might occur when there are indications of suicidal ideation or intent. In such situations it is crucial that you assess very specifically such things as: "Do you have a plan for carrying out this fantasy?" "Have you tried to kill yourself in the past?" "Has anyone else in your family ever tried to kill themselves or succeeded in doing so?" You will notice that these questions would elicit yes–no responses, but for this purpose, that is entirely appropriate.

REFLECTIVE SKILLS

Much of what therapists and counselors do most often is act as a mirror for what the client is saying or doing. Our job is to listen carefully, take in what we heard, and then reflect back our understanding in such a way that we foster a deeper-level awareness and understanding. This might look easy but is also one of the most difficult helping skills for you to master.

There are two main applications of reflective skills; one focuses on the content of the message and the other on the underlying feeling. Both are important components.

In the following verbalization, there is both content and affect, or to say that differently, there is a surface message and an underlying or deeper one.

"I am not really sure how this fits together with what I already know. It seems confusing to me. I think you are trying to cover too much material and too many things in one semester. How am I supposed to learn all of this? Besides, I've got a lot of other things going on in my life right now. You act as if I've got nothing else to do but focus on this one thing. I just don't think your expectations are very fair. And I don't like it."

Whether you are sympathetic or not to this student's point of view, certainly you can understand the source of these thoughts and feelings. In this brief but rich communication, there is a lot of information. Some of it involves the content of the message and the rest contains the essence of the person's feelings. Although in actual situations it would not matter nor be useful to focus only on one dimension or the other, for the purposes of learning the skills involved, it is helpful to label and respond to the different parts. This is especially the case because reflecting feelings is so much more difficult than reflecting content.

In the preceding example, what are some of the major areas of content that were expressed? In other words, on the surface, what was the person communicating?

1. I don't know how this fits.
2. I'm having trouble integrating the material into my life.
3. I'm very busy and overscheduled.
4. Your expectations for me are unreasonable.
5. I'm unhappy with the way this is going so far.

If you chose to focus on the content, these might be some of the parts of the message that you would hone in on and reflect back to the person. The way this might look and sound in the conversation is something like this:

Student: I am not really sure how this fits together with what I already know. It seems confusing to me.
Teacher: So, you've having trouble getting a handle on what we've covered so far.
Student: Yeah, I think you are trying to cover too much material and too many things in one semester. How am I supposed to learn all of this?
Teacher: You don't find that the expectations are realistic. You're having serious doubts about whether you can manage all the work with other things you have going on.

This brief dialogue gives you a sense for the natural rhythm that takes place during a reflective conversation. The teacher is listening carefully and then responding with what is understood so far. This lets the student know that she has been heard and, hopefully, encourages a deeper level of exploration into what might be going on.

There are also a lot of emotions and underlying feelings expressed within the communication. If you chose to identify and reflect back this affect-laden material, what might you select?

1. I'm confused and frustrated because I don't feel in control.
2. I'm feeling very anxious and overwhelmed in my life right now.
3. I'm angry because you are expecting more than I can deliver.
4. I'm feeling helpless because I don't know how to sort things out or center on priorities.
5. I'm feeling better already telling you how I feel.

If during the same conversation the teacher instead chose to go deeper than the content and reflect the person's feelings, this is what it would look and sound like:

Student: I am not really sure how this fits together with what I already know. It seems confusing to me.

Teacher: You sound really frustrated because you can't seem to catch up with what you think I expect, and what you expect of yourself.

Student: Yeah, I think you are trying to cover too much material and too many things in one semester. How am I supposed to learn all of this?

Teacher: You're upset with me because I don't seem to appreciate many of the other things going on in your life. You also sound pretty anxious because you aren't sure about how to catch up.

In this second scenario, the teacher responds by reflecting the predominant feelings expressed. The goal in this case is to lead the student to examine, in greater depth, what he is feeling and what this might mean in the larger context of his life. Perhaps the problem actually has little to do with school at all, but rather this is an overture to get into other areas. Or maybe the student's frustration has been building for some time and is really related to something that happened weeks ago. Or suppose the student is just using this problem as a way to get to know the teacher better. Any and all of these possibilities would reveal themselves as the conversation proceeds.

Reflecting Content

We are going to teach you how to reflect content in a way that will strike you as both artificial and awkward. The rationale behind this method is to introduce you to some very basic behaviors and then slowly build on them, not unlike what we did in earlier chapters on attending and listening skills.

The very first step is called "parroting" because you will sound very much like a parrot that mimics whatever is said. You would not actually ever do this in real life (except if you go brain dead), so rest assured that any discomfort you might feel in learning this "skill" will be short-lived. It is intended only as an intermediate step toward a more complex, advanced set of behaviors.

With parroting, all you do is repeat back exactly what the other person says. Believe it or not, many people can't do this, especially partners in the midst of a couple's conflict. They don't listen to one another because they are so busy preparing to dispute whatever the other says. One exercise that is often used by couples is when counselors require each partner to repeat back exactly what the other person said, to that person's satisfaction, before the person is allowed to respond with his or her own thoughts and feelings. This might sound rather silly to you—except that many people can't do it!

In learning to parrot, all you have to do is follow these steps:

1. Attend fully to the other person, putting into practice what you have learned earlier (remember your body posture, eye contact, facial expression, and cleansing breath).
2. Listen carefully to what the person is saying. Concentrate with all your energy and focus. Gently push aside any distractions that interfere with your attention.
3. Repeat the content of what was said (which is hopefully the same as what you heard).

Here is an (annoying) example of what this is like:

Talker: I've been having a bit of trouble with my car lately. That's why I'm late.

Helper: You've been having trouble with your car and that's been making you late.

Talker: Yeah, I think there's something wrong with the fuel injection system. I need to take it into the shop.

Helper: You think the problem is with the fuel injector and you intend to get it fixed.

Talker: That's what I just said! Are you deaf or just stupid! [gets up and walks out of the room, shaking his head]

Just kidding.

Remember, you wouldn't actually repeat exactly everything your client says; it is just practice getting the rhythm and pace of a reflective frame of mind.

Exercise in Parroting

As with all helping interventions, you always start with that cleansing breath (or whatever else you do to focus your concentration).

With a partner, take turns practicing parroting with one another. One of you agrees to talk for a minute or so (that's about how long you can last without laughing) about something. The other will listen and repeat back exactly what was said, word for word.

Reverse roles so that each of you can practice parroting and being parroted.

As we've said, you would not actually use parroting in a real session, except when you can think of nothing else, but it is a necessary first step in your reflective skill development. You might be surprised to learn, however, that if on occasion you did just repeat what the other person said, they would hardly notice. Most of the time people are concentrating so hard on what they are saying that they rarely listen to what anyone else is saying. We offer this as a reminder to those of you who are unduly hard on yourself about the frequent mistakes you will make. However, there is one time where parroting can be most effective. When you want to emphasize an interesting word or phrase that the client says rather flippantly, repeating the exact word or phrase can slow the client down to elaborate on feelings. For instance,

Client: I can't believe I locked my keys in the car again! I'm so stupid for doing such an idiotic thing. What's wrong with me?"

Therapist: Stupid.

By the therapist repeating such a strong word, the client will often not be able to ignore it. He or she will slow down and think about what you just said. In the worst scenario, he'll look at you funny and continue ranting and raving. However, you will probably have the opportunity to repeat the word again, and after enough repetitions, the client will not be able to avoid your reflection for long. In the best scenario, he'll elaborate on feeling stupid, which may be an underlying theme of most sessions.

Okay, you are now ready to move on to the next step. Thank goodness, huh?

The next skill, which you will use a lot, perhaps more than anything else you do in your work, is called "rephrasing" or "reflecting content." This is where you do essentially what you just tried with parroting, but this time you use different words to convey what you heard and understood. You are taking in what was said, making sense of the essential messages, and then reflecting back what you understand. This accomplishes several tasks simultaneously:

1. It lets the client know that you are listening carefully.
2. It checks the accuracy of what you heard.
3. It helps the client to hear better what he or she is saying, especially the core themes.
4. It helps you to remain actively involved in the conversation.
5. It takes the discussion to a progressively deeper level, at least with respect to the content.
6. It encourages the client to keep going in a particular direction.

In the following interaction, the therapist uses rephrasing almost exclusively to keep things going and track what is going on. Notice that the tone remains on a content level throughout.

Client: I can't seem to concentrate on my studies. I just get distracted so easily.
Therapist: You are losing focus, unable to stick with your work even though you think it is important to do so.
Client: Well, it is important. I agree. But I can't seem to find the time to get the work done. [laughs] Maybe it isn't that important.
Therapist: You are beginning to question your priorities. You have believed that school was more important than anything else, but now you are reevaluating that value in light of other things in your life that are also important to you.
Client: Yeah, like my friends for instance. I hardly ever have time just to hang out, you know, relax, have a beer, listen to music. My friends kid me about that but I know they feel hurt too that I'm ignoring them.
Therapist: You are noticing in many ways that you have been neglecting the people who matter most to you. Even though they say they don't mind, you can tell that it is becoming a bigger problem. And you're wondering what to do about that in light of other commitments you've made.

It is (hopefully) evident that this deceptively easy skill of rephrasing helps the client to explore further what is going on. At first, it seems like a relatively simple matter of poor study habits. But as the two people get into things further, they discover (through the reflections of content) that there are deeper issues involved. This is the beauty of this method. It also has several other advantages you should be aware of:

1. Although potentially quite powerful, it is also relatively benign. Even if you don't help anyone much with reflections of content, you also won't hurt anyone. This should be reassuring to beginners who are afraid they will do or say the wrong thing and somehow provoke a psychotic episode.
2. It keeps a progressive, gradual pace to the conversation, slowly building on what was just said.
3. It is easy to learn. Crisis intervention phone counselors or student peer counselors can learn to use this skill in just a few hours.
4. In the hands of a skilled and experienced helper, you can lead someone to very deep

levels of awareness and understanding. You do this by holding up a mirror and allowing the person to see and hear him- or herself.

Exercise in Rephrasing

As with the previous exercise, meet with the same (or a different) partner. Take turns with one of you being the speaker and the other the listener/reflector. Each of you will spend about five minutes talking about something and the other will listen carefully and then rephrase what was said using different language.

Exercise on Your Own: Take This Skill Home With You

There is nothing that can change your life faster and create more intimacy in all your relationships than the skills of reflection. The fact of the matter is that in most conversations with people you are not listening to them and they aren't listening to you. Reflecting skills provide a structure for constant, hovering attention. You not only listen carefully, but prove you understand what was said. You can't imagine the difference this makes to people.

Try using rephrasing with the people who matter the most to you. Don't just restrict these skills to work. That is the truly amazing thing about this job: Everything you learn not only makes you a better practitioner but also a better person.

At several times during the day—with family, friends, coworkers, fellow students, neighbors, even strangers—make an effort to use rephrasing to let the person know that you are listening and to communicate what you heard. Note the effects.

We warn you that some people will tell you—in jest or seriously—"Stop using that counseling crap with me," but most people are secretly delighted to have the attention. Just keep in mind that this is such hard work that we ordinarily don't like to do this for very long unless we are being paid to do so. Sad but true.

One other warning is that you need to do this when you have time to listen. If you don't, you'll find it's difficult to stop people because they want to be heard so badly. We've been amazed at how a stranger will tell you the most intimate details of their lives in a non-therapeutic setting, when you just reflect.

Reflecting Feelings

We are now going to go deeper, *way* deeper. We warn you that, at first, reflecting feelings will not seem any more challenging than reflecting content (which you have to admit doesn't seem that hard). Indeed, this skill *is* pretty easy to learn the basics, a matter of following a basic formula. Yet even after decades of practice, you will still not be able to do it as well as you would like.

The procedure is not unlike what you have already learned:

1. Listen to what was said.
2. Ask yourself what the underlying message is.
3. Reflect that back.

This time, however, rather than focusing on content you are decoding the underlying feelings expressed. Because emotional reactions are so complex, their nuances so diffused, it is extremely difficult to identify what people are feeling. Then, once you can sort out the label for the feeling, you must ask yourself what the meaning of this might be. Then, just as challenging, you have to figure out a way to reflect this understanding back so that the client will hear you.

As with reflecting content, there are several powerful effects from using this skill:

1. Letting the client know that you understand his or her experience at the deepest possible levels.
2. Bringing attention to previously unacknowledged internal reactions.
3. Fostering exploration of underlying feelings that may be hidden from view.
4. Creating a more intimate relationship through the sharing of self.
5. Slowing the client down to fully experience the feelings being evidenced or reported.

Building on what you have already learned, your task is now to listen to communication on multiple levels. You are not only attending to the nonverbal messages and the surface, content messages, but also to the feelings beneath the surface. Once you can grab hold of some affective material you would then reflect back what you sense, feel, observe, and hear.

Step 1. Listen and look for feeling. In order to go beyond content, you must sensitize yourself to what people are feeling inside. You look for cues in their behavior, their voice tone, manner, nonverbal mannerisms, and certainly the ways they communicate.

Vocabulary Exercise

For each of the three emotion states in Table 6.2, brainstorm (alone or with others) as many other feelings as you can that fit into this category.

TABLE 6.2
Sad, Mad, Glad Vocabulary Exercise

Sad	Mad	Glad

Step 2. Select the label that best fits the feeling. There are limitations to language in trying to describe inner states. Depending on the vocabulary available, you might say that someone is merely annoyed or perhaps a more intense manifestation of anger: The person is enraged or furious. In order for this to work, you are going to have to expand your vocabulary of feeling words (see table 6.2).

Step 3. Find the meaning in the feeling. Once you have identified what you believe is the dominant feeling being expressed, what is the particular meaning of this in the context of this person's experience?

Step 4. Decode the source of the feeling. You may have settled on anger as the most likely emotional force that is currently being expressed in the client's words and behavior. But what is the source of this anger? It isn't enough to simply reflect that the client is angry; it is far more helpful to highlight the origins of the feeling. Instead of merely saying, "You're really angry," you might say, "You're really angry because your friend won't respect your privacy."

Step 5. Reflect the feeling that you hear or sense, supplying the source of the reaction.

It is a good idea to practice reflecting feelings by continuing in small steps. Let's start with the next logical step after using rephrasing. Use the stem sentence, "You feel . . . " to respond to the following client statements:

1. "I am just so tired of all this crap. I wish I could just give up." "You feel _____."
2. "Did you see the grade I got on this assignment! I mean, wow, I really aced it!" "You feel _____."
3. "If he gets on my case one more time, just one more time, I'm going to make sure it's the last time he ever treats someone that way." "You feel _____."

There are several choices possible for these client statements. Here are a few possibilities:

1. Frustrated, helpless, discouraged.
2. Excited, proud, surprised.
3. Angry, resentful, homicidal.

We're just kidding (again) with that homicidal option in number 3 (we just want to make sure you are paying attention). You can see, however, that there is not exactly a correct answer as much as there is a general area to explore. In other words, you don't have to hit the bull's-eye but just the target. This should take some of the pressure off doing this stuff perfectly. That is the amazing thing about these reflective skills; it is certainly better to be on-target every time, but in this work you get credit for trying, even if you miss what you are trying to hit. When you miss, the client will introspect to correct you and give you the right feeling.

In the following example, notice how even though the therapist's skills are not particularly accurate, the client is still able to keep exploring at a deeper level.

Client: If he gets on my case one more time, just one more time, I'm going to make sure he never treats someone that way again.

Therapist: You are so upset you want to punch him.

Client: Well, not that angry. It's just that he has so little respect for me, or anyone else.

Therapist: You wish he would treat you with more respect. It pisses you off that he treats others differently.

Client: I'm not really that special, to tell you the truth. He treats everyone else the same way.

Therapist: So, you feel better about that at least.

Client: I don't feel good about any of this. I just wish I could get him to stop acting the way he does.

Therapist: You are feeling helpless because you don't know what to do next.

Client: I do know what to do, I'm just afraid to do it.

Every single one of this therapist's interventions was off-target. In each case, the client corrected the reflection by stating how she really felt instead of what was articulated. That is what is so amazing about this skill: Even when you are wrong you still help the client to explore more deeply. Of course, if you are wrong every time, or most of the time, the client is going to wonder if you are understanding at all what is going on. If you keep missing the client's feeling, you also have to wonder about calibrating your empathic attunement.

This is what reflections of feeling look and sound like when things are going well:

Student: I'm still having trouble figuring out how all this fits together.

Teacher: You're feeling impatient because this isn't coming together as quickly and as easily as you had hoped.

Student: When you use these skills, they look so easy and effortless, but when I try them I feel like an idiot. I'm waiting for the person to slap me for being so clumsy and transparent.

Teacher: You are comparing yourself to me and then feeling inadequate. Part of you wants to give up, but another part is feeling more determined than ever.

Student: Well, what do you think it takes for me to get this stuff?

Teacher: You are asking me for the answers but you sense that only you can work this out yourself. Although this is hard for you, and perhaps you are not used to this sort of challenge, you recognize that you are going to have to be more patient.

In this 2-minute conversation, the teacher tries to reflect back what she senses and hears in the student who is obviously frustrated. Notice how she deftly avoids the "trap" at the end when the student asks for advice. Nine out of 10 inexperienced helpers would answer that question with some advice or platitude like, "You need to be more patient and realistic about what you can do." Instead, the teacher continues to reflect back what she understands.

Try It Yourself

With these next client statements, reflect the feelings that you hear coming through by (a) selecting the feeling word that you think best fits the emotion, and (b) supplying the paraphrased content. Follow the pattern of the first example.

Client: I haven't been able to sleep well at night. I just keep thinking about stuff.

Helper: You've been feeling anxious because you're worried about some things.

Client: No matter what I do, I just keep tossing and turning.

1. *Helper:* You feel _____ because _____.

Client: I think I know what's bothering me, but, I don't know if I want to talk about it quite yet.

2. *Helper:* You feel _____ because _____.

Client: This is kind of difficult for me. Even kind of embarrassing. It's just not something that I've ever talked about before. Do you know what I mean?

3. *Helper:* You feel _____ because _____ .

Client: I've tried to talk to a few friends about this but they act like they'd rather not get into it.

4. *Helper:* You feel _____ because _____.

In the Helper Response 1, you could have said something like: "You feel frustrated (or uneasy or helpless) because you feel out of control (or because you can't calm down)."

In Helper Response 2, you might have said: "You feel confused (uncertain, uneasy, reluctant) because you're not quite ready to get into this yet (or if you wanted to go a bit deeper: because you're afraid of what I might think or how I might judge you)."

In Helper Response 3: "You are feeling hesitant (frightened, anxious) because this is all new for you (or because you don't know where this will lead)."

In Helper Response 4: "You feel alone right now (sad, disappointed, frustrated) because you haven't been able to confide in anyone (or because people haven't responded the way you hoped)."

Hopefully, the outcome from going through this exercise is that you realize the variety of choices you have when reflecting feelings. There are always at least a half dozen feelings that might be evident in verbalizations, as well as an equal number of content messages that you might rephrase. What this means is that you must give yourself the latitude while you are learning these skills to just say something, reflect something, and then move on. Clients will barely notice what you perceive are mistakes. Just keep the conversation going by showing how closely you are listening and how hard you are trying to understand.

Exercise in Feeling Reflections

With a partner, one of you agree to talk about something that has some strong feelings involved. If you can't think of something, then role-play a client who is upset about something.

During the conversation, the helper is going to concentrate on using only reflecting feelings. That is the only intervention besides active listening skills (head nods, uh huhs, attending). Use the stem sentence, "You feel _____." At several times paced throughout the conversation, say "You feel" and then insert a feeling word. If you can't think of a good one, then insert anything you can think of—it doesn't matter nearly as much as you would think. Your job is to keep the conversation going by reflecting back the feelings you hear.

Exercise in Feeling Reflections: Round 2

Once you have gotten a little comfortable using "You feel," the next step is to add a "because" at the end that summarizes the content expressed: "You feel _____ because _____."

Take turns reflecting one another's feelings by following the steps outlined earlier: (a) listen, (b) identify the feeling underlying the message, (c) decode the meaning of the feeling and its origins, and (d) reflect back what you understand.

PUTTING REFLECTIVE SKILLS TOGETHER

In actual counseling situations, you will combine reflecting content with feelings in a natural way. Because the latter is so much harder to do, you may find yourself using two or three times as many reflections of content as you do reflections of feeling. With practice, you will do this effortlessly and naturally. Within a matter of weeks you will be able to use these skills reasonably well, although it will take years, if not a lifetime, to truly feel like a master.

Reviewing what we have covered so far: In previous chapters you learned about how to listen effectively and how to attend to people when they are speaking. In this chapter you have been introduced to three very important exploration skills: (a) asking questions as prompts and probes, (b) reflecting or paraphrasing the content of communications, and (c) reflecting feelings. You might be surprised to learn that using just these three behaviors, you can demonstrate a significant part of what counselors and therapists do in their work. Depending on the client, the stage in the process, and the particular issue, you might very well use these three skills for more than 75% of your interventions and responses.

In the session that follows, the therapist uses the three skills to facilitate exploration:

Therapist: What would you like to work on today? [open-ended question]
Client: Last time you said we could get more into things with my parents. You know, how maybe the decisions I've made really aren't my decisions but just my attempt to please them.
Therapist: Uh huh. [attending and active listening]
Client: Do you know what I mean?
Therapist: You are talking about the approval seeking that you have done your whole life, not just with your parents, but with others. [paraphrasing]
Client: Well, I've just been thinking that maybe this has been a big problem for me. I mean, I'm almost 30 years old and I'm still acting as if I live at home.
Therapist: You are feeling very uncomfortable realizing the extent you still feel dependent on your parents. [reflection of feeling]
Client: That's for sure. So, where do we go next with this?
Therapist: You're hoping I will tell you what to do just like your parents. Part of you enjoys deferring to others so you don't have to be responsible. [rephrasing, reflection of feeling, and interpretation]
Client: It's just that I don't want to upset them. And they're just trying to be helpful. I mean, they're not trying to intrude or anything . . .

Therapist: What is the latest incident with your parents that is bothering you most right now? [redirective open-ended question]

Client: You just wouldn't believe it.

Therapist: I can see that you are feeling really embarrassed to even talk about the situation because you realize that it only confirms the extent to which you have been dependent on them. [reflection of feeling]

Client: You won't believe this one. I was about to go to bed last night when the phone rang. Of course it was my mother. She calls me every night about this time.

Therapist: You are saying that like it really irritates you. [reflection of feeling]

Client: Well, it does!

In just a few minutes, the client is already well on his way to exploring an important issue of his life. The therapist opened the session with a question and then used this skill only one other time to redirect the focus, when she asked him to supply a specific example of the latest intrusion. She noticed that the client was about to defend his parents, explain their behavior, and go off on a tangent, so she asked the question to help them deal with something more specific. The rest of the time, she used reflective skills exclusively, except for the one deeper-level intervention when she inserted a bit of interpretation: that the client was doing the same thing with the therapist that he does with his parents—wanting to avoid responsibility. This advanced-level skill will be covered in a later chapter.

We want you to see how natural and powerful these few simple skills can be in the hands of an experienced practitioner. Within a very short period of time, you can get into some very important issues and collect all the information you might need to plan an intervention strategy. In the previous example, the therapist was able to find out quite a lot about the client's situation without having to ask directly. At this early stage, she concentrated primarily on mirroring what she was hearing and understanding.

Checking Exercise

There is one important point that we wish to make. It is absolutely critical (read: not optional) that you continuously check with clients to see how things are going and to assess how they are responding to your skills or interventions. You can do this in several ways. First, you can ask the client, but this is sometimes awkward. Second, you can watch and listen to see how the client responds to your interventions. Third, you can review the videotape or audio tape of the session afterward (often with a supervisor or peer).

Allen Ivey and several colleagues developed a procedure called "interpersonal process recall" in which the counselor and client both review the tape of a session to debrief what each was thinking and feeling at the time (this is often led by a supervisor). We would like you to try something similar.

Conduct a 10-minute interview with a partner applying the skills you've learned so far.

Tape the session.

Play back the tape in the company of a third partner who helps you to review what each of you was thinking and feeling, and especially how the "client" was responding after each skill or intervention. Pause the tape at appropriate times to stop the action, and ask one another questions like:

- *What was going on right there?*
- *What did you have in mind when you said that?*
- *I notice an interesting expression on your face. What were you thinking at the time?*
- *Notice how your client is responding after you said that. What do you suppose he was feeling? Okay, let's ask him.*

In this context, we are focusing not so much on your skills as on your client's responses to them. You must get in the habit of constantly checking how your clients respond to everything you say and do, or don't do.

EXPLORING THE PAST

Psychoanalysts are not the only ones who honor the past as a major force that shapes present behavior and current problems. Almost anyone would agree that what we have already experienced and lived through has some influence on what we think, feel, and how we act today. This means that whatever problem or issue a client brings up, you may wonder: How is this related to what he or she has experienced before?

There is not really a set of skills related to exploring the past as much as there is a mindset that guides you in the exploration of relevant history. This gets a little complicated from a theoretical perspective because some approaches (i.e., reality, cognitive, behavioral, strategic, problem-solving, humanistic, existential, Gestalt) appear to stick pretty much to the present and seem to avoid delving too far into the past. Nevertheless, in spite of espoused beliefs, most practitioners spend at least a little time collecting some basic background about what has happened before. At the very least, you might wish to know the following:

- How is what you are experiencing familiar to you?
- What does the present situation remind you of?
- What did you learn growing up that is limiting you?
- What have you already tried that has worked best?
- What have you attempted that has not worked very well?
- How might this story you shared have been influenced by others (parents, culture, gender roles) rather than your own beliefs?
- What are some critical incidents you experienced as a child that are still impacting you strongly today?
- What are some unresolved issues from the past that still plague you today?
- How might your present problem be connected to some of the issues that we have been exploring?

Exercise in Exploring the Past

In small groups or with a partner, one person will talk about a current, ongoing problem. Ideally, this would be a relatively little concern but still one that has been chronic.

> *Ask the person a series of questions like those listed that help him or her to explore the ways this issue might be related to unresolved issues and entrenched patterns of the past.*
> *After the exploration has been completed, ask the person to summarize how this conversation was most helpful and what he or she learned as a result.*

Although many of these questions may appear to be extensions of a particular theoretical orientation (i.e., psychoanalytic, narrative, individual psychology), we believe that these are fairly generic open-ended questions that are often useful to bring up if there is time and the client is amenable to exploring their implications. Essentially, you are operating as an historian. You want to know the context for what the client is experiencing in the present. Although you may not want to spend a tremendous amount of time delving into the past (much depends on your client's needs and interests, your own theoretical leanings, and the length of treatment planned), you will probably check out most of the areas just highlighted.

What is the best way to explore the past? Although we would like to give you the kind of specific direction we offered earlier in the chapter, this process follows a basic inquiry: "I was wondering what we need to look at from the past that might be useful or relevant?"

If you ask this question directly, the client will probably shrug. "How should I know?" the client will think, or say aloud. That is why you may often need to use a series of questions like those listed earlier to structure the search for important material. An example of this process is given in the following case with a woman who is trying to extricate herself from a bad relationship with her second husband.

Client: He was telling me yesterday that he isn't going to make this easy for me, he's going to . . .

Therapist: This is so frustrating for you. Now that you have finally decided to leave your husband, he has only redoubled his efforts to make this as difficult as possible for you. [reflection of feeling and content]

Client: Well, it's not his fault exactly. I mean, I've sort of encouraged him to not give up hope.

Therapist: So, why should he believe you this time? You've given him a lot of mixed messages. [rephrasing]

Client: Yeah. He just thinks I'll change my mind.

Therapist: You're angry at yourself for setting things up so you aren't taken seriously, especially this time when you really mean to do what you say. [reflection of feeling]

Client: Right. I just don't know how I got myself into a mess like this.

Therapist: That's a very good question you asked. I can't help but think that this pattern might be somehow familiar to you. [introducing influences of the past]

Client: What do you mean?

Therapist: This pattern did not just develop out of thin air. And I suspect this isn't the first time you've been involved in a relationship like this. What are some things from your past that help explain why you get yourself into these situations where you aren't taken seriously? [probe and open-ended question]

Client: I'm not sure.

Therapist: Then let's spend some time exploring this further.

With this particular case, the therapist might spend just a few minutes in this area, or perhaps the rest of the session. Other practitioners might devote a significant period of time, even several months, to look at historical patterns. Just to summarize, the main idea is to explore with the client those influences and historical patterns that help explain and account for current difficulties.

SUMMARIZING THEMES

We have just demonstrated the final exploration skill in the previous paragraph. After covering a number of complex topics, we paused to draw together the threads into a concise description that captures the essence of the various messages. Summary statements are inserted at various times during a session:

- When it is time to end the meeting.
- When you have completed a subject and are about to make the transition to another one.
- When the client looks confused or overwhelmed.
- When you need time to regroup and make sense of what is going on.
- When it is time to take stock of what you have been doing and talking about.
- When it might be helpful to organize or structure a conversation that has covered a lot of ground.

It may sound like it is totally the therapist's job to use summarizations whenever the situation calls for it, but a far better strategy is to ask the client to do the work.

Client: I was telling you about how this situation got out of control. Oh, by the way, I ran into that friend I was telling you about, the one who gave me such a hard time . . .

Therapist: One second. Before we get into this new topic, I wonder if we might wrap up what we've just been talking about.

Client: Okay.

Therapist: So, how would you summarize what this has been about?

Client: Just that I have trouble with new situations like this because I wait until the last minute to prepare myself. You were saying that I should maybe think about things ahead of time instead of react impulsively.

Therapist: What else?

Client: Um, that this is the way my parents made decisions too?

Therapist: True. But also that this theme of procrastinating, putting things off until the last minute, is your way of avoiding responsibility for making mistakes.

Client: Right.

Therapist: Okay, so you were talking about your friend . . .

In this brief excerpt, you can see how the therapist starts out by interrupting the client as he abruptly changed the subject. It is important before moving on that the previous topic is completed, or at least wrapped up a bit. Rather than doing the summary herself, the therapist asks the client to do so. Quite typically, the client is awkward and unskilled at doing this, just as you would expect from someone without training. Nevertheless, the therapist draws him out as much as possible, reviewing the main themes covered. Then she finishes the process by filling in the parts that were left out.

In this conversation, just like the previous example demonstrating how the exploration skills all fit together, you can observe the therapist using all the skills that were introduced in this chapter: rephrasing content, reflecting feelings, asking open-ended questions, and then summarizing main themes. All of this exploration leads logically and sequentially to the next stage of the therapeutic process: promoting insight and understanding.

Exercise in Summarizing

1. *Initiate a conversation with a partner about some topic of mutual interest. Spend about five minutes talking about the subject in such a way that you each connect personally with it. In other words, don't just have an intellectual debate but also talk about your feelings related to the issues raised.*
2. *After time runs out, each of you write down on a sheet of paper a summary of what you saw as the essence of this conversation. In just a few sentences, what was this conversation really about?*
3. *Exchange summaries and compare your impressions.*
4. *Reach a consensus between you as to a summary that includes both of your contributions.*
5. *Talk to each other about what this was like.*

PITFALLS AND COMMON MISTAKES

In this chapter, we have demonstrated ways to respond verbally to clients. As a result, the concepts you choose to focus on, the words you choose to say, or even silence directs the session with your client. You might sometimes hear that person-centered therapy is nondirective. However, that isn't quite accurate; it's just less directive than some other approaches. Every response or lack of response will likely facilitate a particular client response. So, you must be mindful of what you say and why you say it. That is why we want to alert you to some common mistakes made by beginning therapists as they learn to respond verbally to clients.

Being Social in Your Demeanor

We have learned a certain way to communicate with others that is socially appropriate. For example, if someone laughs, we smile, even if the content of the information is not funny or happy. We use tenuous language such as "It sounds like . . ." or "It seems like . . ." in order to avoid making a mistake. We talk about ourselves if we have a similar experience to join with the other person. We say things like "I understand" or "I know what you mean" when, in fact, we usually know how we would feel in their situation, not how they actually feel. We are unaware of our demeanor with others, such as usually being enthusiastic and energetic, or usually being stoic and monotoned.

The ways we behave in social situations are often not appropriate when in the role of a therapist. You have to present yourself as a professional with confidence. You have to be flexible in your nonverbals and in the tone of voice you use to match what the client means, not what the client presents. You have to focus on the client, not yourself. For some people, putting on the therapist hat will be simple, and it may be similar to the other professional hats that have been worn. However, for others, learning to present yourself in a new way can be very difficult. I [Leah] had a student tell me that the most difficult part of learning to be a therapist for her was toning herself down. She was a high-energy person, and being calm and still was very difficult for her when her client was talking about serious issues. You will learn to be conscientious and more flexible in the way you present yourself.

Freezing

When you first learn reflective skills, you may believe that you have to do this well, if not perfectly. There will be times when you will freeze, just draw a complete blank. In your role-plays, or with real clients, the person will say something and then pause, waiting for you to respond. You will know that it is time for you to say something—if not a brilliant, deep-level, empathic reflection of feeling, then at least a feeble parroting remark—but your mind is absolutely empty and nothing whatsoever comes out of your mouth. You may start to panic and stutter. The cognitive activity inside your head will be filled with self-castigations about how inept and hopeless you are as a helper.

This is a time to draw one of those cleansing breaths. You will want to remind yourself that almost anything you say, as long as it represents your best response to what you hear and understand, will encourage further conversation and deeper exploration. It does not matter nearly as much as you might think that your reflections are poetic, articulate, profound, and perfectly accurate. Just keep the flow of conversation going by responding, saying something, almost anything. If you can't think of anything else, then you can always repeat verbatim what the person just said. This will give you some time to regroup and clear yourself for what comes next.

The most frequent mistake that beginners make when learning these skills is having expectations that are neither realistic nor even possible. You must be patient with yourself, realizing that it is going to take many weeks, if not months (or years if you are like Leah), until these skills begin to feel natural.

Exercise on Your Own: Listen to Yourself

About the best way to develop proficiency in all helping skills is to become far more aware of your interactive style and its effects on others. Videotape and audiotape yourself as often as possible. Review the tapes with someone more experienced (a supervisor is preferred but even a peer can offer valuable feedback). When there is nobody else available, scrutinize the tapes by yourself, noting things you did well and poorly, behaviors you could have done differently. Take detailed notes about what you intend to change and improve.

Waiting Too Long

You can't just sit around and wait for the perfect opportunity to insert your reflective comments or probes in particular areas. Unlike role-plays in which your partners will politely and considerately pause at regular intervals, allowing you the space to speak, many clients will just talk and talk and talk and talk until (a) the session is over, (b) they run out of ideas or energy, or (c) you interrupt and redirect them. There are many reasons why people do this. They might be rambling as a characteristic style. They might be using a filibuster to keep you from getting too close. They are often just doing what they think you want them to do; they think they are being cooperative by filling the time with as much as they can think of and say in the short period of time. In any case, it is your job to make sure that things stay on course. And if you wait for perfect pauses in the conversation, you may never get a word in.

Each conversation has a different pace, depending on the subject, the mood, and the client's interpersonal style. With some people, it will feel agonizing to keep the conversation going—each session can seem like it lasts days, or even weeks. With other clients, all you have to do is get things going and they will talk, nonstop, without a single pause. You are obviously after some sort of balance in most sessions where there is roughly equal input and a natural exchange of ideas. With clients who speak haltingly and uneasily, you will have to draw them out more. With other clients who talk incessantly, your job will be to offer them structure and clearer focus.

There are times when it is entirely appropriate—and necessary—to interrupt someone. In social situations this might be considered rude, but in the therapy arena where time is so precious, you must provide the kind of structure that is needed. If you find yourself waiting and waiting and waiting in order to reflect back what you hear, it may be time to be more assertive and proactive.

Being Too Cautious

One of the most common errors beginning therapists make is being too cautious. We have heard over and over again, "I'm afraid if I go too deep, the client won't be able to handle it." Sometimes this is just an excuse for not knowing how to go deeper. More often, though, there is fear involved. However, the fear is not really for the client, the fear is that it will get to a point where the therapist feels unequipped to handle the situation.

What you must first understand in working with individuals is that the client will tell you when you are going too far. If you find you are bumping into some resistance, and the client is unable or unwilling to see what you present, then you have gone as far as the client will go. We assure you that most clients who have healthy boundaries and strong egos will let you know directly, or indirectly, when you are going too far. So push a little. Try some things out. If they don't work, just move on. We would recommend you try taking a risk and failing rather than not taking risks at all. And if you still don't feel comfortable with pushing the client a little, then you might need to do your own work around this issue. Sometimes people need a little push, a little encouragement to move forward. They will let you know if you've gone too far. Trust your client to tell you.

Trying to Solve the Problem Too Quickly

We mention this point in almost every chapter because it is such a common mistake of beginners. When you see someone who is struggling, someone in deep pain, someone who is reaching out to you, pleading for assistance, you can't help wanting to do all you can. You want to take the pain away just as fast as you can. You want to make the person feel better. You want to do this because of your own spirit of altruism but also to make yourself feel better. Much of the time in this profession, you will feel utterly helpless. We don't know about you, but one of the reasons we got into this line of work in the first place is because we felt so helpless to resolve our own difficulties that we enjoyed taking care of other people's business. Even if this isn't the case, you will still find yourself trying to fix as many people as you can, just as quickly as possible. Even if it doesn't help them much, it makes you feel better.

We haven't even moved into the insight stage yet, much less action, so in this exploration process you do not want to rush through the data gathering. Except in the cases of single-session therapy or crisis intervention, you will have at least one session (and often much longer) to do some solid exploration before you are expected to organize an intervention.

When watching beginners in action, we often hear the following remarks in the first few sessions:

- "Have you tried . . . ?"
- "One thing that has worked before is . . . "
- "What I'd like you to do is . . . "
- "My advice would be to . . . "
- "So, what are you going to do about this?"

There are times when direct action and advice are indicated (although much less often than you would imagine). Ordinarily, you will not want to push the client to take action until after you have worked your way through the exploration and insight stages.

Spending Too Much Time in the Past

Although it is theoretically consistent to talk about the past in some theories, beginners can get lost in talking about the client's past. As stated before, talking about the past can be helpful to find the origins of the patterns your clients develop. However, clients can tend to tell the stories of the past in the same way without really experiencing any emotion behind it. As a result, if you allow your client to talk about the past in session after session, you might find that you are obtaining interesting history, but the client may not seem to be growing. Furthermore, talking about the past is usually a mere step in reaching the client's goal, not an end in itself simply because you understand the origins of the client's behaviors. A better alternative is to bring the past into the present. Reflect how the client feels right now about what happened then. Another possibility is to bring an exchange from the past into the room with an empty chair technique (discussed in the next chapter). So don't get caught in the trap of talking about the past, reflecting past feelings or experiences. Bring it into the moment where the client can more fully experience his or her feelings to, hopefully, gain depth and insight.

Asking Too Many Questions

We have mentioned this earlier about the dangers of appearing like an interrogator who asks one question after another. Most of the time you can get the same information, or prompt the same behavior, by simply using reflective skills. The best example of this is the often-used question that beginners ask: "How does that make you feel?"

There are several reasons why you will not want to ever use this particular question, the least of which is that it is far more smooth to simply reflect what you sense the person is feeling. Compare these two responses:

Client: I can't seem to get a handle on things. No matter how hard I try, it just seems like I fall further and further behind.
Helper: How does that make you feel?
Client: Terrible.

Client: I can't seem to get a handle on things. No matter how hard I try, it just seems like I'm further and further behind.
Helper: You're feeling really frustrated and anxious because you have so little control over your life right now.

The first response didn't elicit much clarity from the client. The second response exhibited empathy on the part of the therapist. In addition, the first response would likely facilitate the client's thinking process, which is antithetical to trying to get at emotions. Questions place clients into a thinking mode, not a feeling mode.

Another reason not to use the inelegant question, "How does that *make* you feel?" is that it reinforces the idea that feelings are caused by things outside of yourself. As you have learned (or will learn) from cognitive therapies advocated by Ellis (1973), Beck (1976), and others, the language we use inside our heads, and aloud, influences the ways we think. There is, thus, a huge difference between "How does that make you feel?" and "How did you make yourself feel over that?" or even the more neutral, "How do you feel?"

Regardless of how the question is asked, it is still usually better to avoid it when you are trying to promote deeper exploration. Rather than asking how the client feels, make your own best guess as to what might be going on, and then reflect that back. Of course, there are always exceptions such as when you might express concern by asking: "I'm wondering how you are feeling right now?" In that situation, you are not so much even asking a question as you are expressing your own caring. Another appropriate use is by asking: "You are talking about something so sad, and yet you seem cheerful in your descriptions. I'm wondering how you really feel about that." In this situation, you are confronting your client's incongruence.

Exercise in Asking Too Many Questions

First experience what it is like to ask too many questions. One person talks about an emotionally laden topic, and the other simply responds with questions for about 3 or 4 minutes (that's all you'll be able to tolerate). Then switch roles. Talk about your experience.

This time, while one person talks about an emotionally laden topic, the other should

> *reflect content and feelings. Switch roles. Finally, talk about your experience and note any differences.*

Raising Your Voice

In North American English, raising your voice at the end of a statement usually turns it into a question. It also communicates an uncertainty and lack of confidence on the part of the speaker: "You're not doing very well today?" [with rising intonation on the last word] versus "You're not doing very well today" [with an even tone of voice].

The latter example communicates more power, more confidence, and thereby more influence. Remember, you are in the business of impacting people; that is your job. You can't help anyone if you can't get them to look at their lives in new ways and experiment with alternative ways of behaving. People are often resistant to doing so because they feel comfortable with old patterns, no matter how ineffective they might be. So in order to get people to look at themselves more honestly, you must be able to convince them that such a task is in their best interests. Sometimes they will go along kicking and screaming.

You will need all the tools possible to be as influential as possible. This includes using your voice to maximum advantage. If you are raising your voice at the ends of your sentences, you are probably not communicating with as much power and confidence as you could.

There are a couple of reasons why people raise their voices. First of all, it may be a culturally embedded pattern. Canadians raise their voices more than Americans, perhaps as a demonstration of their greater modesty (please excuse our overgeneralizations), and Australians do so even more often. The second reason is that a raised voice is a more polite, gentle way of putting forth an idea, sort of like saying, "Maybe this is what is going on?"

Clients are fully capable of correcting your reflections if they are not accurate, so don't worry that you must offer them in such an apologetic way that they sound "wimpy" and tentative.

Flat Reflections

In contrast to not raising your voice, it's important not to sound monotoned. The volume and tones of your voice should reflect the underlying message the client is trying to convey. For instance, if the client is talking about a sad topic, such as the death of a loved one, even if the client is speaking in a joking manner, you will want to reflect a sad tone when you say, "You miss him very much." Your voice should be congruent with the topic. Another example would be if your client is talking in an even tone about his anger toward his father, you might want to state in a louder and sharper tone with, "You are angry at your dad!" Of course, clients are often congruent in their tone of voice and the topic. If the client is crying while stating her dog ran away last night, you would want to speak softly and slowly to match that tone. So, what we're trying to convey here is that the words you choose are not sufficient to reflect. You must reflect the emotional content, even if the client doesn't. You will be surprised at how the client will match your affect.

Overuse of Summarizing

Summarizing can be very helpful at times, but is best used infrequently. Why, you ask? Well, first of all, if all you do is summarize, then you probably aren't talking frequently enough. You're just listening to a client tell a story, which he or she can do with anyone. You should be interjecting often enough to demonstrate empathy and hopefully, add depth. Second, if you are always summarizing, then you are talking too much when you do talk. If you are going on and on and on about what the client just told you, then the client will likely get bored and/or lost in all of your talking. Finally, summarizing doesn't usually add anything to the depth of the conversation, and it can feel patronizing. Your client needs help in going deeper because of where he or she is stuck at his or her current level. Your client knows what he or she just said. Therefore, your goal is to reflect a deeper meaning behind what is presented by the client to facilitate insight, not to parrot too much.

Using Impersonal Reflections

In order to avoid depth of feelings, in social situations we use "it" or "that." For example, we use "That's hard" or "It's sad" instead of "This situation is hard for you," or "You feel sad." When stating a reflection impersonally, the client can avoid taking responsibility for what was said. However, by simply personalizing the reflection by using "You . . ." the client is more able to feel the feeling and own what you have just said.

Reflecting the Experience of Others Rather Than Your Client

Most of the time, your clients will be talking about relationship issues, whether with partners/spouses, friends, family members, or coworkers. As a result, the client will be making statements about how those other people feel, or think, or behave. It's important for you to remember that what your client presents is only the perception of your client, and not the actual way the other person might think, feel, or behave. Therefore, we recommend you do *not* make reflections about the other person, but rather you reflect your client's feelings, thoughts, or actions. For example:

Client: My husband wants to give me advice when I just want him to listen.
Therapist: He always gives advice.

This is an example of reflecting the client's perception of the husband, which may or may not be true. In addition, you are emphasizing the husband's behavior. This would likely elicit a further elaboration of how he gives advice. A better response would be:

Therapist: You feel frustrated when he gives you advice.

In this example, you are reflecting your client's experience of frustration, which will likely stimulate your client to talk about her frustration. Therefore, check to make sure you are reflecting your client's experiences instead of the experience of the other person. This allows the client to explore more depth of feeling.

Exercise in Reflecting a Client's Experience

In pairs, the person in the client role is to talk about a real or fictional problem he or she is having with another person. The person in the therapist role will practice reflecting the experience of the other person, rather than the client's experience. After 5 minutes, discuss the direction this type of response took you. Then using the same relationship issue, the person in the role of the therapist will correctly reflect the experience of the client, rather than the other person the client speaks about. After 5 minutes, discuss how this type of reflection elicited a different direction in the conversation. Then switch roles of client and therapist and repeat the whole process.

Reflecting Projected Feelings

You may experience a situation where it seems the client is disagreeing with all of your reflections. Sometimes the client is struggling to describe his or her situation. However, more frequently, the error is on the part of the therapist. Remember the exchange where the therapist seemed to be missing the core messages with every reflection?

> *Client:* If he gets on my case one more time, just one more time, I'm going to make sure he never treats someone that way again.
> *Therapist:* You are so upset you want to punch him.
> *Client:* Well, not that angry. It's just that he has so little respect for me, or anyone else.
> *Therapist:* You wish he would treat you with more respect. It pisses you off that he treats others differently.
> *Client:* I'm not really that special, to tell you the truth. He treats everyone else the same way.
> *Therapist:* So, you feel better about that at least.
> *Client:* I don't feel good about any of this. I just wish I could get him to stop acting the way he does.
> *Therapist:* You are feeling helpless because you don't know what to do next.
> *Client:* I do know what to do, I'm just afraid to do it.

When this happens, usually the therapist is projecting his or her own feeling onto the client. What's a projection? First introduced by Sigmund Freud and later utilized by Fritz Perls, projection is the identification of a thought, feeling, or behavior as someone else's when in fact it is yours. Confused? Let's see if we can make this clearer. In the preceding example, the therapist was reflecting how he or she might feel in the client's position. This happens most often when the therapist shares an experience similar to the one that the client is describing. The therapist may have had a relationship where he or she wanted to kill the other person, where the therapist felt treated differently from others, and where the therapist didn't know what to do in that circumstance. The therapist projects his or her own experience onto the client with inaccurate reflections in an attempt to be empathic. However, the therapist is not reading what the client is expressing, and consequently is not being empathic.

Now, just because you make one or two inaccurate reflections does not necessarily mean that you are projecting. You will constantly be off here and there with various clients. However, if you find that it's a pattern with a particular client or with a particular issue that more than one of your clients is experiencing, think about whether you have had a similar problem. If you have, then we recommend you do your own work around the issue so that it does not interfere with your therapy. In addition, getting some supervision or consulting until you feel confident your countertransferences aren't getting in the way is highly recommended.

Going in Circles

There are several reasons that you may find yourself not making any progress with the client. First, you may be only reflecting content. If you are unable to find the feelings beneath the content, then the session is not likely to progress well. Most clients (except those who are extremely emotional) are fearful of exploring feelings and may present content. Presenting content or the facts is much easier than expressing feelings. Thus, check to make sure you are including feelings in your reflections.

Another possible reason for going in circles, assuming you are reflecting feelings, is that you are reflecting at a superficial level, at the level the client presents. An advanced skill is to try to find out what the client is saying and/or feeling beneath the words. One way to do this is to reverse the process. For example, an obvious reflection might be:

Client: In spite of what my parents say, I don't care about making better grades. That's their issue.
Therapist: You believe your grades are good enough.

Versus a deeper reflection:

Therapist: You are frustrated because your parents won't leave you alone.

If you find that you are reflecting both content and feelings at a deep level, and you have reached the point in which you still find yourself going in circles and covering the same ground again, then you know for sure that you've done enough reflecting and exploring. Sometimes the redundancy can begin after just a few minutes; at other times it may not occur in a single hour. There is a point, however, where you realize that you are reflecting back the same feelings and rephrasing essentially the same content. That is a signal that it is time to summarize and move on. Take action. As a matter of fact, we are at that very point right now!

APPLICATIONS TO SELF: LEARNING TO REFLECT WILL CHANGE YOU

We have stated this before, and we'll state it again: Going through the process of becoming a therapist or counselor will change you. It already has! You will become more aware of how you act interpersonally as well as intrapersonally. You will become aware of and hopefully work on many of your issues as you learn new skills and see clients. Most relevant to this chapter is that you will interact with others differently.

You may think that the skill of reflecting is something that you will only use while working with clients. However, we can assure you that this is not so. Once you begin to improve your ability to reflect, once you gain a level of mastery, reflecting will become second nature. You will reflect without thinking, without wanting to. You won't understand why everyone keeps telling you their problems when you're off work, even strangers who don't know what you do. And so there is some good news and bad news.

Lets start with the bad news. Many of your relationships are based on a pattern of interactions, a way of being with people. As you begin to reflect more, if you didn't before, some of your relationships will start to decompensate. By reflecting, you will find the other person goes deeper, and they may not like it, thereby changing or sometimes ending some relationships.

There's more bad news. Some of the people you choose to have in your life help you to work on your issues. This is more difficult to illustrate, but we'll attempt it with an extreme example. If an alcoholic is at a large party, and she is the only one, and a codependent type person is also at the party, and he's the only codependent, then the two of them will find each other. We don't know how they do it, but it seems almost inevitable. They will not only meet, they will fall in love with each other. They will think that the other person is so wonderful! Well, guess what? At some level, we all get attracted to some people because of less healthy aspects of our personality. So where is the other bad news? Well, as you work on your own issues, and these reflection skills can really do it for you, those people won't seem as attractive. They might even complain that you're changing—that you're not the same person, and that would be true.

Okay, so enough with the doom and gloom. The good news! You will become healthier, happier, more balanced and confident. Oh sure, you always have stuff to work on. We can never master it all; that would be boring. But take it from us, you will find much richer relationships. You'll need them, and you'll be prepared to have them with your new-found ability to listen, really listen to others. And you'll be happier than you ever imagined.

SUMMARY

This chapter contains some of the most essential skills to becoming an effective therapist. In fact, you must learn these skills as a foundation to helping clients. We have covered the use of questions, including what good and bad questions are and the frequency with which to use them. We have articulated the process of reflecting content and feelings. This skill is of the utmost importance. You have been exposed to information on how to explore the past as part of the initial stages of therapy. Finally, we have summarized summarizing in therapy. As mentioned at the beginning of this chapter, you will use these skills most early in the therapeutic process. However, you will use them until the last moment with your client. Reflecting especially is essential to demonstrate empathy, to enhance client awareness, and to strengthen the collaborative relationship. Practice, practice, practice.

A CHECK ON WHAT YOU LEARNED

1. What is wrong with the following therapist response? "Was it your elder or younger brother that asked you for help?"
2. What is wrong with the following therapist response? "Tell me why you haven't quit this job that you so despise."
3. What are the two primary types of reflections?
4. What type of reflection elicits the most depth and why?
5. What type of reflection is this? "You feel like it is her fault."
6. What is good about this therapist response? "You're anxious and afraid that you won't get it all done because you are overcommitted and have very little free time."
7. What direction is the therapist attempting to go with the following statement? "Tell me the first time you remember feeling this way."
8. What might cause you to have the experience that the session is going in circles?
9. What are the consequences of asking, "How does that make you feel?"
10. What is wrong with the following reflection? "That's really sad." Rephrase it to make it better.

SUGGESTED READINGS

Goldberg, M. C. (1998). *The art of the question*. New York: Wiley.

Hill, C. E., & O'Brien, K. M. (1999). *Helping skills: Facilitating exploration, insight, and action*. Washington, DC: American Psychological Association.

Sayers-Cowper, G. (2001). *Interviewing and questioning skills*. New York: Spiro Press.

Young, M. E. (2001). *Learning the art of helping: Building blocks and techniques*. Upper Saddle River, NJ: Prentice Hall.

CHAPTER 7

Promoting Understanding
and Insight

This chapter, like this stage in the therapeutic process, acts as a bridge between assessment and exploration, previously described, and action that follows. There are some approaches that advocate the promotion of insight as the main focus of therapy, believing that when this process is carried through in sufficient depth, it alone can lead to lasting changes. Person-centered therapy (Rogers, 1951), psychodynamic theory (Kohut, 1984), Gestalt therapy (Perls, 1969), and existential therapy (May, 1953) are perhaps the best-known advocates of this point of view. They structure the treatment in such a way that increases self-awareness and self-understanding, believing that this more than enough to get the job done. More contemporary constructivist (Neimeyer & Mahoney, 2000) and social constructionist models (Burr, 1995; Gergen, 1991, 1997) also make use of insight, but in a way that is designed to help clients not only to understand the ways they perceive things, but also to change these stories to those that are more helpful.

Rogers (1951) was perhaps the most articulate spokesperson for an insight-oriented perspective when he commented that self-awareness and understanding were both necessary and sufficient conditions for change to occur. There is actually little empirical support for this assumption, and even some question as to whether the therapist is the one who promotes the insights or whether the client is the one who does this outside of the sessions (Tallman & Bohart, 1999).

Reflective Exercise

In small groups, or on your own, consider a time in your life in which you had an epiphany—a major moment of revelation in which some insight or understanding revealed itself to you. This could have been some dramatic insight into the meaning of life, the workings of the world, or perhaps some deeper understanding of yourself. Talk (or think) about what contributed most to this transformation. In addition, discuss what it took for you to remember this lesson and to learn from it.

It may be true that including an insight stage, and using skills designed to promote greater understanding, may not be part of every treatment plan, nor included with every case you see, but you will still provide some forum for exploring the meaning of issues and concerns even if time is limited and motivation is minimal. After all, even the most problem-focused client will still want to have some idea as to what happened and why so future problems of a similar nature might be prevented.

THE USES OF INSIGHT

Insight will come up in a number of ways. Clients may wonder why they developed problems in the first place, or they may wish to understand the deeper meaning of these concerns in the context of their lives. For instance, someone who is depressed might very well be primarily concerned with making these awful feelings go away, but may also wish to have some idea as to the source of this condition. Any of the following explanations may be possible for a case of depression:

- The depression represents a sense of emptiness and meaningless in the person's life because of job dissatisfaction and social isolation.
- The person is experiencing a delayed reaction to sexual abuse that was suffered in childhood.
- There is an overwhelming sense of helplessness and powerlessness that comes from being a member of minority group that was oppressed.
- The person is the scapegoat and "designated client" for a dysfunctional family in which others are the ones who need help but will not seek it.
- The depression is a symptom of a degenerative neurological disease.
- There is an underlying "endogenous," biologically based depression.
- The person is grieving the loss of a relationship that recently ended.

This is but a mere sampling of possible "causes" for the depression. Each might involve a different sort of treatment plan. And each would provoke a very different understanding of the underlying issues and what they mean for that person.

Depending on your theoretical orientation (or the one favored by your supervisor), the particular complaints brought to you by clients, the work setting, and the time you are allotted to offer help, there are a number of options available (surely you aren't surprised) to you for promoting insight and understanding. Table 7.1 summarizes several of these possibilities, each of which makes use of particular skills that will be covered in this chapter.

THE LIMITS OF INSIGHT

Believe it or not (surely you believe that there are advocates for every conceivable position), there are critics who consider attention spent on insight in therapy as largely a waste of time, if not a potentially dangerous digression. Following Milton Erickson's lead, Watzlawick (1997) wrote an article called "Insight May Cause Blindness," in which he reported that there isn't a single documented case he could think of in which a client ever changed permanently as a result of some understanding. Without action, without converting understanding into some form of structured practice, he believed that the time and energy are wasted.

TABLE 7.1

Models for Promoting Insight

Type of Insight	Theoretical Framework	Skill Employed	Example
Awareness of feelings	Person-centered	Reflection of feeling	"You're feeling upset because you don't like giving up control."
Unconscious motives	Psychoanalytic	Interpretation	"The anger you are expressing towards me seems related to feelings you have toward your mother."
Cognitive distortions	Cognitive	Guided discovery	"Even if you don't get what you want, how is that absolutely terrible?"
Inauthenticity	Gestalt	Confrontation	"You say you are really angry about this, but you appear quite calm."
Personal meaning	Existential	Immediacy	"I notice that right now you are withdrawing from our relationship just as you have done with others."
Problem redefinition	Strategic	Reframing	"When you say you have a bad temper, what you really mean is that you are sometimes very passionate."
Family dynamics	Systemic	Restructuring	"I want you to move over there and sit with your wife instead of your children. Talk to one another about what this is like."
Power imbalances	Feminist	Exploring gender roles	"How have you limited yourself by the ways you have defined what it means to be a man?"
Sources of influence	Narrative	Outcome questions	"How did you manage to overcome the anger when it tried to control you?"
Social and language influences	Social constructionist	Re-story life circumstances	"Which roles have you adopted that were not of your own choosing?"
Consequences of choices	Reality	Challenge decisions	"Is what you are doing getting you what you want?"
Family constellation	Adlerian	Interpret early recollections	"Which of your parents do you most resemble?"
Contingency contracting	Behavioral	Identify reinforcers for target behaviors	"What is it that sustains this behavior?"
Reframing	Strategic	Restructure the problem in more helpful way	"When you say that you are shy, what you really mean is that you are sometimes quiet when with strangers."

This may be an extreme point of view, but nevertheless there is considerable evidence to support the reality that people can remain in therapy for a very long time, have perfect understanding of why they are so screwed up, and yet still remain that way without a shred of visible movement in changing their self-destructive behaviors.

The skills covered in this chapter are designed to help your clients to develop at least a minimal level of understanding about the source of their problems and what they mean. Although such efforts may not be enough to help them make needed changes—and make them last—they will provide a solid grounding to help people understand themselves better, and in the best case, prevent future problems through such self-knowledge.

SELECTED SKILLS FOR PROMOTING UNDERSTANDING

It is a gross simplification to think that anything as complex as moments of startling insight can be promoted by the use of a few well-applied skills. When clients arrive at a new place of understanding it is usually the result of accumulated work that has spanned their whole lives. The therapist is merely the midwife who assists in the birth.

Even within the course of therapy, when clients do reach a point of new awareness, it is almost impossible to identify what it was the therapist did or said (if anything) that made the most difference. It is often a big mistake to even ask the client afterward. For one thing, clients don't often know or understand what happened; they will just make up an explanation to satisfy your curiosity. And second, even when they think they do know what happened, you may not like what you hear.

After a particularly moving session, the client discloses how pleased he is with the result. In the best scientific tradition, the therapist attempts to identify the critical factors so that such efforts might be replicated in the future.

Client: I just want to thank you so much for all your help. This was an amazing session. I think I finally understand what is going on now.

What therapist could resist the temptation to ask what happened? Not this one.

Therapist: So, I'm just curious. What made the most difference to you? What would you say helped you the most?

The therapist is reviewing in her head all the possible candidates that might be mentioned. She is almost sure the client will say that it was that wonderful metaphor she created, the one that included several different levels and was constructed to bypass the usual resistance. But perhaps it was that well-timed confrontation in which she was finally able to get his attention and point out what he had been doing that was so ineffective. Then again, it could have been the gentle way that she had supported him in his time of need.

Whatever the client shares, we can almost promise you that it won't be what you expect to hear. All too often, clients are unable to articulate what it was that mattered most. Even when they can do so, it may not be one of the planned interventions but something quite serendipitous. We can't tell you how often we have asked clients this question and heard examples of what we had done that we didn't even remember.

So, humility is the order of the day. Understanding is an accumulative, complex process that builds on previous awareness. Your job is to use those skills that are most associated with helping the development along.

Confrontation

Confrontation has a very bad reputation. It is often associated with being rude or hurtful. Just imagine hearing the words, "I want to confront you about something," and it gets your pulse racing. Confrontation is associated with conflict, with war, with clashes of power.

In a therapeutic context, the best confrontations are so subtle and gentle that the client doesn't even know they happened. Sometimes, in order to get the bad taste out of students' mouths with this word, we call it a reflection of discrepancy because your client is usually exhibiting some sort of discrepancy that you simply notice. In the dialogue that follows, the therapist is merely pointing out some distortion, and is doing it in a way that is unassuming, almost innocent.

> *Client:* I'd like to be able to do something like that, but I'm just not good at that sort of thing. I've never been able to speak up like that with lots of people around.
>
> *Therapist:* I see. I'm a little confused by something though.
>
> *Client:* What's that?
>
> *Therapist:* Well, you say that you can't speak up in front of groups, but last week you were telling me a story about how you gave a toast at your brother's wedding and how moved everybody had been. What do you make of that?

In this interaction, the therapist wished to confront the client with self-limiting statements that were neither accurate nor constructive (i.e., reflecting a discrepancy). Rather than telling the person that he was a liar, or that he was distorting reality, or that he was using this belief as an excuse to hide from taking action, the therapist used a much more subtle approach by simply noting a discrepancy between what the client was saying now and what he had said previously. Then the client was left with the task of sorting this out.

The client could, of course, attempt to ward off this confrontation by denying what he said earlier or minimizing its significance: "Well, that situation was different since it was just with family and close friends." But when the client is open to looking at things in a different way (and it is the client's readiness that matters most), a confrontation like this can go a long ways to provoke changes: "I hadn't thought about it that way. But I guess you're right. It's not so much that I can't speak up as it is difficult for me to do. But I can do it when I have to."

When using confrontation, it is best not to confront the person, but the behavior. You can do this most easily by labeling the behavior that you observe or, most often, by pointing out discrepancies:

1. Between what is said now versus said earlier: "You said earlier that everything in your relationship was going well, but now you are saying that there are some problems."
2. Between what the person is saying versus communicating nonverbally: "You say that you aren't that excited about seeing your friend, but I notice that when you talk about him your voice rises and you start talking really fast."

3. Between what the person says he or she wants and what the person is doing: "I'm a little confused. You say you want to improve your grades, that it is your most important priority, yet you admitted that you spent only one hour studying this week."

There are other instances when confrontation might be indicated, such as when someone is doing something harmful or self-defeating. In each of these situations, the goal is to bring someone's attention to something in a way that it cannot be easily ignored.

Exercise in Confrontation

In groups of three, take on the roles of the helper, client, and observer. The client will talk about a situation in which he or she presents some inconsistency—between verbal and non-verbal behavior or between several statements that don't fit together. The helper will then confront the person by pointing out this inconsistency in the most diplomatic way possible. The observer will then offer feedback on alternative ways this confrontation could have been implemented.

Switch roles until each person has had a chance to practice confrontation.

Disputing Beliefs

One of the contributions that the cognitive therapies made popular is the inclusion of a more challenging set of skills into the repertoire of most therapists. First introduced by Adler (1963) as "basic mistakes," other therapies have taken the same idea as an essential component to their theory, such as cognitive distortions from cognitive therapy (Beck, 1976) or irrational beliefs from rational emotive therapy (Ellis, 1973). When clients show evidence of thinking that is distorted, irrational, or illogical, the therapist may use the opportunity to explore underlying beliefs that lead to these self-defeating patterns.

It is not necessary to embrace rational emotive behavior therapy, individual psychology, or cognitive therapy in order to use disputing skills in your work. There may be times that arise when the level of client cognitive distortion is such that you believe that helping them to examine their underlying thinking may be profitable. This is especially the case in the following circumstances.

When the person exaggerates: Look for uses of "never" and "always" in language usage. *"I never get what I want." "I always end up with the worst end of the deal."*

When the person imagines the worst: Notice the prevalence of words like "awful" and "terrible." *"This is the worst thing that ever happened to me." "This is so awful I can't stand it."*

When the person demands special status. Notice expressions like, *"It's not fair"* and *"Why me?"*

When the person overgeneralizes: *"Because I didn't get an 'A' on my last paper, I'll never earn this professor's respect." "I blew the whole interview; I'll never be a good therapist."*

When the person makes judgmental demands of self or others: Notice the use of the words "must" and "should." *"He shouldn't have done that" "I must get this promotion."*

Ellis (1973) liked to call this "shoulding" all over yourself, or "musterbating".
When the person does not want to take responsibility: Notice the use of the word "made" and "can't" (instead of won't). *"He made me clean the house every week." "She made me angry every time she said that." "I can't learn to type; it's too hard."*

The first skill in this process is sensitizing yourself to notice when people use language that represents underlying dysfunctional thinking. This isn't terribly complicated or involved but will require a certain amount of reading on your part to master the basic concepts. You might consult books by Glasser (1965), Ellis (1973), Beck (1976), Meichenbaum (1977), Lazarus (1973), or Adler (1963) in order to familiarize yourself with the most common beliefs to monitor.

On the simplest level, you can do this by noticing every time a client (or anyone) says something like *"He made me so upset,"* or *"That situation ruined everything."* Ask yourself what is intrinsically irrational about these statements.

Hopefully, you have observed in the first case that other people can't make one upset. Emotions are controlled internally. With a few exceptions, nobody else has the power to make you feel anything without your consent; emotional reactions are the result of interpretations made about various situations. Thus in the second statement, no situation can ruin anything, unless that is the way the person chooses to interpret things.

If, for example, you did get a disappointing grade on an assignment, you could tell yourself any number of things about what this means:

- "This means I'm stupid."
- "The instructor is a jerk."
- "This proves that this department sucks."
- "I'll never be able to succeed in this field."

It is entirely possible, of course, that any of the preceding statements might be true, but is far more likely that the person is overgeneralizing and exaggerating. This would clearly result in rather strong emotional reactions, such as rage, depression, and discouragement.

Another set of possibilities is that the person could say to him- or herself:

- "Gee, this is disappointing. I wonder what I could do to improve my grade on the next assignment?"
- "Just because I received one grade that is lower than I preferred (but still not that bad) does not mean that I am stupid."
- "I wonder if the instructor made a mistake. I'll go talk to her to find out what happened."
- "I'm not crazy about the way some things operate in this department, but I guess that's true of almost any organization."

In this second set of responses you can appreciate that a very different kind of emotional reaction would likely take place. The person is still disappointed, and perhaps even a bit upset, but the intensity of the emotions is more appropriate given the circumstances.

When disputing beliefs, your job is to help clients examine what they are saying to themselves and then, if desired, substitute alternative self-statements that are more reality based.

Some examples of these kinds of interventions might include:

- "I'm not clear how you arrived at that conclusion. How does it follow that just because that one thing happened, this necessarily leads to your conclusion?" This challenges the client to examine assumptions about causes and effects.
- "What are you saying to yourself to cause yourself such misery?" This encourages clients to examine the ways that their chosen interpretations determine how they feel afterwards. By implication, if they changed what they were saying to themselves, they could change the result. Instead of saying, "This is the worst thing that ever happened," the person could say, "This is annoying and disappointing. This is just one of those times I don't get what I want."
- "Where is the evidence to support that belief?" You are asking clients to do a reality check, examining the basis for their assumptions. "You say that you don't have a chance of ever succeeding, but I'm not clear how you arrived at that conclusion."
- "What makes you so special?" When people act as if the forces of the universe have conspired against them, they can be challenged to see that they are no different from others. Although it may sometimes seem as if they got a raw deal, that perception is the result of excessive preoccupation with self.
- "You *should* do that?" When clients use "shoulds" or "musts" this can be brought to their attention so they can use more appropriate language. It is so much more empowering to say "I will do this," instead of "I should do it."

There is a kind of Socratic dialogue associated with the use of these skills. Although there are different styles of intervention, the main goal is to change the ways that people think about their predicaments, and thereby alter the emotional responses.

Exercise in Disputing

With a partner, take turns role-playing the following scenarios in which attempts are made to identify the irrational beliefs implicit in the statements. Once these have been labeled, challenge their validity by using the skills that were introduced.

- *"I can't go to the party. I'm just not good in social situations like that. I'll probably make a fool of myself the way I always do. And even if I did meet someone, things like this never work out for me."*
- *"There's something wrong with the car and they can't find out what the problem is. It's just not fair. There's no way that I can concentrate on anything else until this gets fixed. That's just the way I am."*
- *"He makes me so angry the way he is always manipulating people. He should respect people more."*
- *"If I only had a better education then maybe I'd have a chance to do something with my life. But it's too late for me now. There's just nothing I can do but accept that this is the way things are going to be."*

Interpretation

If disputing beliefs is part of the legacy of cognitive therapy, then interpretation is one of the major contributions of psychoanalytic therapy to generic practice (Kohut, 1984). This is a very different sort of approach to promoting insight, but one that also seeks to alter people's perceptions about their situations.

Through the process of systematic observation and analysis, the therapist develops certain hypotheses about what might be going on and why. Interpretation is the skill that is used to offer these observations to the client with the hope that it will foster a deeper level of understanding into the meaning of the symptoms and their underlying causes (Kohut, 1984).

Interpretations can be made on several different levels:

- Unconscious motives and desires can be made more explicit. "Perhaps the reason why you hesitate to tell her how much you care about her is that you fear she will respond in kind. Deep down inside you don't feel you deserve to be loved."
- Connections can be made between present and past behavior. "You are struggling to establish yourself as someone who is competent and knowledgeable. This reminds me of what you said previously about how inept you felt as a child when you couldn't play any sports well."
- Underlying themes and metaphors can be highlighted. "Perhaps the argument you have been having about who should do which chores around the house is really a struggle for control in your relationship. You have mentioned previously that you used to fight over who would drive the car when you went out together."

There was a time when interpretation was the bread and butter of what many therapists would do in order to promote insight, especially those who were trained in a psychoanalytic background. Because it does place the therapist in the role of expert authority who sees and knows things that are invisible to others, there is a reluctance on the part of some practitioners and theorists to engage in this power-laden skill. Thus, there is a continuum on how to utilize interpretation.

On the one end of the continuum, interpretation is the essence of therapy. For example, in psychoanalysis (Freud, 1936) and analytic (Jung, 1935/1880) psychotherapies, interpreting is a primary function of the therapist. Both of these theories have specific symbols or concepts that are sought out by the therapist to apply to the client, whether from a dream or from catharsis. Learning these symbols and concepts takes years of training on the part of the therapist, especially with analytic therapy.

On the other end of the continuum are Gestalt (Perls, 1969) and person-centered (Rogers, 1951) therapies where interpretation is something that the therapist tries to avoid. The assumption is that the therapist can only project his or her understanding of the problem because the therapist is unable to fully take on the client's paradigm or be completely objective. Therefore, the client must seek his or her own interpretations. Furthermore, if the client arrives at his or her own interpretation, then it will definitely be well timed and accurate. The therapist is at risk of providing an interpretation prematurely or inaccurately. For the stronger personality, if a client hears an incorrect interpretation, he or she can negate it. However, if you have a client who likes to please or has poor boundaries, he or she may not negate it, or worse, may assume it's correct without thinking about whether or not the interpretation seems to fit (called *introjection*).

So let's look at a specific example of these extreme positions before exploring the middle ground. A client reports part of her dream:

> I'm in a big two-story house at the top of the stairs. I walk down the stairs, and at the bottom of the stairway is a table with a large vase full of tall, white flowers. I can smell the sweetness of the flowers, and I feel sad at the sight of them. I stand there frightened, unable to move.

Perhaps the psychoanalytic therapist would interpret the large vase of flowers as some sort of phallic symbol and interpret the client's sadness as an aspect of penis envy. In contrast, a Gestalt therapist would ask the client to report the dream in present tense; once completed, he or she would ask the client to choose something in the dream that stands out most in the dream. Let's assume the client picks the flowers. The Gestalt therapist would then ask the client to be the flowers, to describe the dream in present tense from the perspective of being the flowers, and end with requesting that the client make statements about the flowers, such as, "I am in a vase. I am white. I am pretty. I represent death . . . " When the client begins describing herself as the flowers, she will usually come to her own awareness about what the dream means. This may not be exactly how each of these therapists might work, but we hope you get the idea; in the first example, the therapist imposes his or her own interpretation, and in the second example, the therapist leads the client through a process that allows her to arrive at her own interpretation. So, let's now look at the middle ground.

Exercise in Interpretation

Get into groups of four or five people. Have one person tell a dream for about two or three minutes; if no one has a dream, have someone tell a brief and somewhat bizarre story from a movie. Then, on a sheet of paper, take a minute or two to write down a brief interpretation of the dream or story. After everyone has finished, compare the notes among the listeners. Finally, compare what the dreamer wrote down as his or her interpretation. Discuss the differences.

A more subtle and less direct approach can be taken to help clients look beneath the surface of their behavior. In theories such as individual psychology, interpretation is essential, but is done collaboratively and with a significant amount of supporting evidence before it is submitted to the client (Adler, 1963). Interpretative interventions can thus be employed by making the client more responsible for creating meaning:

- "I wonder what it means that you are so reluctant to tell her how you feel."
- "I suspect that what you are doing now is part of a long-standing pattern in your life. What does this situation remind you of?"
- "This sounds very familiar, given some things you have described earlier. What stands out for you?"

In these instances, instead of supplying the meaning through interpretation, the therapist is helping the client to do the work. Regardless of how the process is introduced, clients are taught to think in ways that uncover underlying themes, recurrent patterns, and significant metaphors that may be instructive. As with all other skills, you will be much more effective if you use the client's language rather than your own preferences when encouraging this deeper understanding. Again, if the client arrives at the interpretation on his or her own, it will be well timed and more accurate.

Providing Information

There are times when clients are struggling because there are things they don't know or understand. I [Jeffrey] remember a couple who came to see me because of sexual difficulties. When I asked them what the problem was, the wife answered meekly that sexual intercourse was so painful that she didn't want to do it anymore.

I asked them to describe for me the way they initiated their lovemaking. They were painfully embarrassed by this discussion, but so desperate they tried their best to be accommodating.

Husband: Well, we just do it.

Jeffrey: Could you be a little more specific please?

Husband: Well, I just kinda tell her that it's time and then we go upstairs and we do it.

Jeffrey: Maybe we could just break this down into smaller steps. First, how do you indicate that it is time for lovemaking?

Wife: He sort of nods his head, like in the direction of the bedroom.

Jeffrey: Okay. Then what happens?

Wife: Like he says, we go into the bedroom and then we do it.

Jeffrey: Again, it would help if you could be more specific.

Wife: Well, I lay down on the bed. Then he pulls down my underpants, and he shucks out of his pants.

Jeffrey: Go on.

Wife: That's about it. Then he gets on top and we do it. It really hurts though, so sometimes we have to stop pretty quick.

Jeffrey: Wait a minute. Let's back up a little. You mean to say that you just lie down on the bed, and he just enters you right away?

Husband: Yessir. That's it. Why? Are we doing something wrong?

When I asked the couple about foreplay, they had no idea what I was talking about. They had little understanding about their bodies and the ways they worked and almost no knowledge about pleasuring one another's bodies. The one and only session I had with them consisted of telling them about leading up to intercourse with a series of lovemaking activities that were designed to arouse and prepare one another. I gave them a few suggestions about books to read. And then I sent them on their way. When I followed up with them by phone a few weeks later, they were delighted with the results. My "therapy" with them consisted solely of providing pertinent information. The "cure" resulted from their applying this new knowledge.

There are several other instances in which problems could arise because clients don't understand something important. Therapists thus take on the roles of teachers to instruct people in areas that are relevant. Examples of this might include:

- Explaining how emotional responses are the result of thinking patterns.
- Instructing people on the short- and long-term effects of their favored mind-altering substance.
- Providing basic information about the best ways to interview for a new job.
- Teaching about the ways that stress can result from unhealthy lifestyle choices.
- Supplying a model for making decisions systematically.
- Giving referral sources for physicians who can do recommended medical tests.
- Introducing a systematic plan for weight loss.
- Explaining the ways that family members can become scapegoats as a result of underlying dynamics.
- Educating about the ways in which people of color are marginalized by the majority culture.
- Explaining how reported symptoms represent normal responses and are not necessarily problematic.
- Warning about risk factors associated with suicide attempts.
- Describing the ways that self-perceptions are shaped by one's culture, gender, and family background.
- Explaining the variables that are most associated with relapses and what can be done to prevent them.
- Teaching people to recognize the signs and symptoms of trouble before they occur.
- Distinguishing between the various kinds of depression and explaining how the client's symptoms fit into this scheme.
- Directing the client to sources on the Internet that will provide additional information.
- Recommending books and movies that might highlight a relevant point.

The key component of the skill associated with giving information is to do it in such a way that you don't come across as a pedantic teacher. It is also far better to teach the client how to get needed information, rather than you doing all the work. For example, if a client is interested in going to college but is unsure how to proceed, rather than telling him or her what to do, it may be better to work with the person about how he or she could find out this information. This way, you are helping the client not only learn about things related to present needs, but also to learn the process by which he or she can find out things in the future.

Giving Feedback

Whenever prospective clients have asked what is so unique about therapy that it is worth the money, a favorite response is that it is the one place you can go to hear the truth. Therapists are in a unique position to observe people and then offer constructive assistance. Where else can someone go to hear how he or she really comes across to others? Who else is going to tell people why they are so annoying? Who can give someone concise and accurate input on what they are doing and understand the effects of that behavior? And who is going to say such things in a way that the feedback can be heard?

It does indeed take considerable sensitivity, as well as honesty, to offer people things about themselves that everyone else knows but is afraid to tell them. To make this much more personal: You consistently do things that are less than effective. You put people off sometimes by the ways you behave. You erect barriers that get in the way of greater intimacy. You engage in defense mechanisms that not only protect you from getting hurt but also insulate you from enjoying life more. Furthermore, most of the people in your life know this about you but they will never tell you.

There are a number of very good reasons why you rarely hear the truth about your self-defeating behavior. People don't want to hurt your feelings. They are afraid you will take things personally and hold a grudge. They don't know how to tell you in a way that you will hear them. And most of all: They are concerned that it won't do much good so what is the point in even trying?

Among the things you will do for your clients, one of the most valuable services is to give them honest and useful feedback about what they do well and not so well. It would not at all be an exaggeration to say that sometimes such comments can irrevocably change people's lives forever. If you can figure out a way to find the core of what people are doing to get themselves in trouble, and if you can bring this to their attention without threatening them too much, it might just be possible for them to make needed adjustments. However, it is very, very hard to offer such feedback without creating high levels of threat and defensiveness.

Giving feedback is one thing; doing it in such a way that it can be heard and accepted is quite another. It's a difficult skill to learn, but as therapists-in-training, you will (hopefully) have good role models as your professors provide you with constructive feedback about your counseling skill level. Notice how they do it and if you think it's done well; mimic what you see and hear.

Good Feedback Is Honest. One of the things that we can do for clients is to tell them about the ways they appear to others. It is as if each of us walks around in the world with a piece of spinach caught between our teeth. Everyone else can see this unsightly mess but nobody is willing to bring it to your attention because it is embarrassing. So they pretend to ignore it, or they whisper about it to others, leaving you in the dark.

When you notice that clients are doing something that is counterproductive, or acting in ways that are off-putting, you can bring this to their attention. Here are some examples of the sort of feedback that might be offered:

- "I notice that when you talk to me you rarely make eye contact or show much animation in your speech. This makes it difficult to make contact with you. I wonder if this might be one of the things that is getting in the way of some of your other relationships?"
- "One thing that might be helpful for you to know is that you continuously interrupt me before I can finish responding to you. This discourages me, and others, from feeling like we are heard by you."
- "You consistently raise your voice at the end of everything you say, communicating that you don't have much confidence in yourself. That may be one reason why you don't feel like others are taking you seriously."

- "It is your right to wear as many body and facial piercings as you want, but if you want to get a job in a traditional setting, you might want to rethink the image you project to prospective employers."
- "Next time you tell your daughter that you disagree with what she is doing with her life, you might want to do it in such a way that she doesn't feel so attacked by you."
- "You strike me as much stronger and more powerful than you give yourself credit for. There are times, like right now, when your passion and enthusiasm seem to take over."

What we attempt to do as part of our jobs is to look at our clients clearly and to tell them what we see. We do not offer this feedback as "the truth," as the way things really are, but rather as an informed, reasonably objective opinion. Certainly we have our own biases, but that is one reason why our own therapy and supervision are so important to help us remain clear-headed and objective.

The Best Feedback Is Specific. Useful feedback includes examples of whatever you are describing. When possible, it includes both supportive and constructive elements. Notice that we have avoided the use of words "positive" and "negative." This is because what might be called "negative" or criticism might just be the most useful thing that anyone could hear. Likewise, what might be labeled "positive," meaning a compliment, would feel good for about a minute but would actually offer very little to the person that is helpful in an enduring way. Ideally, feedback should include elements that cover both strengths and weaknesses: "I really appreciate your warm smile and giving nature. You are the first one to reach out to help others who may be in need. You also neglect yourself and don't do a very good job of taking care of what you need."

Exercise in Feedback

With a partner, or in small groups, take turns giving each other feedback. First, write down each person's name. Next to the name, note several impressions of that person. Include something about them that you especially value and admire, as well as a few things that you think they might work on. Remember, you are not responsible for being "right," but merely to offer what you observe as your opinion. Make the feedback as specific as possible, including an example of what you mean.

Anyone who wishes to hear the feedback may volunteer. It is very important that nobody be forced to receive or give feedback if it is not desired.

The person receiving the feedback is not allowed to respond until after everyone has finished. Then he or she may react by sharing what was most helpful.

Talk about your reactions to this feedback exercise.

Feedback that is too general or abstract is not very useful because the person will not have a clear idea of what you are talking about. Because impressions like this are potentially threatening, people look for any excuse to devalue or ward off what they hear that does not fit their own self-image. Your feedback will carry a lot more weight and power if it is accompanied by supporting examples.

> You don't seem to enjoy hearing anything about yourself that is positive in any way. It is almost as if you prefer to put yourself down, and have others do the same. Earlier when I tried to tell you that I liked what you said, you seemed very uncomfortable. You looked away, shuffled your feet, and laughed uneasily. It felt like you were giving me a clear message that this was definitely something you did not want to hear. I would not be inclined to tell you anything supportive like that again.

In this example, the person giving feedback supplies detailed data to support the impressions. This includes both behavioral descriptions (averted eye contact, shuffled feet, uneasy laughter) and personal disclosures (this pushed me away). As you might imagine, it is far more difficult for someone to ignore or negate feedback like this that comes with specific, supporting evidence.

It Is Easier to Digest Feedback When It Is Concise and Clear. Be careful not to be too wordy and verbose when you give people feedback. The essence of your message may get lost. The experience of hearing feedback is pretty intense and emotional. Your heart is thumping in your chest. Your palms feel sweaty. After all, you are about to hear the naked truth about how others see you.

Imagine that you are sitting in the company of a therapist—an expert, a specialist in giving feedback. This person is well trained, well educated, very experienced, and licensed by the state to help people. Furthermore, this professional is a bit intimidating and seems very smart and knowledgeable. Now this therapist turns her attention toward you. She is about to tell you what she really thinks about you and what she observes about your behavior. Now, tell us you wouldn't be a little nervous.

Under such circumstances, whether in individual or group therapy, the recipient of the feedback is not concentrating as closely as you might prefer. That is one reason to record the feedback or have someone take notes so there is a summary of what was missed. This is also a reason to keep what you have to say as concise and focused as possible. If you go on too long, or try to cover too much ground, the essence of what you have to say will not be heard.

> Rambling feedback: *"I think you need to do a little more to get things going. I mean, you are trying and all, and I think that's good, but you have to do a little more. Do you know what I mean? Like, when you were saying last time that you want to get your grades up, you didn't really do much. You haven't done much so far. You said that your parents were putting a lot of pressure on you and that really bothered you. And you really need to ignore them and concentrate on what you want. That is, if you know what you want. And that's another thing: You should stop listening to what others say and listen to yourself more. That reminds me of one other thing . . . "*

> Concise feedback: *"You have said several times that you want to improve your grades but I've noticed that you haven't followed through on what you claim is so important to you. You speak so much about what your parents say that I rarely hear what you really want."*

Offer Feedback in a Sensitive and Caring Style. The time and energy you spend offering feedback are wasted if the person can't or won't hear what you are saying. It is thus extremely important that you are careful, sensitive, and diplomatic in what you share. You may think that what you are saying is framed in words that are straightforward and honest, but the client may hear something quite different.

You don't want clients to wonder about your motives, believing for a moment that you might be trying to hurt them. Like confrontation, feedback can be potentially hurtful if clients are not adequately prepared for it, nor able to process the input in constructive ways. In the following conversation, the therapist sets up the feedback carefully.

Therapist: You say that you are confused about why it is so difficult for you to make friends. I wonder if you'd like to explore that further.

Client: What do you mean?

Therapist: Well, I've been in a relationship with you for the last few months. I've had the opportunity to know you and spend time talking with you about very personal things. Perhaps I could offer you some feedback on what I've observed.

Client: I guess so.

Therapist: You sound hesitant about this.

Client: I am, I guess. What did you have in mind?

Therapist: Again I sense that you are feeling uncomfortable and a little frightened about what I might say to you.

Client: No, not really.

Therapist: I think it is perfectly reasonable to be curious, and a little apprehensive. After all, it isn't often that you have such an opportunity to hear how you come across to others. And I think after all this time you know me well enough to realize that I will be very honest with you.

Client: Yeah, that's what I'm afraid of.

Therapist: Maybe, then, it would be best if we held off on this until you felt more open to hearing what I'd say.

Client: No, I think I can handle it. It's just . . .

Therapist: It's just that you want to make sure that I'll be gentle.

Client: Yeah, but I know you will.

Therapist: So you do trust me but you are still feeling a little nervous about this. Maybe we could take some time and talk about other times in your life when people have told you things that were difficult to hear and how you processed those experiences. That might give us some guidance as to the best way that we could proceed right now.

This therapist is being very cautious and deliberate in the way the feedback is set up. He senses that this could be a turning point in their work together, but he doesn't want to risk compromising the trust they have built between them by scaring the client away. He also knows that hearing this feedback is absolutely essential to the work they have yet to do, so he has no intention of backing off completely. He just wants to be as sure as he can that sufficient steps have been taken to prepare the client to be as receptive and open as possible.

Many students have complained that they don't want to hurt the client's feelings. They get defensive when we ask them to give constructive feedback or to offer feedback that might be construed as hurtful. This is what they usually imagine: "Your irresponsible behavior seems to get you in trouble a lot." If confrontation isn't your style, another way to frame feedback that can potentially be construed as negative is to reframe it using what is positive and negative about a particular quality. For instance, someone who is irresponsible can also be seen as spontaneous. "You really know how to have a good time, and I also see that your ability to have a good time can sometimes get you in trouble when you don't take care of your responsibilities." Notice how phrasing in this way compliments the client and shows how the extreme of spontaneous can also appear as irresponsible. Try this on your own.

Exercise in Reframing

Get into pairs, and list qualities of former friends or partners (or maybe even current friends or partners) that irritate you. Have your partner reframe them in a way that is gentler. Another example might be in the case of selfishness: "You seem to be really good at self care and setting boundaries to get your needs met, and sometimes you may not be aware of how your actions are affecting your wife." You should be able to do this with virtually any negative quality. Try doing at least five each.

Silence

Silence is not something you might automatically think of as a technique or skill in any part of the therapeutic process. Yet silences are a large part of what we do. How you intervene depends very much on what the silence means. Is the client reflecting on things? If so, it might be best to wait things out. But what if the silence indicates confusion, or frustration, or anger, or withdrawal? In each case, you will have to sort out what is going on and then respond appropriately. The first step, however, is for you to become more comfortable tolerating silence.

Silence is used in all stages of therapy, and when used appropriately, it can be one of your most powerful tools. There will be times when a client says something unexpected, or you state something that is profound. The client will look down and stare, remaining perfectly still. You can see that he or she is really processing something. You may be tempted to respond while the client is reflecting on things. In fact, you might be excited to say something because, by now, you had time to think about a good response. However, whatever you say is not likely to be as powerful as what the client may be thinking or experiencing. Keep quiet until the client makes eye contact again. He or she will most likely tell you what was going on. If not, ask, "What was going on with you just now?"

There are times when silence is inappropriate. How will you know when? You'll know. When the client talks and then stops to look at you, it's your turn to talk, and you may have nothing to say. This will inevitably happen to you. The ball is in your court, and you haven't a clue about how to return. When all else fails, reflect. But if the client is not looking at you, if he or she is looking up and thinking or looking down and processing, don't interrupt. Wait. Be patient. Slow down. The client is working.

Self-Disclosure

This skill just might be the most challenging of all to use appropriately. It either can be used as a powerful impetus for encouraging clients to open up and take risks, or can represent the ultimate in clinician self-indulgence.

You have had experiences in the past when teachers spend excessive amounts of time telling you stories about their lives and about the wonderful things they have done. In some cases, these stories might have been amusing or interesting anecdotes, perhaps even useful in illuminating a particular point. There have been other times, however, when such self-disclosures were a colossal waste of time. You sat there wondering to yourself, "Why are you telling me this? I don't really care."

There are, in fact, several reasons why you might want to use self-disclosure:

1. To bridge psychological distance between yourself and your client: "I remember feeling much the same way that you do when I was your age."
2. To take yourself off the pedestal and make yourself appear more human: "I have also struggled with issues similar to this in my life."
3. To illustrate an example from your life of how you have successfully overcome similar problems that confront the client: "I found that what made the biggest difference was talking to close friends about my struggle as a way to recruit more support."
4. To demonstrate ways of dealing with difficult situations: "When I had a similar problem I found it helpful to stop trying so hard to make things happen."
5. To increase your stature and potential power in the client's eyes: "I have worked with similar situations many times before with great success."
6. To use immediacy to increase intimacy and trust: "After what you shared just now I am feeling closer to you than ever before."
7. To model appropriate ways of thinking, feeling, and behaving: "I started to get angry . . . I mean, I made myself angry over what happened."
8. To demonstrate authenticity and genuineness in order to increase perceived attractiveness: "As I hear your story, I feel a deep sense of loss for you."

Because self-disclosure takes the focus off the client and puts the attention on the therapist, it has certain detrimental side effects, especially for those people who are already insecure and used to deferring to others. Before you ever use the skill of disclosing yourself in session, you must be certain that there is not another way to accomplish the same goal. It is often helpful to ask yourself: How can I get this same point across without taking the attention off the client?

We don't mean to absolutely forbid the use of this valuable skill. We just wish to warn you about how often it is abused by some therapists who are overly self-centered and like to remain the center of attention.

Teaching Tales

A particular kind of self-disclosure involves the sharing of stories from your life that are designed to emphasize or illuminate some crucial lesson. These could be brief heroic stories in which you have overcome some challenge. They could also include examples from your life that illustrate some important point.

We next supply some abbreviated examples of our favorite personal stories that we often employ in our work to inspire or instruct clients, students, or supervisees.

- Risk taking [Jeffrey]: "I rarely had the courage to ask girls out when I was in college because I was so afraid of rejection. Then one day I realized that nobody could hurt me nearly as much as I hurt myself after I avoided taking risks. Once I realized this, I lost all fear about approaching girls. Many of them still declined to go out with me, but I still felt good about myself and what it took to put myself on the line."
- Living in the present [Leah]: "I've always been quite goal oriented. I set a goal, and lived for the attainment of that goal. In other words, I lived in the future. After my mother died at the age of 49, I realized I might not have the time to achieve my goals. I should live in the moment, because right now is all that really exists and tomorrow may not come."
- Failure [Jeffrey]: "For the longest time, I thought I was the only therapist who ever screwed up in sessions. Few of my teachers and supervisors would ever talk about their mistakes so I got the impression that if I didn't know what I was doing (which is my experience of doing therapy some of the time) I was incompetent. I have since learned that all of us are pretending to know a lot more than we really do."
- Letting go [Leah]: "I was told that I could have anything I wanted with a little bit of hard work. So, I made a habit of pushing hard to make things happen the way I wanted. However, as a therapist, that doesn't work . . . at all! I learned that if I let go and stopped pushing, then they actually could gain something each and every session. Over time, the accumulation of small steps resulted in meeting a goal, maybe not the goal that was verbalized at the beginning of therapy, but the goal they needed to meet."
- Adversity [Jeffrey]: "Some of my worst travel experiences have been those that prompted the most growth. And those that went smoothly, with everything going as expected, can barely be remembered."
- Belonging [Leah]: "After completing my undergrad in psychology, I needed a break before continuing to grad school to become a therapist. I worked in several jobs and found that I was miserable in each one. I was bored, unchallenged, and I wasn't able to connect with others. I thought I must have been depressed or something. I was afraid I was incapable of happiness. When I finally returned to school, I found that I felt a real sense of belonging there. The people at school were like me (psychologically minded and deep). The work was interesting and fun. What a relief. I wasn't depressed; I was just in the wrong job."
- Redefining self [Jeffrey]: "I was a mediocre student in school and was told by almost everyone that I would be lucky to graduate from college. Then one day I decided that I wanted to be smart. I started watching people on campus who I thought were smart and I realized that what separated them from me was that they walked around carrying books. And they read them. So I started doing the same thing. And pretty soon everyone started treating me as if I was smart. Then I started to believe it myself."
- Being supportive [Leah]: "I always liked being helpful to others. So when they told me life was bad, I told them it would get better. If they told me they couldn't do it, I told them they could. What I later learned was that I was not being supportive, but rather invalidating their feelings. Once I learned the skill of reflecting feelings and content, I found nothing could be more supportive than that."
- Validation [Jeffrey]: "I thought that if I got a master's degree that this would mean that I was finally good enough, finally smart. Because everyone knows that people with

graduate degrees are smart. When that didn't work, I went on to get a PhD, yet I still didn't feel like I had 'arrived.' So then I thought I'd be a professor because surely they must be smart. Still not enough. The same thing happened when I became an author. The fact is that no matter how much I have accomplished, it has never been enough to feel good enough. This is only something that can be developed from within, not through external sources."

We've got dozens, perhaps hundreds, of such stories that we've collected over the years and kept in our inventories. They are all intended to promote insight by using our own experiences as teaching points.

Exercise in Constructing an Inventory of Teaching Tales

On your own, or in small groups, construct a list of some of your life experiences that might be used to illustrate key points in therapy. You can think in terms of the categories mentioned by the authors, as well as generate several other areas that might arise.

WHAT HAPPENS NEXT?

There are some clients who will come for therapy primarily because they are in search of some deeper level of self-awareness or understanding. Although it is rare in today's climate of man-

---

Diagnostic Checklist

As you begin to promote insight, there are some questions you might consider to check how things are going with your client:

- *What is the cultural context for the client's experience?*
- *What is going on in this relationship that parallels other conflicted encounters that are taking place in the client's life?*
- *What is the client doing that is getting in the way of me knowing, understanding, or becoming close to him/her?*
- *How are the life themes and current difficulties in the client's life being played out during our encounters?*
- *How does the pattern already established appear limiting?*
- *What recurrent issues between us might represent dysfunctional or fully functioning behavior on the part of the client?*
- *What interactional role and relationship position does the client take in the therapeutic relationship?*
- *What interactional therapist role is being evoked by the client?*
- *How has my credibility been compromised?*
- *How has my "humanness" been withheld or diluted?*

aged care, there will even be some cases in which the client is not necessarily interested in changing anything as much as understanding what is going on. Some approaches, such as psychoanalytic and existential therapy, are particularly well suited for this type of work.

The vast majority of your cases will consist of people who not only want to make significant changes in the ways they think and feel and behave, but desperately need to do so. Some will be referred by the courts; unless they stop their destructive behaviors, they will end up in prison. Some people will come to you with their marriages falling apart or on the verge of losing their jobs. Some will be addicted to drugs, prescription medications, or alcohol; they will need to change or they will spin out of control. Some will be so depressed or anxious that they are on the verge of giving up altogether and killing themselves. Still others will be engaging in behaviors that are hurtful toward others. In all of these cases, it is not nearly enough to just help them to understand how they got themselves in these predicaments. You must help them to change the usual ways that they take care of business. In order to do that, you are going to have to help them to make the challenging transition from understanding what might be going on to doing something about it. It is an understatement to say that is a challenging job.

PITFALLS AND COMMON MISTAKES

As we have done with previous chapters, we would like to introduce some common mistakes of beginning counselors that are associated with the skills of facilitating insight. In addition, some pitfalls that occur during this stage in the process will also be mentioned.

Forgetting to Use the Skill of Reflection

Even the best of therapists make this mistake from time to time. You have established the relationship with your client. You have seen your client for several sessions now, and she seems to trust you. You begin to feel like you are doing some work. You confront. You interpret. You give feedback. You use silence. You dispute irrational beliefs. You ask stimulating questions. But you're forgetting something. What is it? Reflecting! It is vitally important that throughout the therapeutic process that you reflect content and feelings. We even teach our students that before you ask a question, reflect what the client said, and then follow with the question. Clients needs to be heard, understood, and to hear what they are saying at all stages of the therapy. The relationship always needs to be fostered and tended to. As the process advances, this is the one area that some students completely forget to do. But when you are testing the relationship with confrontations and honest feedback, you must also nurture it with empathy. Most importantly, nurture the relationship with feeling reflections. This type of response can elicit a powerful reaction in your client at later stages of therapy.

Following Your Own Agenda

Client: I really don't like to go to this church. It's too big and impersonal.
Therapist: You say you don't like it but you attend each week. [confrontation]

Client: I attend because my religious views are important to me.
Therapist: But you just said you don't like this church. [confrontation]
Client: I don't.
Therapist: And yet you go because it's important to you. [still confronting]
Client: Yes.
Therapist: So why don't you go to a different church? [question]
Client: Because this one is close to home, and I hate driving.
Therapist: You would rather be unhappy at this church than be unhappy driving. [confrontation/reflection of content]

Here is an example when the therapist just doesn't seem to be able to gain any depth. He is so tied to keeping his agenda that he can't seem to find a different way to approach the subject. He's not evidencing much empathy for the client's experience either. Sometimes when we think we're onto something, we get excited and try to lead the client with too many confrontations and questions. As a result, the client gets defensive and more determined than ever to hold his or her position.

If you sense your client is getting defensive, take a look at what you are doing. Do you have an agenda? Are you asking a lot of questions? Are you confronting a lot? Are you forgetting to be empathic? If so, slow down and reflect the client's feelings. A better dialogue might go something like this:

Client: I really don't like to go to this church. It's too big and impersonal.
Therapist: You say you don't like it but you attend each week. [confrontation]
Client: I attend because my religious views are important to me.
Therapist: You value the experience of going to church, but you wish this church was smaller and more personal. [reflection of content]
Client: Exactly.
Therapist: Tell me more about your feelings of the church being too big and impersonal. [directing client]

In this second example, the therapist has slowed down enough to understand the problem instead of leading the client into a personally imposed agenda. He is showing empathy and understanding so that the client feels safe enough to explore deeper.

There will be times when you get excited and find yourself directing the session. Don't be too hard on yourself. It happens to the best. Just ask yourself why you have the need to control the session, to lead the client in your own direction. Once you answer that question, you will find that you stop following your own agenda and follow your client's instead.

Interpreting Too Much

As mentioned previously, interpretation is seen as something that should be used with caution. If you find yourself working hard to make connections, or you are providing interpretations to your client and you're consistently off the mark, then you are interpreting too much. You could be way ahead of your client. Your client may not be ready for what you are presenting.

Or you could be wrong because of your own projections. Remember, the client should do the majority of the work, not the therapist.

Another consequence of interpreting too much is that you could foster a dependence from the client who will look to an authority figure to solve problems. In contrast, if the client solves the problem herself, she has added a skill to use for the rest of her life while building self-esteem. A double bonus! In addition, the realization will be at a pace that is appropriate for the client to receive it. Obviously.

Finally, if your client has weak boundaries and likes to please others, your interpretations will mean nothing. He or she will agree with everything you say but not seem to be making any progress. It's like a false insight. It's worthless. For those clients who seem to accept everything you say as truth, who are uncomfortable with disagreeing, or who want to please you too much, don't interpret at all. Let the client do the work. You can lead them with some thought-provoking questions, but be hesitant to ever give too much information away.

We believe that interpretation for some of you will be very tempting. I [Leah] am aware of my need to know things and to share that knowledge. If you are like me, beware. You'll find yourself getting way ahead of your client all of the time. It took me years to learn how to slow down and trust that the client can do it at his or her own pace, and that the client's pace, not mine, was the right pace. I guess because I get to show my knowledge by teaching now, I get that need met and don't have to do it with clients anymore. What will be your solution?

Teaching Your Client Too Much

When I [Leah] was in elementary school, I remember playing teacher. I would line up my stuffed animals and dolls in rows like a classroom. I had a big desk up front, and I would tell them what to do. I would usually teach them what I learned in school that day. However, I never thought that I should teach as a career. I was too young to think about it then. At 12 years old, after overcoming some challenges in my life, I decided to be a therapist. That was the path I pursued. During my master's-level training, I kept getting feedback from my supervisors that I was teaching my clients all the time, and I needed to do that less. I didn't know what they meant, really, until I supervised a group of students in my doctoral studies who all happened to be schoolteachers obtaining a counseling degree to become school counselors. Well, I got it then! The client would present a problem. The student/supervisee would teach the client how to solve it. It was so obvious watching it that I nearly laughed out loud. I couldn't believe that I didn't get it before. I had to find a way to take the teacher out of my supervisees and me, and replace the teacher with a therapist.

So what was the problem with teaching the clients too much? Well, when you teach, you are not doing therapy. They are two very different roles. Let's articulate it as clearly as possible. When you teach, your job is to provide information as an expert on some subject matter the person you are teaching. When you do therapy, you are guiding the client to find his or her own answers, not giving the client yours. You see, when you teach, you assume that there is a correct, objective answer to a problem. However, with therapy, correct and objective do not exist. Therapy is a process of discovery. So although you may need to educate your clients on occasion, like the example Jeffrey gave earlier in the chapter, you do not want this to be your primary role. If you have a hard time overcoming the need to teach, like Leah, become a teacher, too. Then you can do it all!

Inappropriate Use of Self-Disclosure

Client: I'm really nervous about starting graduate school. I never thought I was smart enough to get in.

Therapist: I remember when I started graduate school. It was scary for me, too, but in time I realized I belonged.

In this vignette, the therapist self-disclosed with the client to try to ease the client's anxiety, or maybe to make herself seem more human. However, a response like this can frequently have negative effects on the client. The client may not feel heard or understood. He or she may feel patronized or invalidated. Using a self-disclosure in this type of situation was inappropriate. In addition, the therapist shifted the focus off the client. Although you may feel the need to self-disclose similar situations to your client to bridge the psychological distance with your client, to make yourself seem more human, or to demonstrate a way to deal with a problem successfully, you are at risk of minimizing the client's experience. You are at risk for invalidating the client's experience. You are at risk for making it about you. The client in the preceding scenario could easily respond with, "Really? How long did it take you to feel like you were in the right place?" Now the focus is on the therapist. How is that helpful to the client? It's not.

So when do you do this? You do it with caution, infrequently, and when you have established a relationship with your client so that the client knows this isn't a pattern for you, to talk about yourself. The best time to self-disclose, though, is for the use of immediacy. For example, if a client is having difficulty with relationships, and you experience your client as abrasive, then when the time is right, give your client the feedback as demonstrated in the feedback section of this chapter. But in all cases, you must develop a strong relationship with your clients first so that they know your meeting with them will not be about you—that it will be about them.

APPLICATIONS TO SELF: YOU'RE ALREADY DOING THIS STUFF

Most people, at some time or another in their lives, have a need to find meaning in what's happening at the moment. It could be trying to understand something as difficult and infrequent as the death of a young family member. It could be something as familiar as trying to understand how what you are learning in a particular class is relevant to your life. So searching for meaning and consequently seeking insight are a natural part of what people do.

You may think that these skills associated with seeking insight are new (or maybe not), but they are things we do naturally in our everyday conversations. The only difference here is that we are articulating each type of response, each intention of what is said with a client. When you talk with a friend, words usually flow (at least we hope they do, because you want to talk for a living). You will find that when you talk with a client, at least at first, words will not flow. You might experience awkward silences, stumble, fumble, and sound much less competent than you actually are. Why? Because now, as a therapist, you understand the power of words. How you phrase something, the words you choose all impose some sort of meaning, all facilitate a certain type of response from the other person. Now, as a therapist, you must choose your words carefully. In an instant, you must read the verbal and nonverbal behaviors of your client, interpret them, connect them with previous discussions, translate them into your own words, decide what direction you want to take, and then finally, still in the same instant, respond appropriately. Scared? Well, that's understandable. But at the moment, you already do this to some extent, unconsciously. We hope in this class you will be more conscious of what you say, when you say it, and how you say it. We assume that you have the potential to learn all of this or you wouldn't have been accepted into your program. Have patience with yourself.

All right. So we're telling you that you're already doing this stuff. You just aren't aware of it; you're not doing it mindfully. Let's look at each one, again, here. Confrontation: Tell me you haven't confronted someone, ever. We didn't think you could. Surely you have been confused about mixed messages from someone. "I thought you said to meet you after lunch, not before." Or perhaps you have received bad service somewhere and complained. "I asked for my meat to be cooked well-done and this is rare." These are all confrontations. What makes it different in therapy is that you have to time it appropriately and word it in a way that the client can hear it. That's the skill aspect that needs to be learned.

Let's take the next one. Disputing beliefs: We're going to guess that you came to this field with a certain level of psychological mindedness. You have probably been exposed to, whether from books or your own therapy, the challenging of beliefs. Sometimes it's a belief; sometimes it's an imprecise use of language. In either case, at some point you must have been told or told someone else that "never" and "always" are unlikely situations. We listed several of these in the chapter. Pay attention to the way people speak, the words they choose. If you do this at home, it will be easier as a therapist. Practicing at home will make hearing distorted beliefs sound off like a loud bell in your head. In fact, if you do this enough, you'll have a hard time not confronting this type of language, even at home.

Next is interpretation. Now, we know you've done this one. You don't think so? Well, how many times has a friend talked about a problem with another person, and you told your friend why she said what she said, or why the other person did what they did. "I know you didn't mean it when you said you didn't love him." "When he told you what to do, he was not trying to be controlling. He was trying to be helpful." That's your interpretation. See, you are doing it. It's simply when you apply meaning to a situation. You probably do this every day. The difference here, again, is that as a therapist, you have a greater sense of responsibility with your client because you are in a position of power, because you are perceived as an expert. So you want to be more cautious in making these interpretations, and thus, more mindful of when you use them.

Providing information was the next skill presented. Well, if you have ever been a teacher or a supervisor, you couldn't escape this skill. "You will be expected to arrive at work at 8:00 a.m." If you have a child, you do this all the time. "Don't touch the stove; it's hot." So, how is this different with your clients? When you provide information, you want to make sure what you want to accomplish can't be done in another way. You are not the teacher of your clients, but their therapist. You want to facilitate their ability to find their own answers. However, in some circumstances, you will need to stop and teach them something. You already know *how* to do this one, it's just *when* to do it that's new.

So far so good? You've done all of the above, and we're guessing you have given feedback to someone before, too. "Does this make me look fat?" I wonder if there isn't a single person who hasn't had to answer that question before, even if you ask yourself. However you responded, you were giving feedback. You probably give feedback of some sort all the time. So what makes it different in therapy? Honesty and tact. Face it. We're not always honest with our feedback. "No, that looks good on you." But as a therapist, you will need to learn this most difficult skill, and we say difficult only because to be honest and tactful can be hard. "That dress doesn't flatter you in the best way possible, but perhaps this other dress will accentuate the best attributes of your figure." Start practicing this at home, if you dare . . .

And now for some silence . . . This is one that probably happens much less frequently than the other skills presented in this chapter. Silence makes us uncomfortable. Many people need to fill the space with talking or the television or with music. Even when we are silent on the outside, our minds are full of conversations. "Oh, no! I forgot to lock the door. That reminds me, I need to have the door fixed on the car. I need to call the insurance company. I wonder if my insurance will go up. I can't afford more bills. Oh, the bills. I need to pay bills today . . ." The conversation in your head can be endless. However, you probably have experienced silence, even from your own head. Think about times when you feel dead tired, and you just stare off into space. Hey! If you're doing that now, *wake up*! Just checking. While this may happen at times, it's not something in a dyad or group that we do easily. So you can practice this one at home, too. Try just sitting quietly for five minutes without any noise or distractions. Then once that seems tolerable, try it with a friend. Then when that seems tolerable, try it in the car with a friend. As you get more comfortable with it at home, you'll get more comfortable with it as a therapist.

Finally, we get to self-disclosure. This can be done in several ways. You have probably joined with a person by saying, "I had a similar experience . . . " or been genuine about your experience, "I didn't think the restaurant provided us with good food or good service." Any time you talk about yourself, you are self-disclosing. In spite of being redundant, we'll say it again. You have been using this skill in your everyday life. However, as a therapist you will do it very differently. In your private life, when you self-disclose, you do so for you, to talk about yourself. As a therapist, you only self-disclose when it is helpful to your client. So, you'll have to think before you disclose to make sure you are speaking for the client's benefit, not your own.

There they are: seven skills. You have used each and every one of them. The only difference is that, as a therapist, you will use them in a conscious way to facilitate the growth of your client. We hope you are beginning to see that you already have these skills, but you merely need to refine them and know when to use them as a therapist.

SUMMARY

In this chapter, we introduced some ideas about insight and whether it is necessary and/or sufficient for effective therapy. Some skills and techniques were presented to facilitate insight. However, these skills can be used during any part of the therapeutic process. The skills included confrontation, disputing, interpreting, providing information, giving feedback, silence, and self-disclosure. The next chapter continues with more skills, but these skills may more often be used to facilitate the action phase of therapy.

A CHECK ON WHAT YOU LEARNED

For the first seven responses, what type of skill is the therapist using?
1. "You think that no one believes in you?"
2. "There are several factors that may be affecting your problem with sleeping. For example . . . "
3. "You said you don't have any friends, and yet you have lunch plans with different people each day."
4. [Therapist says nothing, but waits for the client to finish crying.]
5. "You say you don't understand why your family thinks you try to please people too much. However, in session I have noticed that you have yet to disagree with anything I've said, no matter how absurd."
6. "The relationship with your husband sounds a lot like the relationship you have with your father."
7. "I have really enjoyed our time together in therapy, and although I'm sad that our time is coming to an end, I'm also excited that you feel ready to terminate."

8. True or false: People can have insight into their behavior and still, insight isn't enough to facilitate behavioral change.
9. What is the consequence of inappropriate use or overuse of self-disclosures?
10. What is the difference in how you have always used these skills in your personal life versus how you will use them as a therapist?

SUGGESTED READINGS

Anderson, W. T. (1990). *Reality isn't what it used to be*. San Francisco: HarperCollins.

Ellis, A. E. (2001). *Overcoming destructive beliefs, feelings, and behaviors*. New York: Prometheus.

Evans, D. R., Heart, M. T., Uhlemann, M. R., & Ivey, A. E. (1998). *Essential interviewing: A programmed approach to effective communication*. Pacific Grove, CA: Brooks/Cole.

Gergen, K. J. (1991). *The saturated self: Dilemmas of identity in contemporary life*. New York: Basic Books.

Gergen, K. J. (1997). *Realities and relationships: Soundings in social constructionism*. Cambridge, MA: Harvard University Press.

Mander, G. (2000). *Psychodynamic approach to brief therapy*. Thousand Oaks, CA: Sage.

Rosen, S. (Ed.). (1991). *My voice will go with you: The teaching tales of Milton H. Erickson*. New York: W. W. Norton.

Schneider, K. J., Bugental, J. F. T., & Pierson, J. F. (2001). *The handbook of humanistic psychology: Leading edges in theory, research, and practice*. Thousand Oaks, CA: Sage.

Yalom, I. D. (2000). *Momma and the meaning of life: Tales of psychotherapy*. New York: HarperCollins.

CHAPTER 8

Facilitating Action

J ust as all clients are not ready or interested in insight, the same can be true with taking action. You may reach a point in the helping relationship wherein increased awareness of self-understanding takes a period of time to percolate. There is a period of indwelling, or reflection, of taking stock to process what was learned. The client, at this point, may elect to stop the sessions for a while and then return later. If the degree and depth of insight generated are more than the person can comfortably handle, he or she may decide to stop treatment altogether. This does not mean, by the way, that progress ceases; on the contrary, some of the most important work that clients do is accomplished on their own.

Transition From Insight to Action

With most of your clients, it will be appropriate and useful to spend some time helping them to convert their new understandings into some constructive action. This may start with a few important questions.

Therapist: So what?

Client: Excuse me?

Therapist: Now that you understand that the reason you've had so much trouble committing yourself to a long-term relationship is your fear of rejection, what are you going to do about it?

Client: What do you mean?

Therapist: I'm asking you what you intend to do to put what you've learned into action. What are you going to do now that you understand what is going on?

This client is being challenged to examine the implications of his new self-knowledge. The work can very well stop at this point, but it is highly unlikely that entrenched, chronic patterns of interpersonal behavior would be altered by awareness alone. After all, lots and lots of people understand that certain things are bad for them but they keep doing them anyway. And many clients may have attained perfect clarity about what is wrong, and even how to fix it, but they still follow through on precious few of their commitments. This is not just because they may be lazy or afraid, but because they just don't know how to convert what they've learned into action. It is your job to help them make this transition.

Exercise in Not Being Ready

In small groups, talk together about times in your life in which you have realized that you needed to do something but you weren't ready to take action yet (perhaps such a process is going on within you right now). What did it take in order for you to move to the next level and follow through on what you know you needed to do but were reluctant to do?

Exercise in Taking a Risk at Home

We all like to do what's comfortable and predictable. When you go to a restaurant, you probably order the same dishes every time. In order to understand how scary taking a risk can be, go to a really good restaurant and don't choose what you want to eat. Tell the server you will have whatever the chef recommends most and to make it a surprise. Of course, if you have a small limitation (i.e., no fish), that's fine, but choose a place to go where you won't have many limitations at all, if any. If that seems too scary to you, go to the movie theater without seeing what is playing or when it is playing. Just decide to go at a certain time, drive there, and see the next movie that is on, especially if you have never heard of it. If you are too familiar with movies, see a foreign film. When you get back to class, process with the other students what that was like.

DEALING WITH RESISTANCE

We give you fair notice that this is not ordinarily a smooth, effortless transition. Clients don't just respond to our urgings for action by saying, "Okay, what should I do and let's get going?" Even if they do say such a thing, they probably don't mean it. And even if they do mean it (at the time), that doesn't imply that they have the skills and sustained motivation to put their desires into action.

The Gestalt paradigm suggests that all clients are resistant—that overcoming resistance is the purpose of therapy (Perls, 1969). Without resistance, there is no need for therapy. So, it is a normal process. Helping clients overcome resistance is the therapist's job.

A case could be made that there really are no resistant, difficult clients, only difficult therapists (Kottler, 1992). In other words, most clients are doing the best they can to be cooperative under very threatening circumstances; it's just that the ways they are choosing to cooperate are different from what the therapist expects and prefers.

The very first thing that beginning clinicians (and many experienced ones) do when the results are not positive is to blame the client for being resistant and ornery. Often we call them names and assign them scary-sounding diagnoses (especially "borderline") as a way to explain their obstructive behavior. Most of the time, these individuals really are trying to work with us in the only ways they know how. Granted, we may find these "cooperative" behaviors counterproductive and annoying, but they nevertheless represent the person's best efforts at the time.

TABLE 8.1

Forms of Client Resistance

Withholding Communication	Restricting Content
Being silent	Making small talk
Making infrequent responses	Intellectualizing
Making minimal responses	Asking rhetorical questions
Engaging in rambling	Digressing

Being Manipulative	Violating Rules
Discounting	Missing appointments
Being seductive	Delaying payment
Externalizing	Making improper requests
Forgetting	Displaying inappropriate conduct

This is not to say that clients do not engage in behavior that obstructs the progress of therapy, because they do (see Table 8.1). They do this for several reasons: because they don't know better, because it keeps you from getting too close, because it slows down the pace to manageable levels, because they feel empowered, and so on.

When dealing with any form of resistance, the first thing we want you to realize is that these clients are not doing this to make your life miserable. This is often not about you, or even what you are doing, or not doing. Sometimes, however, clients start out cooperative and therapists make them difficult through bungled skills and misjudgments.

Second, identify the source of the resistance. Look in several areas, such as the quality of your relationship and the trust level established. Consider the "secondary gains" the person may be enjoying. These are the benefits that result from remaining stuck, such as the power the person may feel at destroying things on his or her own terms or that the fear of the unknown involved in change is scarier than remaining the same. A certain amount of comfort is involved with what you know. Remember, as well, to consider the pace of progress—you may be moving faster than the client can handle.

When facing resistance in one form or another, you have a number of options that include some of the following:

1. Stop doing what isn't working and try something else.
2. Put boundaries in place and set limits more consistently.
3. Don't over-personalize what is happening but accept responsibility for your share of the conflict.
4. Demonstrate greater flexibility in your methods.

Sometimes there are very good reasons why your clients may be resisting your efforts to push them toward action. Maybe they aren't ready to go where you are guiding them. Pay attention to the signals they are giving you; unless you honor their pace and needs, you will find yourself leading way out in front. Alone.

TABLE 8.2

A Few Models for Promoting Action

Theoretical Framework	Skill Employed	Example
Cognitive	Assigning homework	"What can you do in the next week to convert your insight into action?"
Behaviorism	Setting goals	"What is the first step you can take in learning to assert yourself?"
	Reinforcement	"You feel really good about asserting yourself last week."
	Relaxation	"Take a deep breath, and close your eyes right now. Tell me where you are holding tension."
Psychodrama	Role-playing	"Talk to me as if I was your mother. What would you say to her now?"
Gestalt	Working with the resistance	"You are afraid you will get out of control if you allow yourself to be angry. Keep holding in your anger to be safe and tell me more about losing control."
	Empty chair	"In one chair, play the part of you that wants to get married, in the other chair play the part of you that wants to stay single."
Psychoanalytic	Transference	"You are very frustrated with me, as you have been with your father, for confronting you about being constantly late."
Individual psychology	Acting "as if"	"Right now, act as if you are emotional."

So now that you have in mind the reality of resistance, we would like to introduce some techniques that are helpful in the action phase of the counseling process. Table 8.2 indicates some of the techniques and theoretical orientations from which they come. As in previous chapters, the skills here can be used throughout therapy. However, these skills are more advanced than some of the others previously mentioned. For instance, in a Gestalt approach most practitioners don't see resistance as needing to be overcome but rather as an opportunity to look at something more deeply and to work with it as an ally.

We realize we are giving you a significant amount to learn. You may feel overwhelmed at the idea of learning even more skills when you have already been introduced to so much. But our goal is to expose you to some of the techniques you can master while seeing clients. For this course, your primary focus will be to learn how to perform a good intake, become proficient at providing empathy through the use of reflections, and probably from this chapter, learn to set good goals with your clients. All of the others will develop at their own pace, in your own time. So, be patient with yourself. As we said before, learning the skills to become an effective therapist is not as easy as people may think.

SETTING GOALS

The first step in any action plan is to establish goals. You have already done so as part of your overall treatment plan. In this stage of the process, you are doing a reassessment with clients. After exploring the nature of the problems in depth, and promoting some degree of greater awareness and understanding of what has been going on and why, clients are asked what they would like to do to put their insights into action. Often this involves both short-term goals, those that can be accomplished before the next session, and longer-term goals that are to be attained by the end of treatment.

There are a variety of things that you might help clients to do as an extension of their sessions. These might include writing assignments (keeping a journal), reading assignments (books, articles), social interactions (initiating conversations), behavioral tasks (study skills), lifestyle changes (exercise program), or other activities. (For sources, see Rosenthal's [2001] book of favorite homework assignments by the most prominent practitioners and the *Journal of Clinical Activities, Assignments, and Handouts in Psychotherapy Practice*).

Teaching Goal Setting to Clients

As a general operating procedure, many therapists save the last few minutes of every session for asking clients to summarize what they learned and then guiding them to declare what they intend to work on before the next meeting (Beck, 1976). Depending on how insightful and skilled your clients may be, this can take just a few minutes or half the session. There is usually some period of training involved in which clients are taught how to think in this way. Over time, they will learn to automatically ask themselves the following questions:

- What happened in the session today that was significant and meaningful to me?
- What did I learn that I didn't already know?
- What part of the discussion am I most interested in working on during the next week?
- How can I translate what we talked about into something specific that I can do this week?
- What am I prepared to report next week that I have been able to accomplish during the intervening time?

> **Exercise in Learning**
>
> *Apply the questions just listed that clients ask themselves at the end of their sessions. Ask yourself what you have just learned in this chapter that you didn't yet know. What do you intend to do differently now that you realize these things? What are you going to incorporate into your behavior from now on? What are you going to do today that puts this into practice?*

Like most of the other therapeutic strategies, setting goals is a learned skill that takes considerable practice. It is very challenging to help clients to translate what they have been talking about into constructive things that they are prepared to do. It takes a tremendous amount of sensitivity, diplomacy, and creativity to help people move beyond the talking stage to the action stage.

When helping people to set goals between sessions, you will wish to keep in mind several factors. Effectively set goals should be mutually negotiated; as specific as possible; realistic within time constraints and the client's ability; measurable, so you can determine the extent to which the goal was reached; and relevant to the core issues discussed (Hackney & Cormier, 1994).

Negotiating Mutually Determined Goals

The first and most important thing to keep in mind is that all goal setting should involve a partnership (Hackney & Cormier, 1994). Both of you should be actively involved in determining what will be done between sessions. This requires a degree of negotiation and subtle shaping because clients are not very good at this process initially. You must resist the urge to prescribe goals for your clients, as they will be much less committed to following through on the tasks if they are viewed as homework assignments given by an authority figure.

Therapist: What do you want to work on this week?
Client: I don't know. What do you think I should do?

Rather than falling into this trap of doing the work for the client, the therapist shifts back the responsibility.

Therapist: Let's see if we can figure this out together. First, let's review what you realized today and what you want to do about it.
Client: I'm not really sure. Maybe something about my parents bugging me too much.

Because clients don't know how to do very well what we are asking them, it takes patience to teach them these skills. The therapist needs to help this client expand her vision of what happened.

Therapist: That's true. We did talk about your parents and how they treat you. We also talked about a number of other things like the difficulties you have had throughout your life telling people how you feel. This has been true not only with your parents but also with your best friend.
Client: I guess so.
Therapist: So how else would you summarize the session?

The therapist avoids the temptation to do all the work and instead helps the client to share the load.

Client: Well, I did say how disappointed I am that my parents—okay—lots of people sort of walk all over me. And you pointed out that this may happen because I let it happen. I don't assert myself.

With the summary completed, the therapist next moves to convert this insight into a goal that can be worked toward.

Therapist: Back to the question I asked earlier. Given that you have difficulties asserting yourself with your parents, your best friend, and others, how could you make progress toward your goal this week?

The therapist is gently but firmly leading the client to declare something that she can do during the week that will get her closer to her ultimate goal of being more assertive. It is extremely important that this process be structured in a mutual way so that client feels invested in the outcome.

Imagine what you would say to this client if she returned the following week and said: "Um, sorry, but I just didn't have time to do what you told me to do this week."

If you had prescribed the homework, or it was even remotely conceived of in that way, then clients can act out, rebel, or lash out toward you by failing to follow through on what you told them to do. Sometimes they just never return because they feel embarrassed about not completing the assignment. But if, on the other hand, you clearly reinforce the idea that this is *their* task that they have *chosen* to do, then you have a lot more leverage.

Therapist: No need to apologize to me. This was something that you said you had wanted to do. I guess you changed your mind.
Client: I really wanted to do it. Really. I just didn't get the chance.
Therapist: I notice that you are defending yourself to me and that is not necessary at all. Whether you follow through on your commitments or not, I will continue to support you. Maybe what you learned from this is that you shouldn't say you are going to do something unless you are certain you can follow through.

By emphasizing the mutuality of the goal setting, the therapist makes it clear that the client is the one who is responsible for completing the task. Therapy goes as fast, or as slow, as the client is willing to go.

Structuring Goals That Are Attainable

Another common mistake that beginners make is allowing clients to develop goals that are not reasonable or realistic. Sometimes people become so enthusiastic about changes they wish to make in their lives that they get carried away. In other cases, it may be a lack of experience that leads them to declare goals that are not reasonably attainable within the time parameters established.

Let's say the young woman mentioned in the previous section decided that she wanted to become more assertive with her parents and best friend. She might easily agree that in the very next week she was going to stand up to them and not let herself get pushed around anymore. That is a very admirable objective but one that is not very practical considering that she has been so chronically unassertive in the past. She would need to set intermediate steps on the way to her ultimate goal.

> *Client:* I was thinking that when my friend, Emi, tells me that we're going to a movie this weekend that I would just tell her that I won't go.
> *Therapist:* I'm wondering if you have ever done that before with Emi, stood up to her in that way?
> *Client:* Sure. Well, not exactly.
> *Therapist:* So if you did all of a sudden stand up for yourself in this way, Emi might find it sort of strange. She might not understand what it is you are doing and why.
> *Client:* I guess so.
> *Therapist:* My question for you, then, is how could you set this up with Emi in small steps so that you might prepare her better for the new ways you want to negotiate this relationship?

The therapist is helping the client to scale down her expectations. Rather than going after her goal all at once, and perhaps setting herself up for disappointment or failure, it is often preferable to move a little at a time in the desired direction.

When you ask clients what they want to work on between sessions they will sometimes set ludicrous goals for themselves. Someone who wants to start an exercise program will say that he intends to go to the gym every day for the next week and work out for a minimum of 45 minutes each time. He might very well be able to do this, but if for some reason he skips a day, or cuts a workout short, he may believe that he has failed in his commitment and become discouraged. In this case, it would be your job to get the client to agree to a much more attainable objective—perhaps going to the gym three times during the week instead of every day, and doing a session for 20 minutes rather than 45 minutes. If this goal is easily reached, then it can be raised slowly each subsequent week.

Developing Specific Assignments

Goal setting is a holdover from behavior therapy that emphasizes the importance of therapeutic tasks that are measurable, observable, and specific (Hackney & Cormier, 1994). You may not be as concerned with the first two criteria but it is often advisable to develop goals that are rather specific. That way the client knows exactly what has to be done, when it should be done, with whom it should be accomplished, in which circumstances, and with what consequences. This increases the likelihood that the client will do what was agreed upon and makes it easier to hold the person accountable.

If a client says that he is going to try to do some exercise in the next week, that is a lot different from saying: "I will go for a twenty-minute walk at least three times during the next week. If for some reason, the weather makes it difficult to get all three walks in—and I can't imagine that it would—then I will substitute one twenty-minute session with an aerobics video." This would be a very simple commitment to check out.

Your job is to help clients take fairly complex, abstract, general struggles and convert them into specific therapeutic tasks that can be completed in weekly segments.

Exercise in Setting Specific Goals

On your own, or in a small group, translate these fairly general client goals into more specific homework assignments that could be reasonably completed within a week's time:

- *"I want to stop feeling so stressed and anxious all the time."*
- *"I want to lose weight."*
- *"I'm going to start telling people what I really think."*
- *"I'm going to start studying more."*
- *"I'm going to try to work more efficiently."*
- *"I want to feel better about my marriage."*

Not all client concerns that are brought up in therapy necessarily lend themselves to specific homework assignments, or even structured goals. For instance, some clients may bring up more existential issues related to finding greater meaning in their lives or wanting more life satisfaction. These may not readily translate themselves into a homework assignment.

In other cases, you may inadvertently perpetuate continued self-defeating behaviors for those who are already overly goal oriented. Imagine you are working with a client who works as an electrical engineer in charge of quality control for a company. He attends each of your sessions with a clipboard on his lap to take notes. He brings to each meeting a list of things he wants to talk about, and as each one is covered, he puts a neat checkmark by the item. He ends every session by asking you what he should do the following week, then sits poised with a pen ready to write down the instructions and dutifully follow them through.

At first, you are impressed with his organizational skills, determination, and motivation to get the most from therapy. He is a model client, you think, ready to do most anything you ask of him. The problem, you realize, is that he is seeking help in the first place because of impoverished relationships. His wife is ready to divorce him because she is so sick of his controlling, restricted behavior. His kids rebel against his attempts to impose his notion of an ordered universe on their lives. So when you conspire with him to develop additional structured tasks for his life, you may be inadvertently reinforcing exactly the behavior he most needs to change. For this man, the best thing might be a distinct lack of goals and homework. What he needs most in his life is learning to live without specific objectives.

Make certain that the kinds of goals you help your clients develop are consistent with what they really need most.

Exercise in Goal Setting as a Group

1. *Ask people to think of specific areas of their lives that they would like to work on and make progress toward. Ideally, these would be the kinds of things that lend themselves to small, incremental goals: homework assignments.*

2. *The focus of your group is to have each member declare some goal that he or she is prepared to work on during the next week. These goals will be committed aloud to the group before it ends.*

> 3. *Make the goals realistic and attainable within the time available.*
> 4. *The goals should be reasonably specific so it can be determined whether they were reached.*
> 5. *The goals should be relevant to some core issue rather than just a goal for its own sake.*
> 6. *Make sure the goal is self-declared rather than prescribed by others. People are far more likely to follow through if they came up with it themselves. Don't let group members assign goals to others, but rather to help one another develop them.*

GENERATING ALTERNATIVES

After goals have been delineated and agreed upon, the next step is to help people make initial progress toward their objectives. One thing that gets in the way of this is the client's belief that options available are limited. Sometimes people feel stuck because they don't see other ways that they can get their needs met.

In the following dialogue, the therapist uses several skills you have already learned to promote greater understanding of how alternatives have been limited in the client's life. From there, structure is introduced to increase the number of options available for taking action.

Client: I don't see that I have a choice about what I can do. My job requires me to be at the office at least sixty hours per week. I work out every morning before I go in. I volunteer to work at the church on Sunday afternoons. I've got to take care of my two dogs; they need to be walked several times a day. So I just don't see that I have any time left over for a social life.

Therapist: That's fine if this is the life you want. But we've been talking for the last several weeks about how badly you want more friends in your life, and how you'd like to be married and raise a family. I'm not sure how that can possibly happen if you aren't willing to make yourself available to meet and spend time with people. [confrontation]

Client: Good point. But what am I supposed to do?

At this point, the client is trying to get the therapist to solve her problem, which is not going to happen. (Well, it better not.) Instead the therapist is determined to help her generate other alternatives and, if necessary, to supply prompts and suggestions that might get her to think more creatively and proactively.

Therapist: The way you have framed the problem, you don't have any extra time available. Another way to look at this is that your priorities don't reflect what you say is most important. [reframing]

This reframe defines the problem in a way that allows for more personal control and flexibility. If there is really no time available, no place the client can cut back, then there is no sense talking about other options since there are none possible. But if, on the other hand, the client agrees that she has made certain choices in her life that limit her own options, then she can make different choices.

Client: That may be so, but I still don't see what I can do.

Therapist: Let's pretend that you were starting over. You are beginning a new job. You have no commitments—no pets, no volunteer work, no appointments, no other responsibilities. You could structure your life any way that you wanted. What would this look like?

The therapist is helping the client to visualize a life with more freedom, more options. The insight that would hopefully be generated is the idea that being trapped is a state of mind. Once the client is willing to acknowledge that she has no time available because of the ways she has overprogrammed her life, she will be far more motivated to look at other alternatives.

Therapist: Assuming you could make some different decisions about how you spend your life, what could you do instead?
Client: I'm not sure what you mean. I can't very well stop walking my dogs. That would be cruel.

It is a common response for clients to resist looking at other alternatives. After all, if this were easy, then they wouldn't have sought help in the first place.

Therapist: Okay, rather than looking at what you don't choose to change, let's concentrate on what is possible.

Notice the language the therapist uses to emphasize the choices involved and to focus on what can be done rather than what cannot be changed.

Client: Are you saying that I should stop going to church and stop caring about my career?
Therapist: I'm not saying that you should change anything at all. This isn't about what I want, but rather it's about what you said you want. Right now, you have yourself in a bind. On the one hand, you say your life feels empty because of a lack of intimacy; on the other hand, you don't seem willing to give up or change anything in order to get what you say you want.

The therapist refuses to accept responsibility for this "circular" discussion in which it is clear the client resists making adjustments. It is important that the client be held accountable for the choices made. A summary statement, and then a confrontation, are used as leverage to say to the client: It's your life. What do you want?

Client: You're right. I really have to do things differently. But I just don't know how.
Therapist: You're frightened that once you clear some space in your life, you won't be able to hide anymore from the emptiness you feel. You've been overstructuring your life so you have no time to feel sorry for yourself, and no opportunity to become involved in a relationship in which you might get hurt. You enjoy being in control, but also feel trapped by this predicament.

This reflection of feeling, restatement, and interpretation become a transition from insight to action. The ball is now in the client's court. She is ready either to return the volley, or let the shot pass her by. At this point, the therapist doesn't care about her shot selection, but just wants her to make an effort to swing at the ball.

> *Therapist:* Assuming that you are prepared to make some changes, let's brainstorm some things you might do. I'm not saying that you have to do these things, just that you could do them if you wanted to.

Working as a team, the two of them together make a list of options, some of which are more desirable and practical than others. During any brainstorming exercise, the idea is to generate as many options as possible. Decisions can me made later as to which ones are the best alternatives. There is a power and freedom that comes with the notion that you have lots of possibilities open to you.

Here is a copy of the list:

- Hire a housekeeper who can walk the dogs.
- Cut back on hours at work and slow down the fast-track career plan.
- Change jobs to one that doesn't require such total devotion and leave so little room for outside interests.
- Talk to her supervisor about ways she could cut back her hours.
- Give up volunteering at church.
- Change her exercise routine from working with a personal trainer to taking a class where she would interact more with others.
- Invite people to lunch instead of eating at her desk alone.

It doesn't matter that much which options are listed, as long as they reinforce the idea that there are many possibilities of what could be done. The power from this action strategy comes from helping people to realize that they can make changes. The goal is not necessarily to find the "right" course of action, but rather to put the client in an experimental mood where lots of things may be tried until a good combination has been discovered.

REINFORCING BEHAVIOR

We learned long ago from behaviorists that if you want behavior to continue, it is a very good idea to reinforce it (Wolpe, 1958). Therapists do this unconsciously and subtly in our work. When a client says something that we particularly like, we nod our heads and smile encouragingly. When clients digress or talk about things that are less interesting, we act and look bored, thereby extinguishing (hopefully) this behavior. If subtle cues don't work, then we become ever more assertive in guiding clients to talk about the things that we believe are most useful.

Most therapists have a list of behaviors that they think are good for most of their clients. This may include such things as sharing feelings, being honest, taking constructive risks, increasing intimacy, and so on. When clients engage in these behaviors we let them know that we are pleased, using social approval as a powerful motivator.

Likewise, when clients engage in behavior that is self-destructive, self-defeating, or otherwise counterproductive, we use reinforcement strategies to try and discourage such future actions. Notice in the dialogue below how the therapist attempts to overtly shape the client's behavior in desired directions.

Client: So we went out, had a few drinks, got a little drunk, and then started trashing this place . . .

Therapist: [frowns, shakes his head]

Client: Well, we didn't mean anything by it. We were just having a little fun.

Therapist: [redirecting] Tell me more about the meeting you had with your boss. You said you were going to talk to her about being reassigned.

Client: Oh yeah. I did talk to her.

Therapist: [supporting] That's great! So what happened?

Client: Well, the bitch said . . .

Therapist: [looks startled]

Client: I mean, my boss—and you gotta admit she can be a real hardass sometimes—didn't really want to talk about it.

Therapist: I'm really proud of you that you found the courage to approach her about it. Even though things didn't work out this first time, you showed that you have options other than sitting around waiting for things to happen. I wonder if there are other places in your life where you might do something similar.

Rather than allowing the client to focus on his disappointment, the therapist reinforces the effort. Thus success is defined in terms of things within one's control (taking a risk) rather than the outcome (how others respond).

Whenever clients do things that you want them to continue, you must find ways to support and reward this behavior; whenever they do things that you don't think are good for them, it is important to let them know that as well. Essentially, you are using your power and influence to guide them in directions that are good for them.

Exercise in Guiding Your Clients

1. *Talk about the ethical and moral implications of therapists deciding what is good and bad for their clients. Do you think there is a way to avoid this predicament? Would it be desirable to do so?*
2. *Which behaviors are you aware that your instructor attempts to reinforce in your class? Which specific actions are supported and which ones are discouraged? Supply specific supportive examples.*
3. *Make a list of behaviors that you would like to encourage in most of your clients and those you would hope to discourage.*

USING ROLE-PLAYING

One way to conceive of the value of therapy sessions is that they provide a laboratory for experimenting with new behaviors. If talking is often not enough to promote lasting changes, then opportunities must be provided for helping clients to practice what they are learning in a safe environment and receive helpful feedback for improving their effectiveness.

Role-playing involves far more than a few skills. It actually can be classified as its own style of therapy with a complex set of procedures. Although it is beyond the scope of this book to teach you all the therapeutic techniques and strategies, there are a few generic skills that are part of this modality.

J. L. Moreno (1987) and the other creators of psychodramatic methods had in mind a vehicle that would allow clients to work through unresolved struggles and rehearse alternative ways of dealing with situations. Although often used in group formats because of the increased opportunities for dramatic enactments, interpersonal engagement, and multiple sources of feedback, role-play can be used in any form of treatment from family to individual sessions. Here are some examples of when role-playing might be employed:

1. A client is angry at a family member and wants to work through this conflict.
2. Someone has unfinished business with a parent who died many years ago.
3. A client who is extremely intellectual and emotionally restricted wants help being more expressive.
4. A client has extreme fear of speaking in public and wants to rehearse what might be said and how she might handle things if she loses her composure.
5. A session has just been devoted to learning ways of being less aggressive and offensive.
6. A client has an upcoming job interview.
7. A client demonstrates ineffective interpersonal behavior that puts people off.
8. A client has not been able to muster the courage to ask someone out on a date.
9. There is considerable ambivalence that arises about an upcoming decision in which both choices seem equally attractive.

In each of these situations, or many others that could be listed, the client would be helped to follow these basic steps:

1. Explore and understand the main problem.
2. Recognize that a situation has arisen where rehearsal and practice of new skills could be useful.
3. Define the skill(s) that will be practiced.
4. Invite the client to set the scene and describe the situation that would take place.
5. Conduct a first round of practice.
6. Debrief the client about what went well and what can be improved.
7. Model alternative ways of handling the situation by reversing roles.
8. Conduct a second round of practice.
9. Provide more feedback and debrief the sessions.
10. Connect what was learned to earlier discussions.
11. Structure homework or a therapeutic task that puts the rehearsed behavior into action.

There are many other variations of this basic structure, depending on the context (group, family, individual session), the setting, client, and presenting problem. Here is an example of what this might look like for the case described earlier of the young woman who felt oppressed by her parents and best friend Emi.

Therapist: Let's practice how this conversation with Emi might take place.
Client: What do you mean?
Therapist: I'll be Emi and you tell me what you might say to her.
Client: [giggles] You mean right now?
Therapist: Yeah, talk to me the way you would to Emi.

This sort of reluctance to get started is natural and normal. Most people feel inhibited and uncomfortable with the spontaneous nature of role-playing. That is one reason why you must feel *very* comfortable doing it in order to put others at ease.

Client: You want me to pretend that you're Emi?
Therapist: Exactly.
Client: But you don't look like her. [laughs]
Therapist: Then show me how she acts. How would she sit? Why don't you be her and I'll be you?

This is called "role switching" and it allows the client to demonstrate the ways the antagonist behaves. This accomplishes several things simultaneously. It gives the therapist valuable data that permit a more accurate and realistic portrayal of the person. It also forces the client to get inside the heart and head of the person with whom she is having difficulty. This in itself can often spark some new understandings and insights.

After the client shows the therapist how Emi behaves, her voice tone, mannerisms, posture, phrasing, and language, the therapist is then better prepared to play the part. One other benefit of this structure is that because the therapist has seen the client for some time, it is likely that he or she can play the client very well. The client then sees herself as the therapist sees her, asking: "Is that what I'm really like?"

Therapist: What do you think?
Client: I don't know. I didn't realize that I seemed that . . . I don't know . . . that assured of myself.
Therapist: Let's see what happens when you just be yourself and I'll be Emi.

After this first round, which almost never goes well because of the client's lack of experience and practice with the new strategies, the conversation can be deconstructed, analyzed, and refined. Adjustments can be made for the next round, and then, finally, for the real-life confrontation that will take place during the week.

Exercise in Role-Playing

In small groups, select one person who will be the client. This person agrees to role-play someone who is involved in a conflict with someone (a family member, coworker, friend). The client will then briefly describe the nature of the conflict, including relevant background and contextual information. Other group members will ask a few questions to draw out the nature of the difficulty. Spend no more than 10 minutes in this exploration.

Select a cast. Someone else in the group will play the antagonist. Members may take on the roles of other characters involved tangentially or directly in the situation. Depending on the preferences of your instructor, you may also take on roles of the "auxiliary ego," which is a kind of inner voice that speaks out loud what the client is unwilling or unable to say.

Role-play a scenario in which the client confronts the antagonist by saying some things left unsaid. The antagonist will respond realistically (and perhaps aggressively) to this first attempt.

Debrief and analyze what happened. Give the client feedback and suggestions on other strategies that might be attempted. Perhaps another member can model or demonstrate what is suggested by stepping into the client's role and trying out the strategy with the antagonist.

After the client has again had a chance to practice alternative ways to deal with this person, everyone can process the experience. Discuss what are some things you need to learn better in order to do this in actual therapeutic situations.

You can appreciate that this sort of action strategy requires a different set of skills than those previously learned. You might still use active listening, interpretation, and all the rest of what you've learned, but this situation requires you to use far more spontaneous, dramatic therapeutic actions. You would definitely require advanced-level training and supervision before you ever attempted to do this with clients.

USING THE EMPTY CHAIR

Fritz Perls (1969) really liked the idea of the psychodrama and role-playing we just discussed, especially because he secretly aspired to be an actor. However, because he was acutely aware of the process of projection, he created a similar technique: the empty chair. In the preceding case, he would have the client role-play both parts at once so that the client could gain a perspective of both positions. The assumption is that the problem isn't with the friend, but rather with the client's projection of the friend, the Emi in the client's head. So what better way to reconcile it than by playing both roles? Let's assume the client's name is Kimberly, and the session might go something like this:

Therapist: Kimberly, you have talked about how bossy Emi can be, and specifically, how she made the decision last Saturday to go to a movie you didn't want to see. Would you like to try an experiment in what it might be like to assert yourself with Emi?

The therapist sets this up when a specific situation arises and the client is in the midst of feeling her frustration.

Client: I don't know. That sounds kind of scary. What do you want me to do?
Therapist: I'd like you to imagine that you and Emi are in this room together. You are in one

chair and Emi is across from you. [moving a chair in front of the client] I will sit behind you to be supportive of your position.

Client: Okay. That seems a little weird. I'm not sure I can talk to an empty chair, but I'll try.

Therapist: Then, where would you like to start? With Emi or as yourself?

The therapist gives the client the choice to start where she feels most comfortable.

Client: As Emi.

Therapist: Then I'd like you to close your eyes for a moment and position yourself the way Emi would sit in the chair. Imagine what she looks like, her body posture, facial expressions, what she might be wearing.

The therapist is getting the client into the role of Emi.

Therapist: Good. Now open your eyes and imagine yourself in the other chair across from you. Imagine how you sit, what you might be wearing, how you might seem to Emi. When you're ready start as Emi, tell Kimberly what movie you are going to see this weekend.

The therapist positions herself by squatting behind the client's chair. The client may begin with a specific experience where a lot of emotion is held back. Once the client says everything she has to say as Emi, she will stop to look at the therapist or just start responding as herself. When this happens:

Therapist: Okay, now sit in the other chair as yourself, Kimberly. Look at Emi from your perspective. What would you like to say to Emi?

The therapist facilitates the client moving back and forth. In most cases, either the client will really see things from the perspective of the other person or she will become emotional and say something in her own position that she was not aware of before. The therapist will not have to do much work from here, but will remain behind the client, wherever she sits.

Using the empty chair is helpful because it removes any projection on the part of the therapist out of either position. Another way to use this technique as well would be to have the client play out two polar opposite sides of herself. For example, in one chair may be the part of the client that wants to have intimate friendships, and in the other chair she will play the part of her that is afraid of getting hurt. Sometimes the therapist will suggest something for the client to parrot (or adjust the statement to fit better) when the client seems to be stuck.

There are a few important points that must be made about using this technique. First, as with role-playing, the therapist must have confidence in asking the client to try this. The first time it's done, the client will very likely feel really uncomfortable, so it's the therapist's job to allay the client's awkwardness. In fact, it's sometimes helpful to briefly turn the attention to how strange it would feel to do this, and be fully empathic to that process before proceeding with the experiment.

Second, the client must be ready to perform this exercise. When is the client ready?

- When the client has discussed the issue a lot.
- When the discussion has filtered down to something specific that can be used.
- When both positions (each chair) are fully formed, whether as two sides of the client or whether the client is clear about how her own position differs from the other person's.
- When the client is ripe with emotion.

One word of warning is that using the empty chair technique can elicit a great deal of emotions. It can be a powerful process. So, you must be prepared to deal with a catharsis that can last for moments or for the rest of the session. However, before employing this technique, you may want to see it demonstrated first, and then practice it a few times under supervision.

Exercise in Empty Chair

Get into small groups or do this as a large class. Place three chairs in the middle and the other chairs in a circle around the inner three. One person will need to role-play the therapist, and another the client. This will work best if the client has a real and current issue to discuss. All others in the group will be observers.

Allow the client to describe a specific situation that isn't working with another person or to describe a specific situation where he or she feels pulled in two apparently opposing directions about some topic. The therapist should primarily reflect and clarify at this point. The more feeling reflections the better.

Once the client has described the story, then the therapist can set up the experiment with the client, and try it out.

After the client has finished the process, allow the client to talk about his or her experience. Then allow the therapist to talk about his or her experience of the process. Finally, allow the observers to offer support, feedback, or describe any realizations they came to by observing the process.

USING THE TRANSFERENCE

Frequently clients come to therapy because of some unfinished business with either one of or both of their parents. Because the therapist is in a position of power as the parent was to the child, sometimes the client will perceive the therapist to be like the parent or will react toward the therapist as if he or she were the parent. Freud (1936) identified this process as *transference*. In classical psychoanalysis, transference is one of the most important processes to help clients, whereas other theories acknowledge its existence with much less emphasis.

At times, the client will transfer his or her feelings toward the therapist that are really directed toward another person. This is an excellent opportunity to use immediacy and provide the safe environment the client needs to express what has been previously held back. The therapist does this by facilitating that negative expression by the client directly onto the therapist, and subsequently, the therapist can respond in a way that is new for the client.

Perhaps, for example, the client was not allowed to be angry growing up, and at some point in therapy, the client perceives that the therapist is inhibiting her ability to be angry. The therapist would invite the client to direct his or her feelings, including his or her anger, at the therapist. Consequently, the therapist would respond by taking in the anger and reflecting back empathy. Thus, the client has a new experience of expressing anger with people in positions of power. Hopefully, this would begin to elicit some healing for the client.

You may notice that this is a form of role-playing. However, instead of being set up in a more artificial way, this process can occur more naturally and without as much inhibition on the part of the client, if well timed. In fact, you may notice how these different theories have applied a very similar technique, but only slightly modified it to fit the theoretical frame. First, transference was born, then role-playing. Finally, the empty chair technique was another modification. Because so many theories and therapists use this type of technique, there must be something to it that facilitates client growth. And in our experience, these processes can be powerful indeed.

RELAXATION TRAINING

Stress! Who is not familiar with it? Well, as a graduate student, we imagine you are quite familiar with it. As a result, relaxation training can be helpful for any client (and for you), to help with many therapeutic goals. Although it sounds good, and yes, we know, you already know you should relax more, but (and your excuses follow). However, the need for relaxation is not only a commonsense idea, it is supported by a significant amount of research and data (Bang & Kim, 1998; Benson, 1975; Davidson & Schwartz, 1976; Khasky & Smith, 1999; Lazarus, 1999; Lazarus & Folkman, 1984; Libo & Arnold, 1983; Lichstein, 1988; Meichenbaum, 1985; Peters, Benson, & Porter, 1977; Smith, 1987, 1990, 2001). Before we talk about using relaxation with clients, though, we must emphasize that it is important that the client has had a physical to rule out any physiological illnesses or problems as a source for whatever symptoms seem to be indicating that stress is the problem.

I [Leah] am a biofeedback therapist and became interested in the area of stress reduction because from 8 years old until I learned biofeedback, I had weekly, if not daily, headaches. I was frequently paralyzed by migraines, pain that is so great that I have yet to experience anything worse, and I've broken bones before. So when I stumbled on biofeedback in graduate school as a way to learn how to relax, I was excited by the possibilities. Once I took a course in it and was forced to relax (sounds ironic, huh?), I found my headaches stopped. In fact, I haven't had a migraine since taking that course. I've learned to relax.

When is the best time to use relaxation with the client? When the client's symptoms could be reduced by lowered stress. And what are the effects of stress? Well, there are too many effects to list them all, but let's just name a few:

- Difficulty with concentration. When you tax your body with constant stress, the chemicals in your brain don't fire the way they do when you are relaxed, inhibiting your ability to concentrate.
- Increased risk of depression. When you have experienced long, pervasive stress, or a short but very intense stressor, the cells in your brain seem to permanently change (from MRIs) in a way that increases your chances of depression.

- Creates problems with your health. Chronic stress lowers the immune system and increases your chances of high blood pressure, headaches, Reynaud's disease, and other disorders.
- Affects your mood negatively. Think about when you feel stressed. You are crankier, have a shorter temper, and can tolerate less. That is because your body is prepared to fight or flee a dangerous situation when under stress. The body doesn't know that you don't need those hormones that cause fight or flight when you are waiting impatiently in line. It produces them anyway.
- Interferes with your sleep. Your body has a goal to maintain homeostasis, to remain the same all the time. If you are stressed most of the time, the body will decide that stress is the new way to be. So when you go to bed at night, your body is still wound up, ready to fight or flee from the phantom monster your body has been running from or fighting all day. Your body forgets how to relax, and you can't sleep.

And there are many others. However, because this is not a class in stress reduction, we'll spare you the details of the many consequences and their physiological bases. Instead, we'll tell you how you can teach relaxation to your clients to facilitate a quicker recovery. And we hope you choose to learn stress reduction for yourself too. With less stress, clients tend to be less defensive, less resistant.

Remember the deep breathing exercise in an earlier chapter. That is a wonderful way to transition your body out of its normal stress state into a more relaxed state. When I [Leah] have seen clients for biofeedback-assisted relaxation, they have sometimes reported that they feel relaxed, but the equipment that I have connected to their hand tells me a different story. Relaxed to them is still, objectively, very stressed out. So, starting each session with a deep breath might at least be a good way to transition from the outside world into this one hour of healing for the client.

Without equipment, the best way to reduce stress is to practice relaxation each day. You will want to start by teaching relaxation to your client in the therapy room. In session, keep soft lighting in your office at all times with relaxing images on your walls. If you have a recliner, have the client recline back with his or her eyes closed. If the client is not comfortable closing his or her eyes, have the client look down to relax the eyes. You might say something like this:

> Start with a deep breath and then focus on breathing normally without changing it. Thoughts may float in and out. Pain or itches may come to your attention. Just acknowledge the distraction and return gently to focusing on breath.

This gets the client started and focusing. The next section is called progressive muscle relaxation. Tell the client when he or she tenses the muscle, not to squeeze too tight. You don't want the client to get a cramp.

> Now, starting with the feet, tense and hold, then relax them. Feel the difference when you let go. [pause] Move up to your calves, and tense and hold, then relax them . . .

You continue up through the thighs, buttocks, stomach, hands, forearms, upper arms, shoulders, neck, and face. Tense and hold each muscle, then relax. Make sure and pause after each group is relaxed so the client can feel the difference. Speak in a slow and soft voice. After the client has relaxed the whole body:

> Now allow your body to take over your attention. If there is a particular area that still needs more attention, focus your attention there. Feel yourself letting go. You may feel very heavy or you may feel like you are floating.

When the client focuses the attention on the body, the client will become more aware of tension he or she is holding. This process does not add tension. On the contrary, it makes the client aware of the tension so he or she can let go of the held tension. Then give the client a minute to enjoy the relaxation:

> I'll give you one minute to enjoy the relaxation, and then I'll let you know when it's time to come out of your reverie.

After one minute:

> Take a deep breath and slowly bring your attention back into the room. Know that you can use this at any time to help you relax. When you are ready, open your eyes and stretch.

The first time or two, the client may not feel more relaxed. However, if he or she practices each day, in a few weeks, the client will notice a significant change in the level of stress throughout the day, not just after the relaxation exercise. In fact, at first, he or she may feel tired after each relaxation session. Later, though, the client will feel more invigorated.

What type of homework can you assign? One recommendation is to purchase a relaxation tape at any bookstore. Listen to it at least three times per week for about 20 minutes. This must be uninterrupted time (no phone, no TV). In biofeedback, we suggest the client does this at lunch or after work. It's more effective than when waking or going to bed each day. In addition, do not fall asleep during this time, because being awake and letting go is more relaxing than sleep for someone who is stressed. Other possible ways for you to relax are:

- Set an alarm for each hour, and for 1 minute, take deep breaths with eyes closed.
- Every time you go to the bathroom, take a little time to stop and breathe.
- Each time you are stopped at a light in your car, practice breathing.
- Take 5 minutes of quiet time before getting up, at lunch, after work, and before bed.

As with other techniques, additional training is highly recommended before performing these in your office. However, taking a few minutes each day is recommended for anyone, with or without training.

USING REHEARSAL AND IMAGERY

Usually, behaviorism gets credit for creating the techniques of imagery and rehearsal (Wolpe, 1958). However, the philosopher Vahinger (1925) first introduced this concept in the 18th century, and Adler (Ansbacher & Ansbacher, 1956) brought it into the field of psychology during the time when Freud was ending his career. Adler called it "acting as if." Behaviorism probably got credit for this technique because the paradigm in behaviorism is that if you change the behavior, you have made real change in the client. Well, how do you change behavior? You just go out there and do it. If you feel artificial in your new behavior, act as if it were true. See the connection?

One criticism some therapists make about behaviorism is that you cannot have lasting changes in the client by simply extinguishing a behavior. If the client isn't ready to change, he or she will replace it with another, probably just as ineffective, behavior. Therefore, in order to use this technique, the client must be ready. Usually being ready means the client has a good grasp on where the behavior originated, how it served a good purpose for him or her for a while, and how it's not working now. The client must have a strong motivation to change. And then the therapist can move the client from the insight into action:

> *Therapist:* We have talked a lot about how you have been afraid to assert yourself because you don't feel like you deserve to have your needs met. Let's now consider what it might look like if you acted as if you believed yourself to be deserving of getting your needs met.

The therapist asks the client to act, to pretend as if it were true. Most likely, the client will fail a few times before changing the behavior, and even then, he or she will feel artificial. So, a good way to ease the client into the process is to start by using imagery. Once the client has a clear picture, then the client can rehearse the new behavior in session. When the client has built some confidence in the therapy room, he or she can go out and practice in the rest of his or her life, with others. During each of these steps, the therapist continues to work with the client on changing the thoughts and feelings associated with resistance to change by using a myriad of other techniques. By the time the client starts using it in the outside world, it will feel less and less artificial, more and more a part of who he or she is.

So what is the best way to introduce the imagery? In biofeedback, we know that if the client's defenses are down, if the client is deeply relaxed, then the imagery becomes more vivid, and the client is able to convert that imagery more easily into action (Peniston & Kulkosky, 1989). Therefore, you will want to have already established a strong and safe relationship with your client. When the discussion occurs to start this process of imagery, work with the client to create a script that is as full of as many details as possible, including reference to each of the senses. Make sure to include an entrance into the relaxation and an exit out of it. Once you have written the script together and your client is ready, have the client sit quietly with arms and legs uncrossed, eyes closed. Start with the deep breath exercise introduced in the earlier chapter. Then once the client is ready, read the script slowly in a soft but audible voice until you end. Then discuss with your client how he or she experienced the imagery. You may need to make some changes to the script that make it more accurate for the client's experience. Do this each week in session, and you may even want to record it for the client to use each day at home. The more exposure to the script, the more quickly your client is able to accept the image. A sample script for the client just described might look something like this:

> Sit in a comfortable position with your legs and arms uncrossed, eyes closed. Inhale deeply and feel the cool air enter through your nose and fill your lungs from the bottom to the top. Then exhale slowly, feeling the warm air move out of your lungs through your mouth.

Using the deep breath tells the client's body that it's time to relax and to focus her attention.

> Now, just breathe deeply and rhythmically . . . notice the rise and fall of your abdomen with each breath . . . in . . . and out . . . in . . . and out. You may notice other parts of your body removing your attention or you may notice thoughts floating in. Without judgment, acknowledge their presence and gently focus your attention back on your breath.

Breathing and focusing on breath brings the client to a more relaxed state.

> Now, I'd like you to imagine a door in front of you. What kind of handle does it have? How does it open, toward you, away from you, or does it slide? When you are ready, open the door and imagine a small staircase with ten steps . . . begin stepping down, and with each step, you become more and more relaxed . . . 10 . . . 9 . . . 8 . . . 7 . . . 6 . . . 5 . . . 4 . . . 3 . . . 2 . . . 1 . . . and now you have reached the bottom, and you walk through another doorway onto a beach.

Introducing some image to transition in and out helps the client move through this process more slowly. In addition, the suggestion of going down stairs and relaxing as he or she descends helps the client go into a deeper trance. The therapist counts very slowly.

> On this beach, feel the sand beneath your feet and the warmth of the sun on your face. Hear the sound of the seagulls and the ocean waves crashing to the shore. Smell the fresh ocean air. See the beauty all around you.

The imagery of the beach helps bring the client to a new place to prepare for a new mindset. Notice that each of the senses are acknowledged in this section.

> In this place, you are confident. In this place you deserve to have your needs met . . . feel what it's like to deserve to have your needs met. You feel wonderful and alive. You feel content and happy. See yourself interacting with an approaching friend. You assert yourself by suggesting you both walk along the beach. Your friend readily agrees and is happy to oblige. Feel how satisfying it is to get your needs met with someone who agrees to your suggestions . . . revel in the moment.

This is the part where you interject the work, what the client wants to accomplish. This is the part of the script where you and your client want to work together to use the best and most realistic wording for your client.

Take one minute on your own. At the end of the minute, I will continue . . . [after 1 minute] . . .

A minute is actually a very long time for silence, and the client is given the freedom to do some of his or her own spontaneous work during this time.

Now find your doorway to the stairs . . . open it and as you ascend the stairs, you will feel more and more awake.

Prepare the client to return.

Know that you can bring with you anything you would like from this experience and leave behind anything that no longer works for you.

This is an excellent statement to help the client transition the imagery into reality.

Ascend the stairs to come back into the room 1 . . . 2 . . . 3 . . . 4 . . . 5 . . . 6 . . . 7 . . . 8 . . . 9 . . . 10.

Count very slowly and bring the client back through the same process he or she entered.

When you cross the door at the top of the stairs, you will find yourself here sitting in the room. Feel the pressure of the chair beneath you. Hear the sounds around you. And when you are ready, open your eyes and stretch.

Once the client is ready, discuss the experience and any modifications that might be needed in the script. You can use imagery without a script, but the brain seems to be more receptive to repetitive learning when the repetition can occur in each session as well as at home each day (Basmajian, 1989).

As with the other techniques, it is important that you get trained properly before you use this. Therefore, take a workshop or training class to get the didactic portion, and then make sure you are supervised the first few times you actually execute it. It is possible for the imagery to be sufficient to cause change, but in other cases, it's only the first step. This is where the rehearsal begins, in session, and then acting as if out of the session. In time, your client will learn a new way to be.

BIBLIOTHERAPY

In the last chapter, we discussed how teaching and therapy are different. Because you want to use the time in session for relational type of work, you may not have enough time to teach your clients certain concepts or ideas that might be beneficial. The alternative is to use biblio-therapy: assigning reading for the client to do on his or her own time. In addition, some time in therapy can be dedicated to the discussion of what homework you have assigned the client to read. This helps the client with accountability, and by discussing the information, the client will be more able to process the information in the most useful way possible.

PITFALLS AND COMMON MISTAKES

Once again, we present to you some of the common mistakes that may occur with the skills we have introduced in this chapter. In addition, some of these pitfalls may be more relevant to this stage of therapy. We hope you can avoid some of them with an awareness of them.

Forgetting to Reflect

We said it in the last chapter, we'll mention it briefly here again. You can get so excited about taking some action with the client and meeting some goals that you may forget to reflect feelings and content, but especially feelings. At every stage of therapy, empathy is needed to help gain insight about the current stage and to continue to strengthen the relationship with the client. Remember, you are only human, and at times, your client will get mad at you or feel hurt by you. As a result, you want to have lots of empathy deposited into the emotional bank account so that withdrawals don't cause you to overdraw your account.

Overpersonalization

Do you have problems taking things personally? Do you assume that when someone is in a bad mood that it's because of you? Do we sound like an infomercial? Well, if you do, then you are overpersonalizing, and if you have difficulty with it in your personal life, you are really going to struggle with it as a therapist. Clients will not show, will cancel appointments, will get angry with you for no apparent reason, or will resist your brilliant interventions to foster change. You may assume it's because you did something wrong. There may be some clients who make little progress despite your best efforts. Is it you or is it them? If, every time, you assume that the undesirable behaviors of your clients are about you, you are probably wrong. Clients may not show because they are afraid of therapy. Clients may cancel because they may really be having a series of challenges that does not permit them to attend. Clients get in a bad mood, and may feel safe enough with you to take it out on you. Clients may not be a good fit for your style of therapy. Clients may be fearful of changing. Regardless of the situation, there will be times that it's not about you. It's about your client. In contrast, there may also be times that it is about you. However, if you take it personally every time, especially without exploring the issue more, then you will feel pretty beat up as a therapist. Clients can be thoughtless, inconsiderate, or resistant, and if they are that way at home, they will most certainly be that way with you. What's important is that you check it out. Get some feedback. Collect some evidence before you take it personally.

Making Irrelevant Goals

In your zeal to come up with things that clients can work on, you may develop goals that meet all other criteria but are relatively unimportant and unrelated to core issues. Some therapists so enjoy feeling reassured by the steady progress of their clients that they routinely assign regular homework assignments, whether they are indicated in every case or not. Some therapists ask *all* their clients to read the same books, complete the same journaling assignment, write the same reflective papers, or undertake the same tasks that are believed to be good for everyone. Although it may be true that most people could profit from more exercise, fresh vegetables, and meditation, that doesn't mean that assigning these activities will necessarily address the presenting complaints.

During those times when it is difficult to come up with a "good" goal, that may be because such action steps are premature or contraindicated. Consulting with a supervisor will help you sort out whether this is the case. In the meantime, don't force goals on clients when they don't seem to fit. In such cases, you can actually diminish or compromise the power of what you have already done together.

Being Impatient

We talked about this earlier in the chapter. So, your client is not moving along fast enough.

> He appears resistant. He says he wants to get better, but he seems to do nothing with the insight he has discovered. He won't change.

Your supervisor may tell you to slow down. You're going too fast. Change is difficult, and there are many reasons why clients don't move as fast as we'd like.

- You are striving for the wrong goal. We discussed this earlier in the book. When you set a goal, that goal should be flexible. Frequently, what the client presents as an initial goal and the goal that is reached at the end of therapy are different. Therefore, you will need to periodically make adjustments to the long-term goal to make sure you are on the same page with your client.
- The goal is inappropriate. The goal can be too big and need to be broken down into smaller parts, or maybe it's not specific enough. In either case, reassess to make sure you and your client are specific about where you are going.
- Some aspect of insight is still missing. Just because the client reaches a level of insight does not mean that the level found is the deepest level. More than any other error, we see that students think that once an insight is reached, the client should be ready to make changes, when, in fact, another layer exists below this level of insight. The deepest layers usually are related to self-esteem issues of not being good enough, not deserving, not being valuable, not being a worthy person, and so on.
- The client needs to get comfortable with the insight first. Perhaps you have reached a deep-seated insight. Reaching there is not sufficient. Clients frequently need to simmer at this level, to adjust to the idea. How often have you accepted something at a cognitive

level, but your heart isn't in it yet? It takes time for unpleasant insights to be fully accepted by your client. Work with the resistance, not against it.

- Your expectations are unrealistic. Sometimes you are just too darn impatient. Clients take a long time to go through this process. This is why we recommend you go through your own therapy, so you can really understand how hard it is to change. It's hard to accept change, and it's even harder to take a leap of faith into the unknown abyss. So go at the client's pace, not yours.

- The client prefers the current pain to the pain of changing. On occasion, your client may have thought his or her old way of being wasn't working, but later may decide that it's better than changing. When the change seems to require too much effort relative to the pain of staying the same, the client is free to decide not to change. You must respect that wish.

- You are not prepared to handle this type of issue. Just kidding. Well, kind of. It is possible that you will be given a client or situation in your training which you are not adequately prepared to handle. You may not even know that you're not ready. In these cases, get lots of supervision and/or refer your client to someone who is more qualified to work with that particular issue. It is better, though, to learn how to work with this type of client if you have the luxury to do so under close supervision. The more you learn, the better prepared you'll be for the next client.

In all of these possible reasons for resistance, you may hear one common theme: Slow down! The client needs more time, more space, more readiness for change. We are all impatient at times, and being a therapist will help you to face this need every day.

Reinforcing Too Much

Intrinsic risks are associated with reinforcement. First, if the therapist is trying to enhance or extinguish behaviors to direct the client to act "correctly," we are assuming the therapist knows right from wrong, what is good and bad. Although the therapist may have expertise in human behavior, he or she is not infallible. For example, the client described next reports in session that he has accomplished his homework from the previous week:

Client: I did what you said to do.
Therapist: What did I say for you to do?
Client: You told me to try to start asserting myself.
Therapist: Um hmm.
Client: So when my wife asked me to take out the trash, I let her know that I couldn't because I was working. I let her know I'd have to do it later, after I finished this project.
Therapist: Good. [nodding her head] How was that for you to assert yourself?

Here the therapist is attempting to reinforce the client's behavior to assert himself more. Although this may have been a difficult task for the client to accomplish, we don't know how it was done. The therapist might be hoping that it was done in a polite and tactful way, but what if the therapist is wrong? The client could have yelled this at his wife. He could have sounded exasperated. He could have used foul language. Although we may applaud the ability to stand up for himself, we can never know exactly how it was done. Six months from now, the therapist may be seeing the couple because the way in which the client learned to assert himself was destructive to the relationship. Therefore, reinforcing a reported behavior may have some less than ideal consequences. So, instead of making assumptions before reinforcing any behavior, the therapist may want to get more detailed information about the entire process to look for any potential warning signs that the new behavior wasn't done in an effective way.

Another intrinsic risk associated with reinforcement is that the therapist sets up an external locus of control for the client. Most people love to receive positive reinforcement, and will do a lot to gain the approval of others. Let's face it: Who is really comfortable with someone disapproving of us or our behavior? We want people to approve of us, and your client is the same way. The client may perform in a way to seek the therapist's approval, behaving ingenuinely. In other words, the client will appear to behave one way in the session, and another outside of the session with the intention to seek approval from the therapist. The improvement the therapist sees may be false. In addition, even if the client is performing in a way outside of therapy that is deemed as positive in the therapist's eyes, who will continue the reinforcement for the client when therapy is finished? No one. Therefore, the therapist has facilitated an external locus of control for the client. What's the alternative?

In person-centered therapy, one of the important conditions to good therapy is for the therapist to provide unconditional positive regard (Rogers, 1951). Most other theorists and most practitioners would agree that unconditional positive regard is an essential component. If the client believes the therapist thinks he or she is a good and worthy human being, regardless of behavior, then the client can feel safe to experiment with new behaviors and allow him- or herself to be completely genuine in therapy. You might say, though, that when the therapist uses reinforcement, the therapist is judging the client's behavior, not the client's worthiness as a human. But how does the client know that? The client may or may not, and that is a risk. So how does one reinforce behavior while providing unconditional positive regard so that the client can establish an internal locus of control? Easy. Let's take the vignette above. Instead of the therapist responding with, "Good. [nodding her head] How was that for you to assert yourself?," setting up an external locus of control, the therapist could say, "You feel really good about asserting yourself." Thus, the therapist is using the client's own internal value system to reinforce the behavior. "You feel good about . . ." "You are really proud of yourself." "You liked what you did." All of these are phrases that reinforce the client's behavior using the client's value system, not the therapist's. We might even suggest that you learn to do this as much as possible in your personal life as well, especially with children.

Not Following Up on Homework Assignments

Nothing can be more irritating to a client than constantly assigning homework, and not following up. If your client made the effort to do the assignment, he or she will be eager to share the results. By not following up, your client may perceive that the homework assignment was not important, or that you don't care enough to remember. In addition, if the client does not complete the work, some important information may be missed by not addressing this potential resistance. Therefore, if you assign it, make a note to yourself to follow up the next week.

APPLICATIONS TO SELF: SHARING YOUR CLIENT'S ISSUES

In this chapter, we looked at converting insight into action. Perhaps the best way for you to really understand how this process works is to look at your life, retrospectively. Make a list of all of the major events in your life that have changed you, whether the change was in how you see yourself, others, or the world. For each event, write out the story of what happened. Describe who you were before the event, how you were in the worst of the event, and how you changed after transcending the event. You will find that in each case, most likely, you experienced a great deal of pain. Think of how much pain it took to facilitate that change. On a scale from 1 to 10, with 1 being no pain and 10 being almost intolerable pain, write down the intensity of pain required for your change for each.

Now think about things you know you need to change about yourself. Make a list. I'm sure you can think of three or four things that you'd like to improve. Pick the one issue that seems to interfere with your life the most. Take that one issue and further list all of the ways that it interferes with your life. Did you include that it will interfere with your work as a therapist? Well, it will. You will inevitably get clients who will either trigger your issue or have the same issue. You will think, "I can't even fix this problem myself. How will I help you?" And yet you can't refer every client who shares your issue. So what do you do? You have to do something so foreign and new to you (or at least we assume this). You have to work on it without the intensity of pain. How do you do that? Well, you're a therapist in training, psychologically minded, and smart enough to be in graduate school. You figure it out. Just kidding. When you are able to answer this question, you will be so much more prepared to help clients with their issues.

We have now given you a large toolbox from which to work with clients. But before you use your tools on them, use the tools in your own life. That is what this section of each chapter has been for, for you to apply these skills in your own life. You will become a better person for it. Your relationships will be enhanced. Life will be sweeter. And you will become a stronger therapist.

I [Leah] say to each of my prepracticum classes every semester that there are a lot of therapists out there working: counselors, psychologists, social workers, hypnotherapists, school counselors, marriage and family therapists, psychiatrists. Some are really, really good. Most are just average. We want you to be one of the really, really good ones. To do that, you must, absolutely must do your own work.

SUMMARY

In this chapter, we have introduced you to some techniques from various theories to help foster insight into action. A significant portion of the chapter was dedicated to good goal setting because it's a necessary part of therapy and must be done well in order for everything else to work. If you don't know where you are going, what do you do? We also introduced you to reinforcement, empty chair, transference, relaxation training, and rehearsal and imagery. We are now approaching the issue of evaluating how you are doing and terminating with your client, discussed in the next chapter.

A CHECK ON WHAT YOU LEARNED

For the following eight client statements, what type of action skill might you use?
1. "There is one part of me that would like to confront my father, but there is another part of me that wants to defend him."
2. "I'm really afraid to tell my friend she hurt my feelings, but I have to do it. I just don't know how."
3. "By the end of my drive home, I'm so wound up from the traffic, I just yell at everyone."
4. "I've been doing my imagery homework each day, and I'd like to try it now."
5. "You are just like my mother; you have to tell me everything I do wrong."
6. "Imago therapy sounds very interesting and may be something that helps me to understand why I keep getting into abusive relationships. Where can I learn more?"
7. "To actually talk in front of a group seems terrifying. I don't think I'll be prepared for it next month."
8. "I was able to ask Janet out on a date last week! I finally had the courage to do it!"

9. True or false: Resistance is something to avoid in therapy.
10. What are three qualities that should be taken into consideration when setting goals?

SUGGESTED READINGS

Cormier, S., & Nurius, P. S. (2003). *Interviewing and change strategies for helpers* (5th ed.). Pacific Grove, CA: Brooks/Cole.

De Jong, P., & Berg, I. K. (2002). *Interviewing for solutions* (2nd ed.). Pacific Grove, CA: Brooks/Cole.

O'Hanlon, B., & Beadle, S. (1999). *Guide to possibility land: Fifty-one methods for doing brief, respectful therapy.* New York: W. W. Norton.

Rosenthal, H. G. (Ed.). (1998). *Favorite counseling and therapy homework assignments.* New York: Brunner-Routledge.

Wiener, D. J. (Ed.). (1999). *Beyond talk therapy: Using movement and expressive techniques in clinical practice.* New York: Guilford.

Wubbolding, R. E. (2000). *Reality therapy for the 21st century.* New York: Brunner-Routledge.

CHAPTER 9

Maintaining Progress
and Evaluating Results

You may not ordinarily consider that figuring out how you are doing with a client is a therapeutic skill, but unless you can do so effectively your efforts are not likely to be very helpful. You must devise ways in which you can determine accurately and consistently the impact of your interventions. You must be able to tell how well things are going. And you must be able to figure out adjustments that need to be made in order to increase the power of your work.

In this chapter we discuss the skills that are involved in evaluating the results of your helping efforts. In other words: How are you doing?

SOME ASSESSMENT CHALLENGES

There are several reasons why measuring the effectiveness of your work is far more difficult than you might imagine.

1. *When you think you might be helping people, they might not be doing nearly as well as you believe*. Therapists cannot judge accurately how well things are going. At times some of your best interventions will fall on deaf ears; other times, you will think the session went horribly yet the client will report it was really helpful.

2. *People lie when they report on their progress*. You can't necessarily trust what clients say is going on. First of all, they might not really know how they are doing but they want to please you so they make something up. Second, because they may not want to let you down, they will tell you things are going a lot better than they really are. Third, they may also play down how well they are doing because they enjoy the benefits of having lower expectations.

3. *How clients are doing in sessions is not necessarily a reliable indicator of how they are doing outside*. Some clients perform like trained seals during sessions—they say and do all the right things, they thank you profusely for how much you helped them, and they repeat exactly what you most want to hear about what they learned. Then they leave the office and don't do a darn thing to change anything. They can

remain in therapy for years like this. If this isn't confusing enough, some clients will perform miserably in sessions, acting uncooperatively, appearing resistant, yet they may be making consistent and significant progress in their lives—without you even knowing what is going on.

4. *Sometimes the results of therapy don't make themselves fully known until many months later.* Some interventions can have a delayed effect that will come out a long time later. After all, how many times have you finally integrated an insight even years after you first were exposed to the ideas? Clients can even leave therapy as supposed treatment fails and then later integrate what was learned.

What all this means is that you must have a *lot* of humility and caution when it comes to assessing the outcomes of your work. There are certainly ways you can learn to become more proficient in measuring the impact of your skills, but part of that development includes understanding the limitations of our assessment tools. That is one reason why you will want to rely on multiple measures of therapy outcomes, including client self-reports, observations of client behavior, therapist intuition, reports by family members and significant others, and objective measurement of specific behavior and declared outcome goals. In other words, the following is *not* an acceptable means by which to measure the results:

Therapist: So, how are you doing?
Client: Just great!

Exercise in Measuring Outcomes

Your instructor has devised several ways to measure how much you learned in this class. These could include submitting audio tapes, videotapes, transcriptions, process papers, and so on. This is a challenging task because it is difficult to get a clear sense of how much you have developed your skills. How do you measure such a thing? Based on how much you report you learn? Based on what the instructor observes?

Meeting in small groups, discuss alternative ways that your therapeutic skills could be measured and assessed accurately. Think of creative ways other than the more traditional methods just mentioned.

SKILLS OF EVALUATING OUTCOMES AND MEASURING RESULTS

It is not so much a skill as an attitude that you are prepared to look at your work honestly. Often therapists and counselors attempt to disown their failures and negative outcomes by blaming the client for being resistant. Unless you are willing to accept some degree of responsibility for your sessions that don't appear to go well, there is little opportunity to learn from the experience (Kottler & Blau, 1989). In fact, bad therapy can actually be your best teacher, especially if you are willing to look at your role in the poor result (Kottler & Carlson, 2003).

In order for any assessment skills to be of use, you must be prepared to examine outcomes as objectively and honestly as possible. This takes training, of course, but also a degree of commitment. This is the only way that you are going to improve your skills.

Self-Monitoring Strategies

One of the most logical ways to assess how therapy is going is to make the client responsible for this task. This means teaching clients to be assertive consumers and to look objectively at how things are proceeding. This could be introduced in the following way:

> It is your job to let us both know the extent to which the therapy is meeting your needs. Ultimately, you are the best judge of this since you must live with the consequences of what happens. After every session, you must ask yourself the questions: Did you get what you wanted? To what extent have you made progress towards your self-declared goals? Ultimately, you will want to know: Is this working for you?
>
> In order to make this assessment on a regular basis you will want to monitor carefully the progress of our work as it unfolds. It even helps to collect some data systematically, which means that you will want to measure the results on an ongoing basis.
>
> I must warn you that progress does not always proceed in an orderly, sequential way. There will be relapses. There will be times when progress may be slow. But there should be some improvement within a reasonable period of time.
>
> I am dependent on your feedback in order to customize what we do in here. I don't watch you in your world outside of sessions. I can't tell what you are really thinking and feeling inside, only what you report to me. I don't know about how well (or how poorly) things are going. We must spend considerable time in here talking about what is working for you and what is not. It does little good if you complain to others about your dissatisfactions and frustrations; you must bring them in here so we can review them together and make adjustments as they are needed.

With an introduction similar to this, the therapist is educating the client about how important it is to work together to review progress on an ongoing basis. There are several means by which clients can help with this process.

Journaling

Keeping a journal in therapy is *not* like keeping a diary in which events are merely recorded. In the best possible circumstances, journaling becomes an extension of therapy, an integral part of the process in which clients continue their work on their own. In a sense, journaling eventually becomes the therapy once regularly scheduled sessions are stopped.

Pennebaker (1990) wanted to measure the effects of journaling, and did an interesting experiment that suggested that journaling had benefits. He had asked people who had been laid off of their jobs to participate in his study. Group 1 did the usual outplacement work receiving advice on how to look for a job, interview, or write a strong resumé. Group 2 received the outplacement services, and they were asked to write for several days about their experience of being laid off—in most cases, how angry or resentful they felt about being laid off. Both groups received about the same number of interviews, but the second group was given offers more quickly than the first group. One possible explanation for this was that the group who journaled were able to express negative feelings, helping them to interview better than the group who did not journal those feelings. In another interesting study, he had university students write about their feelings toward someone with whom they felt infatuated. He found that after writing about their infatuation several times, their interest in the other person waned significantly more quickly than for members of a group who did not journal and only talked about their infatuation. Therefore, there may be something to this journaling thing.

Like any other skill, clients don't know how to journal effectively. It is not enough to simply ask people to do this. Remember, if it is merely an assignment that you give to them, they will not feel all that committed to doing it on a regular and consistent basis. You must "sell" the importance of this structure and emphasize how critical it is to the work you are doing together. Basically, you can say that therapy takes as long as the client wants it to: if it is preferred that things move more quickly and efficiently, then clients must have a way to continue the work between sessions.

Like anything else you teach to clients, it sure helps if you can practice what you preach. In order to encourage clients to use this self-monitoring structure effectively it is preferable that you speak from personal experience—meaning that you keep your own journal on a regular basis to process your continued growth and development.

There are several different kinds of journal entries that clients can initiate, each of which complements what you are doing in sessions.

Progress Notes. Just as therapists keep progress notes on sessions, clients can construct their own narrative about what was covered in each meeting. Clients can even be encouraged to bring their notes into the session and review them as part of the check-in at the beginning of the session.

> Today we talked about the ongoing problem I have asking for what I want. As usual, I tended to overgeneralize and say that I do this with everyone but it was pointed out that I could assert myself pretty well with my friends (except for Dorrie). The main area that I have to focus on is related to my family. We looked at how I learned to be this way and drew some connections to the way my parents were raised according to a similar pattern in which the role of women is to serve men. We looked at how this belief continues to interfere with the relationship with my husband and my son. I agreed that I would talk about this with my mother this week and find out more about these so-called family legacies.

Critical Processing. This is a further (and deeper) process analysis of what is transpiring in therapy and how the person feels about it. The objective is to be as honest and frank as possible, about one's own behavior, about the therapist's actions, and about the way sessions are going. If "progress notes" are mostly descriptive, then these types of entries are much more critical.

All in all, it was a pretty good session but a painful one. I noticed that I defer to my therapist just like I do with others. There were several times when I agreed with him just because it was easier and I didn't want to disappoint him. I can tell he gets upset with me when I don't move as fast as he wants. I realize this is part of the same pattern that we were discussing. I plan to say something to him about this next time.

Insights. Journals can used to keep track of new understandings, new insights, things that the client wishes to remember and hold onto. Entries might include particular ideas that are memorable, metaphors that seem especially useful, quotes that are especially powerful, or anything else worthy of remembering.

That was pretty interesting the way my therapist pointed out how my expectations set up my disappointments. As long as I have such insanely unrealistic notions about what I want from people I will never get what I want. I set them up to fail me. I need to remember the Zen idea about staying clear and centered, expecting nothing, and then being delighted with whatever life brings me.

Goal-Setting. It is often useful to write down both short-term and long-term goals as they arise in sessions. Journaling about them is a way to commit oneself, in writing, to follow through on what was declared. Clients are held accountable for what they declare they wish to do. These written goals also help them to track progress.

For the first time, I heard myself say out loud that I am not happy in my job and want a change. So, what that means is that I need to make some changes even though they really scare me. What I told my therapist is that I want to try something else, something different from what I'm doing. But it's really much more than that. I'm afraid to say it to anyone, but what I'd really like to do is go back to school and get another degree that would finally allow me to do what I've always wanted to do.

I suppose the first step would be to look into what programs are available. I've also got to figure out my expenses to see what I can afford. In the short-run, though, I've got to start making plans to cut down my expenses so I can afford to live on less income during this transition.

Exercise in Journaling

If you have not already done so, begin a journal of your journey as a therapist in training. Record several times a week what you are learning, what you are struggling with, and what you want to remember. List areas of weakness that you intend to work on. Explore unresolved personal issues that are triggered by the work you are doing. Write down feedback you are hearing about your interpersonal and helping skills. Discuss what puzzles, confuses, excites, and interests you the most. Write about what frightens you. Talk about the transformations in your personality, your behavior, and your relationships that you are noticing.

> *Make an effort to write at least a page every day, or at least several times each week. Examine your resistance and excuses for avoiding or postponing your journaling. Talk about that with your instructor or classmates.*
>
> *Remember that you cannot in good conscience ask your clients to do something that you have been unable or unwilling to do yourself.*

Recording Progress

If a journal is a narrative about the therapy experience, and progress that is being made, then other more objective means can be used to record progress. Clients can be taught to graph their progress in cases where specific behaviors have been identified as in need of change. They can be encouraged to plot their weekly successes and failures as they unfold. Depending on the nature of the presenting complaint, and how specifically it may be defined, the client may be directed to monitor changes in behavior.

A couple comes to therapy because they fight a lot. In fact, they fight so much and so loudly that neighbors complain and sometimes the police are called in to intervene. Although things have never escalated to the point that any physical abuse has taken place, the verbal sparring and screaming are quite toxic. This couple is difficult for anyone to be around very long because they bicker so much of the time.

An initial assessment determines that the couple is quite committed to staying together and neither one has entertained serious thoughts about leaving the relationship (although they quite often threaten divorce). They enjoy a satisfying sexual relationship and have many interests in common. They don't even seem particularly bothered by their fights—it is more a problem for others around them.

The therapist has encouraged them to keep a detailed record of when the fights occur and to include: (a) the time of day the fight took place, (b) how long the skirmish lasted, (c) what they were fighting about, (d) what happened right before the fight began, and (e) how the outcome of the dispute ended. They were each asked to keep separate records and then compare them at the session. Not surprisingly, they started to fight about what constituted a fight.

The therapist intervened to keep them on track and negotiated a consensus on their record from the previous week. They found that they had a total of 41 "fights" during the previous week, averaging more than 6 per day (one of the days they hadn't been together at all so there were no fights recorded).

You can appreciate that the act of looking at their fighting behavior would already have had an impact on the pattern. The process of examining carefully what they were doing made them more aware of what they were doing. Furthermore, it is hard to have a proper war with one another when one or both people are busy taking notes on what is going on.

Using 41 fights per week as a baseline, the couple was responsible for keeping score on their "performance" during the ensuing weeks. They were thus able to measure changes that occurred as a result of several different interventions that took place. For instance, when they were asked to schedule all their fighting during specific intervals of time that were prearranged, the frequency went down to less than 30. When they were taught other ways of handling dispute resolution, the number went down further. After each session and a different method of disrupting their pattern, the results could be measured. This allowed both the therapist and the couple to assess what was working and what was not.

As it turned out in this case, the best strategy was actually the assessment process itself. The couple became much more aware of their behavior to the extent that they couldn't engage in fighting anymore without it being labeled. They would fight about that too, of course, but the frequency and intensity of conflicts steadily decreased to one-third the previous levels (but alas, still not eliminating the fighting completely).

Exercise in Recording Your Own Progress

In previous chapters we have asked you to keep copies of your tapes and the associated feedback of your sessions. For at least three tapes that are spread apart as far as possible, review 10 minutes of each one to assess your level of improvement. Score yourself on a scale from one to five as follows:

1. *Poor.*
2. *Needs improvement.*
3. *Satisfactory.*
4. *Good, above expectations.*
5. *Excellent, far exceeds expectations.*

Score each of the tapes on the following areas:
Nonverbal:

1. *How are your facial expressions (congruent with the client's content)?*
2. *Evaluate your eye contact (good, but not staring).*
3. *Evaluate your body posture (relaxed but professional).*
4. *Do you use minimal encouragers appropriately (vocal)?*
5. *Evaluate whether you are nodding appropriately.*

Building the relationship:

6. *How frequently are you reflecting?*
7. *How well are you reflecting content?*
8. *How well are you reflecting feelings?*
9. *How are your reflections (depth of understanding)?*
10. *How are you using questions (open-ended questions and infrequent)?*
11. *How are you at conveying unconditional positive regard?*

Facilitating insight and action:

12. *How are you at working at the client's pace?*
13. *How are you fully exploring emotionally laden content?*
14. *How are you at taking risks (trying interventions other than reflecting and questioning)?*
15. *How are you at avoiding advice giving?*
16. *How are you at avoiding overteaching?*
17. *How are you at using the skill of interrupting the client?*
18. *How are you at confronting your client?*
19. *How are you at disputing beliefs?*
20. *How are you at disclosing appropriately?*

> *Once you have assigned numbers to each, add the numbers for your total score in each category and then total the categories for a final score of your tape. The higher the score, the better you are doing. If you want a more objective opinion, have the classmate that may be role-playing your client do this for you. Look at your totals to assess where you have improved most, and where you still need to improve. You can receive a maximum score of 100, but at this level, we might expect your most recent tape to be around 80.*

Transcription Exercise

One of the techniques we use in our classes is to have counseling students transcribe about 10 to 12 consecutive exchanges between themselves and their clients. After each helping response, the student looks at the response, identifies its intended purpose, and determines how it could have been improved. We then ask beginners to write a better response and support why the new response is preferred. In addition, the student is required to write how many of the following responses were made: reflection of feeling, reflection of content, open question, closed question, summary, giving information, providing feedback, supportive (saying "That's good" or "I'm proud of you"), silence, small talk, giving advice, and directing client behavior.

Try this activity on your own (with a partner or volunteer client). Record a conversation with someone in which you attempt to be as helpful as possible. Following the guidelines just described, transcribe parts of the session and complete the activity by noting how you could have improved on your helping responses. We realize, of course, that this requires a colossal commitment of time and effort. But then who ever said that learning to be a fine helper was going to be easy?

Discourse Analysis

Another way in which you can evaluate your progress is by completing a discourse analysis. A discourse analysis also requires that you audio tape your session on occasion and transcribe it, but this time you transcribe the session completely (Steiden, 1993). After transcription, look for repetitive words, phrases, or meanings used by you or the client. You can look for trends from the client to find something you might have missed in session, or you can look for trends in how you typically respond. Evaluating what you and your client says within a single session or over two or three consecutive sessions will help you to see trends you might not see in the moment and will make you aware of how you might improve your work with your client.

Continuing Education

You may already know that once you receive any license or certification, continuing education will be a requirement to maintain that credential. Why? For three primary reasons. First, attending conferences will expose you to new research about the effectiveness of certain techniques as well as to changes that may occur in the field. It is important to keep up-to-date.

Second, by attending conferences, you can learn new ways to work with clients and consequently become a more effective therapist. Many of us can be quite creative in coming up with
new ways to help clients; many of us are more likely to only perform those techniques that we
have already learned. In either case, exchanging ideas about new ways to work with clients
increases our repertoire of skills, making us more prepared to work with the clients we do have,
and also prepares us to work with new populations unseen. Finally, at conferences we can
develop new relationships to help support us, whether for consultation or just for fun.

Consultation

As just stated, one of the reasons that going to conferences and workshops can be so valuable is
that you can develop relationships with other professionals in your area. As you meet people
with whom you have respect, you can develop a consulting relationship whereby if either of
you gets stuck with a client, you can discuss it together to get a fresh opinion. Consultation is
not only helpful, though, when you get stuck; it is also helpful just to make sure you stay on
top of things with your client. We can often get into ruts in the way we do therapy or look at
clients, and a fresh perspective can help us to grow and prevent burnout.

Supervision will become a large part of your weekly professional development, not only in
your skills but in conceptualizing cases. The eventual goal of these consultations is for you to
reach a point where you naturally and consistently engage in self-supervision to supplement
your sessions with other experts (Morrissette, 2002).

Exercise in Getting the Most From Supervision

*Just as learning to be a good client takes practice, so too does learning to get the most from
supervision. Before you begin the kind of intensive supervision that will be part of your later
clinical courses and field placements, it would be highly profitable for you to speak to experienced practitioners and supervisors to get their advice on the best ways to use these consultation services. This is not as easy as it sounds because you may very well feel a certain
amount of ambivalence talking to a supervisor who may serve multiple roles as your confidante, advisor, tutor, and counselor, but also as your evaluator who decides on your continued suitability for the profession. How much should you share with your supervisor about
your fears, your feelings of inadequacy, your self-doubts, your mistakes and misjudgments?
It all depends on the trust you feel in the relationship and whether you believe the supervisor is acting in your best interests.*

ENDING THERAPY EFFECTIVELY

Therapy can end in one of several ways. A judgment can be made about whether it ended
successfully or badly. Another way of looking at closure is whether it was done according to
plan or took place prematurely. You might think that successful endings might always be related to how intentionally and strategically the relationship was terminated, but that is not
necessarily the case.

The reality is that many clients you will see simply stop coming. They may cancel an appointment and never call back to reschedule. You can't necessarily assume this relationship ended unsuccessfully, or even that there was more work to be done. Some clients just have trouble saying goodbye so they may initiate this process by walking away without looking back. A case could be made that it is, in fact, a very successful outcome. The problem, however, is that you may never find out what happened. And you have to live with that uncertainty.

One of the things for which therapists are often singularly unprepared is how to deal with failures and disappointing endings (Kottler & Blau, 1989). Yet learning from our mistakes not only presents opportunities to get better at what we do but is actually quite necessary to prevent further misjudgments in the future (Dillon, 2003). In one study of the worst mistakes of the world's best therapists, it was found that what most interferes with a clinician improving professional competence are such things as overconfidence, arrogance, narcissim, rigidity, and a marked refusal to acknowledge own one's errors (Kottler & Carlson, 2003). It is crucial for you to have a safe place to consult with supervisors and peers about what you've done that did not work, and thereby learn from these failures.

In ideal circumstances, or at least according to the preferred plan, clients are prepared for termination as soon as they begin treatment. This is to minimize dependency issues that may occur, but also to equip clients to understand the natural progression that takes place in the relationship. Often the closure process may take place during the last scheduled appointment, although ideally the whole ending process takes place over many weeks.

Several distinct skills are involved in ending therapy effectively. Many of these closure strategies involve adapting skills you have already learned and applying them to this distinct stage in the process.

Exercise in Good and Bad Endings

In small groups, talk to one another about learning experiences that ended on the best and worst possible notes. Describe a class, workshop, or helping relationship that ended in such a way that the momentum of what you learned continued long after things ended. Describe another relationship where your progress ended abruptly as soon as the help stopped. Talk about what made the difference between these two kinds of experiences.

Negotiating Closure

There are several different ways that termination issues may be addressed. In one scenario, clients may state that they are ready to end; in another, the therapist suggests that sessions be stopped in the near future. Regardless of who brings up the issue, there is usually some form of negotiation involved in deciding when therapy will stop. Remember that both parties will have some difficulty letting go of a relationship that has been so significant, intense, and intimate.

Client: I've been thinking lately, that uh, um . . .
Therapist: Go on.
Client: Well, I was kind of wondering if, maybe, if I don't need to come back anymore.

Therapist: You're feeling really good about the progress you've made and thinking that the time is ready to start preparing for going out on your own.

Client: Yeah. What do you think about that?

Therapist: Well, for one thing I'm feeling a bit sad because we've gotten very close to one another, but on the other hand, I'm really excited for you that you are feeling confident enough to deal with things more on your own.

Client: I'm feeling a little uneasy about this too. But I think I'm ready.

Therapist: I do too! So let's talk about how we can best bring our work to a close.

In this case, it might only require another session or two to complete the therapy and then work toward closure. With other clients, you may need many weeks to facilitate this process. It all depends on the client, the amount of work left to do, and your mutual assessment of where things stand.

Summarizing Themes and Reviewing Content

Some time is spent toward the end of the relationship helping clients to put things in perspective and reviewing what they have learned. This is a time to ask them to compare where they are now to where they started, and also to consider the extent to which they have reached their previously stated goals. Such a process would look something like the following:

Therapist: This is our last session, at least for awhile.

Client: Yeah.

Therapist: I'm wondering what you have been thinking and feeling anticipating our meeting today.

Client: Well, kind of excited actually. It has been a long haul.

Therapist: Yes, it has been a tough journey for you.

Client: I'm also feeling kind of sad.

Therapist: It's hard for us to say goodbye after having spent so much time together talking about such intimate things.

Client: I kind of wonder what it's going to be like without coming here every week.

Therapist: I'm going to miss seeing you as well. We've been through so much together.

Client: For sure.

Therapist: I'm looking at you now and remembering what you were like when we first met. You remember that first session?

Client: [laughs] I wish you wouldn't remind me.

Therapist: Seriously, what were you like then compared to what you are like now?

So far, the therapist is checking out how the client has been feeling anticipating the last scheduled session. This would provide clues as to whether the person is truly ready or not to move on. In this case, the client seems to be feeling a healthy balance of sadness and exhilaration. Notice that we say "seems to be," because you can't know for sure what is going on merely from listening to client reports. From observing this client, it appears as if his behavior is congruent with what he is saying.

Although the therapist touches on their feelings toward one another, before pursuing that further he or she would like to dig deeper into what was learned from the therapy.

Client: Well, I can hardly recognize myself now. I'm just not the same person anymore.
Therapist: Say more about the specific ways this is the case. Exactly how are you different?

By asking the client to articulate how he is different, the therapist is continuing the process of assessing the outcome.

Client: For one thing, I don't complain and whine so much anymore. I've accepted that there are some things I can't change no matter how much I would like this to be the case.
Therapist: You are referring to your previous efforts of trying to get your boss to change rather than concentrating on what you could do to respond to her differently.
Client: Absolutely.
Therapist: How else are you different?

Again the therapist presses her client to define, as specifically as possible, what is different now. This is an excellent way to get the client to articulate what has been accomplished, and does so in a way that they can end on an upbeat note.

Next on the agenda is to ask the client to summarize the main work that was accomplished. Clients are generally not that skilled at covering all the material so the therapist would be free to fill in what was missed.

Client: I'd say that I have more patience now than I used to. I don't seem to get so frustrated with people when they don't do the things I'd prefer.
Therapist: I like the way you said that: "the way you would prefer." That implies that you remember that you can't make people behave a certain way, and just because they don't comply with your preferences, that doesn't mean you can't accept this and take care of yourself.
Client: Yeah, but I still get upset when my daughter doesn't listen to me. I mean, for God's sake, she's only 15 and already she thinks she's an adult.
Therapist: Let's hold off on that for a minute and get back to what else you've learned.

The client starts to move into other things that are not fully worked through, but the therapist redirects the discussion back to the high points first. In the next stage they can talk about further work that needs to be done.

Client: Well, that thing you taught me to do so I don't get so stressed out at work.
Therapist: You mean the relaxation training?
Client: Yeah.
Therapist: Okay, what else?
Client: I don't know. I guess that's about it.

Now it is time for the therapist to fill in what the client left out. This will prompt further review by both parties to list as many things as possible that were accomplished in their sessions together. Some therapists may take notes and write down what is listed during the review or, better yet, ask the clients to do so. Some other clinicians may record this last session and give the tape to the client as a parting gift. This acts as a reminder of what they did together and what is left to do.

Identifying Unfinished Business

No matter how many weeks, months, years, or even decades spent in therapy, there will always be things left unfinished. Human beings are just so infinitely complex that it is impossible to cover everything that needs to be addressed. But if the therapy has been effective, then clients have internalized the skills to continue work on their own. It could be said, in fact, that the ultimate purpose of therapy is to teach clients to be their own therapists.

This stage of the closure process involves helping clients to assess the work that is left to be completed. It is sort of an inventory taken of goals that still need to be reached and continued work that must be followed through.

Therapist: You were saying before that you still have trouble dealing with your daughter, especially when she is so strong-willed.
Client: She can be so stubborn sometimes. She won't listen to anyone. It drives me crazy.
Therapist: She sounds a lot like you in many ways.
Client: [laughs] I guess that's true.
Therapist: So, you still have some work cut out for you in handling conflict in your relationship. We've also discussed how a certain amount of disagreement between parents and their adolescent children is not only normal but also healthy. You remember why?
Client: Well, you said it's because it helps them to separate from us.
Therapist: That's what I said. What do you think?

In reviewing one unresolved issue, the therapist is giving the client a quiz of sorts, asking him to repeat what he has learned and reminding him of what he must practice doing in the future. It is usual that there would be several areas of unfinished business to identify.

Client: No, I agree with you. It's just that it's so hard to remember this stuff when she starts ripping into me about something.
Therapist: Of course it's hard. But that's not to say that you can't make things proceed in a way that is less upsetting to both of you.
Client: Right.
Therapist: What else is left over?

The therapist continues to dig with the client into areas that have only been marginally excavated. The goal is definitely *not* to stir things up more, especially at this late stage. Rather, the objective is to remind one another about potential trouble spots that might arise at some later time. The client may elect to return for follow-up sessions, but far better is to apply what was already learned to new situations. After all, if transfer of learning is to be successful, the client must adapt what he already knows to other challenges.

Therapist: So, let's say that your daughter comes home from school today and tells you that she doesn't feel like doing her homework and she's going out with friends.

Client: Please don't remind me. I can feel a headache coming on just thinking about it.

Therapist: Then let's stop for a moment and you can practice your relaxation skills.

Client: Very funny. I guess what you're reminding me is that what I do with my boss I can do with my daughter as well.

Therapist: And not just with your daughter, but anyone with whom you find yourself in conflict.

During this phase of closure, the therapist structures time for the client to review not only what has been done, but also what is left to do. This leads logically to planning for the future work.

Constructing a Plan

Based on the nature of the unfinished business, a specific aftercare plan should be developed that provides alternative support and structure needed. You cannot just close therapy with a client and expect that things will end happily ever after. After the initial feelings of elation and relief, there may also be strong feelings of abandonment. Even when therapy has gotten into a rut, when the conversations are repetitious, there is still the advantage of a regularly scheduled appointment to review on progress. When that ceases, the client may lose momentum because he is no longer held accountable.

The therapist and client together structure a plan of action for continuing the work left to do. This might involve referral to a support group, but may also involve looking at alternative ways that the functions of therapy can be met elsewhere. Examples of this might include regularly scheduled meetings with friends, journaling, attending classes or workshops, reading books of a particular nature, continuing exercise programs, and so on.

Saying Goodbye

This might sound like the simplest of steps but is actually among the most difficult. You have spent many hours together talking about the most intimate things imaginable. There is a lot of ambivalence tied up in this relationship that is now coming to an end. You want to say goodbye on an upbeat note, but also one that acknowledges the bittersweet nature of any ending.

Just think about entering into the most intimate relationships with people, learning their deepest secrets and darkest fears. You spend hours together, talking only about meaningful content. You develop emotional attachments to one another; you even come to look forward to your meetings. An even more complicated factor is that if you are in private practice, you might also be dependent on the income clients provide. Then, one day, it is time to say goodbye, perhaps forever. You may act like this is no big deal, as if this sort of thing happens all the time (which it does), but that does not stop the pain and loss associated with ending a relationship— even if it is for the best of reasons.

Scheduling Follow-Ups

You will want to leave the door open for further issues that may come up in the future. It is also considered sound practice to schedule checkup sessions that are designed to make sure the client is continuing to make steady progress. In the same way that a surgeon will want to see patients a few weeks or months after a wound has healed, just to make sure that the mending has continued, therapists and counselors will do the same.

Follow-ups can be handled in a number of ways. You might schedule another session a few weeks or months thereafter; you may even have started to taper off the frequency of sessions from weekly to biweekly to monthly as a way to minimize closure trauma. Another possibility is that you could send follow-up letters or make an aftercare phone call just to check to see how things are going and communicate your continued interest and care. You would want to be careful not to give the impression that you are pressing the person to return—merely that you want him or her to know that you are still in his or her corner.

Handling Relapses

The best way to prevent relapses is to plan for them because some degree of backsliding is inevitable. Programs can be implemented to plan for and prevent relapses (Kottler, 2001b). Several steps are involved in this process, each of which requires its own set of skills.

1. *Identify high-risk situations.* Help the client to recognize those situations that will be the most tempting. Someone who has worked on controlling his anger may realize that he is in special jeopardy for relapsing when he drives alone in rush-hour traffic.
2. *Identify triggers.* What has set the person off in the past? A woman has tended to feel bad about herself whenever someone comments about her appearance.
3. *Develop coping skills needed to deal with these situations.* Prepare clients with whatever behaviors they need to deal with the challenges they will face. In the first example, the man may need anger management and stress reduction techniques. In the second case, the woman may need to learn self-talk methods to counteract perceived criticism.
4. *Rehearse responses.* Whether through imagery, fantasy exercises, or role-plays, it is a good idea to help clients to rehearse how they will respond in potential relapse situations. The man with anger control problems may be asked to imagine himself caught in a traffic jam and then be guided through ways he can respond as an alternative to blowing up.
5. *Practice new skills.* Before the therapy ends, you will want to structure opportunities for clients to deliberately slip backward so they can prove to themselves they have the power and skills to recover at will. We are not saying that you should urge a recovering alcoholic to have a drink, but rather that you should help the person to practice putting himself in stressful and challenging situations (going into a bar) and then dealing effectively with the temptations.
6. *Generalize to new situations.* Help your clients to apply what they have learned with the

presenting problem to other areas of life. The woman who can talk to herself effectively to counteract criticism from others can also use this strategy in other situations she faces.

7. *Build resilience and adaptability.* The one thing that you can count on is that things will change. Clients will face new challenges they had not ever considered. They will encounter difficulties that were not planned for. Help clients to prepare for surprises so they can recover with minimum interruption in their continued growth.

8. *Increase frustration tolerance.* Help clients to deal with disappointments and setbacks in such a way that they become minor annoyances rather than major disruptions.

9. *Develop support systems.* Build in sources of support that can be available as needed. These could include self-help groups, sponsors in 12-step programs, friends and family members who will pitch in, and referrals to other professionals.

10. *Make needed lifestyle changes.* Assist clients to make alterations in their routines in habits in such a way that they encourage and support changes that were made. These might involve significant changes in friendships, social activities, spending habits, and so on.

11. *Learn from mistakes.* Remind clients that setbacks and failures are inevitable and unavoidable, yet they don't have to represent significant difficulties as long as you recognize what is happening and learn from the mistakes.

Exercise to Reflect on Failure

In order to help clients to make the most from their mistakes and learn from their failures, it helps if you are skilled at doing the same. No matter how skilled a therapist you might be, how well-prepared and trained you are, how experienced you become, how good your supervisors might be, you will still face situations where you can't help people to the extent you would prefer. Some of your clients will leave unhappy customers. Some will even become worse no matter what you try to do to help them. And somehow you must learn to acknowledge your limitations and weaknesses as a clinician if you ever hope to get better.

In small groups, talk about some of your most disappointing failures and regretful mistakes in your life. Share what you learned from these experiences and how they made you stronger and more skilled in the future.

Talk to one another about some of your fears and apprehensions related to making mistakes in your work. How do you intend to work through these blunders when it is often not safe to admit your imperfections and lapses to others?

PITFALLS AND COMMON MISTAKES

In this last chapter before approaching work with families and groups, there are only a few common mistakes we see with beginners. However, because endings are just as important as beginnings, you will want to attend to avoiding these pitfalls as well.

Forgetting to Evaluate Your Progress

Several reasons exist as to why a licensed therapist might cease to obtain supervision. While you are in school and during your internship for licensure, you will be required to be evaluated at least once per week individually and/or as part of a group. Sometimes these evaluations are quite formal. At other times, evaluations will be done surreptitiously while your supervisor listens to you talk about your cases and reads your case notes. However, once you are licensed, supervision is no longer a requirement. In fact, unless you work for an agency, obtaining external supervision at your skill level is difficult at best. Even if you work for an agency, your supervisor may not be looking to help you improve so much as making sure your clients are not dissatisfied. As a result, many practitioners get comfortable working with their clients without supervision, and unless they have difficulty with a client, they cease to get supervision. They forget. What's worse is that after not having supervision for a long period of time, the practitioner may become somewhat insecure about his or her skill level and fear receiving any supervision, imagining that another professional will discover that he or she is an imposter, not a good therapist at all. And so a terrible cycle begins of not obtaining supervision.

A more dangerous situation is when the therapist loses all humility and believes him- or herself to be an excellent therapist, not needing to improve on any skill or become educated in any new areas. Typically, if a therapist finds him- or herself in this position, the therapist will frequently become burned out. This therapist can lose why he or she came to this field in the first place. The person will feel stagnant and bored, thankful when a client no-shows or cancels. If a therapist believes that each client becomes a burden, it doesn't seem likely he or she will be able to provide good therapy.

Furthermore, seeking to evaluate your performance requires that you be able to receive constructive feedback (i.e., criticism) throughout your career, which can be quite difficult at times. Therapists cycle through feeling competent and incompetent, whether with or without supervision. At first, you may feel incompetent because this is a new skill. You may be more forgiving of yourself as a trainee until you feel like you have finally mastered the first level of skills. Then you feel competent, good about your abilities. An event happens, such as you see someone else's work, you receive a new supervisor, whatever, and suddenly, you feel incompetent again. It's difficult. Many students don't always realize that they are now trying to master a more advanced skill level, and feel instead that they are starting from the beginning. They are quite hard on themselves. So after cycling through this a few times and receiving a license, a therapist may feel too raw to receive any more supervision; this is especially true if the supervision he or she received was inadequate, where the supervisor only offered information about weaknesses without also pointing out strengths. Obviously the reverse can also be just as dangerous, where the supervisor only points out strengths without regard for areas for improvement. The therapist may falsely believe he or she no longer needs to evaluate progress.

Finally, even if the therapist would like to obtain supervision after licensure, doing so requires some additional work and, consequently, time, a valuable commodity. Finding creative ways to self-supervise or to consult without losing confidentiality is difficult and time-consuming. Obtaining information from your clients in session can take away time from your client's need to talk. Assessing information outside the session takes time away from other activities. So what does a therapist do? Many therapists just don't do anything, which is rather sad for the clients who see those therapists. Many therapists may just become mediocre at helping clients. However, you can be different. You can become a phenomenal therapist if you continue to evaluate, if you commit to taking the extra time and effort required. If you truly intend to change one life at a time, you must be open to continual evaluation. Your clients will be happier, and so will you.

Terminating Prematurely

In some situations, terminating with your client may be unavoidable. For instance, while you are in school, you may only have one semester with a client, who will need to be referred to next semester's students if he or she is not ready for termination. When you leave an agency from your internship to start earning an income, you may have to terminate prematurely. These are situations that are not preventable. Yet, you can let the client know in advance and work within these limitations.

However, even without these externally imposed systems, you may find yourself terminating prematurely. When?

- *When you don't particularly care for a client because he seems like a difficult case for you.* For instance, imagine a client who has a history of domestic violence and is sent to you by the probation department, for anger management. He may yell at you, take absolutely no responsibility for his outbursts, and resist your best attempts to help him. He continues to come because he is require to stay if he wants to keep out of jail, but he's not that committed to changing. As you can imagine, clients who are involuntary can be quite challenging, but you must find a way to work with them. Perhaps you won't accomplish a lot, but for those clients with whom you do, imagine how rewarding that progress could be: much more fulfilling than the easy client.
- *When you find the client triggers a countertransference feeling in you.* Just imagine that you are going through a difficult period in your marriage. Your wife just can't keep a job, yet she spends money like it's going out of style. You have tried everything at home to be supportive and yet be assertive to take care of your needs. Then a client comes in who says she is frustrated with her spouse because he won't let her spend money on new clothes for a new job she just started. Your client has always known that her husband was conservative with money, but this just feels ridiculous to her. As you listen, you find yourself aligning with the husband. Your questions are leading in a certain direction. You can't be objective; you're too angry with your own wife to even see this client's perspective. You are aware enough to know that your own issues are getting in the way. What do you do? Refer? No, you work on it. You are experiencing a countertransference, a situation that happens in therapy when your client triggers something in you similar to another relationship in your life (Kohut, 1984). The best way to combat this reaction, and it will happen, is for you to receive your own therapy or obtain supervision or consult with another professional. You cannot refer every client who has money problems. You must get help. So the bad news is you have to work on your own stuff. The good news is that you aren't likely to become stagnant with your problem and may

even find an acceptable solution. And by overcoming yet another challenge in your life, you will grow personally and professionally.

- *When your client has vastly different values than you that may even be offensive to you.* Let's assume you have grown up in a conservative Christian environment with strong Christian values. A client comes to you and says that the reason he needs therapy is because he can't seem to find a woman to whom he is attracted. Through the process of therapy, he comes to realize that he has always been attracted to men, even as a child. What do you do if you believe that homosexuality is wrong because it is against your religion? Do you try to convince the client it is a choice? No, you realize your ethical guidelines require that you not impose your values. Do you try to convince your client to become asexual? You realize that's not likely to work. Do you refer? Maybe, but we hope not, because you realize that by you referring, the client may be hurt by your rejection because you have already established a therapeutic alliance. Instead, we hope you can learn to see the world through your client's eyes, see from his phenomenological perspective, and work with your client from that foundation, not from your own. If you can master this skill with something so extreme, imagine how much better you will be as a therapist. You will really enhance your empathy skills with as little of your own projections as humanly possible. And just imagine how wonderful your clients will feel and how they will foster your ability to not only really see them, but to accept them as well.

Your ethical codes state that you can refer a client, when necessary, and you will need to at times (AAMFT, 2001; ACA, 2002; APA, 1992; NASW, 1999). Referrals on occasion are appropriate and in the best interest of you and your client. However, at what point to you stop referring clients? Do you only keep the ones you like, the ones who are psychologically minded, who self-pay, who are responsible, and who work hard? Not likely, because you won't get a lot of people like that. You'll go broke first.

So rather than referring or terminating prematurely, you must continue to do your own work, as a therapist and personally. If you find yourself talking your clients into termination over and over, you may want to take a look at what might be going on. Instead of asking yourself why all of these clients don't want to terminate, ask yourself, what do those clients have in common that seems uncomfortable for you? You may need to take responsibility when you see trends and own your part. Most likely, you will find that you have an issue that needs some attention. If you do, get your own therapy. Therapists who obtain their own therapy are not unusual because the nature of the work requires that you be as healthy as possible. It's normal and natural for a therapist to be in and out of therapy for the rest of his or her career. Therefore, just succumb to the fact that you will probably need therapy from time to time until you retire. You'll be better for it.

Not Reminding the Client of Upcoming Termination

Try to imagine this situation. You having been working with a client for 13 weeks, and it is the end of the session. Suddenly, you remember that next week is your last session together.

Therapist: Well, we have about ten minutes left, and I wanted to remind you that last week
     will be our last session.
Client: What? Next week? But I still have so much work to do. I'm just getting started.

You can imagine how frustrated and betrayed the client might feel. She is totally unprepared for termination. Even if she has a week to think about it, she may not return because of
her anger. Worse, she may regress, knowing that her primary support will be taken away in
only one week. How is she to cope with such short notice? And now she has a new issue,
abandonment!

As stated earlier, sometimes you know in advance that you will need to terminate with
your client on a predetermined date. When you first meet with the client, you should let the
client know that your time with him or her is limited so that she can decide if she wants
therapy with someone more long term. In addition, by your letting the client know in advance,
he or she can be well prepared when the time for termination approaches. Having a predetermined date may even be an advantage because the client realizes he or she must get the work
done within a prescribed amount of time. The client can't take his or her sessions with you for
granted.

The client should also be reminded of the termination date at least three sessions in advance so that the client has time to process the information. In the last few weeks, you may
want to give your client sufficient time to discuss his or her feelings with you so that you can
say goodbye well. Saying goodbye is something we don't always do well, even when the feeling
is mutual. Furthermore, if your client has some abandonment issues (and who doesn't to some
degree?), then you will want to help your client find new ways to cope with the parting. By
mistakenly not providing the client with sufficient notice, you may exacerbate the client's issues and never know the consequences.

Stringing the Client Along

So, you finally made it. You have had your license for years, and you have had a booming
private practice. But then the economy changes and people are getting laid off of work right
and left. Your best clients can no longer afford the luxury of therapy because they are unem-
ployed, like thousands of others. You have only a few clients left who self-pay, and you know
that most of your HMO or insurance-paid clients will only have six sessions. How will you
make ends meet?

When seeing clients becomes your bread and butter, your only income, you may be tempted
in difficult times to string your clients along, keeping them in therapy way longer than necessary. You may find yourself rationalizing that the client still has work to do. You may find
yourself convincing many clients to continue therapy even if they think they are ready to
terminate. If that happens, we recommend you really become clear about whether you want
the client to continue therapy for your sake or for the client's sake. Continuing therapy because
issues still exist is not necessarily in the client's best interest because, as we have stated before,
your clients will always have issues. This is why setting goals (discussed in the last chapter) can

be so helpful. Goals will help you and your client know when it is time to terminate. Clients need time to go into the world with their newfound skills and use them, refine them, and, hopefully, build some self-confidence as a result of them. Your job is to work yourself out of a job, even if it is inconvenient for you. That's not to say that you won't have some clients who want long-term therapy. You might. However, very few clients, especially when you need them most (in economic hard times), will have this luxury. Terminate when the client is ready. Terminate because the goal has been met. It's your ethical obligation.

Exercise in Values

Sometimes a client may find that therapy is so helpful and rewarding that he or she wants to keep that relationship as a style of life, rather than as a temporary support to overcome a specific problem. As a result, this client may be able to afford your time each week except when you take a vacation. Having a client like this is helpful financially. Also, clients who prefer indefinite therapy may be psychologically minded and consequently, fun to work with. At the same time, some practitioners see the job of the therapist as to teach the client to become self-sufficient and not become dependent upon the therapist.

In small groups, discuss whether you think continuing therapy indefinitely is ethical or not. Support your argument with a list of reasons.

APPLICATIONS TO SELF: CLOSURE ON CLOSURE

One of the most difficult challenges you will face as a clinician is mastering the art and science of ending the therapy effectively. There are a lot of feelings that will be stirred up inside you as you say goodbye to people you have grown close to—sadness, loss, frustration, abandonment, relief, excitement, pride, and a dozen others. These feelings are not unlike those that parents feel when their kids leave home.

Closure is difficult to manage because the client may also be experiencing tremendous ambivalence about ending the therapy. There is relief, of course, at just saving the time and expense involved. The client may also feel a degree of pride graduating from a very challenging program—some might say, the most painful and growth-producing structure for learning that is available.

When bringing therapy to an end, you must help clients to come to terms with their reactions, and also to help them to continue their work on their own. In addition, you must learn to come to terms with your own losses after experiencing such intimacy with your client.

Think about how you have ended relationships in the past. Create a list of four or five important relationships that have ended. Write how each one ended: abruptly, slowly, on good terms or bad, willingly or unwillingly, and so on. Read back through what you wrote. Do you see a trend? Many times we get in the habit of doing things the same way over and over, and endings are no exception to that rule. What makes most of us especially clumsy about ending relationships is that we are not taught how to do this well, neither didactically nor by example. So, learning to be okay with ending these most intimate relationships will help you to do it in your life outside of the therapy session.

SUMMARY

In this chapter, we have covered the importance of evaluating your progress with your clients. Related to evaluating progress is deciding when to terminate and how to do that effectively. We hope, at this point, that you feel like you have a foundation for working with clients in an individual setting. In the next two chapters, we introduce you to working with two other client types: families and groups. Each of these requires many of the skills you have learned up to this point but also requires some additional skills to focus on interpersonal relationships in a therapeutic setting.

A CHECK ON WHAT YOU LEARNED

1. Why is measuring your progress with a client difficult?
2. What are some reasons you might not continue to evaluate the progress of your client?

For the following skills, determine whether (a) they are ways to self-monitor or evaluate your progress as a therapist or (b) they are skills to end therapy effectively.

3. Identifying unfinished business.
4. Saying goodbye.
5. Consulting.
6. Constructing a plan.
7. Continuing education.
8. Making the client responsible by journaling or recording progress.
9. Summarizing.
10. Negotiating closure.
11. Transcribing your sessions.
12. Following up.

SUGGESTED READINGS

Dillon, C. (2003). *Learning from mistakes in clinical practice.* Pacific Grove, CA: Brooks/Cole.

Falvey, J. E. (2002). *Managing clinical supervision: Ethical practice and legal risk management.* Pacific Grove, CA: Brooks/Cole.

Hubble, M. A., Duncan, B. L., & Miller, S. D. (Eds.). (1999). *The heart and soul of change: What works in therapy.* Washington, DC: American Psychological Association.

Kottler, J. A., & Carlson, J. (2003). *Bad therapy: Master therapists share their worst failures.* New York: Brunner-Routledge.

Morrissette, P. J. (2002). *Self-supervision: A primer for counselors and helping professionals.* New York: Brunner-Routledge.

Tryon, G. S. (2002). *Counseling based on process research: Applying what we know.* Boston: Allyn and Bacon.

PART III

CHAPTER 10

Skills of Family Intervention and Consultation

T his chapter and the one that follows, on group leadership skills, look at the ways that counselors and therapists use their generic training to work in specialized treatment modalities. Both family and group strategies share a number of core assumptions in that they work with multiple people at the same time. The main difference, of course, is that a family is a group in which all members are related to one another.

Family therapists use the same basic skills favored by clinicians who see individual clients, plus a number of others that are geared for this unique situation. If you had a family in session, for instance, you would most likely reflect individual members' feelings, challenge their dysfunctional thoughts, examine underlying intrapsychic issues, and confront discrepancies in behavior, just as you would if you were seeing the client alone. But you would also do a lot of other things in ways you would not dream of doing in individual therapy.

Imagine, for instance, that you are interviewing a couple and asking the husband first what he sees as the main problem.

Husband: I think it's just a matter of my wife having expectations in our relationship that I could never meet.

Wife: Now that's a lie and you know it. The real problem here is that I don't trust you. And you know why.

Husband: That's not true, dear. We've been over this before . . .

In the first 30 seconds you can appreciate that merely reflecting content and feelings will not be helpful to this couple, and you will quickly lose control of the session unless you introduce a very different structure and style of communication. This is the main challenge of family therapy (and group therapy in the next chapter): all the while you are attending to the needs of one person, you have others present who may have very different agendas and interests.

A DIFFERENT WAY OF LOOKING AT THINGS

When we speak of family therapy, it sounds like we are talking about some kind of single entity that is universally accepted in the profession. You probably know better by now than to expect such simplicity in this field. Just as there is in individual therapy (and group therapy), there are dozens of different ways that family therapy may be defined and structured (see Brock & Barnard, 1999; Gladding, 2002; Goldenberg & Goldenberg, 2001; Nichols & Schwartz, 2001).

Some family therapists believe that it is preferable to bring in as many members of the family, the whole clan, as possible: the more participants, the better. Other therapists like to work with only the nuclear family unit, leaving out the aunts, uncles, cousins, and extended kin. There are therapists who identify only the most powerful member in the family and initiate changes through him or her. Other therapists pick the weakest family member and attempt to bolster his or her position in the tribe. Still other therapists believe that all therapy is family therapy, even if you are doing only individual sessions, because when you change one person you change the whole family system.

Regardless of which family members the therapists wants to see, and which theoretical approach is favored, there are still some universal assumptions that most practitioners share. These beliefs would guide not only which skills you would select in a given clinical situation but also how you would use them.

Circular Causality

In a systemic approach you don't subscribe to simple cause–effect phenomena in which one person causes another to act in a particular way. Instead, behavior is seen as infinitely more complex and interactive. One person's actions are likely to be both the cause *and* effect of another's behavior. In any conflict situation, nobody is solely at fault for the problems but rather each contributor does something that provokes continued tension (Brock & Barnard, 1999).

An adolescent boy and his father respond to the therapist's invitation as to why they came to therapy:

> *Father:* My son can never get home on time. He's always breaking his curfew.
>
> *Son:* If you didn't have such unreasonable expectations, I could be on time.
>
> *Father:* I think that being home by 11 p.m. on weekends is perfectly acceptable. There's nothing you can do after that that can't be done earlier. And anyway, when I have extended your curfew, you were still late.
>
> *Son:* That's not true and you know it! It's not fair, my friends don't have to be in until midnight.
>
> *Father:* I'm not their dad, nor do I care to be.
>
> *Son:* That's it, isn't it? You just hate my friends and you'll do anything to make me lose them, like expecting me to come home at such an early hour.
>
> *Father:* Your curfew has nothing to do with that; 11 p.m. is late enough. It's what my father required and it kept me out of trouble.
>
> *Son:* See, you do think I'll get into trouble. You just don't trust me.

As you can see, this conversation is going nowhere. The two people clearly have made assumptions about each other's position and are responding to those assumptions. The father maybe had the same curfew and thinks it's reasonable. The son, on the other hand, may assume that his dad is just trying to keep him away from his friends because he doesn't trust him to make good decisions. Regardless of the reasons, the therapist is not likely to help these two by only focusing on one person's position. The therapist must explore both positions while teaching the people how to communicate.

System and Subsystems

What family therapists look for are the underlying structures of family systems (Brock & Barnard, 1999). This means the way the family is organized and also how communication takes place. Within the larger family unit, there are also smaller units called subsystems or coalitions. There are also boundaries in place, both between the various coalitions and between the family and the outside world. There is a whole new vocabulary associated with this approach that talks about families that are *enmeshed* (meaning overly dependent) or *disengaged* (overly isolated).

For example, a mother may be enmeshed with her eldest son, creating one coalition. She gives him lots of positive attention and sometimes talks about her marriage problems. The father may be closer to his daughter. He is involved with her extracurricular activities and buys her gifts spontaneously. The youngest son is not close to either parent (is disengaged) and continually gets into trouble. Each parent blames the other for his or her youngest son's trouble.

Family Life Cycles

Just as an individual life progresses through a series of predictable, sequential stages, so too does a family (Gladding, 2002). You will see the same things in the life of any group in the next chapter. This means that family therapists carefully trace the stage of a family, whether it happens to be in the early childhood or empty nest period.

We could go on and on about this stuff, but most programs offer at least one course, and usually more, to prepare you to do family therapy. Family therapy is among the most popular treatment approaches for a variety of reasons:

1. Family therapy is more consistent with many cultural backgrounds (Asian, Latino, Indigenous) that value family values over those of the individual.
2. Many of the most effective brief therapies currently in use are designed as family approaches.
3. Family therapy has potential to be more powerful and influential because all the "players" are in attendance.
4. Family systems theory recognizes the importance of interpersonal and interdependent relationships that are so much a part of life.

STRUCTURING A FAMILY INTERVIEW

Although we have discussed in previous chapters the ways that interviews are to be structured, several significant adjustments must be made in the ways that family sessions are conducted. For one thing, you have multiple clients present, each with his or her own agenda. For another thing, there is almost always a certain degree of chaos going on, especially when there are three or more people in the room and some of them happen to be children. Unless you are prepared to exert some control and structure, the situation can spin out of control rather quickly.

Although there are so-called humanistic, nondirective family therapists, we do not recommend that you try such an approach as a beginner. You must establish sufficient safety and boundaries to make sure that each family member is heard, that each person has the chance to talk, and that conversations do not deteriorate to the point where things become disrespectful or abusive. Remember that families in distress come to you in the first place because they are conflicted, disorganized, and often out of control. It is your job to establish needed structure.

Exercise in Family Chaos

In small groups, role-play a family in which the following situation exists: (a) The father and mother don't like one another at all—they bicker and argue and blame one another; (b) the grandmother (father's mother) takes her son's side and is aligned against the mother, except when her son turns on her; (c) the oldest adolescent child is sullen and angry and resents being there; and (d) the younger child is hyperactive and distracting.

One person will attempt to restore some order to the situation and try to maintain control over the situation so that family members take turns talking and respect one another's point of view. We say "try" because such an effort is not likely to be very successful. That is fine, however, because at this point in your training we just want to give you a taste for how important it is to use your therapeutic skills in very different ways when counseling families.

Join the Family

In order to help the family you have to develop collaborative relationships with them in order to be trusted and to influence them. Salvador Minuchin (1974) felt this was especially important, to become part of the system that you intend to influence. This is also important when you consider that you are going to ask people to do things that they won't want to do or that they will find very difficult. Joining the family gives you the leverage to undertake the therapeutic changes that you believe are necessary in order to restructure the way decisions are made and the way communication takes place.

So, what does it mean to "join" a family? Essentially, this involves using all your charm, caring, and acceptance—plus your clinical skills—to get members to trust and respect you. You do this by demonstrating that you are fair and that you are concerned for everyone's welfare. You present yourself as caring and kind, but also as firm and dependable. In a nutshell, you get everyone (or almost everyone) to like and respect you, to consider you one of them. You become an honorary member of the family as a function of the intimate time you spend together.

One area in which beginners often feel confused is how to "join" the family, that is, to become accepted as a trusted member of the unit, yet also maintain appropriate professional boundaries at the same time. This is indeed a challenge that can be discussed openly with family members as the relationship evolves. As with all forms of therapy, you must walk a line (it is not necessarily a fine line) in which you present yourself as caring, trustworthy, and dependable, at the same time that you communicate that you are there as a paid professional.

Ask Yourself (and Your Clients) Some Questions

Part of your assessment process in family therapy is to ask a series of questions that help you to locate better what the problem is and what needs to be done to address it. Here are some questions you might consider:

1. *What is the problem?* If you ask each family member, you are likely to get a different answer. That is not only expected (and interesting) but useful in getting varied perspectives.
2. *When does the problem occur?* Just as importantly, when does the problem not occur? In other words, when is the problem most and least evident?
3. *Where does the problem occur?* You are gathering more information about the specific settings and situations in which the problem takes place. This gives you information about context and reinforcers.
4. *With whom does the problem occur?* It is always interesting to discover that the problem is activated by the presence of some people and not by others. What does that mean? How does this guide your understanding of what might be going on?
5. *What are the effects on others?* Thinking systemically, you are interested in the interpersonal and reciprocal effects of behavior. You wonder about what happens when the problem occurs. How do people respond? How might this behavior be reinforced inadvertently?
6. *What are the payoffs that the person enjoys?* Behavior does not persist unless it is helpful in some way. Even dysfunctional and self-destructive behavior presents some benefits to people. They get sympathy and attention. They don't have to feel responsible. They have an excuse for not getting on with their lives. They can focus on the problem so they don't have to think about other things that are even more challenging.
7. *Who in the family has had similar problems?* The answer to this question will give you some clues as to how the presenting complaint is related to other family history.

Assess Family Dynamics

When you are thinking systemically (as all family therapists do), you are looking at the characteristic ways that members relate to one another (Gladding, 2002). You check out who is aligned with whom. You note who has the power, and who doesn't. You assess who is the scapegoat. You look at how decisions are made. You examine the ways that people communicate with one another, as well as identify the underlying messages that are implicit in what they say and do. You identify the metaphors embedded in their behavior. You assess the stage the family is operating at in its life cycle. The big picture is that you are looking at the family as a unit, as a system, as a living thing.

Family therapists collect this information and form their observations using a variety of methods. We use "genograms," or pictorial maps, to gather family history. We watch the family in action and note patterns that emerge. We observe where people sit, who talks to whom, and in what tone. We watch how the family makes decisions. We plot the communication patterns in evidence. We look for evidence of codependence. We search for weaknesses in the family system, but also strengths: What resources are available to this family? How have they managed to keep things together in the face of their problems? What are some of the family legacies that have been passed on from one generation to the next? These would be limiting in some ways, but also helpful to the members in organizing their lives.

Assessing Domestic Violence and Child Abuse

Although we could have covered this earlier in the book, any sort of abuse is usually looked at in a family context. As part of your assessment process, you will be especially vigilant about any evidence of physical, sexual, or even verbal abuse going on in the family. In whatever jurisdiction you live, there will be mandatory reporting laws that require you to protect the safety of people, especially children who can't protect themselves.

In addition to reporting some forms of abuse to protective services, you must also report suspicions of neglect, that is, when family members are deprived of basic needs (AAMFT, 2001; ACA, 2002; APA, 1992; NASW, 1999). Remember that it is not your job to determine whether the abuse or neglect is going on, but rather to report your suspicion of this activity. Even though such reports are confidential, once authorities become involved, it obviously changes the therapeutic options available to the family.

Most places require you to have some specialized training in this area in order to be licensed, but the main features to look for include emotional symptoms (sadness, guilt, anxiety, low self-worth), physical signs (bruises or injuries), and behavioral indices (phobic reactions, age-inappropriate sexual knowledge, clinginess, regression).

Doing a Couples Assessment

Although we've covered some of the skills and mechanics for doing family interviews, there are some more specific strategies that might be applied to working with couples. In one sense, doing couples therapy is just a specialized form of family therapy but with only two people present who often have conflicts related to the "Big Three": money, sex, and kids.

To give you an idea of how you might conduct a session with more than one person present, we present one format for how you might approach a couple during a first interview.

1. Ask each person for presenting complaints.
2. Ask each person for expectations for treatment.

3. Hear the story of how they met.
4. Find out a brief history of their relationship.
5. Assess current functioning as individuals (personality, personal issues, interpersonal skills, developmental functioning, etc.) and as a couple (communication, roles, power, intimacy, differentiation, sex and money issues, decision making, etc.).
6. Check out family configuration (coalitions, boundaries, etc.).
7. Identify significant others.
8. Dig for family of origin issues.
9. Ask what is going right and what is working well.
10. Find out their respective degree of commitment to the relationship (rate on a 1–10 scale).
11. Discuss goals for treatment.
12. Invite feedback and initiate summary.
13. Negotiate mutually agreed homework (if indicated).
14. Reflect on what you observed, heard, sensed, felt, and experienced.

Exercise in Doing a Couples Interview

It might be fun (as well as useful) for you to practice doing a couples initial interview in which you begin probing the presenting issues and collect basic background. This is quite similar to the kind of intake session you would do with an individual client, only (a) you are keeping two people engaged at the same time, and (b) you are focusing on relational and interactive concerns between them rather than only their individual struggles.

Organize yourselves in groups of four in which two people role-play a couple that is coming in for a first session. This could be a married couple, a cohabitating couple, or a gay or lesbian couple. While the "couple" is deciding on how they wish to present themselves, the two cotherapists should spend a few minutes talking about how they wish to proceed.

Take 30 minutes to interview the couple in order to: (a) build a working relationship, (b) assess the dynamics between them, (c) identify core issues that might be worked on, and (d) collect background information. Here is a sample of questions that you might ask:

1. *On a 1 to 10 scale, how would each of you rate how committed you are to working on this relationship? Note: A low score by either member of the couple does not bode well for a favorable prognosis.*
2. *Ask each partner: What is it that you would most like to work on in this relationship?*
3. *How is it that you decided to seek help at this time?*
4. *What have you tried to do so far to resolve your difficulties?*
5. *How did you meet one another? Tell the story of how you met.*
6. *What initially attracted you most to one another?*
7. *How and when did you first become aware that there were some difficulties that needed to be addressed?*
8. *How do the two of you usually address conflicts and disagreements? Give a recent example of this.*

9. *What are the best parts of your relationship? What do you especially appreciate about your partner?*
10. *What did you learn about one another, and about yourself, during this conversation?*

Form Diagnostic Impressions

You would use everything you already know to diagnose individual disorders that you observe in family members. You may notice, for instance, that the mother has a substance abuse disorder, the father an explosive personality disorder, the grandmother a chronic neurological condition, and the child has a developmental disorder. All of these issues would obviously play a significant role in whatever brought the family into treatment.

Thinking systemically, you would also examine a number of other issues (Brock & Barnard, 1999):

1. How are emotions expressed in the family? How do members respond to one another emotionally?
2. What is the state of individuation among members? How is codependency present? To what extent are members disengaged or enmeshed with one another?
3. How is power distributed?
4. What are the family rules and how are they enforced?
5. How are conflicts and disputes resolved?
6. How is information shared?
7. What are the family myths?

This last question about myths refers to the historical legacy and traditions of the family. How do members of the family view their unit? How do they describe their family to others? What rituals are used as part of the family functioning?

Exercise in Identifying Family Myths

In small groups, talk to one another about your own family identification. How would you best describe your family? What are some of your unique rituals in which you participate together? What would a therapist need to know and understand about the way your family functions in order to be helpful to you?

In addition to these general considerations, you will want to check out the usual areas you would in any interview. How are people functioning in terms of basic skills? What is the drug/alcohol use among family members?

Among partners or spouses, you will also want to look closely at how they are doing together with the Big Three: money, sex, and children (Goldenberg & Goldenberg, 2001). In other words, how do they make decisions in these areas? What is their degree of satisfaction in the way they handle these issues?

Set Up Rules and Boundaries

Have you ever seen an argument with the following process?

> *Wife:* Where were you? I cooked dinner and we all ate hours before you got home last night. You knew that I would have dinner ready at six, but you had to work late.
> *Husband:* Don't jump down my throat! I wasn't really working late, it's just that . . .
> *Wife:* I know, I know. Your most important client called at the last minute and . . .
> *Husband:* No, that's not it at all. When I left the office, I had to . . .
> *Wife:* You forgot to do something absolutely urgent. I'm really tired of your excuses.
> *Husband:* But you haven't given me a chance to even tell you what happened. [talking to the therapist] Do you see what I have to put up with?
> *Therapist:* I can see that you are feeling really frustrated, and . . .
> *Wife:* Oh, so you're siding with him!

Notice how neither of them will allow the other to complete a sentence, much less a thought. All too often when people are angry, they work so hard to prepare their next argument that they don't listen to each other at all. We could probably assume that this couple does this at home, too, and if the therapist allows this to proceed, the therapist will find that they will get nowhere.

At the point where we ended, if the therapist said something about not interrupting, the wife might feel put off, unless a ground rule was established at the beginning of therapy. Furthermore, the therapist should have allowed the husband to finish his thought at the beginning. Perhaps the sessions would have gone in this direction:

> *Wife:* Where were you? I cooked dinner, and we all ate hours before you got home last night. You knew that I would have dinner ready at six, but you had to work late.
> *Husband:* Don't jump down my throat! I wasn't really working late, it's just that . . .
> *Wife:* I know, I know . . .
> *Therapist:* Sally, remember our agreement, that we would allow the other person to finish speaking before responding?
> *Wife:* Okay.
> *Husband:* As I was saying, I was not working late. I was home late because I was taking care of some personal business. Something for us, for you.

Well, you can see how this might be more helpful to allow each person to finish speaking. Some practitioners set up a rule where they not only require that the first person finish speaking, but that the recipient of the information has to repeat back what was heard until it is perceived correctly. We talked about this earlier. For instance, to continue the preceding scenario:

> *Wife:* You were late because you were working, again, for me?
> *Husband:* No, that is not what I said. I said I was taking care of personal business, something for you and me, not for the office.
> *Wife:* You were doing work that was for us. So, you were working late.

Husband: No, it wasn't work. It was . . . well . . . I wanted to make it a surprise, but I was buying your anniversary gift, and it took longer than I expected.

Now, you might imagine that this conversation will take an entirely different turn than the first example. Now the explanation is much more clear than before. With this understanding, the wife's anger might be diffused.

Even more so than in individual sessions, you must establish and enforce rules for how people behave. Either these can be presented to clients or you can negotiate them as a collaborative exercise. Here is one way this idea could be presented:

Therapist: Before we begin our work together, I'm wondering what rules we need to agree on together.

Adolescent: Rules? Why do we need rules? I thought we were here to speak our minds.

Therapist: Good point. So let me ask you: Why do we need rules?

Mother: Well, for one thing so we don't end up arguing like we do at home.

Younger child: Yeah, and so I get to talk too. You guys are always yelling so much that I don't even get to say anything.

Father: Okay, enough of that. It's not that bad and you know it.

Therapist: So far you've mentioned that you have problems working out conflicts at home because voices are sometimes raised, you don't listen to one another, and not everyone gets a chance to talk.

Younger child: You can say that again.

Mother: Hush now!

Younger child: See that? She's doing it again. They never let me talk.

Therapist: Another rule that might be important is not interrupting one another . . .

Younger child: I'm for that one.

Therapist: . . . just like you did now.

Whether you negotiate the rules or simply explain the ones you know are critical from prior experience, you will need to alert participants about: (a) the importance of being respectful, (b) the need to listen before responding, and (c) the requirement that people attend sessions promptly and consistently. These rules should be established at the first session, and should be applied consistently so that the therapist is seen as treating everyone equally.

Get Everyone Involved

In family sessions (and in groups, mentioned in the next chapter), you must keep everyone engaged in the process. Doing family (or group) therapy is not the same as doing individual therapy in front of an audience. Even if there is one person who is the "identified client"—the one with the problem—when you look at things systemically you view the situation from a more global perspective. The systemic approach looks at the interdependence between people and the ways their behavior is affected by reciprocal, circular influences (Brock & Barnard, 1999). Blame is moved away from the individual and instead focus is centered on what the family can do to restructure itself.

Since there are multiple persons in the room, you must use your eyes and attending skills to keep everyone fully present. Rather than talking to you, you will instruct members to speak to one another. You will draw in members who are quiet. You will restrain those who are overly controlling or talkative. You will balance the contributions, the energy, and the pace so that things move along in a way that meets the needs of everyone present. If you think this is easy, you haven't been paying attention. That is why some family therapists elect to work with a partner whenever possible.

Use Directives

Since family therapists have the ambitious goal of trying to restructure the way a family operates, it is virtually impossible to do so during sessions alone. Directives or therapeutic assignments are often prescribed (or negotiated) so that members work on things between sessions. These could either be direct tasks ("Do something nice for one another each day") or paradoxical directives ("I want you to keep arguing with one another, but next time I want you to do it nonstop for an hour").

Directives can be designed along a number of lines. They could be structured to change the way members communicate with one another. They may be created to change the power structure in the family. They may also be employed to directly address the presenting problem.

What all this means is that when you are doing family therapy, you are more active, directive, and initiating than you might be ordinarily during your individual sessions. You have a slightly different role that is designed not just to help individuals but to help restructure the way the family functions.

Using directives in therapy would be considered advanced-level skills that are not intended for beginners. In fact, some clinicians prefer not to use them at all because they may keep power and control in the hands of the therapist and could be seen as manipulative. Once you manage to become reasonably comfortable with the basic skills previously introduced, you can later add directives to your repertoire. You can also learn to adapt these powerful skills in a way that is more collaborative.

Sex Therapy Skills

Another specialized area in which counselors function is in dealing with sexual dysfunctions and personal issues related to sexual behavior. These are relatively common difficulties, as roughly one-quarter of women report difficulties having orgasms and one-quarter of men ejaculate prematurely (Mah & Binik, 2001). Then there are problems related to value and moral issues, inhibitions, and a variety of physical problems related to achieving or maintaining erections in men or responsiveness issues in women.

Sex therapy skills are often educational in nature, in which clients are taught to heighten their awareness of their senses and bodies, create greater intimacy in their relationships, enhance their pleasures, and eliminate dysfunctional thinking that is getting in the way. Although it would not necessarily be classified as a "skill," a huge part of doing sex therapy work involves monitoring your own attitudes and comfort with the subject. If clients sense that you are in any way uneasy about your own sexuality, or talking about sex, they are likely to feel uncomfortable as well. That is why much of sex therapy training involves not only learning the methods for treating various sexual dysfunctions, but also addressing your own unresolved issues related to sex. The goal is to get to the point where you can talk to people about any facet of sexuality and do so easily.

Exercise in Sexual Values

In the margin of the book, in your journal, or a separate piece of paper, write out what it would be like for you to respond to each of the following clients who presented their problems to you in a first session:

- *"I like to dress up in my wife's underwear and I think about doing that when I am having sex with my wife. I'd like to talk about this with her but I'm afraid of what she might think."*
- *"I have never felt comfortable as a man; it's always seemed to me like I'm a woman in a man's body. I want to explore the possibility of having a sex-change operation."*
- *"I am a lesbian and involved in a long-term relationship with my partner. We would like to adopt children but first we want to get couples counseling to have us look at what might be involved in this."*
- *"I have been having a sexual relationship with my younger brother since we were teenagers. We still get together on occasion. Although I feel a little guilty about this, I'm not sure if it is wrong that we continue this relationship. We both like it."*
- *"I am having an affair but I don't want my husband to know about it. I don't think it really hurts my marriage; in some ways it takes some pressure off because my husband doesn't like sex as often as I do."*
- *"I can only have erections to the point of orgasm when my wife and I watch pornographic videos. She says it bothers her but I don't see what the problem is if it adds spice to our relationship."*
- *"My husband doesn't know this but the only way I can have an orgasm is with a vibrator. If the truth be known, I'd much prefer to masturbate instead of have intercourse."*

Talk about your reactions to these presenting problems in small groups. Pay particular attention to areas where you might need to do some work in order to deal with some of your biases and unresolved issues related to sex.

The actual skills in doing sex therapy are considered "add-ons" to what you would do with any couple: develop a solid relationship with the partners, earn their trust, explore the context of the problem in relation to other factors, and figure out the particular meaning of the symptoms. For instance, a man who prematurely ejaculates may be communicating anger to his wife ("Ha, ha, I got off and you didn't"). A woman who does not have orgasms with her partner may be communicating similar anger ("You are not good enough to excite me"). We are not saying this is the case, just that often the presenting symptoms are saying things that may not yet have been heard by the other partner.

Some other things to keep in mind when doing sex therapy or dealing with sexual issues are:

1. Rule out any organic cause. Many sexual dysfunctions are not psychological in origin but result from underlying diseases, substance and alcohol abuse, physical problems, or side effects from medications.
2. Look at the problem in the context of the relationship.
3. Help the couple to tell one another what their needs and preferences are. This includes what they like and dislike.
4. Provide relevant information when indicated. Some people are remarkably ignorant about their bodies and about how sex works.
5. Use directives to help the couple reduce anxiety and address their problems. These often involve "sensate focus" exercises in which the partners pleasure one another in nondemanding ways without feeling pressured. For instance, a man who has difficulty attaining and maintaining erections would be asked to pleasure his partner, and be pleasured in return, but *without* attempting intercourse.
6. Encourage deeper communication. Facilitate open discussions about how things are going, how each partner feels and thinks about what is happening.

CHILD COUNSELING SKILLS

In one sense, everything that you have already learned about therapeutic skills in general also works with kids. Children of any age respond well to being heard and understood. As long as language and communication are adjusted and adapted to the particular age and developmental stage of the client, you can use almost any intervention. For instance, cognitive therapies hold sacred the belief that the way you feel is determined, to a large extent, by how you choose to interpret the situation and how you talk to yourself (Beck, 1976; Ellis, 1973; Meichenbaum, 1977). When working with adults, you would use skills of disputing beliefs and challenging thinking along the lines of what was presented earlier. Yet even preschoolers can understand the idea embedded in the children's rhyme: "Sticks and stones will break your bones but names can never hurt you."

Not only must the sort of language you use and your style of communication be adjusted for kids of various ages, but so must your basic strategies. If you remember what you learned about developmental theory, then you know that before certain ages children lack the capacity for abstract thought (Jean Piaget's theory) or lack the reasoning processes to resolve moral dilemmas beyond basic avoidance of punishment (Lawrence Kohlberg's theory). This means that you must take into consideration the particular functioning of each client in terms of moral, emotional, cognitive, physical, and psychosocial development. The skill involved here is being able to accurately assess a child's level of functioning in each dimension and then adapting your helping strategy in a way that it is most likely to be received.

Exercise in Adapting Skills to Children

On your own, with partners, or in small groups, discuss how you would use active listening skills to respond to the following statements by children of various ages. Role-play the interaction that is begun by the initial client statement.

Eighteen-year-old honors high school student: "My parents won't leave me alone. They are always on my case. It's like whatever I do is never good enough for them."

Fifteen-year-old freshman football player: "My parents say I better have a good season this year or I'll never make the varsity team next year. I think I can do it. At least I hope I can. But there's some pretty big guys out there."

Eleven-year-old girl who never speaks in class: "Um, my parents can't come to the conference like you asked. I think they have to work or something. Um, is that okay?"

Eight-year-old boy with chronic stomachaches: "My parents say that I'm just too nervous all the time. I get upset about things. I can kind of feel my tummy hurting right now. My mom says if I relax, it'll get better."

Four-year-old girl who throws temper tantrums: "My mommy won't let me go to playgroup today. She says I was bad. But she's the one who is bad. She's mean."

Because younger children cannot easily express what they are thinking and feeling, at least in the language that therapists would prefer, play becomes their primary means of communication (Axline, 1964). Play therapy is a desired modality that allows children to express themselves through a variety of modalities other than speech. They may use puppets, or songs, or drawing, or building, or acting out roles, in order to "speak" through their actions and "talk" about what is bothering them. Likewise, therapists may respond at the same level of communication.

THE ROLES YOU TAKE AS A THERAPIST

As a therapist, you will need to take on various roles regardless of your environment, such as mediator or consultant. Sometimes these roles will be required as a therapist; the skill of mediation is frequently required of you as a family therapist, for example. Sometimes you may choose to pursue additional roles to your role as a therapist for extra income, such as a consultant or personal coach.

Mediation Skills

Also known as *alternative dispute resolution,* this procedure is very different from usual counseling goals even though many of the skills are the same. Just as in individual or family counseling, the mediator would use active listening and summarizing skills, but the goal is not to stir up emotional issues but rather to calm them down so that constructive decisions can be made.

You would be functioning more in the role of consultant or problem solver rather than therapist during this professional activity. You are supposed to be the objective, neutral, impartial third party who resolves disputes and helps conflicted parties negotiate to the point of a mutually acceptable solution. This could be in matters of divorce or child custody, in disputes between business partners, in conflicts between employees, or in legal problems in which both parties need help coming to an agreement.

Therapists operating in a mediator role have received specialized training and certification in this profession. Although therapist and counselor education provides a solid background in active listening and responding skills, many mediators come from very different jobs such as the practice of law. Obviously, mediation requires both knowledge of the legal process as well as solid helping skills (see Moore, 1996; Winslade & Monk, 2000).

Steps in the mediation process require the mastery of several helping skills. Many of these would already be part of your repertoire, and others would require additional training.

1. *Relationship building.* You must establish trust with the participants and earn their respect just as you would do in family therapy (or any helping relationship). You do this through the joining process described earlier and by presenting yourself as fair, objective, and concerned. You are trying to do two things simultaneously: establish good rapport with the parties and also establish your credibility as a source of influence.

2. *Gathering background.* Just as you would do in therapy, you want to help each person to tell his or her story and share his or her version of the situation. You will need to use limit-setting and blocking skills to ensure that people are not interrupted and that they are allowed to speak fully. You would also use questioning and reflecting skills to draw people out.

3. *Building collaborative relationships.* Until you can get the parties to listen to one another, they are not likely to agree on much (that's why they are seeing you in the first place). You must keep the atmosphere sufficiently under control so the conflict is not intensified and the parties are not further aggravated. This means making expectations and norms very clear and enforcing them consistently.

4. *Negotiating.* This set of skills forms the core of the mediation process. This is where you help parties to explore the issues, understand one another's position, and try to foster compromise. In order to do this you will have to uncover hidden agendas, identify underlying issues, and help people to work them through. When a couple argues heatedly about who gets to keep the silver cup collection, they are obviously struggling about some other important issue. When two business partners are fighting over their expense accounts, they are really struggling with trust issues.

5. *Generating options.* When people come to mediation, they are stuck. Your job is to help them generate other alternatives and solutions. This might mean increasing their awareness of possibilities, suggesting ideas that had not been considered, and helping them to let go of strategies that have not been working so they are free to discover new ones.

6. *Get an agreement.* This is where you help parties to reach a final settlement that both are willing to live with. You would want to formalize this commitment in writing and also come up with ways that the agreement will be enforced.

You can appreciate that the mediator may be using therapeutic-type skills but is operating according to very different professional guidelines and after a different sort of outcome. As in forms of family therapy, the "client" is not an individual but rather a relationship. What therapists bring to the mediation process is a greater sensitivity to process as well as outcome. This means that in addition to working toward an acceptable solution to the problem you would also be concerned about the way people feel and think about the experience.

Exercise in Getting Unstuck

Working with partners, one of you decide to talk about an area of your life in which you are feeling stuck and can't seem to resolve a problem. The other partners will function as problem solvers.

The first step is to help the person figure out what he or she is doing already that is not working very well. After the "client" gives some brief background on the problem (5 minutes), ask the person to list the things he or she has tried that have proven consistently ineffective.

Get the person to agree not to do those things anymore. There is often resistance at this point to letting go of favored strategies—incredibly, even when they don't work. But until the person agrees to let go of methods that aren't helpful, there is little room to try anything else. At the very least, get the person to surrender at least a few of the most ineffective behaviors.

Brainstorm together an exhaustive list of other alternative strategies that could be tried. As with any such exercise, the more options you generate the better. Creative, far-out, and innovative possibilities are especially encouraged. It happens that in an exercise like this, the specific solutions are less important than the feeling the person leaves with: that there are many, many other options available besides those that are currently being used unsuccessfully.

Afterward, talk about what this experience was like for all the participants and how you might use this in your lives and work.

Consultation Skills

As you can readily see, the roles of a family counselor are somewhat different than those played during individual sessions. In many ways, the clinician functions as much as a consultant as a therapist. You are looking at the underlying processes and dynamics of a system rather than just those of a single individual. The same is true during those times when you are asked to intervene on the systemic level of a larger group or organization.

The consulting role is playing an increasingly important part in what counselors and therapists do in their work. Most school counselors, for example, spend far more time consulting with teachers, administrators, and parents than they do actual counseling with children in ongoing relationships. Therapists who work in community and private practice settings are often called upon to consult with organizations, to initiate systemic changes, and to work in concert with other professionals. Finally, specialty areas that are developing in mediation and coaching rely more on consultation-type roles rather than that of the traditional therapist who goes after deep, emotionally laden material.

Consultation skills are similar in some ways to therapeutic-type skills, especially what is involved in practicing good listening and responding behaviors. Likewise, consulting activities also make use of principles and strategies that are included as part of doing family and group therapy, especially the emphasis on systemic thinking. Yet consultation skills are also quite different in some ways as well.

Differences Between Therapy and Consulting Skills

A number of distinctions between consultation and therapy have been noted (Parsons, 1996). First of all, similar to family therapy, the "client" is not an individual but is rather the organization. Although individual needs are valued and respected, the primary goal of consultation is to help the larger unit to function more effectively and in such a way that individual interests are improved.

Second, although in therapy or counseling the client comes to the clinician, in consultation the professional does the work on-site, within the most natural setting possible. This means that a school counselor involved in consultation activities would not be sitting in his or her office waiting for people to come visit; instead, he or she would be roaming through the hallways, visiting with kids on the playground, talking to teachers in their classrooms and staff lounge. Another example is that a therapist practicing consultation in schools would not necessarily mediate a dispute in his or her office but would go visit the work setting where the conflict is taking place.

Third, consultants are problem solvers. Even when they don't intervene directly to fix what is wrong, they act to help others to do so. The focus is not on so much on emotional issues or prompting personal insight as on improving performance.

Finally, consultation activities are unique in that the professional acts as a catalyst for change, often working behind the scenes and operating indirectly to get other people to do the work. As you will see, the consultant is more like a coach and teacher rather than a therapist.

Personal Coaching

One of the hot new areas in helping professions is that of personal coaching or life coaching. This is a very unique consulting role in which professionals work outside the usual parameters that we think of in our work. They may spend their time visiting clients on their jobs or at home. They may communicate on a daily basis via the Internet and telephone. And they violate one of the most important prohibitions in practicing therapy: They give lots of advice.

The personal coach develops close consulting relationships, one on one, with a client—sets goals, offers feedback, teaches new skills, gives advice, helps with decision making, aids in job searches and personal marketing (Grosso, 2001). The coach may direct clients to dress differently and present themselves to the world in new ways.

Personal coaches (and other consultants) use a number of specialized skills in their work, such as those that are part of the organizational development field. As one example, they rely a lot on Internet communications, a strategy that presents a new set of challenges. For one thing, the exchanges can be more anonymous, and certainly more convenient, but there are also visual cues missing that help us to interpret what people mean and to adjust our responses to fit their changing needs.

Some professionals have even launched careers as "virtual shrinks," consultants and coaches who operate exclusively online. This has been identified by the media as one of the new, emerging areas in mental health and service industries. Several distinct advantages of this modality have been identified in popular outlets promoting the service, including greater efficiency, anonymity, cost-effectiveness, comfort, and ongoing record keeping of the transactions. Needless to say, this unregulated industry also has a number of risks and ethical problems related to protecting confidentiality and client safety.

PITFALLS AND COMMON MISTAKES

Just as mistakes can be made in working with individuals, mistakes can also be made in working with families. Here we cover mistakes specific to family therapy.

Assuming You Can't Change Your Client Format

If you typically see only individuals, you may not think that bringing in other members of the family or friends might be appropriate; or if you work primarily with families, you may not consider that seeing one person individually would be appropriate. However, sometimes it's not only appropriate to change your client format, but fruitful as well. One of the advantages I [Leah] had in working at one of my internship sites was that we had a lot of therapists who needed clients. We had a family of four children and their mother who came in for family therapy to deal with the recent death of the husband/father. The children seemed to be coping poorly, and the mother was concerned. The children ranged from 6 to 18 years in age. After watching an initial family assessment under the particular conditions of bereavement and with such different issues of the children, we decided to have a 45-minute session as a family, and then to see each person individually, including the mother. Within 8 weeks, this family prospered. They were able to get the individual attention they desperately needed, especially because the mother wasn't able to give each child individual attention the way she wanted. At the same time, they were able to do some work as a family and learn new ways to interact with each other.

If you decide to work with children, you will find that it's not uncommon that parents will bring their child in for you to "fix" him or her. However, many times, the parents need as much work in parent education or in dealing with their own stressors related to their child's problems as the child. So, if you work in a facility with others, we strongly recommend that you encourage the parents of the children to participate in either parent education classes and/or their own therapy. The best time to approach the subject is before you see the child. You might say something like this:

> I understand you are struggling with Johnny's anger outbursts. You don't know where they are coming from or how to deal with them. You must feel extremely tired and frustrated yourself, trying to cope with this new problem. [if the parent agrees] At our agency, we have found that when parents participate in parent education and/or do their own therapy, the child seems to progress

much more quickly. Because you will be sitting here anyway in the waiting room, I would like to strongly recommend you see your own therapist. You can choose to undergo parent education, which may give you some skills in dealing with Johnny's particular problem, or you may choose to just talk to a therapist about your own frustration. Which do you think might be better for you now?

You may notice how no blame was placed on the parent, and in fact, the therapist provided empathy and used that empathy to encourage therapy. In addition, you may have noticed the therapist gave an "either/or" choice rather than asking a "yes/no" question, increasing the possibility that this parent might participate in something. Most parents really want their kids to get better and, if the invitation is worded correctly, will agree to participate in therapy as well. So, you might make it a habit to try and encourage parents to participate in therapy as well.

Another common situation is when you are doing individual therapy, and issues with another person are continually the topic of conversation. Sometimes, your client may want to say something to the other person, but does not have the courage. As a result, you may want to bring the other person in the room to provide support to your client while he or she speaks to this other person. This is especially typical when working with an adolescent who needs to confront a parent. In addition, it is sometimes helpful to allow an adolescent to bring a very close friend with them to therapy for one or two sessions. Watching them interact can provide you more information than working with the adolescent alone. Usually the friend will give you more information than your client can about himself or herself, and you can strengthen the relationship with your client by joining with him or her and the friend.

Anytime you have the potential to occasionally add or remove people from the therapy, you may create a unique experience that otherwise might not occur in your usual format. However, it is essential that you remember who your client is (the family, the individual, the couple) and keep your primary focus on your client or client unit. As long as you keep this in mind, you are only limited by your creativity.

Aligning With One Person or Against Another Person

When we are working with a couple or a family, sometimes we want to align with one person or work against another because of our own issues. For instance, imagine that a couple comes to see you about their marriage. He had an affair 10 years ago, and he is frustrated because his wife still does not trust him. If you had been in a situation similar to the husband, you might find yourself aligning with him. Or perhaps you see a family with four children. The family consistently blames the mother for not being at home enough, and you find yourself joining with the rest of the family in berating her. You can see the implicit problems with doing this. So, you might be saying to yourself, "Obviously, I want to be as objective as possible." However, we frequently find ourselves aligning with or against people in session. To prevent this, you may want to ask yourself how you feel about each client. Who do you like and not like? Why? By taking a moment to reflect on this after each session, you can at least be aware of your biases. Without awareness, your biases might interfere with your objectivity.

There is one exception to alignment. Some therapists purposely align with or against a particular person as a therapeutic technique. It's a more aggressive way to get a point across, and should be used with great caution. One way in which a therapist might use this technique is when one member of the family bullies the other members and thus holds too much power. The therapist may choose to bully the bully so that the person feels what it's like to be the recipient of this interpersonal style. And after the bully realizes what is going on, it is important for the therapist to articulate what he or she just did so that all of the clients understand that the therapist is not partial to one person, but rather was trying to get a point across. Nevertheless, using this technique can be quite dangerous and should only be used after sufficient training and supervision.

Waiting Too Long to Intervene

One of the biggest challenges I [Leah] struggle with is balancing the time for each person to talk. I remember I once had a couple come in, and when I asked what brought them to therapy, the wife started to speak. Now, this has been a quite common experience for me, that the wife starts, but in this particular case, she never stopped. I had to actually stop her at one point to get the husband's perspective. Until I invited him, he did not make any attempt to speak and his nonverbal communication was completely blank. I was astonished. He didn't even have a problem. He was there to find out why she wanted them in couples counseling. The wife could have taken over the entire session, and he might have been perfectly fine about it. As it turned out, the wife actually realized she was unhappy not with her marriage, but with herself. She ended up doing individual therapy, which proved to be much more beneficial for her.

How is it that a therapist might allow a client to go on for too long? Well, one example might be when one party wants to talk and the other has difficulty with verbal expression. Another situation might be when the therapist gets so wrapped up in the story that he or she forgets to check out what's going on with the other members of the family. Finally, as we have stated before, we have been taught that interrupting is rude. As a therapist, that standard cannot be followed. A therapist must frequently interrupt, especially in family or group settings when one person monopolizes, when an argument gets too intense, or when the clients need to be reminded to treat each other with respect and not resort to name calling. Interrupting is an essential part of the process.

Leading the Child Too Much

When working with children, we sometimes forget to consider their level of development when interacting with them. We may even go so far as to try and provide a talk therapy format to little children. This is not always the most beneficial way to help children with their problems. The following scenario is not uncommon:

Therapist: What would you like to talk about today?
Child: I don't know.
Therapist: Well, how was school today?

Child: Fine.
Therapist: Did you get in trouble with your teacher again?
Child: Yes,
Therapist: Tell me what happened.
Child: She was mean to me.

Clearly, this therapist isn't going to get too far with this line of questioning. In addition, the child is not receiving any empathy and may feel interrogated. That is why we recommend play therapy for children. As stated before, play is the language of children, and invariably, under the right conditions, children act out and work through their issues in the playroom (Axline, 1964). Even when new therapists work with children in the playroom, they may get impatient when they allow the child to lead because it sometimes takes two or three sessions for the child to feel safe in the playroom with you. Therefore, the therapist becomes too directive, and the child will not have the opportunity to work through his or her issues. For example, the therapist may decide what task to engage in for each session.

Therapist: Do you want to play pickup sticks today?
Child: Okay.
Therapist: Do you want to go first?
Child: Okay. [the child begins playing] Hey! You're better than me. That's not fair.

As you might imagine, this can't go anywhere. Pickup sticks is not as fruitful as what the child might choose to play with. Another way therapists can be too directive is when playing with the children.

Child: Let's play with the dolls.
Therapist: Okay. I'll be this doll.
Child: No, I want to be that doll.
Therapist: Then I'll be this other doll.
Child: I want to be that doll, too. You be this ugly doll.

Instead of choosing what doll to be, this therapist might do better to ask the child which doll he or she should be. In addition, as the dolls begin to interact, allowing the child to lead permits the child to set up the exact environment they need.

Child: I want to be the teacher and you be the student.
Therapist: Okay. Where would you like me to sit?
Child: Over here. Now I want you to pay attention and listen to my story today. I'm going to read you a story. Do you understand?
Therapist: [whispering] What should I say?
Child: [whispering back] Say, "No, I don't feel like it."

The therapist's natural inclination may be to say, "Okay, I understand," when in fact the child wanted the therapist to disagree, playing out, perhaps, something that happens in the child's class. The more you allow the child to lead, the more the child will blossom in therapy.

As much as possible, allow the therapy room to be the time for the child, for the child to choose his or her method of play, and for the child to choose how to play directing your behavior. It can be the one place where the child can be the boss, which in and of itself is powerful. This isn't to say that you don't set up some boundaries. This must be done, too, but must be done as liberally as possible.

Like other techniques and skills we have introduced, this is one method of therapy that requires training and supervision to be done well. Many programs offer courses in play therapy, but if your program does not, and you plan on working with children or with families, we recommend you attend some workshops. Just as working with individuals and families, there are several theoretical orientations to working with kids. Our bias here is more humanistic because this is what we believe can benefit the child most.

APPLICATIONS TO SELF: AWARENESS OF YOUR OWN FAMILY DYNAMICS

Family therapy will test you in ways that individual sessions never would. With more people in the room, more complex dynamics, conflicting agendas, long-standing battles, and overheated emotional energy, things can easily spin out of control. All your own unresolved issues will be triggered. And that is one reason why you *must* work through your own stuff before you attempt to do this sort of work.

You may have noticed that much of what we recommend in this section of each chapter is for you to do your own work to enhance your skills as a therapist as well as for your own growth. Doing your own work will help you to gain better insight into your work with clients. Well, the skills involved with family therapy are no different. You will want to evaluate your family dynamics, look at coalitions, and identify patterns and where those patterns might have originated.

To start this process, we recommend you do a thorough genogram of your family. Start by identifying your personal issues, which should be clear by this time, assuming you've been following the other recommendations in this book. Then identify your immediate family. For some this process might be brief; for others, where a lot of divorces or deaths have occurred, this may be a complex process. Once you have outlined the primary people involved in the process, identify the subsystems within the family by marking coalitions and enmeshed and disengaged relationships. Mark divorces and deaths. Now go back at least to the generation of your grandparents and do the same thing.

After you have identified the relationships, using your issue and how someone might have an opposite issue, notate these for the whole family tree. For example, if you have a tendency toward particular kinds of love relationships, note others in the family who follow a similar pattern. Or if you are someone who needs a lot of control, mark all the controlling individuals and all the irresponsible individuals. Once you have completed your picture, look for patterns. How are you influenced by patterns in your family? How might those patterns be affecting your children?

We hope you are able to identify some new information by using this technique. What do you do with this information? Well, think about how, as a therapist, you might approach your family. Where would you start? What homework might you assign to this family? How might you need to mediate the process of doing family therapy with your immediate family?

By thinking about your own family, you can gain some insight about who you are. Consequently, you may be more prepared to work with similar families after thinking about your own. If possible, attend a few family sessions just to see what it might be like. It couldn't hurt.

SUMMARY

In this chapter, and the one that follows on group leadership skills, you are introduced to specialized helping behaviors that require advanced training. We are presenting them to you now so that you can get a head start using them in your work. Because family counseling has now become so universal and generic in practice, the skills included here are now part of the repertoire of every clinician.

A CHECK ON WHAT YOU LEARNED

1. Skills required in individual therapy are applied with families as well; however, one primary difference in working with families is what?
2. When one person's actions are likely to be both the cause and effect of another's behavior this is called _____.
3. Define a family subsystem.
4. One way to gain influence into the family is to _____ as a member of the family.
5. With regard to child abuse, your job is which?: (a) to determine whether or not abuse is occurring, or (b) to report your suspicion that abuse may be occurring.
6. In establishing rules of communication with families, you will need to cover what three important areas?
7. Members of the family should do which of the following?: (a) talk to you, or (b) talk to each other.
8. When you are in the role of a consultant or problem solver, you will use what skill?
9. _____ is the language of children and the recommended modality for providing therapy.
10. What are the differences between consulting and therapy?

SUGGESTED READINGS

Axline, V. (1964). *Dibs in search of self.* New York: Ballantine.

Brock, G. W., & Barnard, C. P. (1999). *Procedures in marriage and family therapy.* Boston: Allyn and Bacon.

Brown, J. H., & Brown, C. S. (2002). *Marital therapy: Concepts and skills for effective practice.* New York: Brunner-Routledge.

Carlson, J., & Kjos, D. (2001). *Theories and strategies of family therapy.* Boston: Allyn and Bacon.

Gladding, S. T. (2002). *Family therapy: History, theory, and practice* (3rd ed.). Columbus, OH: Merrill.

Goldenberg, H., & Goldenberg, I. (2001). *Counseling today's families.* Pacific Grove, CA: Brooks/Cole.

Kleinplatz, P. J. (Ed.). (2001). *New directions in sex therapy: Innovations and alternatives.* New York: Brunner-Routledge.

Moore, C. W. (1996). *The mediation process: Practical strategies for resolving conflict* (2nd ed.). San Francisco: Jossey-Bass.

Nichols, M. P., & Schwartz, R. C. (2001). *The essentials of family therapy.* Boston: Allyn and Bacon.

Winslade, J., & Monk, G. (2000). *Narrative mediation: A new approach to conflict resolution.* San Francisco: Jossey-Bass.

CHAPTER 11

Group Leadership Skills

In many ways, group leadership skills are not that different from those used in individual or family or couples sessions, or even organizational settings. In all of these helping situations, you rely a lot on active listening, reflecting feelings and content, open-ended questions, and summarizing what was heard and understood. Likewise, you bring in a lot of your general clinical training to read nonverbal behavior, to identify problem areas, and so on. Yet there is also a lot of specialized content and skills in group leadership, which is one reason why you will have one or more additional courses focused solely on this clinical specialty.

We don't want to replicate needlessly the content that is covered in other courses, but we briefly mention some of the added content and skill areas that you will need in your work. Nowadays, every practitioner is expected to be thoroughly competent in applying therapeutic skills to various group settings. You will want to check out training manuals specifically related to group therapy and counseling skills. These books will give you an overview of core knowledge areas in understanding the stages of group development, group dynamics, and group treatment models.

GROUP STAGE DEVELOPMENT

Just as there are predictable, sequential developmental stages that individuals progress through, so too do groups follow a series of incremental steps. There are lots of names for these stages and lots of different models. Tuckman (1965) introduced the most widespread system, calling the stages forming, norming, storming, performing, and adjourning. Other stage models were introduced as well (see Corey & Corey, 2002; Kottler, 2001b). Basically they may be simplified into three basic stages: a beginning, a middle, and an ending.

In the beginning stage (also called the "forming" and "norming" stages), you build cohesion, address trust issues, establish constructive norms, and help members to create a solid working environment. You will also elicit content and establish treatment goals for each participant. This is an awkward stage because people are trying to learn to work together. They are asking themselves questions like:

Is this a safe place?
Does the leader know what he or she is doing?
Who can I trust here?
What do these people think of me?
What will I reveal and what will I hide?
Do I want to come back next time?

Needless to say, during this critical beginning stage you will do all you can to make the group experience as safe, interesting, and productive as possible. You are likely to apply exploration skills learned earlier to let group members know they have been heard and understood and to model these behaviors so that others will use them.

The middle stage is also known as the "working" stage. Once cohesion and trust have been established, it is safer for people to take risks. This is also known as the "storming" stage because members feel safer challenging the leader, confronting one another, and behaving in more natural ways. This is the stage where most of the work gets done and where the clients pursue their individual treatment goals. You will use almost all of your other therapeutic skills in this stage, but you must adapt them to fit the rather unique circumstances of working before an audience.

In the final closing stage, members work toward letting go. Unresolved issues are worked through (some of them, anyway). People say goodbye. Codependency issues are addressed. A follow-up program is structured so that clients have a structure for continuing their progress after the group ends. One of the unique challenges you will face in leading groups is that it is especially difficult to keep momentum going once the sessions have disbanded.

Consistent with most developmental models, it is fairly important to be able to assess accurately at which stage a group is operating so that therapeutic steps can be taken to facilitate progress to the next, deeper level.

GROUP DYNAMICS

There is an extensive body of literature and research on group behavior. Contributions are made from sociology, social psychology, organizational development, and related disciplines to describe and explain why and how people act the ways they do in interpersonal situations. You will be using some specialized observation skills to check some of the following areas:

Proxemics. What are the physical distances between people? How close or far away do people sit or stand from one another and what does that mean?

Nonverbal behavior. What are various group members communicating with their posture, their eyes, facial expressions, and gestures?

Coalitions. Who is aligned with whom? What are the cliques in the group?

Silence. There will be inevitable pauses in group that have different meanings. Are people bored? Confused? Resistant? Thoughtful?

Conflict. Where are the points of tension and competition? Where are struggles for power and control?

Group roles. Who is playing which roles in the group? Who is the scapegoat? Who are the leaders? Who has been marginalized?

Cultural identities. Which ethnic backgrounds, sexual orientations, gender identities, and similar cultural backgrounds shape the norms that have evolved?

Applying group leadership skills, you will constantly be observing member behavior to notice interesting or relevant patterns. At times, you will simply file away what you notice and use this information at a later time; other instances will require immediate intervention.

Exercise in Group Skills

You are in the midst of leading a group when, out of the corner of your eye, you notice that a usually talkative member has pulled his seat back and averted his body to the side. He is looking down and shuffling his feet, nervously flitting his eyes around the room and then looking down again.

What are some possible hypotheses that you can generate about what this behavior might mean? Don't settle on just one possibility from this limited data. Remember, you don't know the context for these actions, nor do you understand the relevant history. Caution and humility are in order.

Discuss some possible ways that you might intervene in this situation (if you think some action is desirable).

GROUP TREATMENT APPROACHES

Just as there are more than two dozen major theoretical approaches to therapy, so too are there a similar number of models applied to group leadership. Some of these approaches are virtually identical to what would be employed in individual sessions. For instance, the cognitive therapist would address the same dysfunctional beliefs in groups that she might when working with single clients (Corey & Corey, 2002). The existential therapist would explore universal themes of personal responsibility, freedom, and search for meaning. The behavioral clinician would still work on specific, identifiable goals.

Some therapeutic models evolved as group therapies before they were ever used with individuals. Gestalt and person-centered therapies are examples of approaches that were primarily field tested by Fritz Perls and Carl Rogers (respectively) in groups and later refined further for individual therapy. Other theories have been more specifically adapted from individual to group (and family) settings. Psychodynamic theory is one good example of this since it had been used for many decades with individuals before systematic group approaches were introduced (Corey & Corey, 2002).

Although it is beyond the scope of this book to cover this material in depth, you should realize that certain leadership skills are connected to their theoretical origins. So, for example, psychodynamic group leaders may be more inclined to use interpretation skills, humanistic practitioners would use lots of reflective skills, and cognitive therapists would favor challenging belief systems. Based on what you already understand about the influence of various theories on our profession, this should come as no surprise.

Some Differences to Keep in Mind

Although we have been emphasizing that there are indeed a lot of similarities between group and individual therapeutic skills, there are also some distinct differences to keep in mind. For one thing, group leadership requires even more multitasking skills. There are always a dozen, a hundred, maybe even a thousand things going on at the same time. While you are talking to one group member, everyone else in the group is reacting in some way. There is a barrage of stuff going on inside you—hunches, observations, feelings, thoughts, and only some of it is relevant. You have to sort out which things to attend to, both inside you and in the group. You have to track what the person-in-focus is saying to you, responding appropriately, and yet you must also manage the experience for everyone else present. Needless to say, this is a job that will test you in ways that you never imagined.

Building Cohesion

Unless you manage to create a climate and conditions that are conducive to trust and sharing, nothing much is going to happen in a group. It thus takes some effort to structure the environment in such a way that group members are likely to feel safe and disclose personal material in need of work.

Cohesion-building skills take place over the life of a group and are designed to help people to feel close, respectful, and caring towards one another (Kottler, 2001b). In a sense you are trying to build a community in which participants support one another, yet feel safe enough to be honest and confrontive.

Cohesion is built by using many of the skills that follow, in addition to those you have already learned. Essentially, you are looking for every opportunity to make connections between people, to guide them from a position of "I" to a more universal stance of "we."

There are specific structures and techniques that are often helpful in building cohesion. One such example that is often used requires members to reveal something personal about themselves, something a bit risky. This is presented as sort of the price of admission. Once you can get everyone to share a significant part of themselves, your next step is to develop what is called universality—a searching for common experience.

In the following example, the group leader uses an opportunity to build cohesion in a group:

> *Natalie:* I can't seem to get motivated to do this. I know I keep saying it's important but I don't seem to find the time to follow through.
> *Candy:* Then maybe it's not important.
> *Jose:* Yeah, I remember once when I had a problem like that . . .
> *Leader:* Candy and Jose, you are both offering something useful to Natalie but I wonder if we might go in another direction instead. I am wondering how the rest of you are relating to similar struggles in your own lives.
> *Jose:* Yeah, well I can definitely relate. What Natalie was talking about . . .
> *Leader:* [pointing] Tell Natalie.

So far, you can see that the leader is moving people away from advice giving, and even confrontation ("Maybe it's not important"), at this early stage. Instead she is trying to get other members to lend support to Natalie by talking about the ways that they have similar problems. This does several things simultaneously; it helps Natalie to not feel so alone, and it helps other members to talk about their shared issues. These are the bricks and mortar from which trust is built.

Cohesion can be facilitated further by providing opportunities for members to give support to the member-in-focus, as well as sharing more about their own experiences. This is how a community of caring is constructed.

> *Jose:* I just wanted to say to you, Natalie, that I have been having a problem like that in my life. What worked for me . . .
>
> *Leader:* Thanks Jose. Who else would be willing to tell Natalie about how you feel towards her since she shared this problem with you? Talk directly to her rather than to me.

By politely and firmly intervening after Jose's initial comment, the therapist is again trying to stop advice-giving (this "blocking" skill is discussed later) in favor of promoting more personal sharing to one another. The goals here are to help Natalie to feel proud of taking a risk and to help other members to feel closer to one another as a result of this sharing. Cohesion and trust often result from such instances when people reveal themselves in an honest and authentic way, and feel better about it afterwards.

Modeling

In all forms of counseling, therapy, and teaching, some modeling takes place. This is when clients learn new skills and attitudes as a result of watching the professional and internalizing what is observed (Kottler, 2001b). Often this takes place unconsciously and in very subtle ways.

In groups, where a lot of vicarious learning takes place anyway as a result of some members watching others work, modeling plays a more significant role. Remember that many group members don't know what is expected or how to behave. They don't know how to be effective participants. Your job is to teach them this by demonstrating appropriate behavior by the ways you present yourself.

Modeling skills can take many different forms. When the therapist intervenes with someone who is talking too much, the other members are watching carefully to see how this is done; they will be inclined to imitate the behavior in the future. When the therapist uses self-disclosure or tells a personal story designed to illustrate a point, this may encourage others to follow the lead.

Although we could list a number of other specific ways that modeling can be done, the general principle is that all clients watch carefully what you do, how you behave, and who you are. If they are drawn to you, if they respect you, if they admire you, then they will be likely to imitate your style and behavior and values. What this means is that who you are is as important as what you do. Modeling is not so much a skill (although it does require being skillful) as it is a way of being.

Exercise on Modeling

Make a list of those specific behaviors, values, attitudes, and personal characteristics that your instructor models in class. Among these dimensions that you have identified, which of them would you most like to include in your own style?

In small groups, compare notes about what features you have identified. Come to a consensus about which modeled behaviors have been most powerful and influential on your own thinking and behavior.

Capitalizing on Vicarious Identification

One of the remarkable things that happens in groups is that while one person is working and is the focus of attention, others are identifying strongly with what is going on. Imagine, for example, that someone is talking about a problem with his boss. This authority figure is reported as being arbitrary, capricious, unfair, and at times even verbally abusive and disrespectful. Time is taken in the group to help this person to work on the issue, role-play a possible confrontation, understand the underlying issues, connect this problem to others in his life, and then finally to commit himself to take constructive action. The vicarious identification skill that next takes place occurs when the therapist asks other group members to talk about how they have personalized or identified with the issue that was presented. This is some of what people said:

- "I don't have a problem with my boss. In fact, I like my boss a lot. But this reminded me of the crap I get from my father, who still tries to control my life. I've decided it's time to do something about this."
- "I was thinking about the way I feel treated by an instructor. She always seems to cut me off when I make comments in class, as if she doesn't like me or value what I have to say. I'm going to talk to her."
- "Gee, I was reminded that some of the people who work for me may feel the same way that you do toward your boss. I sure hope not but I intend to check this out with them."

Like many of these leadership skills, there is no single specific behavior that can be learned so much as an overall strategy that is different from that of individual sessions where you don't have to be concerned about these additional challenges. Remember that in groups even though you may be working with one person at a time, you are doing so before an audience in which each person is asking him or herself: "What does this have to do with me and my life?"

Linking

This skill involves making connections between members as well as searching for common themes that have emerged (Corey & Corey, 2002). As mentioned earlier, linking often leads to cohesion and trust building but may also be used in a more general sense of connecting material from various members to find common themes.

Cassie: I just feel so out of control lately. I can't seem to sleep or eat right. I walk around like a zombie.

Luis: I know what that's like. I've been working three jobs trying to keep my head above water.

Leader: So Luis, you can identify with the stresses that Cassie has been going through even though your pressure results from a different source. I wonder if others might say something about how they identify with what Cassie and Luis have mentioned?

The therapist is trying to universalize Cassie's disclosure so she doesn't feel so alone and also to help members remain engaged in the process. The best way to think about linking skills is that you are trying to build as many points of connection as possible between members. This is important not only in group work but also in family counseling sessions.

Exercise in Linking

Get together in small groups. Each of you present separate personal issues that are either real or role-played. Take turns making linking statements to draw connections and find common themes in issues that were presented.

Scanning

In group and family sessions you must juggle the needs of multiple clients at the same time. You have less control over what's going on and less time to attend to the individual concerns of each person. For this reason, it is important to monitor carefully how each person is doing and how each one is reacting to what is going on at any moment in time.

Scanning is the skill of continuously observing each member of the group, using your eyes to let each person know that you are aware of him or her (Kottler, 2001b). It is sort of like you are continuously taking the pulse of each person, communicating that you are watching to make sure they are okay.

Scanning is a safety measure but much more than that. It is what allows you to keep the group functioning as a unit, reading problems when they first manifest themselves nonverbally. Who is nervous? Who is reluctant? Who is excited? Who is about to talk? What wants to say something but needs some encouragement? Who is restless and bored? Who is sending signals to others? Who is frustrated? Who is in trouble?

Scanning involves simply periodically "making the rounds" of a group with your eyes, checking in with each person. When you are leading a group by yourself (as opposed to having a coleader), you will already have enough to do just helping individual members work on their issues. It takes additional energy to remember to scan the group to see what else is going on while you have been focused on one person who was talking.

> ### Exercise in Scanning
>
> *Make an effort to scan periodically around your class or in other groups of which you are a member. Notice the nonverbal behavior around you, the variety of ways that people are reacting to what is going on. Notice who is bored, who is frustrated or puzzled, who wants to talk and is waiting for an opening. Who is agreeing most with what is going on? Who is disagreeing? Make scanning a habitual part of your natural behavior.*

Cuing

One of the unique aspects of doing group therapy over individual therapy is that you are trying to get members to do most of the work. Initially, you may model appropriate ways of intervening, showing people how to respond sensitively, how to explore issues, how to confront someone, how to let people know they have been heard and understood. Whenever possible, it is best to cue members to intervene rather than trying to do everything yourself (Kottler, 2001b). There are several reasons for this: it helps clients to learn helping skills, it diffuses reactions to authority, and it spreads around responsibility for the work.

If you are scanning consistently and effectively, then you will notice members who are having strong reactions to what is going on and what is being said. You can use these observations to cue members to talk at appropriate times. This is often far more effective than you having to do the work.

For instance, someone in the group is consistently talking too much. You know this is a problem because you want to draw out the quieter members instead of letting this one person continue to dominate. But if you are the one to intervene, there are certain side effects. For one, the person may likely feel publicly censured by the authority figure. Besides, people generally need practice confronting others and this would be a perfect opportunity.

So, when you notice this monopolizing behavior going on, rather than saying something about it, you might look around the group and see who else is bothered or disturbed. You notice that a quiet man is shaking his head and muttering to himself.

Leader: Excuse me, Dan, but I couldn't help but notice that while Melinda was talking, you were shaking your head. What's going on?

Dan: Nothing.

Leader: It might be my imagination but you seemed to be annoyed about something when Melinda was talking.

Dan: Well, it's just that she talks . . .

Leader: Don't tell me. Tell her.

The therapist has cued Dan to confront Melinda rather than doing so himself. Ironically, Melinda is far more likely to hear such a confrontation from another member, where she will not feel so threatened than if it had been the therapist who intervened.

Blocking

Unlike in individual counseling situations, you are not in complete control of what happens in a group. Some members may say things that are mean, or even hurtful. Some people may talk too much or attempt to act in manipulative ways. Sometimes you may even end up with severe personality disorders in a group, individuals who may wish to disrupt the process for their own sense of power or entertainment. Less severe but still challenging are those clients who simply lack interpersonal skills or socially appropriate behavior. They may disrupt proceedings and become distracting if their behavior is not checked. This means that you *must* set limits and enforce these boundaries consistently.

There are specific times when you must intervene to prevent people from hurting one another, or themselves.

When Someone Is Being Disrespectful or Abusive. You must prevent members from being verbally inappropriate or hurtful to others. This is part of the group norms that you would establish from the beginning. Examples of such behavior that you would need to block include any instance when members are rude, hurtful, or disrespectful to one another. This might occur because the person is insensitive, ignorant of consequences, malicious, or malevolent.

You can block this behavior directly by labeling what is going on and intervening to stop it: "Excuse me, but speaking to him with your voice raised and using that language are not tolerated in here." Another way of handling the situation is to structure an opportunity to give the person feedback at the same time that the "victim" is given a chance to do some work.

> *Freda:* Look, bitch, I don't give a shit about this crap. And I'm tired of listening to you and hearing you whine all the time.
>
> *Leader:* Freda, I can see that you are feeling rather strongly about Teresa and what she has been saying. [reflection of feeling] But speaking to Teresa in this way is not okay. [blocking] Teresa, I wonder if you'd be willing to talk to Freda about what that felt like. [cuing]
>
> *Teresa:* She was mean. And that hurt. But I'm not surprised . . .
>
> *Leader:* Talk to Freda. [redirecting]
>
> *Teresa:* Freda, I don't like it when you talk to me that way. It hurts. If you've got some problem with me, then . . .
>
> *Freda:* Look, you talk too damn much. Nobody else can get a word in . . .
>
> *Leader:* Freda, I don't think that Teresa is hearing you when you use that tone of voice. [blocking] I wonder if you could try it again but phrase it in a way, and in a tone of voice, that might be easier for Teresa to hear you.

When Someone Is Incessantly Complaining. Remember, group members don't know the rules and norms for how to behave. Some members will whine and complain about all the people in their lives who they believe are making them miserable. Even if this were true (which it rarely is), there is still little you can do to change anyone else's behavior. Unless you block this behavior, you can easily eat up all the time in the group with people going on and on about others who are annoying.

The intervention usually takes the form of saying something like, "Because this person is not in the group, there is little we can do to help him or her. What about you?"

Energizing

Leading groups is considerably different than individual counseling because you must juggle so many tasks at the same time and keep so many different people (with different needs) fully engaged in the process. At times, this job seems overwhelming.

Based on scanning and other therapeutic skills, you must keep the group members interested throughout the proceedings. When a client is talking about something that is not of obvious interest to others, they may check out. When someone rambles too much, then people tend to tune out what is going on. When people are tired or when routines become too predictable they may also lose interest and motivation. These are times when the pace of the group will diminish and energy will lag.

At such times you must take steps and use all your skills to change the energy level. There are a lot of very creative ways to do this that are limited by your own imagination. Sometimes, the most direct way to deal with the problem is to bring it up to the group: "I notice the energy level seems to be flagging right now. What's going on?"

By naming what you see (or feel) happening, you present the group with the problem to solve; after all, it is *their* group. If they are bored or disengaged, then it is their responsibility to do something to liven things up.

Facilitating Feedback

If a client is to receive feedback about dysfunctional behavior, the therapist is the only one who can offer it during individual counseling. But in group work, a distinct strength is that a person may receive feedback and input from multiple sources. There is nothing more useful, and exciting, than hearing about how one is perceived by others. Your job is to structure things in such a way to make this happen. This can be as simple as asking the client who received attention if he or she would like to hear feedback, or it can involve a far more complex activity that involves everyone.

Giving feedback is a skill that must be learned like any other. In order to teach this skill to others, you must first be an expert yourself. This means that you must work hard at learning to hear feedback yourself in a way that you do not feel defensive and can make changes based on what was offered. It also means that you must learn to give feedback to others so that that they don't shut down or ward off perceived threats. And make no mistake: It is very scary to hear honest reactions from people about how you are perceived.

Here are some guidelines to keep in mind:

Be Honest and Frank. Solid feedback must be on target. This is not time for watering down the truth or hedging for the sake of being polite. A group is supposed to be the one setting where participants can finally find out what others think and feel about them. Our whole lives we walk around in the world doing some stupid, ineffective, and annoying things but few (if any) people will ever tell us this. They will whisper behind our backs. They will think their most private opinions about us. They will tell others. But rarely will you hear such remarks to your face. It is as if the whole world knows something about you that is hidden from your own view. How many times, for instance, have you looked at people and wondered how they could not possibly realize how annoying some trait is? In groups you have to create ways that people can hear out loud what people are thinking.

As we stated in the previous chapter, make sure to include both supportive and constructive elements. Ordinarily, this might be labeled as "positive" and "negative" feedback, but these terms are neither accurate nor useful. It so happens that what might be called "negative," that is, critical, might actually be the most constructive thing that could ever be offered to you. Let's say, for example, that you have some irritating trait that is off-putting and that compromises your credibility. Maybe you raise your voice at the end of each statement, turning it into a question. Or perhaps you end every sentence by saying, "Do you know what I mean?" Or maybe you avert your eyes from others, communicating a lack of confidence. Everyone in your world knows this about you, but until you hear from others how this behavior affects them, you are not going to do much to change it. So, what this means is that what you might ordinarily think of as "negative" feedback is really quite positive and constructive.

Likewise, so-called "positive" feedback, the kind that is generally supportive and complementary, might feel good for a few minutes but may not give you anything solid that you can work on. If we tell you that you are a nice person, that you are smart or lovely or kind, that would certainly feel good. But what can you do with that? What does that give you to work on?

So, the best feedback contains elements that are both supportive and constructive. Here are some examples:

> I really like the way that you assert yourself and speak up for your rights. One thing I struggle with, however, is that you sometimes come across to me as overly aggressive and self-centered.

> I love the way that you are always there for all of us. You are the first one to jump in whenever anyone needs help or support. But I also notice that you don't take care of yourself. It is almost as if you are trying to hide in other people's problems so you don't have to deal with your own.

Use Descriptive, Personalized Language. Feedback is more valuable when it is adapted to the person you are offering it to. You will want to be as specific as possible and to supply examples of the behavior you are describing. Compare these two ways that feedback could be presented to someone who is acting inappropriately intrusive in the group, pushing people to do or say things that they are not yet ready to reveal.

> Although I know that you mean well, and you are just trying to be helpful, you can be pushy at times. I wish you'd back off sometimes.

> You play an important role in the group of being one of the lead persons to help others explore their issues. Sometimes, however, you seem to push harder than would seem necessary. For instance, just a few minutes ago, Claire said

clearly that she wasn't sure she want to go any further with this, yet rather than hearing and respecting her reluctance, you continued to press her to reveal more and more. You can and should check this out with Claire, but my sense is that she shut down because you pushed her too hard.

Generally speaking, the more specific the feedback the better, and the more concrete the examples, the easier it is for the person to act on what is being said.

Be Sensitive and Caring. Remember that hearing feedback is often very frightening and threatening. Offer it in the most loving way possible, as if you are giving someone a precious gift (which it is).

Exercise in Feedback

In order to become more expert at teaching group members to give and receive feedback you will need to gain as much experience as possible—and as much feedback on your feedback as you can get. You must make this a priority, not only for improving feedback ability but all your therapeutic skills.

With partners or in small groups, practice giving feedback to one another that meets the most important criteria—that is, that you are sensitive, caring, supportive, honest, descriptive, and provide specific examples.

Afterward, give one another feedback on the feedback. In other words, help one another to become more effective in using this skill in the future.

WORKING WITH A CO-LEADER

Another unique facet of group or family therapy is working with a partner as a co-therapist. There are a number of reasons to use this format. First, it provides greater coverage of the group. While one leader is working with a client, the other leader can be scanning and monitoring other members. Second, the co-leaders can model the way cooperative partners (surrogate parents) work together. This increases the possibilities for members to have a positive identification with a therapist. And finally, it gives the therapists a forum for comparing notes and supervising one another. As you will discover, there is a no more lonely job sometimes than being a therapist, and especially a group therapist because there is so much to process afterward.

There is a special set of skills employed when working with a co-leader. It is crucial that you work together as a team, that you synchronize efforts so as to present a consistent, unified front. That is not to say that you can't and shouldn't disagree with one another in front of the group, because that could be instructive if done respectfully.

Sit Opposite One Another for Maximum Coverage. You want to be able to scan opposite sides of the room. You also will want to see one another so you can signal one another and make eye contact to communicate throughout the session.

Develop a Signal System. Spend some time with one another ahead of time so you feel comfortable working together. Agree on signals that you might use during the group to indicate when time is running out, when you are confused, or when you want to move on to something else.

Make Sure You Are Equal Participants. Co-leader teams are a lot less effective when they don't work together as equal participants. Make sure that you and your partner get equal time to participate in the group process.

Take Time-Outs as Needed. When you are at cross purposes or don't understand where things are going, feel free to take a time-out in order to talk across the group about what is going on, or not going on. Here are some examples of when this might take place:

"I'm not sure where you are going right now."
"I'm confused what this silence means. Where should we go next?"
"I don't think that Tim is ready to go on much further with this. I think we should move on."
"I could use some help right now."
"I really like the way you did that."

Of course, there is also modeling going on in that group members are seeing two partners discuss things openly and make decisions cooperatively.

Exercise to Co-lead a Group

Team up with a partner to practice the co-therapy model and experience what it is like to work together as part of a treatment team. One way to do this is in a role-play situation in which one person plays a client (or presents a part of oneself) and two others interview the person together. Find a couple of opportunities in which to take a time-out and talk to one another to make sure efforts are coordinated.

UNIQUE ETHICAL CHALLENGES

When you are applying group skills, it is important to understand the special ethical considerations involved. These are in addition to the usual things you must watch out for in any therapeutic encounter.

Confidentiality

Although in individual sessions communications can be kept private and sacred, there are no guarantees that this is the case in groups. You can urge members to respect others' privacy. You can stress how critical this privilege is for the group to work. You can prepare members for potential violations. But you can't ensure that everyone will honor the rules. Some violations may occur inadvertently, and others may result from malicious motives.

Informed Consent

As with all forms of treatment, you are required to inform clients about the risks, cautions, contraindications, and dangers so they can make informed choices about whether and how to participate. This would include mentioning the limits of confidentiality, but also other issues like the inevitable peer pressure and possible coercion that can take place. In most, if not in all groups, participants pressure perceived "deviates"—those who are different from the norm—to comply with the majority values. Individual rights must be protected and members given the opportunity to pass. Research on group work has shown that casualties most likely occur when people are pressured to do things that they are not ready or prepared to do. Once some group members take risks and reveal themselves, they want others to do so as well so they aren't left hanging out there alone. The idea is that I opened myself up to you; now you reciprocate so I have something on you and you can't betray me without fear of retribution.

Control

One other ethical challenge has to do with less control you have during the process. In individual therapy, if something goes wrong it is because of your lapse or mistake, but in groups anyone present can do something hurtful. That is why you must receive additional training in group work because the skills are so specialized. You have seen how the other skills you have learned must also be adapted in order to work effectively.

Exercise in Group Skills

If you have not already had experience as a group member in a therapeutic type group, we would urge you to make this a major priority in your training and personal development. Even though you will likely take a course (or two) in leading groups, we still strongly recommend that you gain experience sitting in the client's chair. That is the only way you can fully appreciate what your clients will go through when they appear cautious, reluctant, or hesitant to go along with your planned program.

PITFALLS AND COMMON MISTAKES

Most of the pitfalls that occur with individuals and families apply with groups as well, and we next cover some of these again but from the paradigm of a group. However, as a group leader of a group of strangers, you may have some unique opportunities to mess up, too, and we cover those as well.

Trying to Do Too Much

We talked about this in previous chapters, and we cover it again here with groups. As with individuals, you may find yourself working harder than the group. You may have also noticed that while working with a group, you have more information to attend to and more people to attend to. So, in a way, you will have more work to do. However, once you establish the boundaries and set up the culture of the group, you can use other members to do the work. You would do this by first modeling how to communicate and behave, and then by linking, scanning, cuing, and blocking. Eventually, the members catch on and do this automatically. Sometimes a member of the group begins to act as the leader. Then, by the time the group culture is established, your work should be much easier than when you started.

Failing to Establish Boundaries

As with working with families, establishing group ground rules is essential at the beginning of the group. You will want to cover confidentiality and that while you expect each member to keep confidentiality, you cannot guarantee it. You will want to cover some of the same ground rules you did with families, such as respecting each other (not calling each other names), letting people finish what they have to say before responding, and attending on time and consistently. There may be other rules that you consider important for running the group, but many of these can be addressed indirectly, such as blocking advice giving. Whatever boundaries you want to establish, you must use them consistently to avoid the appearance of favoritism, just as you do with families. Without these boundaries, a group of strangers can quickly decompensate. The slightest threat to safety can set a group back for weeks.

Failing to Keep the Monopolizer in Check

More often than not, you will have at least one group member who will monopolize the session if you let him or her. He or she will talk incessantly, commenting on anything anyone else says. The monopolizer will not allow silence to simmer. He or she will always want to talk. If you don't keep this person in check, the other members will become frustrated. They will not feel their needs are getting met. They may not return. However, if, instead, you use your scanning and subsequent cuing skills, the group can help you to keep this person in check. In fact, once cohesion has been established and the group feels safe, this person will likely get confronted by other members and have a unique opportunity to understand how he or she comes across to others. In individual therapy, you don't have this advantage. Thus managing the monopolizer not only helps the monopolizer learn new ways of communicating, but keeps the group functioning better.

Not Dealing With Silence Well

We mentioned this with individual therapy, and if you think it's challenging to allow or facilitate silence with individual therapy, group silence will really feel like torture. In a group, nearly all silence is productive in some way. Of course, in the first few sessions, because you are establishing the group, you may want to avoid awkward silences where no one knows how to proceed. But when working in the later stages of the group, silence can be powerful. Just like in individual therapy, sometimes silence allows one person or several people within the group to process information. It will be important that you give time for that to occur by attending to the person who is processing. If you look around the room, slowly, others might want to talk to fill in the silence. At other times, the group will feel stuck and go silent. You may want to "save" them and say something, but allowing the silence to hang can be good for the group. It's part of the process. After these types of silences, you might want to process what that was like for each member.

Being Too Cautious

Because working with groups might facilitate strong negative emotions in proportions greater than with individuals, you may feel cautious. You may do things in a group to avoid arguments or confrontations, if you are uncomfortable with them. You may interrupt important interpersonal conflicts that involve the expression of negative emotions. If you are not comfortable with anger or tears, you will really struggle in a group. One of the most valuable advantages of a group is to have group members work through conflict. Your role as therapist is not to avoid these conflicts, but rather to teach members how to disagree or confront well. And don't be surprised if at some point, you get to be the center of attention. Sometimes this can be the most difficult group process to deal with. It is not unusual for groups to get frustrated that they have revealed so much of themselves, and yet you, the leader, have revealed nothing. Occasionally, they can get downright angry with you. If you can remember that your purpose is to accept the expression of their anger but in a way that is most constructive, you will not have to take it personally.

All ranges of emotions should be allowed in a group. Sometimes your job will be to facilitate these feelings that are usually withheld. Try to gather the courage to experience intense feelings so that the members can learn how to direct those feelings in a constructive way.

Pushing Too Much (Before and After Cohesion)

In contrast to being too cautious, you also can err in the other direction. You can push your group or each member too much. There are two particular areas where you may want to be sensitive to pushing too hard. First, if the group has not formed cohesively enough yet, if it's not yet safe, then you probably don't want to facilitate anything before the members are ready. You cannot expect in the first, second, or even third session that group members are ready to confront each other. If you notice, for example, that when Sally speaks, Jane rolls her eyes, just make a mental note of it. Once the cohesion is established, then cue Jane to tell you what her expression is about. The opportunity will surely arise later.

Even when the group is fully cohesive, you still can push too hard. When you are doing individual work, pushing is a little safer in that the likelihood the client will feel humiliated is limited. However, in a group, humiliation is easily accessible. Clients have not only you to think about, but how the group perceives them as well. Therefore, you will want to gently push clients when you can. In a group more than with individual therapy, if you push too hard, the group member may not return. In addition, other members may not think it is safe to be vulnerable either, so your group goes back to the first stage where the members will reveal little.

Not Working Well With a Co-leader

While you are in training, you may get assigned to work with another leader in a group. In fact, most agencies require that your first group experience be with a co-leader who has more experience than you. Therefore, your personal styles of running a group or assumptions about how a group should be run may differ.

For example, you may find yourself working in a domestic violence agency where you are assigned to work with batterers. The group may be primarily psychoeducational, but you prefer to be more humanistic. Imagine that you are paired with a co-leader who likes to be by the book in teaching this group about the cycle of violence. You find yourself talking over each other, giving each other dirty looks, and losing direction and focus within the group because of your power struggle. Or because you are new, you just sit quietly and allow your co-leader to completely dominate. How do you think this will affect the group? Remember, everything you do is a model of interpersonal communication for group members. Although some members may mimic your styles of interpersonal communication, others might just feel frustrated with the palpable tension between you.

The best way to avoid co-leader problems is to start by discussing your style of leading groups and what process you would like to facilitate. After each group session, take some time to talk about any snags, any misunderstandings, or negative feelings. You must be able to assert yourself and not fall into the passive-aggressive game. If you do, you not only hurt your growth as a therapist, you hurt the group as well. So talk it out and be honest. It's another opportunity to practice giving feedback.

Being Too Serious

As the group forms cohesion and starts doing serious work, you may find that suddenly the group stops working. You may want to facilitate a more serious conversation, but the group won't have anything to do with it. This may be because the previous session was too serious or too deep, and the group needs to lighten up a bit to balance the depth that occurred in the previous session. Another way the group can be too serious is just if the nature of the group tends to be serious. After a while, this can get draining to the group members, and to you. We highly recommend using humor when you can to lighten the situation. The best thing we can do is learn to laugh at ourselves. Of course, this must be done at appropriate times. But if done correctly, varying the mood of the group will keep it more lively and interesting for you and the other members.

Not Balancing Individual Needs and the Needs of the Group

One unique challenge to working with groups, including families, is to balance individual needs with the needs of the group. You may remember at the beginning of the chapter, we mentioned that the group is a unit, a client unit that functions as a whole. It has its own culture, its own unique personality and identity. Therefore, you have an opportunity to focus on what is good for the group as a whole, to facilitate the movement through stages, to get the individual members to do the work, or to keep the best interest of the larger group in mind. You can do this to a point where you forget to consider the individual differences.

For example, imagine that one of the members begins to talk about her experience of being raped in college. She describes feeling powerless and having no control. In the midst of her sorrow, you think, "Ah, a time to link using feeling powerless," and you try to link this feeling. You have begun to invalidate this one person's experience. You must let them go where they need to in the conversation for some period of time before attempting to link. It's only when they start to monopolize that you might want to shift the direction.

In contrast, you may be primarily an individual therapist and get tempted to just do individual therapy while the other members watch. This extreme is not good either. In some counseling programs, one requirement of the group class is that each student must participate as a group member with classmates where the group is led by teaching assistants. Under these conditions, it is not unusual for one member to self-disclose, and all other members, including the leader, to do therapy with that person. The next week, the same process occurs, but with a different person revealing something personal. This process is basically sequential individual therapy. It's therapy for one person and eight therapists. Consequently, allowing this process to occur for too long loses the primary advantage of being in a group: working through interpersonal issues. And if you find that one member really does need individual attention, it is appropriate to recommend privately to that person that individual therapy might be helpful. This way the individual can get his or her more intense issues dealt with in a more appropriate venue, and use the group for more interpersonal challenges.

APPLICATIONS TO SELF: YOU ARE ALREADY IN A GROUP

One of the first things that most group textbooks cover is that being in a group is the most natural thing in the world. You are constantly in a group whether you are with your family, with friends, in class, in line at the grocery store. In some way, you could be defined as being in a group most of the time. Therefore, you should have ample opportunity to practice these skills outside of class. Let's look at each one.

Think of a group of friends you might have made recently. You may use the students in this class as an example. What stage are you in with your group? If this is your first semester together and you haven't done a lot outside of class, you may still be in the first stage of getting to know each other and determining what and who is safe. If you have been together a lot prior to this class and/or met outside of class a lot, you may be in the second phase where you can confront each other and can survive conflict. Or because this is the end of the semester, you may be finding ways to part and say goodbye in the ending stage of the group. Identifying the stages can sometimes be quite obvious, but sometimes it's more difficult as members move between the first and second stages for a while before everyone feels safe.

In addition to the observation skills you learned in one of the earlier chapters with individuals, groups offer additional challenges for you to attend to. Think about the last time your family gathered. As the memory forms and becomes clear, think about a particular moment in the group. What were the proxemics? Did you notice the nonverbal behavior of some of the people who were not talking? Where were the coalitions and conflicts? Was there silence, and if so, what was the meaning of the silence? What roles do each of the family members typically take? How has culture influenced the norms of this group, your family, as compared with another family you know? We imagine you might feel a bit overwhelmed with having to attend to so much, and it is difficult. However, the more you practice, the more these things will become second nature. Now let's move on to other skills.

Think back again to a new group, which has formed recently. Perhaps you will use this class or another class of fellow students. After reading about the importance of cohesion, think about how you have formed cohesion in this group so far. What else can you do to facilitate more cohesion? Perhaps you could risk revealing something risky, something personal. Perhaps you already have. In fact, think of groups where you have revealed something personal as compared with groups you have not. We might make a guess that more cohesion formed in those groups where you showed some level of vulnerability. This can be used as an important tool if you want to increase the cohesiveness in groups.

Think about this particular class and compare it with another class with a different instructor. We can guess that there are some differences in how you participate in the class, whether due to the content of the class, or to different personal styles. How have your instructors modeled appropriate behavior? What have they done to facilitate certain behavior and extinguish other behaviors? Think about whether the instructors seem to communicate in a way that they teach you to communicate. As you form these impressions, you can become more conscious of this very subtle skill. Therefore, you will want to be aware of how you come across as the group leader, because whether you intend to or not, your behavior will set up a foundation for how to behave in the group.

Linking can sometimes be difficult for students at first. It's not always something that comes naturally, but with practice, it can become second nature. Everywhere you go, listen to the ways in which people talk. Pay attention not only to the content of information but the process, how they communicate. When you focus on both content and process, you will find it easier to make connections between people. This is a skill you can practice everywhere: at school, with friends, with family, in a restaurant.

We already suggested how to use scanning. When you are in class, scan the room to check how people are responding. For instance, if you find yourself reacting to something strongly, look around the room to see if anyone else seems to be responding as well. Pay attention to the nonverbal behaviors of those around you. Your natural inclination will be to focus on the person who is talking, so this might be difficult at first. However, this, too, will become a habit with practice, and it is most essential in working with groups.

In class, notice how your instructor cues different people to talk. He or she may call names, make eye contact and nod, or say something to indicate it's appropriate for you to speak. Also, go somewhere where people gather and watch how they communicate in groups. How does each person know when it's their turn to speak? Sometimes one person monopolizes the conversation, making it difficult for others. At other times, members of the group intentionally elicit from quieter members. Regardless of the situation, notice the process of who talks when and how they know it's their turn. Then use what you learn to cue group members when you notice something interesting from scanning.

Blocking can be a more difficult skill because we are inclined to not interrupt in social conversations. However, this is a skill that is quite essential as a group leader to prevent feelings from being hurt unnecessarily and to enhance the safety and cohesion of the group. We have a more difficult challenge for you on this skill. The next time you are with a group of friends or family members, and one person seems to get attacked, take the risk to interrupt in some way to block the process. We realize this will not be done in a way that is exactly like in group counseling, but try it nonetheless. Assert yourself to protect the underdog. If you can do this with your friends or, more challenging, with your family in a way that is productive, you will be a master of using blocking in a group.

Finally, energizing a group can be important when things come to a lull. As stated before, you may notice that a group doesn't seem very energized. Sometimes this happens after a particularly intense group experience, or sometimes it happens when the group feels less safe for a moment. You may notice that with longer friendships, you have had times where the energy in the friendship has waned. Your natural inclination might be to just deal with it. However, try doing something different. Bring it up. Say that you've noticed a change and see what comes of it. A single statement is all you need to stimulate a conversation: "I've noticed we don't laugh as much anymore."

We have now reviewed nine skills associated with running groups that you can practice in class, with friends, or with family members. If you haven't had your group class yet, getting started now will put you ahead of your class so that you can work on more advanced skills. Get the basics down. And remember, you can use these skills to help work in other environments, such as families, couples, with schoolteachers, or at home with the people closest to you.

SUMMARY

In this chapter, we introduced you to some of the ways in which working with groups is different than working with individuals. We briefly covered some the major concepts associated with group work; such as group stages and terms such as *proxemics*. Several skills have been included that are specific to working with groups. Finally, we covered some skills associated with working with a co-leader, and the unique ethical considerations involved in doing group therapy. Now we move on to the last chapter, on what's next.

A CHECK ON WHAT YOU LEARNED

1. How many stages are there in group development, according to the authors? What are they? Describe each stage.
2. Paying attention to the physical distance between people is called what?
3. What two theories were applied to groups before they were used with individuals?
4. List the ways in which cohesion can be built.

5. The style in which you communicate and behave will be copied by the members of the group. This technique is called what?
6. Making connections and searching for common themes is called what?
7. What skill helps you in knowing what's going on with all members at any given time, especially the members not currently speaking?
8. One way to get members of the group to do most of the work without having to assert your power as the leader is to do what?
9. What are two times when blocking might be appropriate?
10. How might you energize a group that seems bored or disinterested?
11. True or false: When working with a co-leader, it is appropriate to disagree in front of the group.

SUGGESTED READINGS

Barlow, C. A., Blythe, J. A., & Edmonds, M. (1999). *A handbook of interactive exercises for groups.* Boston: Allyn and Bacon.

Capuzzi, D. (2003). *Approaches to group work: A handbook for practitioners.* Upper Saddle River, NJ: Prentice Hall.

Corey, G. (2000). *Theory and practice of group counseling* (5th ed.). Pacific Grove, CA: Brooks/Cole.

Corey, M. S., & Corey, G. (2002). *Groups: Process and practice* (6th ed.). Pacific Grove, CA: Brooks/Cole.

Gladding, S. T. (2003). *Group work: A counseling specialty* (4th ed.). Upper Saddle River, NJ: Merrill.

Haney, H., & Leibsohn, J. (2001). *Basic counseling responses in groups.* Belmont, CA: Wadsworth.

Kline, W. B.(2003). *Interactive group counseling and therapy.* Upper Saddle River, NJ: Prentice Hall.

Kottler, J. A. (2001). *Learning group leadership.* Boston: Allyn and Bacon.

Posthuma, B. W. (2002). *Small groups in counseling and therapy: Process and leadership.* Boston: Allyn and Bacon.

Yalom, I. (1995). *The theory and practice of group psychotherapy.* New York: Basic Books.

CHAPTER 12

Where to Go Next

It is perfectly reasonable, and perhaps appropriate, that you would feel a certain degree of apprehension about using your new skills in actual sessions with real people. In fact, if you are enjoying excessive confidence at this point, you might want to examine some possible feelings of arrogance bordering on grandiosity. We don't mean to imply that with solid skills training, excellent supervision, and the work experiences you may already have under your belt, you are not entitled to feel good about how far you have come in your professional development. But we do wish to stress that even with 10 or more years experience in the field, many practitioners still feel a degree of trepidation when facing a new client. This is not only normal but expected; it is part of the exhilaration that makes this job so much fun.

Soon you will not be role-playing anymore, nor doing pretend exercises. You are about to see clients in pain who desperately need your help.

We remember all too clearly the terror we felt waiting to be assigned to our practica and field placements after we completed our skills training. Thus far, we had been able to fool our professors and classmates pretty well, pretending that we were far more confident about our abilities than we actually felt. But now with the prospect of seeing actual live people coming in for help, the game was about up. We would have to 'fess up that we had no idea what we were really doing. There was this one reoccurring fantasy that went something like this:

Client: So I was saying that I was really upset about the way this was going . . .

Me: You were feeling anxious because you weren't sure what to do.

Client: That's the best you can do?

Me: Excuse me?

Client: That is the poorest excuse for a reflection of feeling that I've ever heard. I've seen a lot of therapists in my life and I gotta tell you that you are absolutely the worst.

Me: I am?

Client: Damn right! Your attending behaviors stink. Your reflection was shallow, and besides that, it missed the mark completely. I wonder if you were even listening. You look so nervous you are making me feel worse.

Me: Gee, I'm sorry about that. But I'm just a beginner at this . . .

Client: You're sorry? That's the best you can do? I'm feeling so discouraged by your low level empathy skills that I feel like killing myself. In fact, I think I will . . .

Okay, maybe this fantasy is a little exaggerated. But you would be perfectly entitled to have more than a few disastrous images of what could go wrong when you start seeing clients. Most of your fears are ungrounded, but it is still understandable that you will feel anxious before you start any new challenging enterprise.

The reality of doing counseling is that clients are so involved in their own stuff that they are barely paying attention to what you do anyway. You will be your harshest critic. Besides, as you have hopefully already learned, most of what you do to be helpful is not related to the perfect execution of your skills, but rather your overall presence with the people you are helping and the quality of the relationships you develop.

There are a number of common apprehensions and fears often expressed by students at this point in their development.

What If I Don't Know What to Do?

Time to burst *that* bubble. It is a certainty that much of the time you *won't* know what to do in a given situation. As you have learned, therapy is so complex, the clinical choices so limitless, that whatever you do at any moment, you will be flooded with other paths you could have taken instead.

The question is not so much what to do *if* you don't know what to do, but *when* you face this challenge every session. And the answer is that you do the best you can. You trust the process. You remind yourself that the client is the one who does most of the work; you are the facilitator. And the only way you will ever get better at this stuff is to be honest with yourself—and your supervisor—about what you don't know and cannot yet do. Mostly, just strengthen your ability to build the relationship with your client through attending and being empathic. Your clients will be your teachers and will do the rest.

What If My Supervisor Finds Out How Little I Know?

So much of your continued learning and growth will be related to the quality of your supervision. Unless you feel a degree of trust toward your supervisors, you are not likely to be very open and honest with them about areas in which you most need help. If you feel like you have to hide your weaknesses and cover up your mistakes to win your supervisor's approval and respect, you may be able to fake your way through the experience but at a very high cost. That is why you should choose your supervisor carefully and why you should be open with him or her about the things you need to work on.

We ask our students to bring us not their best tapes, but their absolute worst ones. Furthermore, we ask them to cue the tapes to the parts where they are most bumbling, awkward, and incompetent (or at least when they felt most that way). This is not an exercise in humiliation, but rather our intent is to teach beginners to get in the habit of scrutinizing their skills critically.

Until you are prepared to talk about the worst examples of your work, you will make little progress improving those skills.

What If I Hurt Someone?

This is a legitimate concern. One of the hallmarks of our profession is that even if you don't help anyone, you want to make sure you don't hurt them. That is one reason why good supervision is so important to monitor your progress and safeguard your clients.

You should know that most clients are far more resilient than you might give them credit for. Even when you do make mistakes, or use your skills awkwardly, you will have plenty of time to recover. That is where a good relationship comes in so handy: clients become very forgiving of your lapses once they trust and respect you. Note in the dialogue below how it takes the therapist several tries to find the right intervention.

Client: I just don't think I'm ready to start dating yet. It has only been a year.
Therapist: You are still feeling pretty raw recovering from your last relationship. [inaccurate reflection of feeling]
Client: Well no, not exactly. It's just that I don't want to give up my freedom. I love being on my own right now.
Therapist: You say that this is about freedom, but I sense that you have some concerns about putting yourself in a position to be abandoned again. [ill-timed confrontation]
Client: How can you think that about me? After everything we have talked about together. Do you really think I'm that weak?
Therapist: Not at all. In fact, right now I can feel your power in standing up to me, asserting yourself, telling me that you feel misunderstood. [effective use of immediacy]

So it goes. Perhaps half of your skills and interventions (on a good day) will fall on deaf ears, be misunderstood, or ignored. But that's okay: You have plenty of time and lots of opportunities to find the right combination of things that will get through to the person.

What If I Don't Have What It Takes?

This might be the scariest fear of all—that when all is said and done, you are not cut out for this kind of work. That is indeed a possibility. Once you get out in the field, and start seeing clients, perhaps you will discover that this job is not for you. But we would suggest that it is just as good to learn what you don't want to do as it is to learn what you do like.

What *does* it take to succeed in this business? You must master the basic skills learned in this class, but that mostly takes practice and solid feedback. We can think of very few students who actually could not do this, although more than a few elected to give up. But if you are determined, and dedicated, and persistent, you can get better and better in your skills.

What else does it take to succeed? You have to learn to not take things so personally or you will burn out quickly. You must be able to metabolize the daily stresses in such a way that you don't take them home with you. You must be forgiving of your imperfections. One of the wonderful tenets of individual psychology seems most appropriate here. Your job is to learn how to accept your inferiorities (Manaster & Corsini, 1982). We all are inferior in many ways, and if you can acknowledge your weaknesses, personally and professionally, and commit to overcoming them, you are on the right track.

What we find, more often than not, is that beginners don't so much wash out of their training as move on to something else because they have discovered that what they are doing is not a good match for who they are and what they do. If that is what happens with you, so much the better; it means you have found something better suited to your unique gifts and skills.

Exercise in Strengths

On your own, make a list of 10 of your strongest skills and qualities that will help you as a therapist. We know, we know. Ten is hard, but you can do it, and don't proceed until you do. We trust you have 10 strengths.

SOME ADVICE ABOUT WHERE TO GO NEXT

The transition between the skills class and your practica/internship is a critical time in which you prepare yourself for applying what you have learned to the real world. If you have been doing your work all along, we still cannot in good faith reassure you that you will be ready. In truth, you will *never* be ready.

Bet you didn't expect we'd tell you that. You thought we were going to give you a rah-rah speech about going out there and doing it for the team. You thought we would tell you that you are well prepared and can handle whatever comes your way. But that would be a lie. Even after all these years, we still don't feel as ready as we would prefer to help the people who come to us. So, welcome to the team of humility. But there are still a few more things you can do to get yourself as ready as you can.

Keep a Journal

If you haven't already begun a journal to talk about your development as a therapist and to work through personal issues that come up, we would highly recommend that you do so. I [Jeffrey] began such a journal when I started my first practicum 30 years ago, and I'm still writing in it. I talk about cases that confound me. I work through personal issues that are triggered by my work. I jot down some of my best metaphors and stories that I might want to remember (and include in a book someday). I set goals for myself about areas that I want to improve. I plot my progress in several areas that I have been working on throughout my life. I make notes to myself about things I want to hold onto. I process new insights that come up in sessions. In short, my journal has become a lifelong partner and "peer" supervisor that has kept me accountable. It has offered comfort as well during some very difficult times.

Watch Videos of the Masters

You can learn a lot by watching master practitioners in action. There are thousands of such videos that have been published, presenting the most distinguished clinicians demonstrating their skills with real clients. Apart from understanding their theories better, viewing these demonstrations allows you to watch the ways that highly skilled practitioners use all the generic skills that you have just learned.

You will find yourself unconsciously and (almost) effortlessly imitating the behaviors you see modeled by the masters. Without having to think about it, or even plan for it, you will find yourself in the middle of a session blurting out something that seems to come out of someone else, someone not quite you. The fact is that you can learn a lot about therapy by watching very good professionals do it.

Get Into Therapy as a Client

Even better than watching therapy is to experience it as much as you can, especially sitting in the client's chair. The more different kinds of therapy you can experience—in groups, individual, family formats, by practitioners of different approaches—the more you will learn about what works best.

As we've said before, most of the therapeutic skills are now so universal and generic that practically every clinician relies on the same basic helping behaviors. The true beauty, however, is in experiencing how they work with you. How do you respond to confrontation best? When do you most appreciate someone who proves they have heard and understood you? When do you find self-disclosure instructive versus indulgent? What kinds of interpretations work best with you? When do you find you most need some sort of summary? In other words, which skills do you most appreciate when you are a client? The answers to these questions will go a long way to guiding your own choices about when to use which interventions.

Another substantial advantage to getting into your own therapy is that you will start to work on your own issues that tend to hold you back as a therapist. You will experience fewer countertransferences, or at least be aware of it when it happens. You will also realize that change is difficult and perhaps have more realistic expectations about how quickly your clients can change. Finally, you will be a healthier person by learning more about yourself.

Get Tapes Critiqued

In preparation for your practica/internships it would be a good idea to get used to being taped. This is one of the best learning modalities of all for improving your skills.

It is a strange experience indeed to watch yourself continuously. You will notice your annoying mannerisms, your characteristic gestures, every nuance related to how you present yourself to the world (and to your clients). You will hear what your voice sounds like to others, and if this sounds strange to you, then consider all the other ways you are out of touch with the ways that others hear and see you.

Your job is to become a student of yourself, as well as of others. This means that by watching your sessions on video you can monitor carefully all the hundreds, if not thousands, of things that you do and say that can be improved. We are not suggesting that it is possible to track everything, but just that watching yourself is an important part of this process.

Apart from your usual supervisors, ask knowledgeable friends and coworkers, those more experienced than yourself, to listen to or watch your tapes and give you feedback. Sure, this is a time-consuming imposition on them, but they will understand how important this is to your continued development. The more feedback you can get from the maximum number of good practitioners, the better.

Exercise in Opportunities for Improvement

Make a list of five skills you think must be developed next, and prioritize them. Next to each one, write how you can commit to developing each skill in order to develop a sense of mastery with it. Keep this list and your list of strengths in a safe place and refer to it often . . . perhaps in the front of your new journal.

Be a Good Consumer of Supervision

You may notice that supervisors with whom you work have different styles and philosophies if you ask them to describe what good therapy looks like. We recommend that you take full advantage of the differences you experience with each supervisor. While you are with your first supervisor, master what he or she is trying to teach you. When you go to your second supervisor with a different style, master that different style. In a way, you may be thinking that it might be frustrating to be a chameleon, but the only way you will develop your own style is by trying on the styles of your various supervisors. Developing your own style of therapy is something that takes time to develop, and it's dynamic; it's constantly changing.

One last word about supervision: You have the right to good supervision. What is good supervision? Well, ideally, your supervisor will observe or listen to actual recordings of your sessions each week. Your self-report of the session is not sufficient to improve your skills. So take the initiative to record sessions if your supervisor does not require it, and ask them to listen to at least 10 minutes of at least one session per week. Ask them to explain to you what you did well (which you will want to repeat) and what you could have done better and how (so you can change it).

You also have the right to no less than 1 hour per week of uninterrupted individual supervision and preferably at least 1 (or 2) hour(s) per week of uninterrupted group supervision. With individual supervision, you can monopolize that hour for all your supervision needs. With group supervision, you have the advantage of learning from other people's mistakes, "borrowing" cool interventions from others that went well, and of hearing the views from a variety of people on how to help your client best.

Finally, your supervision experience should provide you with information about what you do right and what can be improved upon. If you are only getting feedback about what's right, you won't be able to improve much. If you are only getting feedback about what needs improvement, you'll feel really beat up each week. If you are not getting any of these needs met, assert yourself by asking for what you need. Supervision is one of the most essential processes needed to develop your skills to help one life at a time. Make sure to get what you need and use the information well.

Attend Workshops and Conferences

We have mentioned before the advantages of attending workshops and conferences, but we think it's worth mentioning again. First of all, the organizations with whom your department is affiliated usually have at least one annual national conference. Many organizations also have regional (groups of states), state level, or local groups who gather each year. Join at least one, if not two organizations and get involved. Join maybe the primary national organization in your field and perhaps a group that supports the theoretical orientation you are interested in or a group that specializes in the type of client with whom you would like to work. You can meet some of the important people in your field, and you can make friends with other professionals who can offer support when you feel stuck or just need someone with whom to talk.

Another advantage to attending workshops or conferences is to get more specific information about the areas that interest you. Perhaps your program doesn't offer a course in a particular area. Or perhaps you won't have the money or time to take all the courses you were interested in while in school. You may also start to develop new interests as you progress through your education where you may want to submerge yourself. Workshops and conferences are the best way to get new information about techniques, skills, research, and trends in the field.

Finally, joining some organizations will lead you to external training groups where you can develop your skills even further. I [Leah] noticed that the professionals who I thought did the best therapy were affiliated with a particular theoretical orientation. I got to know some people, and eventually found out about a local training group that was affordable. It was one of the most growth-inducing experiences of my professional and personal life. Because of the nature of this training group and the wonderful members who participated with me, I was able to work on many of my own issues while concurrently developing my skills as a therapist. We cannot impress on you enough that the more good training and supervision you receive (and are receptive to), the better you will be at being a therapist. At this point, you may finally realize that doing therapy is no easy task. Additional training can really help.

Practice Everywhere

One of the great things about learning helping skills is that you can use them everywhere, in every interaction, in every conversation. You may have noticed that within each chapter, we have suggested exercises for practicing these skills in class or at home. In addition, we have a section in each chapter (Applications to Self) where we talk about how the skills can or already do apply in your personal life. Take some time to read each of them again after you finish this semester. Make a list of what you can do, and start practicing them now, every day, if you haven't already done it. Just because the semester has ended does not mean that your learning has to end. Remember practice makes . . . okay, not perfect, but instead . . . practice will make you better.

Remember Your First Priority in Helping: The Relationship

If you take nothing else from all we have given you, remember that the most essential task you must accomplish with your client is to build the relationship. Developing the relationship includes improving your skills to:

- Attend to nonverbal behaviors.
- Attend to nuances in the client's language.
- Attend to the content of the client's communications.
- Attend to the process of how your client communicates.
- Provide empathic responses in a genuine and caring way.

If you can do these things while being sensitive to and accepting of cultural differences, you have the foundation. As we have said before, this foundation is most of what you need in all stages of therapy for your client to grow. In fact, think of it this way: if you do nothing but give the client a positive experience of being heard, understood, and accepted, you will have helped your client, even if you didn't accomplish the goals that were articulated in the early stages of therapy. A healthy relationship can go a long way.

Be Gentle With Yourself

Finally, we would like to encourage you to be gentle with yourself. Learning the skills involved with becoming a therapist are as difficult as training for a new sport. Instead of developing your body, you are learning to attend to many aspects of your client and to your own reactions to your client, then deciding how to respond in a way that you deem is most beneficial for your client. It is a skill, not a talent. It takes practice and is not a common way of communicating interpersonally. You will have many victories and many failures, and with each failure, be kind to yourself. Becoming a therapist is a difficult but rewarding process that never ends. Enjoy it.

Final Exercise

Break into small groups of three or four and discuss:

1. *What aspects of this class met your expectations?*
2. *What did you learn that you didn't expect?*
3. *What do you feel you still need to learn?*
4. *How can you learn what you still want to learn?*
5. *How do your other courses in your program apply to being a better therapist?*
6. *How can you take advantage of your remaining courses to develop your skills as a therapist?*
7. *How has going through this course changed who you are?*
8. *How has going through this course changed your relationships?*
9. *How have the people in this group been supportive to you?*

SUMMARY

Well, we hope we have given you some tools to utilize as you start your adventure as a thera-pist. In the process, we also hope that we haven't overwhelmed you, too much, although we know you must be feeling a little anxious. Your anxiety is good. It simply indicates that you care enough to do well, and will work to improve on this foundation you are building. We wish you the best in changing . . . one life at a time!

SUGGESTED READINGS

Corey, G., & Corey, M. S. (2002). *On becoming a helper.* Pacific Grove, CA: Brooks/Cole.

Kottler, J. A., & Hazler, R. (1997). *What you never learned in graduate school.* New York: W. W. Norton.

Kottler, J. A., & Jones, P. (2001). *Doing better.* New York: Brunner-Routledge.

Skovhold, T. M. (2001). *The resilient practitioner: Burnout prevention and self-care strategies for counselors, therapists, teachers, and health professionals.* Boston: Allyn and Bacon.

Sussman, M. B. (1992). *A curious calling: Unconscious motivations for practicing psychotherapy.* Northvale, NJ: Jason Aronson.

Yalom, I. (2001). *Gift of therapy: An open letter to a new generation of therapists and their patients.* New York: HarperCollins.

Answers to
"A Check on What You Learned"

Chapter 1

1. Reading minds.
2. The ability to instill hope and power/influence.
3. The therapist is blamed for the negative results and consequently loses power.
4. The client becomes dependent on the therapist and loses faith in her/himself to find his/her own solutions.
5. They have to.
6. Placebo effect.
7. The healing relationship.
8. Intuition.
9. Apply what they learn in therapy to their daily lives.
10. (a) What clients experience; (b) a comprehensive inventory of complaints and symptoms; (c) a reasonable hypothesis about the origins of their problems; (d) a diagnostic formulation that pinpoints the core issues; (e) the cultural, familial, and contextual background for the client's experience; and (f) a treatment plan for what will be done and how it will be done.

Chapter 2

1. Individual differences.
2. Gender, socioeconomic status, sexual orientation, religion, and ethnicity.
3. African American and Caucasian.
4. Acculturation.
5. Value of family; individual focus versus group focus; gender-role stereotypes; religion; social structures; and emotional expression.
6. Be a good client.
7. Knowledgeable; respect.
8. Training for the specific population of client; training in the use of assessment instruments; and no dual relationship is likely.

9. Intent to harm self; intent to harm others; reports of abuse to a child, an elderly person, or a person with a disability; if records are subpoenaed; if the client requests the records be released; and if you are recording the session.
10. Becoming clear about your own values.

Chapter 3

1. Active listening and the use of "I" messages.
2. Diagnosis and treatment; techniques.
3. Three: beginning, middle, and end.
4. Building the relationship with the client.
5. False.
6. Important; valuable.
7. Motivation; momentum.
8. Expected; normal.
9. Choice; use.
10. Theory.

Chapter 4

1. Diagnostic aid.
2. Unfinished business.
3. Authentic engagement.
4. Yourself.
5. Establish and enforce boundaries; reduce your need for distractions.
6. Body posture; eye contact; facial expressions; and minimal encouragers.
7. Take a deep breath.
8. Matching client content.
9. Build collaborative relationships.
10. Practice them at home in your everyday life.

Chapter 5

1. Mental status exam.
2. Waiting room.
3. Ground rules.
4. False.
5. Drug/alcohol abuse/use; physical/sexual abuse; suicide risk.
6. Medical.
7. Thinking too much.
8. Engage.
9. False.

10. If the advice fails, the client will blame you. If the advice succeeds, you are reinforcing the belief that the client can't solve his or her own problems.

Chapter 6

1. It is a closed instead of open question where the therapist is directing the conversation. In addition, it doesn't help the client any.
2. Clients often aren't able to answer "why" questions. If they knew the reason, they might behave differently.
3. Content and feeling.
4. Feelings, because once the client hears the feeling reflected, he or she can fully get into the emotion for more depth of exploration.
5. Content.
6. It includes both content and feelings.
7. Exploring the past.
8. You're not reflecting feelings enough, or your reflections lack depth, or it is time to move forward and take action.
9. The question does not exhibit empathy, and the client must think to answer the question, which does not elicit feelings, and the word "make" implies that feelings are externally driven.
10. The reflection is impersonal. "You feel sad."

Chapter 7

1. Disputing beliefs.
2. Providing information.
3. Confronting.
4. Interpretation.
5. Giving feedback.
6. Interpretation.
7. Self-disclosure.
8. True.
9. The client may not feel heard or understood, or may feel invalidated or patronized.
10. In therapy, you will use the skills in a more mindful and purposeful way to facilitate client exploration.

Chapter 8

1. Empty chair.
2. Role-play.
3. Relaxation.
4. Rehearsal.

5. Transference.
6. Bibliotherapy.
7. Imagery.
8. Reinforcement.
9. False.
10. Mutual, attainable, and specific.

Chapter 9

1. You may think you are helping, but the client doesn't think so; clients may not tell you the truth; progress in session is not always indicative of progress outside of session; and sometimes the effects have a delayed reaction.
2. The client is difficult; you have countertransference issues; and you have value difference.
3. B
4. B
5. A
6. B
7. A
8. A
9. B
10. B
11. A
12. B

Chapter 10

1. With families, you have to attend to the agendas and interests of many people.
2. Circular causality.
3. Smaller units of coalitions within the family.
4. Join.
5. B
6. Teach each member to be respectful of each other; listen to each other's side before responding; and attend sessions promptly and consistently.
7. B
8. Mediation.
9. Play.
10. The client is an organization or group; the therapist goes to the client's natural setting; consultants are problem solvers; the consultant is more like a coach than a therapist.

Chapter 11

1. Three: beginning, middle, and end.
2. Proxemics.
3. Person-centered and Gestalt.
4. Have a member reveal something personal, facilitate member support, and reduce advice giving.
5. Modeling.
6. Linking.
7. Scanning.
8. When a member is abusive or disrespectful or when a member complains incessantly.
9. Notice it out loud.
10. True.

References

Acebo, C., & Thoman, E. B. (1992). Crying as social behavior. *Infant Mental Health Journal, 13*(1), 67–82.

Adler, A. (1963). *The practice of theory of individual psychology.* Paterson, NJ: Littlefield Adams.

American Counseling Association. (2002). *ACA code of ethics and standards of practice* [Electronic version]. Retrieved June 25, 2002, from http://www.counseling.org/resources/ethics.htm

American Psychiatric Association. (2000). *Diagnostic and statistical manual of mental disorders* (4th ed.). Washington, DC: American Psychiatric Association.

American Psychological Association. (1992). *Ethical principles of psychologists and code of conduct* [Electronic version]. Retrieved June 25, 2002, from http://www.apa.org/ethics/code.html

American Association for Marriage and Family Therapy. (2001). *AAMFT code of ethics* [Electronic version]. Retrieved June 25, 2002, from http://www.aamft.org/resources/LRMPlan/Ethics/ethicscode2001.htm

Anderson, W. T. (1990). *Reality isn't what it used to be.* San Francisco: HarperCollins.

Ansbacher, H. & Ansbacher, R. (Eds.). (1956). *The individual psychology of Alfred Adler: A systematic presentation in selections from his writings.* New York: Basic Books.

Atkinson, D. R., Morten, G., & Sue, D. W. (1989). A minority identity development model. In D. R. Atkinson, G. Morten, & D. W. Sue (Eds.), *Counseling American minorities* (pp. 35–52). Dubuque, IA: W. C. Brown.

Axelson, J. A. (1999). *Counseling and development in a multicultural society* (3rd ed.). Pacific Grove, CA: Brooks/Cole.

Axline, V. (1964). *Dibs in search of self.* New York: Ballantine Books.

Bang, S. C., & Kim, K. H. (1998). The effects of guided imagery on state and trait anxiety. *Korean Journal of Health Psychology, 3,* 156–168.

Baruth, L. G., & Manning, M. L. (2003). *Multicultural counseling and psychotherapy: A lifespan perspective* (3rd ed.). Upper Saddle River, NJ: Prentice Hall.

Basmajian, J. (Ed.). (1989). *Biofeedback: Principles and practice for clinicians* (3rd ed.). Baltimore, MD: Williams & Wilkins.

Beck, A. (1976). *Cognitive therapy and the emotional disorders.* New York: International Universities Press.

Beecher, H. K. (1955). The powerful placebo. *Journal of the American Medical Association, 159,* 1602–1606.

Benson, H. (1975). *The relaxation response.* New York: Morrow.

Bowen, M. (1978). *Family therapy in clinical practice.* New York: Jason Aronson.

Brock, G. W., & Barnard, C. P. (1999). *Procedures in marriage and family therapy.* Boston: Allyn and Bacon.

Burr, V. (1995). *An introduction to social constructionism.* London: Brunner-Routledge.

Buss, D. M. (1999). *Evolutionary psychology.* Boston: Allyn and Bacon.

Carkhuff, R. R. (1969). *Helping and human relations.* New York: Holt, Rinehart, & Winston.

Carkhuff, R. R., & Anthony, W. A. (1979). *The skills of helping.* Amherst, MA: Human Resources Development Press.

Carkhuff, R. R., & Berenson, B. G. (1967). *Beyond counseling and therapy.* New York: Holt, Rinehart, & Winston.

Carlson, N. (1998). *Physiology of behavior* (6th ed.). Boston: Allyn and Bacon.

Corey, G. (2001). *Theory and practice of counseling and psychotherapy* (6th ed.). Pacific Grove, CA; Brooks/Cole.

Corey, G., Corey, M. S., & Callanan, P. (2003). *Issues and ethics in the helping professions* (6th ed.). Pacific Grove, CA: Brooks/Cole.

Corey, M. S., & Corey, G. (2002). *Groups: Process and practice* (6th ed.). Pacific Grove, CA: Brooks/Cole.

Cormier, S., & Nurius, P. S. (2003). *Interviewing and change strategies for helpers: Fundamental skills and cognitive behavioral interventions* (5th ed.). Pacific Grove, CA: Brooks/Cole.

Cottone, R. R., & Tarvydas, V. M. (2003). *Ethical and professional issues in counseling* (2nd ed.). Upper Saddle River, NJ: Prentice Hall.

Davidson, R. J., & Schwartz, G. E. (1976). Psychobiology of relaxation and related states: A multiprocess theory. In D. I. Mostofsky (Ed.), *Behavior control and the modification of physiological activity* (pp. 399–442). Englewood Cliffs, NJ: Prentice Hall.

De Jong, P., & Berg, I. K. (2002). *Interviewing for solutions* (2nd ed.). Pacific Grove, CA: Brooks/Cole.

Dillon, C. (2003). *Learning from mistakes in clinical practice.* Pacific Grove, CA: Brooks/Cole.

Downey, N., & Roush, K. (1985). From passive acceptance to active commitment: A model of feminist identity development for women. *Counseling Psychologist, 13,* 695–709.

Egan, G. (2002). *Exercises in helping skills for the skilled helper.* Belmont, CA: Wadsworth.

Ellis, A. (1973). *Humanistic psychotherapy: The rational-emotive approach.* New York: McGraw-Hill.

Erikson, E. H. (1950). *Childhood and society.* New York: W. W. Norton.

Fish, J. (1973). *Placebo therapy.* San Francisco: Jossey-Bass.

Freud, S. (1936). *The ego and mechanisms of defense.* New York: International University Press.

Gergen, K. J. (1991). *The saturated self: Dilemmas of identity in contemporary life.* New York: Basic Books.

Gergen, K. J. (1997). *Realities and relationships: Soundings in social constructionism.* Cambridge, MA: Harvard University Press.

Gladding, S. T. (2002). *Family therapy: History, theory, and practice* (3rd ed.). Columbus, Ohio: Merrill.

Glantz, K., & Pearce, J. K. (1989). *Exiles from Eden: Psychotherapy from an evolutionary perspective.* New York: W. W. Norton.

Glasser, W. (1965). *Reality therapy: A new approach to psychiatry.* New York: Harper & Row.

Goldenberg, H., & Goldenberg, I. (2001). *Counseling today's families.* Pacific Grove, CA: Brooks/Cole.

Gordon, T. (1970). *Parent effectiveness training.* New York: Peter Wyden.

Gordon, T. (1974). *Teacher effectiveness training.* New York: Peter Wyden.

Gottman, J., & Lieblum, S. (1974). *How to do psychotherapy and how to evaluate it.* New York: Holt, Rinehart, & Winston.

Grosso, F. (2001). *Complete applications of law and ethics: A workbook for California marriage and family therapists.* Santa Barbara, CA: Frederico C. Grosso.

Hackney, H., & Cormier, S. (1994). *Counseling strategies and interventions* (4th ed.). Boston: Allyn and Bacon.

Haley, J. (1973). *Uncommon therapy.* New York: W. W. Norton.

Harrison, J. (2000). *The beast that God forgot to invent.* New York: Grove.

Havens, R. (1996). *The wisdom of Milton H. Erickson: Human behavior and psychotherapy* (Vol. II). New York: Irvington.

Helms, J. (1984). Toward a theoretical explanation of the effects of race on counseling: A black and white model. *Counseling Psychologist, 12*, 153–165.

Hoff, L. A. (2001). *People in crisis: Clinical and public health perspectives* (5th ed.). San Francisco, CA: Jossey-Bass.

Horgan-Garcia, M. (2003). *The four skills of cultural diversity competence*. Pacific Grove, CA: Brooks/Cole.

Ivey, A., & Ivey, M. B. (1999). *Intentional interviewing and counseling: Facilitating client development in a multicultural society* (4th ed). Pacific Grove, CA: Brooks/Cole.

Ivey, A. E., D'Andrea, M., Ivey, M. B., & Simek-Morgan, L. (2002). *Theories of counseling and psychotherapy: A multicultural perspective* (5th ed.). Boston: Allyn and Bacon.

Jung, C. (1935/1980). The Tavistock lectures. In *Symbolic life: Miscellaneous writings. Collected works* (Vol. 18, pp. 1–182). Princeton, NJ: Princeton University Press.

Keeney, B. (1996). *Everyday soul*. New York: Riverhead.

Khasky, A. D., & Smith, J. C. (1999). Stress relaxation states, and creativity. *Perceptual and Motor Skills, 88*, 409–416.

Kirschenbaum, H. & Henderson, V. (Eds.). (1989). *The Carl Rogers reader*. Boston: Houghton Mifflin.

Kohlberg, L. (1976). Moral stages and moralization: The cognitive-developmental approach. In T. Lickona (Ed.), *Moral development and behavior* (pp. 31–53). New York: Holt, Rinehart & Winston.

Kohut, H. (1984). *How does analysis cure?* Chicago: University of Chicago Press.

Kottler, J. A. (1991). *The compleat therapist*. San Francisco: Jossey-Bass.

Kottler, J. A. (1992). *Compassionate therapy: Working with difficult clients*. San Francisco: Jossey-Bass.

Kottler, J. A. (2001a). *Learning group leadership: An experiential approach*. Boston: Allyn and Bacon.

Kottler, J. A. (2001b). *Making changes last*. New York: Brunner-Routledge.

Kottler, J. A. (2002). *Theories in counseling and therapy*. Boston: Allyn and Bacon.

Kottler, J. A., & Blau, D. S. (1989). *The imperfect therapist: Learning from failure in therapeutic practice*. San Francisco: Jossey-Bass.

Kottler, J., & Brown, R. (2003). *Introduction to therapeutic counseling: Voices from the field* (5th ed.). Stamford, CT: Brooks/Cole.

Kottler, J. A., & Carlson, J. (2003). *Bad therapy: Master therapists share their worst failures*. New York: Brunner-Routledge.

Kottler, J. A., & Montgomery, M. (2001). Theories of crying. In A. Vingerhoets & R. Cornelius (Eds.), *Adult crying: Psychological and psychobiological aspects*. New York: Brunner-Routledge.

Kottler, J., Sexton, T., & Whiston, S. (1994). *The heart of healing: Relationships in therapy*. San Francisco: Jossey-Bass.

Lazarus, A. A. (1973). Multimodal behavior therapy: Treating the BASIC I.D. *Journal of Nervous and Mental Disease, 156*, 404–411.

Lazarus, R. S. (1999). *Stress and coping*. New York: Springer.

Lazarus, R. S., & Folkman, S. (1984). *Stress appraisal and coping*. New York: Springer.

Lewis, J. A., Dana, R., & Belvins, G. (2002). *Substance abuse counseling* (3rd ed.). Pacific Grove, CA: Brooks/Cole.

Libo, L. M., & Arnold, G. E. (1983). Relaxation practice after biofeedback therapy: A long-term follow-up study of utilization and effectiveness. *Biofeedback and Self Regulation, 8*, 217–227.

Lichstein, K. (1988). *Clinical relaxation strategies*. New York: Wiley.

Lum, D. (Ed.). (2003). *Culturally competent practice*. Pacific Grove, CA: Brooks/Cole.

Mah, K. & Binik, Y. (2001). The nature of human orgasm: A critical review of major trends. *Clinical Psychology Review, 21*(6), 823–856.

Manaster, G., & Corsini, R. (1982). *Individual psycholgy: Theory and practice*. Chicago: Adler School of Professional Psychology.

Meichenbaum, D. (1977). *Cognitive behavior modification*. New York: Plenum.

Meichenbaum, D. (1985). *Stress inoculation training*. New York: Pergamon.

Mikulas, W. L. (2002). *The integrative helper.* Pacific Grove: CA: Brooks/Cole.

Minuchin, S. (1974). *Families and family therapy.* Cambridge, MA: Harvard University Press.

Monk, G., Winslade, J., Crocket, K., & Epston, D. (1997). *Narrative therapy in practice.* San Francisco, CA: Jossey-Bass.

Moore, C. (1996). *The mediation process.* San Francisco: Jossey-Bass.

Moreno, J. L. (1987). *The essential Moreno: Writings on psychodrama, group method, and spontaneity.* New York: Springer.

Morrissette, P. J. (2002). *Self-supervision: A primer for counselors and helping professionals.* New York: Brunner-Routledge.

National Association of Social Workers. (1999). *Code of ethics of National Association of Social Workers* [Electronic version]. Retrieved June 25, 2002, from http://www.naswdc.org/pubs/code/code.asp

Neimeyer, R. A. (Ed.). (2001). *Meaning and reconstruction and the experience of loss.* Washington, DC: American Psychological Association.

Neimeyer, R., & Mahoney, M. (Eds.). (2000). *Constructivist psychotherapy.* Washington, DC: American Psychological Association.

Nichols, M. P., & Schwartz, R. C. (2001). *Essentials of family therapy.* Boston: Allyn and Bacon.

Okun, B. F. (2002). *Effective helping* (6th ed.). Pacific Grove, CA: Brooks/Cole.

Parsons, R. D. (1996). *The skilled consultant.* Boston: Allyn and Bacon.

Peniston, E. G., & Kulkosky, P. J. (1989). Alpha-theta brainwave training and beta-endorphin levels in alcoholics. *Alcoholic Clinical Experiences Residency, 13*(2), 271–279.

Pennebaker, J. (1990). *Opening up: The healing power of confiding in others.* New York: William Morrow and Company.

Perls, F. (1969). *Gestalt therapy verbatim.* Moab, UT: Real People Press.

Peters, R. K., Benson, H., & Porter, D. (1977). Daily relaxation response breaks in a working population: Effects on self-reported measures of health performance, and well-being. *American Journal of Public Health, 67,* 946–953.

Piaget, J. (1967). *The child's conception of the world.* Totowa, NJ: Littlefield Adams.

Prieto, L. R., & Scheel, K. R. (2002). Using case documentation to strengthen counselor trainees' case conceptualization skills. *Journal of Counseling and Development, 80,* 11–21.

Prochaska, J. O., & Norcross, J. C. (2003). *Systems of psychotherapy: A transtheoretical approach.* Pacific Grove, CA: Brooks/Cole.

Remley, T. P., & Herlihy, B. (2001). *Ethical, legal, and professional issues in counseling.* Upper Saddle River, NJ: Prentice Hall.

Rogers, C. (1951). *Client-centered therapy: Its current practice, implications and theory.* Boston: Houghton Mifflin.

Rogers, C. (1961). *On becoming a person.* Boston: Houghton Mifflin.

Rosenthal, H. (1998). *Before you see your first client.* Holmes Beach, FL: Learning Publications.

Rosenthal, H. (2001). *Favorite counseling and therapy homework assignments.* New York: Brunner-Routledge.

Ruiz, A. (1990). Ethnic identity: Crisis and resolution. *Journal of Multicultural Counseling and Development, 18,* 29–40.

Seligman, L. (2001). *Systems, strategies, and skills of counseling and psychotherapy.* Columbus, OH: Merrill Prentice Hall.

Slife, B., & Williams, R. (1995). *What's behind the research? Discovering hidden assumptions in the behavioral sciences.* Thousand Oaks, CA: Sage.

Smith, J. C. (1987). *Relaxation dynamics: A cognitive-behavioral perspective.* Champaign-Urbana, IL: Research.

Smith, J. C. (1990). *Cognitive-behavioral relaxation training.* New York: Springer.

Smith, J. (2001). *Advances in ABC relaxation: Applications and inventories.* Chicago: Roosevelt University Stress Institute.

Snyder, C. R., Michael, S. T., & Cheavens, J. S. (1999). Hope as a psychotherapeutic foundation of common factors, placebos, and expectancies. In M. A. Hubble, B. L. Duncan, & S. D. Miller (Eds.), *The heart and soul of change* (pp. 179–200). Washington, DC: American Psychological Association.

Sommers-Flanagan, R., & Sommers-Flanagan, J. (1999). *Clinical interviewing* (2nd ed.). New York: John Wiley & Sons.

Spitzer, R. L. (2002). *DSM–IV–TR casebook*. Washington, DC: American Psychiatric Press.

Steiden, D. (1993). Self-supervision using discourse analysis: Playing with talk about talk. *Supervision Bulletin, VI* (2), 2.

Sue, D. W., & Sue, D. (1973). Understanding Asian Americans: The neglected minority. *Personnel and Guidance Journal, 51*, 386–389.

Sue, D. W., & Sue, D. (1990). *Counseling the culturally different: Theory and practice* (2nd ed.). New York: John Wiley & Sons.

Summers, N. (2003). *Fundamentals for practice with high-risk populations*. Pacific Grove, CA: Brooks/Cole.

Tallman, K., & Bohart, A. C. (1999). The client as a common factor: Clients as self-healers. In M. A. Hubble, B. L. Duncan, & S. D. Miller (Eds.), *The heart and soul of change* (pp. 91–132). Washington, DC: American Psychological Association.

Tseng, W. S., & Streltzer, J. (1997). *Culture and psychopathology: A guide to clinical assessment*. New York: Brunner/Mazel.

Tuckman, B. W. (1965). Developmental sequence in small groups. *Psychological Bulletin, 63*, 384–399.

Vahinger, H. (1925). *The philosophy of acting "as if": A system of the theoretical, practical and religious fictions of mankind*. New York: Harcourt, Brace.

Vivero, V., & Jenkins, S. (1999). Existential hazards of the multicultural individual: Defining and understanding "cultural homelessness." *Cultural Diversity and Ethnic Minority Psychology, 5*(1), 6–26.

Watts, R. E., & Carlson, J. (Ed.). (1999). *Intervention and strategies in counseling and psychotherapy*. New York: Brunner-Routledge.

Watzlawick, P. (1997). Insight may cause blindness. In J. Zeig (Ed.), *The evolution of psychotherapy: The 3rd conference*. New York: Brunner-Routledge.

Welfel, E. R. (2002). *Ethics in counseling and psychotherapy: Standards, research, and emerging issues*. Pacific Grove, CA: Brooks/Cole.

Winslade, J., & Monk, G. (2000). *Narrative mediation*. San Francisco: Jossey-Bass.

Wolpe, J. (1958). *Psychotherapy by reciprocal inhibition*. Stanford, CA: Stanford University Press.

Yalom, I. D. (1980). *Existential psychotherapy*. New York: Basic Books.

Young, M. (2001). *Learning the art of helping*. Upper Saddle River, NJ: Prentice Hall.

Zimmerman, M. (2002, July/August). Tour de force. *Men's Health*, p. 73.

Index